CORPORATE LAW FOR ONTARIO BUSINESSES

Farah Jamal Karmali

CARSWELL®

ISBN: 978-0-7798-5167-6

A cataloguing record for this publication is available from Library and Archives Canada.

Printed in Canada by Thomson Reuters

Composition: Computer Composition of Canada Inc.

CARSWELL, A DIVISION OF THOMSON REUTERS CANADA LIMITED

One Corporate Plaza
2075 Kennedy Road
Toronto, Ontario
M1T 3V4

Customer Relations
Toronto 1-416-609-3800
Elsewhere in Canada/U.S. 1-800-387-5164
Fax: 1-416-298-5082
www.carswell.com
E-mail www.carswell.com/email

Acknowledgements and Dedication

I have been fortunate to have the support of several friends, family members and colleagues in writing this book and its additional resources. I am grateful to the friends and family members that encouraged me as I wrote the book, while still meeting my responsibilities as a full-time Professor, mother of two young children, and spouse. It was not an easy task, but I feel immensely rewarded by having achieved my goal, and incredibly grateful to those individuals who have expressed their pride in and support of my achievement.

My colleagues and the management at Humber College have shown enthusiasm and support for this book, and for that, I am truly grateful. Paul Kupferstein was particularly helpful in introducing me to Fast Company, a corporate database program that I have written about in this book. He was both helpful and supportive in many ways. Kirk Rintoul and Rose-Ann MacGillivray have also provided suggestions and have shown enthusiasm for incorporating this book into their courses. I look forward to their feedback so that I can continue to improve upon the book in future editions.

Gregory Ham at Do Process Software was an invaluable resource who arranged for me to have access to Fast Company in order to evaluate it for this book, and was kind enough to provide additional information and support. I appreciate his help, and I am grateful to Do Process Software for providing me with permission to include their precedents in this book. Finally, I have been fortunate to work with Lisa Gordon and an excellent editorial team at Carswell. Thank you for all your hard work and assistance.

When all is said and done, it is those that we are closest to that provide us with the energy to meet a challenging goal. Writing this book has been a personal achievement that I did not think would happen at this stage in my life, because of competing responsibilities. With the support of my loved ones, however, I was able to accomplish a lifetime goal, and I hope they are proud of me for it.

This book is dedicated to my children, Aaniqa and Aayan Karmali. They are the light in my life, and everything I do is ultimately for them. Despite the fact that Mommy was not available to play as often as I would have liked in the past year, I hope that, as they grow older, they will be proud of their mother. I want them to know that, if they make goals in life and work hard to achieve them, they can be and do anything that they dream of. Moreover, I pray that they will achieve much more than me, as it is the hope of every generation that their children will surpass them – in achievement, contribution to mankind, and ultimately, in happiness. Aaniqa and Aayan, this is for you.

Farah Jamal Karmali
May 12, 2012

PREFACE

As a young lawyer who had done well in law school, I was surprised at how inadequate I felt when I started articling. While my legal education had provided me with an invaluable skill – the ability to think and reason in a legal framework – it had not provided me with the practical details about how to run a legal practice. Fortunately, I learned those practical elements from many seasoned professionals, both lawyers and law clerks, over time. When I started teaching Corporate Law as part of the Law Clerk Diploma Program at Humber College, I realized that students could not understand the textbooks that were available on the market. Law school textbooks lacked the practical components of a real corporate law practice, and college textbooks tended to be very detail oriented, dense, and difficult to understand. It was difficult for my students to see the forest for the trees, and many simply gave up on using the textbook as a learning tool.

My goal in writing this book has been to provide a resource that is valuable to both lawyers and college students, because it combines the theoretical and practical aspects of learning corporate law. I have tried to write it with simple language, because I want readers to understand what is being conveyed. I believe that, if the area of corporate law is demystified, readers will find it both understandable and genuinely interesting, as I do. In an effort to make this a valuable learning tool, I have provided a Workbook for readers to apply their knowledge. The Workbook provides useful precedents and review exercises, to ensure that readers have grasped the concepts in the main textbook. It can be used in the classroom, or by lawyers or law clerks that need to know how to complete government forms. Of course, instructors can use the Workbook as an important resource in teaching their course, both for in-class exercises and assignments.

The material in this book is accurate at the time of writing, but readers should be aware that certain things – like screen shots from websites – tend to change frequently, and may change by the time the book is published. Every effort has been made to provide enough information to forward readers to the correct sources, even if those sources look different by the time readers refer to this book.

This textbook, Workbook and the accompanying Instructor's Manual are the result of many long days and nights of hard work. I am confident that the result will be a valuable resource for students, instructors, law clerks, lawyers, and even business people that want to understand corporate law in order to make wise business decisions. I hope that you will enjoy reading this book.

Farah Jamal Karmali
May 12, 2012

TABLE OF CONTENTS

TABLE OF CASES

CHAPTER 1: INTRODUCTION

Overview:

- What is corporate law?
- Finding corporate statutes
- *Business Corporations Act*
- *Canada Business Corporations Act*
- Why do we need corporate law?
- Business in Ontario
- Role of legal professionals
- Our clients – scenario
- Workbook:
  - Review Exercise

1. Introduction

Corporate law is a subject that can provoke a strong reaction from students and legal professionals who are unfamiliar with it. It conjures up images of piles of paperwork to deal with, or possibly, a boardroom full of high-powered individuals negotiating complex deals. Either way, many individuals who are new to corporate law fear that it will either be boring or overwhelming. It is the goal of this textbook to convince you that corporate law is neither of those things.

This textbook is for a legal professional or student who has little or no background in corporate law. It is designed to demystify this area of law, and to present material in a straightforward and simple way, without compromising essential principles. The focus of this textbook is practical, so that it can assist a lawyer or law clerk in the everyday practice of corporate law.

The material in this textbook will focus on businesses in Ontario. We will examine different types of corporations, but will focus on Ontario and federal corporations, as these are the two types of corporations that most legal practitioners will deal with in Ontario. We will examine the two key corporate statutes (described later in this chapter,) and will also discuss cases that illustrate legal principles and provide a basis for discussion.

While corporate law principles do not change very often, the practical aspects of this area of law do change more quickly. For example, forms, processes and certainly websites, change over time. The information in this textbook has been verified as of the date of publication, but an attempt has also been made to guide you to sources that will help you to ensure that the practical details are still accurate at the time that you are reading this textbook.

Finally, one of the best ways to learn about the law is to put yourself in the shoes of the client. At the end of this chapter, we will introduce a scenario that will be used throughout the textbook to guide your analysis and discussion of the corporate law principles that are explained. It will also form the basis of exercises that are included in the Workbook, so that readers can learn the practical aspects of corporate law while learning the theory.

2. What Is Corporate Law?

Corporate law is simply the area of law that relates to corporations, and a corporation is just one way that a business can choose to operate within our legal system. We will explore corporations and other types of business organizations in greater detail later in the textbook.

In Ontario, law comprises of statutes, regulations and cases. This means that, to understand the law in any area, you must familiarize yourself with the statute or statutes that relate to that area, check related regulations where required, and read cases that show you how the courts have applied those statutes and regulations in real life situations.

The primary statute that governs Ontario corporations is the *Business Corporations Act*,[1] which is often referred to as the "*BCA*" or "*OBCA*". Federal corporations are governed by the *Canada Business Corporations Act*,[2] commonly referred to as the "*CBCA*".

---

1 R.S.O. 1990, c. B.16.

3. Finding Corporate Statutes – The *BCA*

To read a current version of the *BCA*, you should access the e-Laws website. E-Laws is a government of Ontario website that provides free access to most Ontario statutes. It is currently updated every two business days. Information about the currency date of a particular statute, like the *BCA*, is also provided on e-Laws.

In addition, the *Legislation Act, 2006*[3] provides that a law printed by the Queen's Printer and laws accessed from the e-Laws website are considered "official". An "official" statute is one that is considered to be an accurate statement of the law, unless otherwise proven. The Queen's Printer (that is, the Ontario government printer) prints paper copies of statutes and regulations in annual statute volumes, revised statute volumes (the last revision being in 1990), in the Ontario Gazette, and in the form of consolidated statutes and regulations. As of November 30, 2008, an on-screen display of a law viewed or downloaded from e-Laws, or a print-out of a law viewed in HTML format or in Microsoft Word format, is also considered "official." This makes it much more convenient to access relevant provisions of the *BCA*, if required.[4]

To find the *BCA* on e-Laws, you can:

1. go to <http://e-laws.gov.on.ca>

2. click on the grey box titled "Search or Browse Current Consolidated Law"

3. click on "B" under "Browse Current Consolidated Law"

4. find *Business Corporations Act* in the alphabetical listing of statutes

---

2 R.S.C. 1985, c. C-44.
3 R.S.O. 2006, c. 21, Sched. F.
4 "Frequently Asked Questions", online: e-Laws<http://www.e-laws.gov.on.ca>.

5. to view regulations, click on the "+" beside the name of the statute

6. to download a copy of the statute in Microsoft Word format, click on the Microsoft Word symbol

7. to view the legislative history of the statute or a regulation, click on the "H" on the far right of the screen.

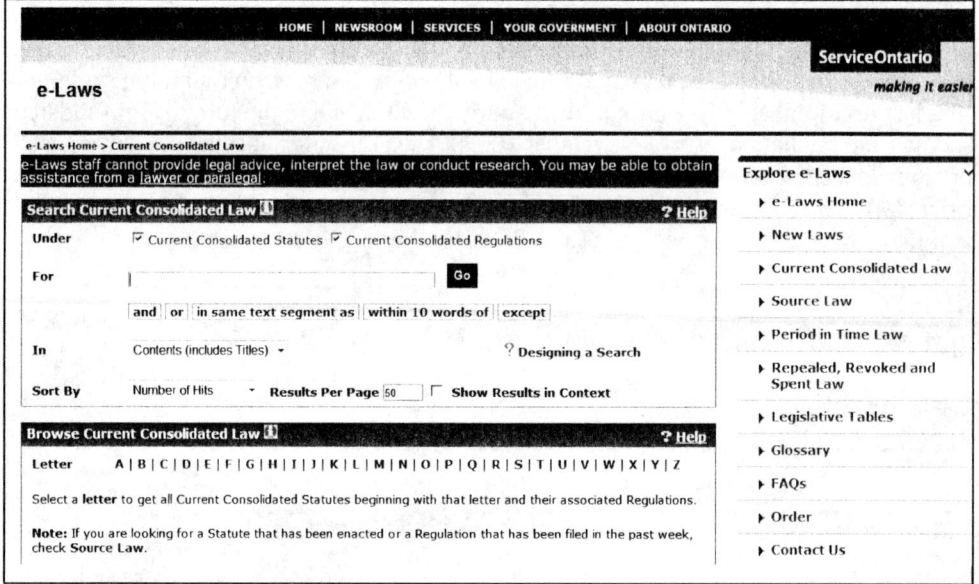

Note that you can also use the "Search Current Consolidated Law" function and type in keywords such as:

business "and" corporations

However, the results of the search are not as easy to read, and do not provide the option to view legislative history. Note that keyword connectors such as "and" must be clicked on (not typed in) below the search box.

Browse Current Consolidated Law 🔒   **? Help**

Letter   A | B | C | D | E | F | G | H | I | J | K | L | M | N | O | P | Q | R | S | T | U | V | W | X | Y | Z

Select a **letter** to get all Current Consolidated Statutes beginning with that letter and their associated Regulations.

Note: If you are looking for a Statute that has been enacted or a Regulation that has been filed in the past week, check **Source Law.**

Click on the plus sign (✪) beside the Statute Title to get all the Regulations under that Statute.

Found 19 items   ⬩ **Page 1 ▾ of 1** ⬩   **Items 1 - 19 of 19**

Current Consolidated Law (HTML)	Download	Legislative History
✪ Bail Act, R.S.O. 1990, c. B.1	W	H
✪ Bailiffs Act, R.S.O. 1990, c. B.2	W	H
✪ Barrie-Innisfil Boundary Adjustment Act, 2009, S.O. 2009, c. 29	W	H
✪ Barristers Act, R.S.O. 1990, c. B.3	W	H
✪ Beds of Navigable Waters Act, R.S.O. 1990, c. B.4	W	H
✪ Beef Cattle Marketing Act, R.S.O. 1990, c. B.5	W	H
✪ Bees Act, R.S.O. 1990, c. B.6	W	H
✪ Blind Persons' Rights Act, R.S.O. 1990, c. B.7	W	H
✪ Boundaries Act, R.S.O. 1990, c. B.10	W	H
✪ Brain Tumour Awareness Month Act, 2001, S.O. 2001, c. 19	W	H
✪ Bridges Act, R.S.O. 1990, c. B.12	W	H
✪ British Home Child Day Act, 2011, S.O. 2011, c. 14	W	H
✪ Broader Public Sector Accountability Act, 2010, S.O. 2010, c. 25	W	H
✪ Building Code Act, 1992, S.O. 1992, c. 23	W	H
✪ Bulk Sales Act, R.S.O. 1990, c. B.14	W	H
⊖ Business Corporations Act, R.S.O. 1990, c. B.16	W	H
O. Reg. 289/00 FORMS	W	H
R.R.O. 1990, Reg. 62 GENERAL	W	H
O. Reg. 665/05 HEALTH PROFESSION CORPORATIONS	W	H
✪ Business Names Act, R.S.O. 1990, c. B.17	W	H

Once you find the *Business Corporations Act*, click on the name of the statute and you will be taken to the HTML version of the statute. This version allows you to click on a section in the Table of Contents, and be taken directly to that section in the statute.

(If you want to print a copy of the statute – or parts of it – click on the Microsoft Word symbol. To view the legislative history of the statute or one of its regulations, including the date it came into force, click on the "H" on the right side of the screen.)

Once you are viewing the HTML version of the *BCA*, click on "e-Laws currency date" to determine the last time that the statute was updated on e-Laws. If the e-Laws currency date is January 1, 2012, that means that the version you are reading has incorporated any changes made to the law, up to and including changes made on January 1, 2012.

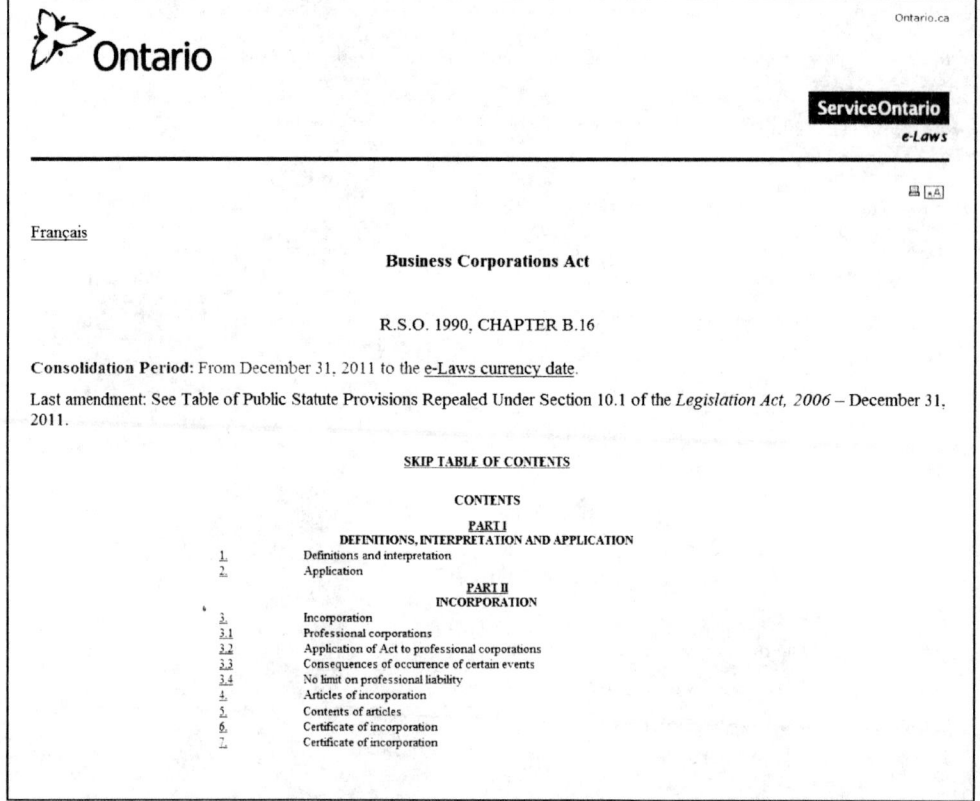

4. Finding Corporate Statutes – The *CBCA*

A client may also choose to incorporate a business in Ontario as a federal corporation. In this case, the legal professional advising this business must be familiar with the *Canada Business Corporations Act* (*CBCA*). While the *CBCA* and the *BCA* are very similar, there are some significant differences, making it important to refer to the correct legislation.

The Justice Laws website is provided by the government of Canada – specifically, the Department of Justice. To find the *CBCA* on the Justice Laws website, you can:

1. go to <http://www.laws.justice.gc.ca/>

2. Click on "English"

3. Click on "Consolidated Acts" under the heading "Laws"

4. Click on "C" at the top of the screen

5. Scroll down until you find the link to the *Canada Business Corporations Act*, R.S.C. 1985, c. C-44

6. To download a copy of the Act, click on "PDF" on the right side of the screen

7. To view regulations, click on the "R" on the right side of the screen

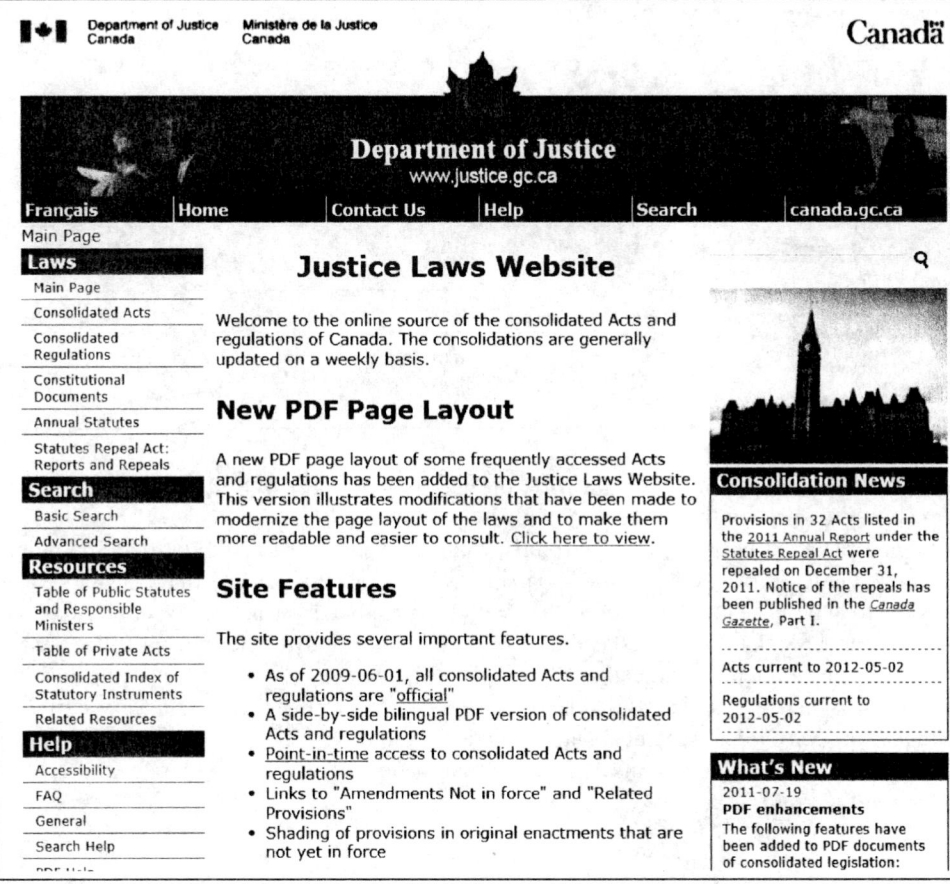

Department of Justice www.justice.gc.ca					
Français	Home	Contact Us	Help	Search	canada.gc.ca

Main Page > Consolidated Acts

Laws

Main Page

Consolidated Acts

Consolidated Regulations

Constitutional Documents

Annual Statutes

Statutes Repeal Act: Reports and Repeals

Search

Basic Search

Advanced Search

Resources

Table of Public Statutes and Responsible Ministers

Table of Private Acts

Consolidated Acts

\# A B **C** D E F G H I J K L M N O P Q R S T U V W X Y Z

Campobello-Lubec Bridge Act
S.C. 1958, c. 23   PDF [133 KB]

Canada Agricultural Products Act   R
R.S.C., 1985, c. 20 (4th Supp.)   PDF [213 KB]

Canada Border Services Agency Act
S.C. 2005, c. 38   PDF [347 KB]

Canada Business Corporations Act   R
R.S.C., 1985, c. C-44   PDF [1389 KB]

Canada Consumer Product Safety Act   R
S.C. 2010, c. 21   PDF [405 KB]

You can also search for the *CBCA* through the Basic Search or Advanced Search function provided on this website.

The Justice Laws website is currently your best source to find the *CBCA* (and other federal statutes,) for several reasons. First, it is a free access website that provides easy access to federal statutes. Second, the website is updated on a weekly basis, and all statutes and regulations are consolidated. Each statute and regulation will provided a notation (in the header) indicating the date of the last consolidation. While the Justice Laws website is not updated as quickly as the e-Laws website, it is still very current. Finally, all consolidated statutes and regulations found on the Justice Laws website are considered "official" as of June 1, 2009, which means that they are accurate and can be presented in court.[5]

---

5   "Frequently Asked Questions", online: Justice Laws Website<http://laws-lois.justice.gc.ca/eng/FAQ/>.

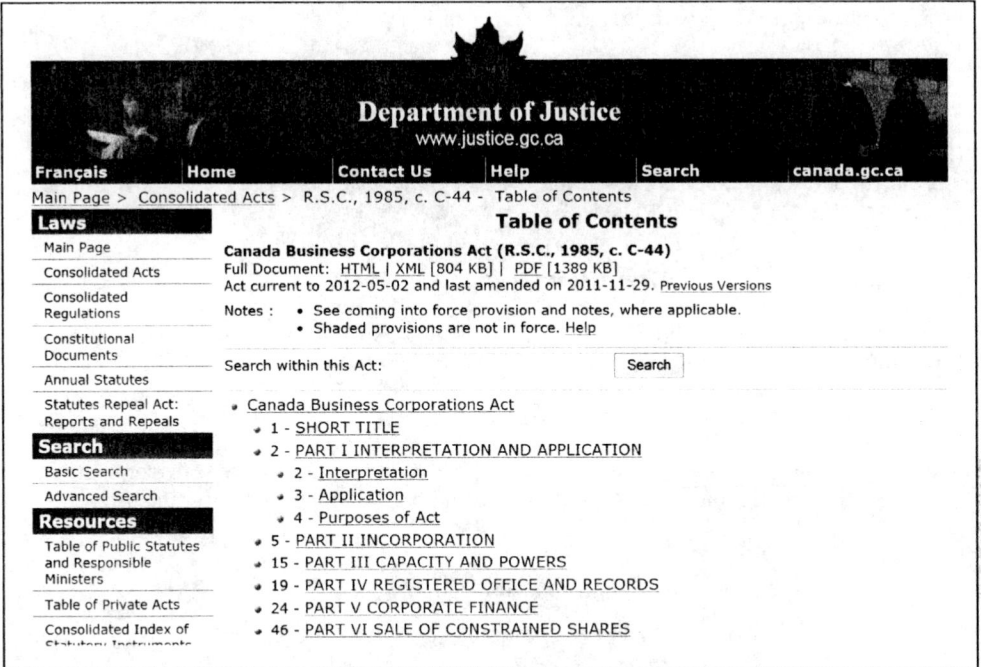

5. *Business Corporations Act*

The *BCA* applies to every corporation with share capital that has been incorporated in Ontario, with certain exceptions. Corporations created pursuant to the *BCA* are often referred to as "Ontario corporations".

Section 2 of the *BCA* reads:

2. (1) This Act, except where it is otherwise expressly provided, applies to every body corporate with share capital,

(a) incorporated by or under a general or special Act of the Parliament of the former Province of Upper Canada;

(b) incorporated by or under a general or special Act of the Parliament of the former Province of Canada that has its registered office and carries on business in Ontario; or

(c) incorporated by or under a general or special Act of the Legislature,

but this Act does not apply to a corporation within the meaning of the *Loan and Trust Corporations Act* except as provided by that Act. R.S.O. 1990, c. B.16, s. 2 (1).

(2) Despite *The Railways Act*, being chapter 331 of the Revised Statutes of Ontario, 1950, and subject to subsection 168(6), this Act applies to a body corporate with share capital that is a company as defined in that Act but that is not engaged in constructing or operating a railway, street railway or incline railway. R.S.O. 1990, c. B.16, s. 2 (2).

(3) This Act does not apply to a body corporate with share capital that,

    (a) is a company within the meaning of the *Corporations Act* and has objects in whole or in part of a social nature;

    (b) is a corporation to which the *Co-operative Corporations Act* applies;

    (c) is a corporation that is an insurer within the meaning of subsection 141 (1) of the *Corporations Act*; or

    (d) is a corporation to which the *Credit Unions and Caisses Populaires Act* applies. R.S.O. 1990, c. B.16, s. 2 (3).[6]

6. *Canada Business Corporations Act*

Similarly, the *CBCA* applies to all corporations incorporated or continued under the Act, with certain exceptions. Corporations that are governed by the *CBCA* are referred to as "federal" corporations.

Section 3 of the *CBCA* reads:

3 (1) This Act applies to every corporation incorporated and every body corporate continued as a corporation under this Act that has not been discontinued under this Act.

(2) [Repealed, 1991, c. 45, s. 551]

(3) The following do not apply to a corporation:

    (*a*) the *Canada Corporations Act*, chapter C-32 of the Revised Statutes of Canada, 1970;

    (*b*) the *Winding-up and Restructuring Act*; and

    (*c*) the provisions of a Special Act, as defined in section 87 of the *Canada Transportation Act*, that are inconsistent with this Act.

(4) No corporation shall carry on the business of

    (*a*) a bank;

    (*a.1*) an association to which the *Cooperative Credit Associations Act* applies;

    (*b*) a company or society to which the *Insurance Companies Act* applies; or

    (*c*) a company to which the *Trust and Loan Companies Act* applies.

(5) No corporation shall carry on business as a degree-granting educational institution unless expressly authorized to do so by a federal or provincial agent that by law has the power to confer degree-granting authority on an educational institution.[7]

7. Why Do We Need Corporate Law?

In general, laws are rules that society creates in order to promote harmony and prosperity amongst its citizens. Over time, corporations have become an important engine for economic growth and power. With power, however, comes the potential for abuse. Corporate laws ensure that the individuals who incorporate and operate corporations are

---

6 *Business Corporations Act*, R.S.O. 1990, c. B.16, s. 2.
7 *Canada Business Corporations Act*, R.S.C. 1985, c. C-44, s. 3.

required to do so in a way that is fair to the various parties involved, and in a manner that allows them to be held accountable by members of the public.

For example, almost every business in Ontario is required to register with the Ontario government, which essentially means that it is required to disclose information that becomes part of a public database. If a member of the public wanted to sue that business, he or she might find important information (such as the names and addresses of the owners of the business) on the database. Similarly, one party – a shareholder, for example – may feel that another party – a director, for example – is acting in a manner that is unfair or against the best interests of the corporation. Corporate laws would give the disadvantaged party the ability to sue the other party for damages in certain circumstances.

Since the *BCA* and the *CBCA* govern most types of corporations in their jurisdiction, they also provide some uniformity in the law (thereby reducing confusion and theoretically increasing fairness.)

Section 4 of the *CBCA* reads:

4. The purposes of this Act are to revise and reform the law applicable to business corporations incorporated to carry on business throughout Canada, to advance the cause of uniformity of business corporation law in Canada and to provide a means of allowing an orderly transference of certain federal companies incorporated under various Acts of Parliament to this Act.[8]

In essence, corporate laws ensure that individuals who incorporate run their corporations in a manner that will provide individuals and society with the level of protection that the government deems appropriate. There are individuals who criticize corporations for operating against societal interests; however, there is no doubt that the corporation has been and continues to be a major tool for business and economic growth in Ontario and beyond.

8. Business In Ontario

A legal professional who works in the field of corporate law plays a critical role in ensuring that a business person operates in a manner that complies with legal requirements, but also helps to achieve their business goals. For example, the choice of which type of business organization to operate (which we will discuss in Chapters 2 to 4) can be a critical choice that a legal professional can guide a client through. Therefore, a lawyer or a law clerk who keeps the client's business and other goals in mind can provide better assistance to the client.

A business is an enterprise created by one or more individuals to provide a product or a service to the public, in order to generate a profit. The strength of the business sector in any country is a key determinant of individual prosperity. The Economist Intelligence Unit has identified Canada as the best of the G7 countries to do business in from 2010 – 2014. (The G7 includes Canada, France, Germany, Italy, Japan, U.K. and U.S.A.) The Organization for Economic Co-operation and Development (OECD) identified Canada as having the highest Gross Domestic Product (GDP) of all the G7 countries in 2009.[9]

---

8 *Ibid.*, s. 4.
9 "Canada Strong Against Rest of G7", online: Ontario Canada <http://www.sse.gov.on.ca/medt/investinontario/en/Pages/coca_303.aspx>.

While this has not always been true, Canada certainly has a strong business sector – with many of those businesses operating as corporations.

As of October 2010, Canada's banking system ranked #1 in the world, according to the World Economic Forum. Canada is #1 amongst the G8 in the growth of health research patents, and ranks 4th overall in the world. Canada is also the 3rd largest exporter of automotive products, the 4th largest exporter of agricultural products, and the 5th largest aerospace producer in the world.[10] For more information on Canadian industry, visit the Invest in Canada website at http://investincanada.gc.ca.

There is no doubt that Ontario is the economic engine of Canada. Ontario's GDP is one of the ten largest in North America, and is larger than the GDP of countries like Belgium, Sweden, Switzerland, and Ireland.[11] Ontario is also the leader of Canada's manufacturing sector. In the advanced manufacturing machinery (AMT) industry, there are over 397 firms that employ approximately 73,000 people. The aerospace industry boasts some of the world's advanced companies, with sales exceeding $4 billion annually. Ontario's automotive industry includes 6 of the world's top automakers, producing more cars than any other North American jurisdiction. Ontario also ranks as the 3rd largest food processing jurisdiction in North America, with annual sales of more than $32.3 billion.[12]

In the information technology (IT) sector, Ontario is also a strong player. There are more than 5,500 IT companies in Ontario, including global leaders such as Research in Motion, Cognos, and others. The industry includes companies in every sector, including telecommunications, software development and services, digital media and microelectronics.[13]

Finally, the *Global Competitiveness Report* gives ranks Canada highly in the financial services sector, and gives it top marks for the relatively quick procedures it has established to start a business. *Forbes.com*'s has also ranked Toronto, Ontario, as one of the top ten "World's Most Economically Powerful Cities," indicating that "along with London, Toronto is the fastest growing G7 Financial Centre."[14] For more information on business and industry in Ontario, visit the Ontario Canada website at <http://www.sse.gov.on.ca>.

9. Role Of Legal Professionals

Lawyers can only give legal advice to their clients, but understanding a client's business can help a lawyer to give better legal advice. Each business – and the industry that it operates in – has unique opportunities and challenges, and certain industries have unique regulatory requirements.

The role of a legal professional is to understand the legal framework that pertains to a client's business, and to ensure that the client:

---

10 "Canada's Industry Strengths", online: Invest in Canada <http://investincanada.gc.ca/eng/industry-sectors.aspx>.

11 "Canada Strong Against Rest of G7", online: Ontario Canada <http://www.sse.gov.on.ca/medt/investinontario/en/Pages/coca_303.aspx>.

12 *Ibid.*

13 *Ibid.*

14 *Ibid.*

1. follows all the rules and regulations that relate to his/her business, and

2. benefits from all the advantages or opportunities that the law may provide for his/her business.

The role of a law clerk is to understand the principles of corporate law, so that he/she knows why things have to be done a certain way. Certainly, a law clerk will need to know what forms to complete and how to complete them, but if this is the only focus of the law clerk, then he/she will not be able to assist the lawyer when unique situations arise.

For both a law clerk and a lawyer, corporate law can be very exciting if you view it as a tool to assist a client in achieving their business goals, within a legal context.

10. Our Clients

In this textbook, we will use a hypothetical scenario to help understand the legal issues related to starting a business, and to illustrate certain corporate law principles.

Meet our clients: Javid Khan, Helena M. Madej, and Mike Alexander Smith. All three have recently graduated from a local community college, and would like to open a nightclub together.

* Javid has graduated with a 90% average as has received a Business Administration diploma. He comes from a wealthy family, and has a large inheritance which he can use to start the business. He also has family members who are willing to lend him additional money and advice, if required. One of his uncles, Sam Khan, runs a successful nightclub in another province, and is willing to act as a guide or mentor to help Javid start his first business.

* Helena is a hard-working, young woman who has put herself through college, despite no family support and very little savings. She has no formal business training, but has worked in a nightclub part-time for the last 4 years. She is reliable and friendly, but has no money to contribute to the business.

* Mike is a very social person. He was the President of the student government at his college, and although he did not do too well in his Business Management program, he did pass and graduate. Mike attributes his low grades to a very active social life, which included several impressive projects as student government president. For example, he was able to plan, market and implement a fund-raising event that generated more revenues than it had generated in the last 5 years. Mike has strong connections in the entertainment industry, and is a hard worker – but he is terrible at finances and has no savings to contribute to the business.

These are our clients. In the rest of this book, we will join them on the exciting journey to starting and, eventually, selling or closing their business to move on to other ventures.

CHAPTER 2: SOLE PROPRIETORSHIPS

Overview:

- What is a sole proprietorship?
- Advantages and disadvantages of a sole proprietorship
- Registering a sole proprietorship
  - *Business Names Act*
  - Restrictions regarding the business name
  - How to register
- Workbook:
  - Review Exercise
  - Form 1, *Business Names Act*
- Appendix to Chapter 2:
  - *Business Names Act*
  - *Restrictions Respecting Names* (Regulation)

1. What is a Sole Proprietorship?

The concept of a "corporation" is easier to understand if you compare it to other, simpler forms of business organization. The simplest way to organize a business is to create a sole proprietorship – but even a sole proprietorship has to follow certain rules established by government.

Basically, a sole proprietorship is a business operated for a profit by one owner. That owner may employ others to assist in the business (although once the owner does this, it may make sense to incorporate, for reasons that we will discuss later in this book.) Think of a convenience store or a small retail establishment in a strip plaza – many of these (and other) types of businesses are operated as sole proprietorships.

2. Advantages and Disadvantages of a Sole Proprietorship

> In Chapter 1, you were introduced to our clients – Javid, Helena and Mike. Which one of these clients could decide to start a nightclub on his/her own? What would be the advantages and disadvantages for doing so?

Generally speaking, the main advantages of establishing a sole proprietorship include:

- a simple, inexpensive and quick process to establish the business
- few legal requirements (as compared to other forms of business organization)
- complete control for the owner
- no separate tax records for the business (because the business income is included in the owner's personal income for taxation purposes)
- the owner owns all of the assets of the business
- the owner keeps all of the profits from the business

Some of the key disadvantages of a sole proprietorship include:

- unlimited, personal liability for the owner
- the sole proprietor is responsible for all the debts and obligations of the business
- complete responsibility for anything that goes wrong – the owner bears all the risk and loss from the business
- the business may require long hours and responsibilities that cannot be shared with another owner
- the skills and resources of the sole proprietor may be limited
- usually, a smaller pool of capital with which to start the business (because the more owners you have, the more capital they can bring to the business)

Essentially, the sole proprietor is the business – the law makes no distinction between the assets, liabilities, profits and expenses of the business, and those of the sole proprietor. That is why the business is not required to file a separate tax return to the government;

instead, the sole proprietor simply adds the corporate income and expenses to his/her own tax return. There is no difference in the law between the person who runs a sole proprietorship, and the business itself. As we continue to discuss the features of sole proprietorships and corporations, you will see that the first disadvantage named above – unlimited, personal liability – is the main reason that many individuals consider incorporating.

What does "unlimited, personal liability" mean? The term "unlimited" indicates that the sole proprietor has complete responsibility for everything related to the business – both good and bad. On the negative side, the sole proprietor must accept responsibility for all the debts and obligations of a business. As illustrated by the *Metroland Printing*[1] case in this chapter, the sole proprietor must pay any debts owed by the business. "Obligations" typically relate to contractual obligations – for example, the obligation to supply a product, or the obligation to pay for a product. It is the sole proprietor's responsibility to ensure that all the obligations of the business are satisfied.

The term "personal" is also very significant. It indicates that, if the business is not able to generate sufficient income itself, the sole proprietor must pay for the debts and obligations of his/her business out of his/her own personal assets. In other words, in the *Metroland Printing*[2] case, the defendant would have had to pay damages of $140,807 out of her own personal assets if her business, Liquidation Event, did not have enough money to pay that amount. It is for this reason that sole proprietors consider declaring bankruptcy when they fear that they will be sued personally for a substantial amount. The decision to declare bankruptcy is a very serious one with long-term consequences, however, and should be evaluated by a legal professional.

It should now be clear why "unlimited, personal liability" is the most serious disadvantage for operating a business as a sole proprietorship. For this reason, many legal professionals automatically advise clients to incorporate their businesses. (As discussed in Chapter 4, incorporating addresses this problem to some degree.) However, a legal professional should analyze each client's circumstances to determine if incorporation is advisable.

Metroland Printing, Publishing & Distributing Ltd. v. Isabella, 2009 CarswellOnt 1769 (Ont. S.C.J.)

The plaintiff corporation operated a community newspaper called Mississauga News. From June 2006 to January 2007, it published ads and distributed flyers for a business called Liquidation Event. As of January 2007, Liquidation Event owed the plaintiff $140,807.05 for these services. There was no written contract between the parties, and the business was operated by the defendant's deceased husband.

However, the court relied on a Business Names Report issued by the Ontario government, which indicated that in March 2006, a sole proprietorship was registered by the defendant, under the name Liquidation Event and at the address of the defendant and her deceased husband. The defendant had also opened a bank account for Liquidation Event and had sole signing authority. She had signed cheques for over $50,000.

---

1 *Metroland Printing, Publishing & Distributing Ltd. v. Isabella*, 2009 CarswellOnt 1769 (Ont. S.C.J.).

2 *Ibid.*

The defendant claimed that her deceased husband ran the business, and that she opened the account because her husband could not open a bank account himself. (The defendant did not elaborate on the reasons for this.)

In its analysis of the matter, the court emphasized that a sole proprietor is fully responsible for all the debts and obligations of a business. The court quoted the textbook *Advising the Family-Owned Business*, authored by Robert Halpern, in which the author states "the sole proprietor, as the owner of the business owns all of the assets of the business, is entitled to all of the profits and is also personally responsible for all of the debts. Since there is no distinction at law between the individual sole proprietor and his or her business, third parties who contract or deal with the business entity are entitled at law to look to the sole proprietor personally to comply with the terms of the contract."

The court held that there was an oral contract between the plaintiff and the defendant, and that the defendant – as the registered sole proprietor of the business, Liquidation Event – was liable. The plaintiff was granted judgment for $140,807 plus pre-judgment interest and legal costs.

Assume that your client, Tomas, is a part-time college student studying graphic design. He does not own a car, a home or any other significant assets, except a computer and some graphic design software. He has very little cash in the bank, and no other savings. Tomas decides to start a small graphic design business on the side, to supplement his income while he is studying. On the weekends, he provides graphic design services to a photocopy shop. He makes approximately $10,000 in the first year that he runs this business.

Would it be advisable for Tomas to operate as a sole proprietor, or would it be better to incorporate? Why or why not?

Incorporation provides an owner with protection from liability, but it involves more time and expense than running a business as a sole proprietor. The process is more complicated, and requires payment of government fees, legal fees and fees for preparing corporate tax records. For someone who has very few assets and little cash on hand when he/she starts a business, it may make sense to operate as a sole proprietorship initially, and to consider incorporating the business later. In addition, many businesses fail in the first six months of operation – so, for someone with few assets to protect from liability, it may make sense to wait until the business has established an income stream before incorporating. However, if the business is one that has a high degree of risk, or one where lawsuits from customers or others are likely, it would be prudent to consider incorporating from the start. In each case, it is the legal professional's responsibility to conduct a risk-benefit analysis to determine whether it is advisable to incorporate the business immediately, or to wait until a business has generated significant income.

It turns out that Tomas is an excellent graphic designer, and his services are in great demand. Although he is still studying part-time, he is able to provide graphic design services to 10 different photocopy shops in his second year, and as a result, he generates an income of $50,000 that year. He has purchased a car, and has invested in more sophisticated computer equipment. He rents an apartment close to his college, and works on his graphic design business from that apartment.

Would it be advisable for Tomas to continue operating as a sole proprietor, or would it be better to incorporate at this stage? Why of why not? If you think he should wait before incorporating, what circumstances would have to change to make it worthwhile for him to incorporate?

If a sole proprietor decides to incorporate after operating his/her business for some time, it is critical that adequate notice is provided to all customers, suppliers and anyone else dealing with the business. It is not enough to simply go through the legal process of incorporation in order to avoid unlimited, personal liability. All debts and obligations must be assigned to the corporation, and all business records, invoices and other forms must be maintained in the name of the corporation. In addition, it would be prudent for the sole proprietor to provide written notice of incorporation to all customers and suppliers, and to ensure that all future contracts are signed by the owner as an agent for the corporation (not in his/her own personal capacity, as would be the case in a sole proprietorship.) Failure to provide adequate notice of incorporation can have dire consequences, as the case described below illustrates.

Data Business Forms Ltd. v. MacIntosh (1986), 76 N.S.R. (2d) 418 (N.S. T.D.)

In 1976, the defendant entered into a contract with the plaintiff (an Ontario corporation) to supply business forms through the defendant's business, MacIntosh Business Systems. This business was operated as a sole proprietorship. In 1980, the defendant incorporated Maritimes Business Forms Ltd. ("Maritime") to continue running the business. However, the defendant did not advise the plaintiff that he had incorporated the business. The only indications of incorporation were that cheques were written in the name of Maritime and a letter was written to the plaintiff under Maritime's letterhead. The plaintiff did respond with two memos to the defendant, addressed to "Maritimes Business Forms". The plaintiff made no changes to the defendant's account, and no new credit application was required. Eventually, Maritime went out of business, and the plaintiff sued the defendant personally to obtain payment of $14,155.71 owed to the plaintiff. The defendant admitted that no express notice of incorporation had been provided to the plaintiff, but argued that knowledge of incorporation should be imputed by the use of Maritime's corporate cheques and the memos written by the plaintiff. The defendant did not dispute the fact that a debt was owed to the plaintiff, but argued that the debt was owed by the corporation, and not by him personally.

The court held that, in view of all the circumstances, the plaintiff had not provided adequate notice of incorporation to the plaintiff, and as such, he was personally liable for the debt owed by Maritime to the plaintiff. All the invoices and purchase orders were in the name of the sole proprietorship, and the court felt that this was more significant than the presence of cheques and memos in the corporate name. The court stated that "a person who changes his status from sole proprietor to an agency relationship must do more than just hope that the new letterhead will be observed and absorbed by a person it is dealing with in a contractual relationship as showing a change in status." Judgment was granted to the plaintiff, with interest and costs.

3. Registering a Sole Proprietorship

(a) *Business Names Act*

The requirement to register the business name of a sole proprietorship comes from the *Business Names Act*.[3] Other types of businesses, including corporations, also need to register their business names pursuant to this Act, but for this chapter, we will limit our discussion to the requirements for sole proprietorships. For convenience, a copy of the Act is provided in the Appendix to this chapter. However, a current copy of the *Business Names Act* can be viewed on the e-Laws website (which was introduced in Chapter 1.)

The *Business Names Act* has three regulations (at the time of writing):

1. *General*, O. Reg. 121/91

2. *Restrictions Respecting Names*, O. Reg. 122/91

3. *Refund of Fee for Electronic Application for New Registration*, O. Reg. 18/07

Copies of these regulations can also be obtained from the e-Laws website. It is important for a legal professional to review these regulations – as well as the Act – before advising a client who is starting a business.

The general requirement to register a business name is provided in subsection 2(2) of the *Business Names Act*, which states:

> No individual shall carry on business or identify his or her business to the public under a name other than his or her own name unless the name is registered by that individual.[4]

The term "business" is defined in the Act as "every trade, occupation, profession, service or venture carried on with a view to a profit",[5] and "person" is defined as:

> an individual, sole proprietorship, partnership, limited partnership, unincorporated association, unincorporated organization, trust, body corporate, and an individual in his or her capacity as a trustee, executor, administrator or other legal representative.[6]

While there are specific sections that address partnerships, corporations and other types of businesses, the *Business Names Act* generally imposes a requirement on most business entities to register their business name before doing business in Ontario. As indicated in section 2(2), a sole proprietor that operates a business in his or her own name does not need to register under the *Business Names Act*. However, if that sole proprietor operates under a different name, there is a requirement to register under the Act.

---

3 R.S.O. 1990, c. B.17.

4 *Business Names Act*, R.S.O. 1990, c. B.17, s. 2(2).

5 *Ibid.*, s. 1.

6 *Ibid.*

One of the purposes of this registration process is to provide a public record that can be searched by any "person", as that term is defined in the Act. This can be a source of important information in the event that a plaintiff seeks to sue a business, or in other circumstances where an individual needs information about a business. The Act provides that the Registrar must maintain a record of all registrations made under the *Business Names Act* and the *Limited Partnerships Act*, and that any person may examine these records during normal business hours.[7]

Note that a registration under the *Business Names Act* is effective for 5 years, and can be renewed before it expires. Anyone who registers under the Act must file an amended registration within fifteen days of a change in the information provided in the previous registration.[8]

Many business people are not aware of the need to register their business name under the *Business Names Act*, but the consequences for not registering can be serious. Section 7 essentially takes away the person's right to sue in an Ontario court (with respect to business matters) if that person is operating a business without registering under the *Business Names Act*.

Section 7 states:

> A person carrying on business in contravention of subsection 2 (1), (2) or (3) or subsection 4 (4) or (6) is not capable of maintaining a proceeding in a court in Ontario in connection with that business except with leave of the court. . . .
>
> (2) The court shall grant leave if the person seeking to maintain the proceeding satisfies the court that,
>
> (a) the failure to register was inadvertent;
>
> (b) there is no evidence that the public has been deceived or misled; and
>
> (c) at the time of the application to the court, the person is not in contravention of this Act or the regulations.[9]

Note, however, that a sole proprietor cannot use the fact that he/she has not registered under *the Business Names Act* as a way to get out of a contract.[10] Finally, it is critical that the information provided pursuant to the *Business Names Act* is complete and accurate. The Act provides that a person who provides false or misleading information in relation to a material fact can be charged up to $2,000, or if the person is a corporation, up to $25,000.[11]

(b) Restrictions Regarding the Business Name

As mentioned previously, there is a regulation to the *Business Names Act* that deals specifically with the name that the business chooses to operate under. The regulation begins by specifying the type of alphabet, numerals and punctuation marks that can be

---

7 *Ibid.*, s. 3(3)–(4).
8 *Ibid.*, s. 4(4).
9 *Ibid.*, s. 7.
10 *Ibid.*, s. 7(3).
11 *Ibid.*, s. 10.

used in a business name. More importantly, it specifies that a person **cannot** register a business name that is:

- immoral or obscene (in any language)

- against public policy

- prohibited by statute

- a combination of words and numerals that is similar to a corporate number name

- something that would suggest that the business is a form of organization that it is not (for example, a sole proprietor cannot use the word "Limited" in the business name, because that implies that the business is a corporation)

- the name of a specific person (except in certain circumstances)

- connected to the government (federal or provincial), the Crown, a municipality, a government agency (unless the registrant obtains prior permission)

- comprised of the words "college", "institute" or "university", unless the Minister of Colleges and Universities gives prior consent.[12]

Please refer to the regulation, *Restrictions Respecting Names*[13] in the Appendix to this chapter for full details on what may and may not be registered as a business name. Note that a current copy of this regulation may be viewed on the e-Laws website.

If a business name is refused upon registration, the registrant may appeal this decision to the Divisional Court within twenty-one days of receiving notice of that refusal. In addition, the Registrar may cancel a registration that was accepted in error; in other words, a business name may be cancelled if it is later discovered that it does not meet with the prescribed requirements.[14]

One of the questions that clients often ask is whether or not the client can register a name that is the same or similar to the name of an existing business. While the *Business Names Act* does not specifically prohibit this, it does provide several disincentives for registering an existing name. Section 6(1) states:

A person who suffers damages by reason of the registration of a name that is the same as or deceptively similar to another person's registered name is entitled to recover compensation from the registrant for damages suffered because of the registration."

(Note that this section is to be repealed and substituted with the following section, on a day to be named by proclamation of the Lieutenant Governor:

6(1) A person is entitled to recover compensation from a registrant for damages the person suffered by reason of the registration by the registrant of a name that is the same as or deceptively similar to,

    (a) a name registered by the person; or

---

12 *Restrictions Respecting Names*, O. Reg. 122/91.
13 *Ibid.*
14 *Business Names Act*, R.S.O. 1990, c. B.17, s. 4(7), 4(10)–(11).

(b) the person's name, even though the person is not required to register that name under this Act. 2010, c. 16, Sched. 5, s. 2(1).[15]

Section 6(2) continues: "for the purposes of subsection (1), the compensation is limited to the greater of $500 and the actual amount of damages incurred."[16] In addition, a sole proprietor who registers a business name that is the same or similar to another business name is taking the risk that he/she will be sued by the business that registered the name first. The cost and other consequences of a lawsuit suggest that it is wiser for individuals to select a unique business name, rather than taking the financial and legal risks of using an existing name.

For this reason, a legal professional should consider ordering a Business Names Report through the Service Ontario website (Services for Business) at <http://www.ontario.ca/en/services_for_businesses> (Click on "Search for Business Names").

Four types of reports can be obtained:

1. Detailed Business Names Report ($8)

2. Certified Detailed Business Names Report ($16)

3. Statement of No Match Found ($8)

4. Certificate of Non-Registration ($26)

The costs indicated above are for each business name searched. Note that these searches only related to unincorporated businesses. (To search corporate names in Ontario, you must order a NUANS search, which is discussed in Chapter 5 of this textbook.) A Detailed Business Names Report indicates business names registered or renewed in

---

15 *Ibid.*, s. 6(1).
16 *Ibid.*, s. 6(2).

the last 5 years, including information filed on amendments and cancellations. A Statement of No Match Found indicates that there is there is no record of the business name registered under the *Business Names Act* or the *Limited Partnerships Act* within the past 5 years. A Certificate of Non-Registration is a certified version of the Statement of No Match Found.

(c) How to Register under the *Business Names Act*

There are three options for registering a business name under the *Business Names Act*:

1. Registering in person

2. Registering by mail

3. Registering online

Each of these options will be now be explored, with an emphasis on registering online.

(i) Registering in Person or by Mail

Registration by person or by mail requires the legal professional to complete Form 1 under the *Business Names Act*. Current versions of many government forms are easily accessible on the internet through the Ontario Central Forms Repository at <http://www.forms.ssb.gov.on.ca>.

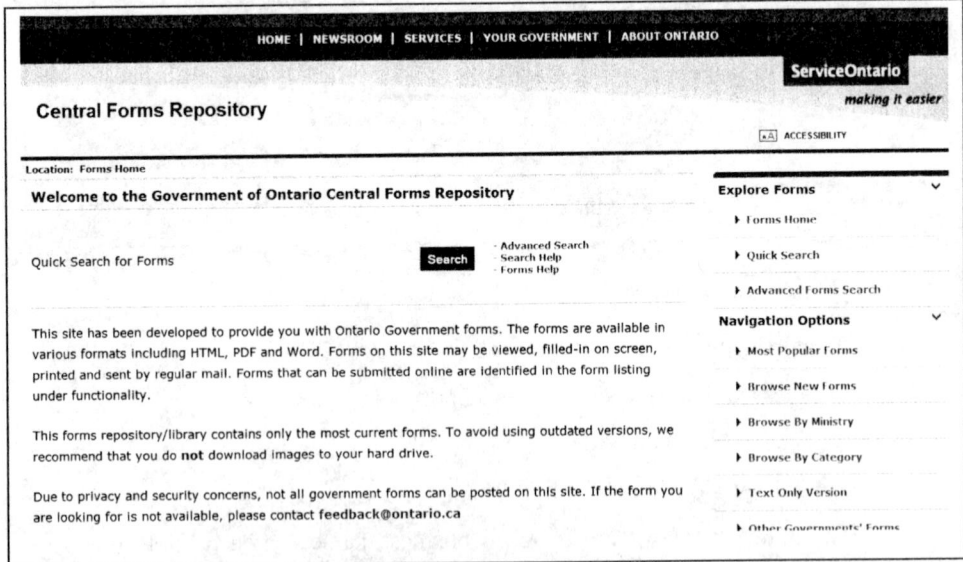

You can type a simple search (such as "business name") in the field called "Quick Search for Forms", or click on "Advanced Search" to see the following screen:

HOME | NEWSROOM | SERVICES | YOUR GOVERNMENT | ABOUT ONTA

Central Forms Repository

Location: Forms Home > Forms Search

Form Search

Browse forms by letter:

A-B-C-D-E-F-G-H-I-J-K-L-M-N-O-P-Q-R-S-T-U-V-W-X-Y-Z

or find forms where:

Form contains:

or Form Number contains:

and restrict search to:

Ministry: Select All

Branch/ABC: Select All

Program: Select All

☐ Show only New forms

Sort Results: by Form Title ▼

Limit output to: 10 results ▼

Start Search   Clear Search Values

In this screen, type "business name" in the search field called "Form contains:" and you will have the option to click on a number of links. Click on the link that states:

Registration Form 1 under the Business Names Act – Sole Proprietorship/Partnership

Note that this form applies to both sole proprietorships and partnerships, but not to other forms of business organization. Form 5 under the *Business Names Act* applies to partnerships and limited partnerships, and Form 6 under the *Business Names Act* applies to an Ontario limited liability partnership.

Central Forms Repository

Location: Forms Home > Advanced Forms Search > **Forms Search Results**

Form Search Results

Form Title	Form Number	Ministry
Application for Amendment to Extra-Provincial Licence Form 3 Extra-Provincial Corporations Act	007-07066	Government Services
Articles of Amendment Form 3 Business Corporations Act	007-07119	Government Services
Business Name Approval Form	022-58-1683E	Training, Colleges and Universities
Registration -Form 2 under the Business Names Act - Corporations	007-07197	Government Services
Registration Form 1 under the Business Names Act - Sole Proprietorship / Partnership	007-07219	Government Services
Registration Form 5 under the Business Names Act - Partnership/Limited Partnership	007-07215	Government Services
Registration Form 6 under the Business Names Act - Ontario Limited Liability Partnership	007-07193	Government Services

Showing   1 - 7 (of 7 forms)

Once you click on the PDF version of the form, you are ready to complete it online. Note that it is a "fill and print" version of the form, so you can type information directly onto the form online. A copy of Form 1 is provided in the Workbook (Chapter 2, Exercises).

It is always important to read the instructions for forms carefully, as mistakes may cause a delay in the registration process. The instructions for Form 1 are found at the end of the form. You should note the following:

1. The form must be completed in capital letters using black ink.

2. You can complete the form online and then print it. You will not be able to save the completed form in an electronic format.

3. There are instructions for completing each section of the form. Always read the instructions first, if you are not familiar with this form.

4. When you are providing a description of the activity to be carried out under the business name, try to be general enough to accommodate related activities, so that there is no need to file an amendment to the form if there is a slight change to the business.

5. Form 1 is the same form that you must submit if you are filing an amendment to information that has previously been provided in relation to a business name registration.

6. The government fee must be paid in cash (if submitting the form in person,) money order or cheque, payable to the Ontario Minister of Finance.

7. You must submit two copies of the form. (One will be returned to you.)

8. The forms must be mailed (along with the requisite fee) to the Ministry of Government Services, at the address provided on the form. At the time of writing, the address was:

Ministry of Government Services
Central Production and Verification Services Branch
393 University Avenue, Suite 200
Toronto, ON M5G 2M2

9. To search and register a business name in person, go to:

Companies and Personal Property Security Branch
Ministry of Government and Consumer Services
Second floor, 375 University Ave.
Toronto, ON M5G 2M2

10. The fee for registering or renewing a business name is $80 by mail, $80 (manual form) or $60 (electronic form) in person, or $60 through ServiceOntario (online). The most payment options are available for registration in person, including cash, debit, credit card, cheque or money order.

11. There are private service providers who can conduct business name searches and registrations for you, for an additional fee. Go to the Service Ontario website (<www.ServiceOntario.ca>) for a list of providers who have a contract to perform these services with the Ministry of Government and Consumer Services.

(ii) Registering Online through ServiceOntario

The most efficient way to register a business name in Ontario is online, through the ServiceOntario website. There are private service providers who will incorporate a company for you, but the ServiceOntario website makes it relatively easy, quick and affordable to do this yourself. As mentioned above, it is less expensive ($60 instead of $80) to register online as compared to registering by mail, and online registration has a service guarantee. It takes approximately 30 minutes to complete a registration online.

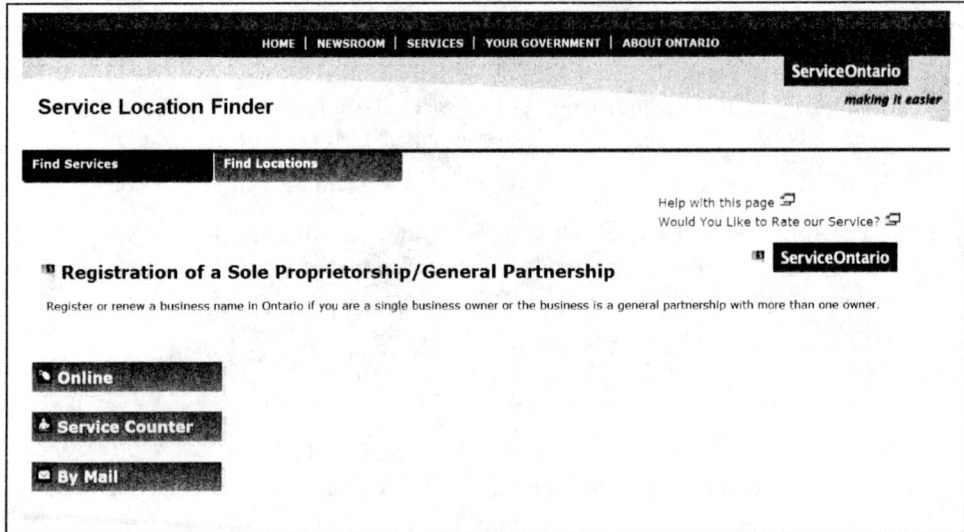

If you register a **new** business name through ServiceOntario, you can benefit from its two-business day service guarantee. In other words, you will receive an electronic copy of a Master Business Licence (eMBL) within two business days by email, as long as you register correctly and provide a valid email address. In fact, if you register during regular business hours, you will receive the eMBL immediately upon successful completion of the online registration process. The eMBL can be stored electronically and printed at any time. If you do not receive your eMBL within two business days and you meet all the necessary conditions, you can request a refund of the $60 registration fee. This service guarantee has been established pursuant to one of the regulations to the *Business Names Act*, which you can read online on the e-Laws website. Please refer to the following regulation: *Refund of Fee for Electronic Application for New Registration*.[17]

A Master Business Licence (MBL) is an important document for the sole proprietor or his/her legal advisor to keep. The MBL confirms that a business name has been successfully registered with the Ontario government, and provides two important pieces of information:

1. The expiry date (so that the sole proprietor or his/her legal advisor can renew the registration before that date), and

2. the Business Identification Number (BIN)

The MBL is proof of business registration, and may be requested at financial institutions, government programs and other places. The BIN will be required in subsequent government filings. Just like a student number at a post-secondary institution allows a college or university to keep track of all the grades for one student, a BIN allows the government to keep track of all information submitted to the government about that business.

---

17 O. Reg. 18/07.

To begin a business name registration or renewal online, go to the following page on the ServiceOntario website: <http://www.ontario.ca/en/services_for_business/STEL02_039990.html>

Click on "Register or renew your business name" for information about the registration process. This process will allow you to register your business name, apply to the Ontario Ministry of Revenue for the Employer Health Tax (EHT) and apply to the Workers Safety and Insurance Board (WSIB) in one step. Registration for the EHT and with the WSIB is free. When you have completed the registration process, you will receive an MBL, a summary of your registration, and a receipt for the business name registration.

To start the registration process, scroll down the page shown above and click on "Do It Online Now". You will now be taken to the Integrated Business Services Application page.

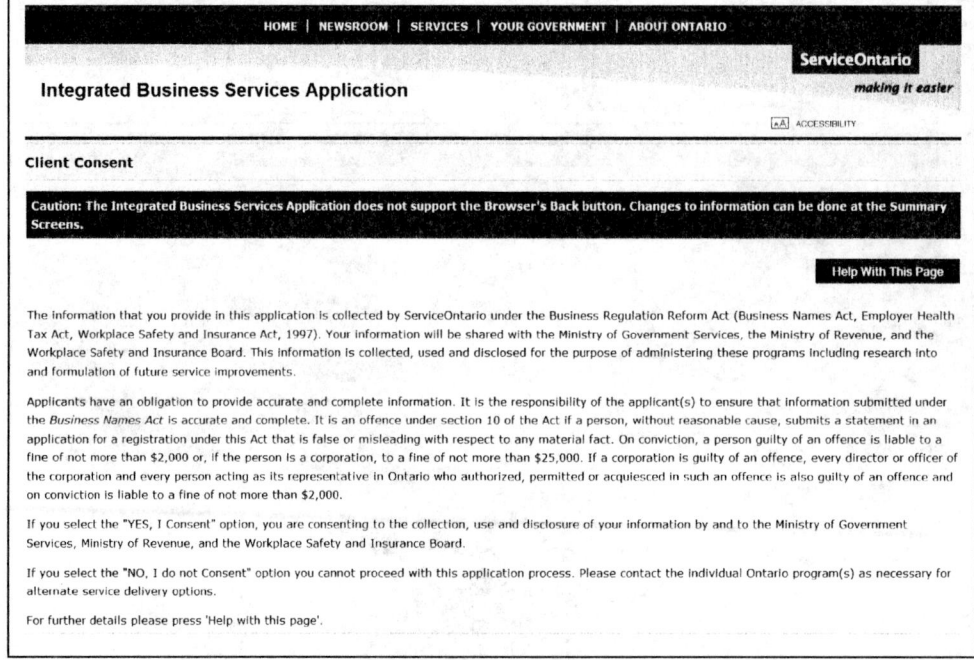

You will be required to click "I consent" at the bottom of the page. This indicates your consent to the collection and disclosure of information by the Ministry of Government Services, Ministry of Revenue and the Workplace Safety and Insurance Board.

On the next page, you will be required to choose between performing an "Enhanced Business Name Search" or a "Business Name Registration". You cannot select both options at the same time. An Enhanced Business Name Search will show you whether or not a business name has been previously registered with the Ontario Ministry of Government Services. Searches can be done on a specific business name, or even on words in business names. You can also search for information about a business through its BIN number. If you select "Enhanced Business Name Search", you will be given the option to select a number of reports described earlier in this chapter, such as a Detailed Business Name Report or a Statement of No Match Found. The cost for each report is also provided. Note that this process only pertains to business names registered by sole proprietors, general partnerships, corporations (trade/style name), limited partnerships, Ontario limited liability partnerships, and certain other business entities. (You may also wish to consider performing a NUANS search, which will be discussed in Chapter 5.)

If you select "Business Name Registration", you will be asked to indicate the type of business entity you are registering for (such as a sole proprietorship or general partnership.) Once you select "sole proprietorship", you will be asked to answer questions that determine eligibility for the EHT and WSIB. After these questions, you will be prompted to provide the same type of information as is found on Form 1 of the *Business Names Act*. (Please refer to the copy of Form 1 provided in the Workbook.) If you have questions during the registration process, you can click the "Help with this Page" box at the top of each screen for detailed explanations. Once you have provided all the information relating to the business registration, you will be provided with a summary to review, and then payment options.

(d) Other Issues to Consider

In addition to the legal processes described above, a sole proprietor must consider the following to start his/her business:

1. Opening a bank account for the business

2. Applying for any licenses required for this business

3. Considering insurance that may be required or may be advisable

4. Registering with the Ministry of Revenue for payment of Harmonized Sales Tax (HST), payroll deductions and/or import/export accounts.

The ServiceOntario website does provide links to the Business Registration Online service provided by the Canada Revenue Agency (CRA). You may also go directly to CRA's website for this service. This is an important step to ensure that the sole proprietor has met all the requirements for starting his/her business in Ontario.

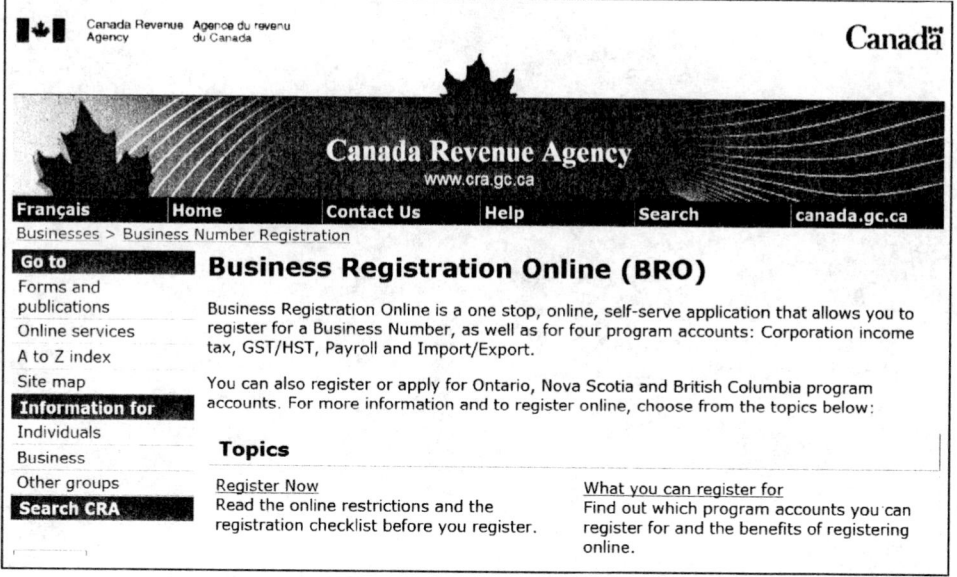

APPENDIX:

Business Names Act, **R.S.O. 1990, c. B.17**

BUSINESS NAMES ACT

R.S.O. 1990, c. B.17 as am. **S.O. 1994, c. 27, s. 72;** 1998, c. 2, s. 9; 1998, c. 18, Sched. E, ss. 33–39; 2001, c. 9, Sched. D, s. 13; 2004, c. 19, s. 4; 2006, c. 35, Sched. C, s. 9; 2010, c. 16, Sched. 5, s. 2, Sched. 8, s. 2 [Sched. 5, s. 2 not in force at date of publication.]; 2011, c. 1, Sched. 5, s. 2

1. Definitions — In this Act,

"business" includes every trade, occupation, profession, service or venture carried on with a view to profit;

"corporation" means a corporation wherever or however incorporated;

"Minister" means the Minister of Consumer and Business Services;

"Ministry" means the Ministry of the Minister;

"person" includes an individual, sole proprietorship, partnership, limited partnership, unincorporated association, unincorporated syndicate, unincorporated organization, trust, body corporate, and an individual in his or her capacity as trustee, executor, administrator or other legal representative;

"prescribed" means prescribed by the regulations;

"Registrar" means the Registrar appointed under section 3;

"registered" means registered under this Act;

"regulations" means the regulations made under this Act.

1994, c. 27, s. 72(1); 2001, c. 9, Sched. D, s. 13

Registering name

2. (1) — No corporation shall carry on business or identify itself to the public under a name other than its corporate name unless the name is registered by that corporation.

Idem

(2) — No individual shall carry on business or identify his or her business to the public under a name other than his or her own name unless the name is registered by that individual.

Same

(3) — No persons associated in partnership shall carry on business or identify themselves to the public unless the firm name of the partnership is registered by all of the partners.

Same

(3.1) — No persons associated in partnership shall carry on business or identify themselves to the public under a name other than a firm name registered under subsection (3) unless the name is registered by all of the partners.

Non-application

(3.2) — Subsection (1) does not apply to prohibit a corporation from carrying on business or identifying itself to the public by a name other than its corporate name if the name is set out in a partnership registration under subsection 4(1) or a declaration under the *Limited Partnerships Act*.

Same

(3.3) — Subsection (3) does not apply to prohibit persons associated in a limited partnership from carrying on business under the firm name in accordance with the *Limited Partnership Act*.

Exception

(4) — Subsection (3) does not apply to prohibit persons associated in partnership from carrying on business or identifying themselves to the public under a name that is composed of the names of the partners.

Idem

(5) — This section does not apply to prohibit the use of a name that contains characters from an alphabet other than the Roman alphabet if the name is used in conjunction with the registered name.

Name to be set out

(6) — A corporation and such other persons as are prescribed carrying on business under a registered name or, in the case of a corporation, identifying itself to the public under a registered name, shall set out both the registered name and the person's name in all contracts, invoices, negotiable instruments and orders involving goods or services issued or made by the person.

1994, c. 27, s. 72(2)

Extra-provincial limited liability company

2.1 (1) — In this section,

"extra-provincial limited liability company" means an unincorporated association, other than a partnership, formed under the laws of another jurisdiction that grants to each of its members limited liability with respect to the liabilities of the association.

Registration

(2) — No extra-provincial limited liability company shall carry on business in Ontario unless it has registered its company name.

Use of "Limited"

(2.1) — Despite any other Act, the word "Limited" or any abbreviation of that word or any version of it in another language may be used in the registered company name of an extra-provincial limited liability company.

Use of registered name only

(3) — No extra-provincial limited liability company shall carry on business in Ontario under a name other than its registered company name.

Exception

(3.1) — Despite subsections (2) and (3), an extra-provincial limited liability company may carry on business or identify itself to the public under a name other than its company name, if the name is set out in a partnership registration under subsection 4(1) or a declaration under the *Limited Partnerships Act*.

Laws of other jurisdictions

(4) — The laws of the jurisdiction under which an extra-provincial limited liability company is formed shall govern its organization and internal affairs and the liability of its managers and members.

Service

(5) — A person may serve a notice or document on an extra-provincial limited liability company at its Ontario place of business, if any, or its address required to be maintained under the laws of the jurisdiction of formation or its principal office address.

1998, c. 18, Sched. E, s. 33; 2010, c. 16, Sched. 8, s. 2

Registrar

3. (1) — The Minister shall appoint a public servant in the Ministry as the Registrar.

Delegation of powers

(2) — The Registrar may delegate any of the duties or powers of the Registrar to any public servant employed under Part III of the *Public Service of Ontario Act, 2006*.

Records

(3) — The Registrar shall maintain a record of every registration made under this Act or filed under the *Limited Partnerships Act*.

Available to the public

(4) — Any person is entitled to examine, during normal business hours, the records maintained by the Registrar.

1994, c. 27, s. 72(3); 2006, c. 35, Sched. C, s. 9

Registration

4. (1) — Upon payment of the required fee, any person may register a name for the purpose of complying with section 2 or section 2.1 or section 44.3 or 44.4 of the *Partnerships Act*.

Period

(1.1) — The registration is effective for five years from the date that it is accepted for registration by the Registrar.

Idem

(2) — The Registrar shall not accept for registration a name that does not comply with the prescribed requirements.

Idem

(3) — Only letters from the Roman alphabet, Arabic numerals or a combination of letters from the Roman alphabet and Arabic numerals together with punctuation marks and such other marks as are prescribed may form part of a registered name.

Changes

(4) — If there is a change in information set out in a registration, the registrant shall register, in the prescribed form within fifteen days after the change, an amended registration showing the change.

Correcting information

(5) — If the Registrar has grounds to believe that information registered is not correct or current, he or she may give notice to the registrant requiring that the information be corrected or updated within the time specified in the notice.

Idem

(6) — A registrant receiving a notice under subsection (5) shall comply with the request in the notice or provide evidence to the Registrar that the information registered is correct or current, as the case may be.

Cancelling registration

(7) — The Registrar shall cancel a registration,

(a) if a name was accepted for registration that does not comply with the prescribed requirements;

(a.1) if the registrant fails to pay a fee required by the Minister under section 10.1; or

(b) if the registrant requests the cancellation.

Idem

(8) — The Registrar may cancel a registration if the registrant is given a notice under subsection (5) and does not comply with subsection (6).

Entering cancellation

(9) — The Registrar shall indicate, on the record, every cancellation under subsection (7) or (8).

Notice of cancellation

(10) — Before cancelling a registration other than on the request of the registrant or pursuant to a Court order, the Registrar shall give the registrant twenty-one days notice of the intention to cancel.

Appeal

(11) — A person whose application to register a name is refused may appeal to the Divisional Court within twenty-one days after the day of the refusal.

Idem

(12) — A registrant who receives a notice under subsection (10) may appeal to the Divisional Court within twenty-one days after receipt of the notice.

Idem

(13) — If a notice under subsection (10) is under appeal, the Registrar shall not cancel the registration unless a final determination is made upholding the Registrar's decision.

1994, c. 27, s. 72(4); 1998, c. 2, s. 9; 1998, c. 18, Sched. E, s. 34; 2004, c. 19, s. 4

Renewal of registration

5. (1) — A registrant is entitled to renew a registration before it expires upon paying the required fee.

Late renewal

(2) — A registrant is entitled to renew a registration within sixty days after it expires upon paying the required fee for late renewal.

Effective date

(3) Effective date — A renewal made under subsection (1) and (2) is effective on the day immediately following the expiration day of the registration being renewed.

1998, c. 18, Sched. E, s. 35

Liability for damages

6. (1) — A person who suffers damages by reason of the registration of a name that is the same as or deceptively similar to another person's registered name is entitled to recover compensation from the registrant for damages suffered because of the registration.

Proposed Amendment — 6(1)

(1) *Liability for damages* — A person is entitled to recover compensation from a registrant for damages the person suffered by reason of the registration by the registrant of a name that is the same as or deceptively similar to,

(a) a name registered by the person; or

(b) the person's name, even though the person is not required to register that name under this Act.

2010, c. 16, Sched. 5, s. 2(1) [Not in force at date of publication.]

Idem

(2) — For the purposes of subsection (1), the compensation is limited to the greater of $500 and the actual amount of damages incurred.

Proposed Amendment — 6(2)

(2) *Same* — The compensation under each of clauses (1)(a) and (b) is limited to the greater of $500 and the actual amount of damages incurred.

2010, c. 16, Sched. 5, s. 2(2) [Not in force at date of publication.]

Cancelling registration

(3) — In giving a judgment for a plaintiff in an action brought under subsection (1), the court shall order the Registrar to cancel the registration that was the cause of the action.

Ability to sue

7. (1) — A person carrying on business in contravention of subsection 2(1), (2) or (3) or subsection 4(4) or (6) is not capable of maintaining a proceeding in a court in Ontario in connection with that business except with leave of the court.

Idem

(2) — The court shall grant leave if the person seeking to maintain the proceeding satisfies the court that,

(a) the failure to register was inadvertent;

(b) there is no evidence that the public has been deceived or misled; and

(c) at the time of the application to the court, the person is not in contravention of this Act or the regulations.

Contracts valid

(3) — No contract is void or voidable by reason only that it was entered into by a person who was in contravention of this Act or the regulations at the time the contract was made.

Certified copies

8. (1) — Upon the payment of the required fee, the Registrar shall issue to any person applying for it,

(a) a certifed copy of the record with respect to any name registered; or

(b) if a name is not registered, a certificate so stating.

Idem

(2) — A certified copy or a certificate issued under this section is admissible in evidence in all courts as proof, in the absence of evidence to the contrary, of the contents of the document or of the non-registration of a name, as the case may be, without proof of the appointment or signature of the Registrar.

Idem

(3) — For the purpose of this section, the signature of the Registrar may be printed or otherwise mechanically or electronically reproduced.

1998, c. 18, Sched. E, s. 36

Form of records

9. (1) — Records prepared and maintained by the Registrar may be in bound or loose-leaf or electronic form or in a photgraphic film form or may be entered or recorded by any system of mechanical or electronic data processing or by any other information storage device that is capable of reproducing any required information in an accurate and intelligible form within a reasonable time.

Idem

(2) — If records maintained by the Registrar are prepared and maintained otherwise than in written or other form, the Registrar shall furnish any copy required to be furnished in intelligible written form.

Idem

(3) — A report reproduced from records prepared and maintained otherwise than in written form that purports to be certified by the Registrar is, without proof of the Registrar's office or signature, admissible in evidence.

Copies

(4) — The Registrar is not required to produce the original of a document if a copy is furnished in compliance with subsection (2).

Idem

(5) — For the purpose of this section, a document is a copy of an original if it contains all the information contained in the original.

1994, c. 27, s. 72(5)–(7)

Delivery of notices, etc.

9.1 (1) — A notice or other document that is required or permitted by this Act to be sent by the Registrar may be sent by ordinary mail or by any other method, including registered mail, certified mail or prepaid courier, if there is a record by the person who has delivered it that the notice or document has been sent.

Same

(2) — A notice or other document referred to in subsection (1) may be sent by telephone transmission of a facsimile of the notice or other document or by another form of electronic transmission where there is a record that the notice or other document has been sent.

Deemed delivery

(3) — A notice or other document sent by mail by the Registrar shall be deemed to have been received by the intended recipient on the earlier of,

(a) the day the intended recipient actually receives it; or

(b) the fifth business day after it is mailed.

Same

(4) — A notice or other document sent by the Registrar by a method referred to in subsection (2) shall be deemed to be received by the intended recipient on the earlier of,

(a) the day the intended recipient actually receives it; or

(b) the first business day after the day the transmission is sent by the Registrar.

Fax delivery

(5) — Subject to the regulations, a registration may be sent in duplicate to the Registrar by telephone transmission of a facsimile.

1994, c. 27, s. 72(8)

Offence

10. (1) — Every person who, without reasonable cause, contravenes section 2 or 2.1 or subsection 4(4) or (6) or submits a statement in an application for a registration under this Act that is false or misleading with respect to any material fact is guilty of an offence and on conviction is liable to a fine of not more than $2,000 or, if the person is a corporation, to a fine of not more than $25,000

Idem

(2) — If a corporation is guilty of an offence under subsection (1), every director or officer of the corporation and every person acting as its representative in Ontario who authorized, permitted or acquiesced in such an offence is also guilty of an offence and on conviction is liable to a fine of not more than $2,000.

1998, c. 18, Sched. E, s. 37

Powers of Minister — (0.1) Minister's regulations

10.1 — The Minister may make regulations,

(a) governing the registration of forms in electronic format, including the manner of acceptance of forms and the determination of the date of receipt;

(b) governing the registration of forms sent by telephone transmission of a facsimile;

(c) governing the custody and destruction of registrations and certificates.

Fees

(1) — The Minister may by order require the payment of fees for registrations, late renewals, search reports, or copies of documents or information, or other services under this Act and may approve the amounts of those fees.

1998, c. 18, Sched. E, s. 38; 2011, c. 1, Sched. 5, s. 2(1)

Registrar's regulations

10.2 — The Registrar may make regulations prescribing forms and providing for their use.

2011, c. 1, Sched. 5, s. 2(2)

Regulations

11. — The Lieutenant Governor in Council may make regulations,

(a) prescribing information to be contained in a registration;

(b) prescribing the duties of the Registrar;

(c) [Repealed 1998, c. 18, Sched. E, s. 39(1).]

(d) [Repealed 2011, c. 1, Sched. 5, s. 2(3).]

(d.1) [Repealed 2011, c. 1, Sched. 5, s. 2(3).]

(d.2) [Repealed 2011, c. 1, Sched. 5, s. 2(3).]

(d.3) authorizing the Registrar to enter into an agreement with any person respecting the use, disclosure, sale or licensing of records maintained under this Act and prescribing terms and conditions for any such agreement;

(e) exempting any class of person or business from the application of section 2, or any provision in the regulation, and prescribing conditions for any such exemption;

(f) prescribing and prohibiting the use of connotations, suggestions, words, expressions or phrases in a name shown in a registration;

(g) [Repealed 2011, c. 1, Sched. 5, s. 2(3).]

(h) [Repealed 1998, c. 18, Sched. E, s. 39(1).]

(i) prescribing any matter required or permitted by this Act to be prescribed for which a specific power is not otherwise provided.

1994, c. 27, s. 72(9); 1998, c. 18, Sched. E, s. 39; 2011, c. 1, Sched. 5, s. 2(3), (4)

Transition

12. (1) — A name or designation that is stated in a declaration or a renewal thereof filed under section 1 or 9 of the *Partnerships Registration Act*, being chapter 371 of the Revised Statutes of Ontario, 1980, shall be deemed to be registered under and in accordance with this Act and the regulations.

Idem

(2) — A registration of a name or style or a renewal thereof that is filed under section 2 of the *Corporations Information Act*, being chapter 96 of the Revised Statutes of Ontario, 1980, shall be deemed to be a registration under and in accordance with this Act and the regulations.

Consolidation Period: From March 30, 2011 to the e-Laws currency date (Thursday, February 23, 2012)

Business Names Act - *Restrictions Respecting Names*, O. Reg. 122/91

ONT. REG. 122/91 RESTRICTIONS RESPECTING NAMES

made under the *Business Names Act*
O. Reg. 122/91 as am. O. Reg. 247/05

GENERAL

1. The first character of a name shown in a registration must be a letter of the Roman alphabet or an Arabic numeral.

2. (1) For the purposes of subsection 4(3) of the Act, the following are prescribed as the punctuation marks and other marks that may form part of a registered name:

" # $ % & ' () * +,. / :; **lesser than angle bracket** = < ? [] /, ^ ' @

(2) A name shown in a registration must not consist only or primarily of a combination of punctuation marks and other marks.

(3) A name shall be set out in a registration with only one space between each word.

O. Reg. 247/05, s. 1

3. If the name contains characters from an alphabet other than the Roman alphabet, the name shown in the registration must consist of a translation of the name into a language which contains only letters from the Roman alphabet.

PROHIBITED USAGE

4. (1) A name shown in a registration must not include, in any language, a word or expression that is contrary to public policy, including a word that is scandalous, obscene or immoral.

(2) A name shown in a registration must not use a word or expression that would suggest that the registrant is engaged in an activity that is contrary to public policy.

5. A name shown in a registration must not include a word, an expression or an abbreviation the use of which is prohibited under a federal Act or an Ontario Act.

6. A name shown in a registration must not use Arabic numerals or a word or expression that would suggest that the name is a corporate number name.

7. A name shown in a registration must not use a word or expression that would suggest that the registrant is a form of organization that the registrant is not.

RESTRICTIONS

8. (1) A name shown in a registration must not include the name of a specific individual,

    (a) unless, at any time before or during the period of the registration of the name, the individual has or had a material interest in the business or activity carried on by the registrant; and

(b) unless the individual consents in writing to the use of his or her name.

(2) For the purpose of clause (1)(b), if the individual is deceased and his or her death occurred within thirty years before the name is registered, the heir, executor or administrator of the individual may consent in writing to the use of the individual's name.

(3) This section does not apply if the individual is deceased and his or her death occurred thirty years or more before the name is registered.

9. A name shown in a registration must not include a word, expression or abbreviation the use of which is restricted under a federal Act or an Ontario Act unless the registrant satisfies the restriction.

10. (1) Subject to subsection (2), a name shown in a registration must not include a word or expression that suggests that the business or activity of the registrant is connected with,

(a) the Crown in right of Canada or in right of a province;

(b) the Government of Canada, of a territory or of a province;

(c) a municipality; or

(d) an agency of the Crown, government or municipality.

(2) If the registrant obtains the written consent of the applicable Crown, government, municipality or agency, a name shown in a registration may include a word or expression described in subsection (1).

11. A name shown in a registration must not include in any language the word "college", "institute" or "university", if the use of the word would suggest that the registrant is a post-secondary educational institution, unless the Minister of Colleges and Universities gives written consent to the use of the word.

EXCEPTIONS

12. (1) Sections 1, 2, 3, 6, 7, 8, 10 and 11 do not apply with respect to a name shown in a registration if, on the 30th day of April, 1991,

(a) the registrant was using the name; and

(b) the registrant was not required to file a declaration under the Partnerships Registration Act (R.S.O. 1980, c. 371) respecting the name.

(2) Sections 1, 2, 3, 6, 7, 8, 10 and 11 do not apply with respect to a name shown in a registration,

(a) if the registrant was using the name on the 30th day of April, 1991; and

(b) if the registrant was required, on the 30th day of April, 1991, to file a declaration under the Partnerships Registration Act (R.S.O. 1980, c. 371) respecting the name before the 1st of July, 1991.

COMMENCEMENT

13. This Regulation comes into force on the 1st day of May, 1991.

Last amendment: 2009, c. 33, Sched. 2, s. 57.

Consolidation Period: From June 1, 2005 to the e-Laws currency date (Thursday, February 23, 2012)

CHAPTER 3: PARTNERSHIPS & OTHER FORMS OF BUSINESS ORGANIZATION

Overview:

- General partnerships
  - The nature of a partnership
  - Advantages & disadvantages
  - The relationship between partners and others
  - The relationship of partners to one another
  - Dissolution of partnership
- Limited liability partnerships
- Limited partnerships
  - Filing a declaration
  - Extra-provincial limited partnerships
- Other types of business associations
  - Joint ventures
  - Franchises
  - Not-for-profit organizations
- Workbook:
  - Review Exercise
  - Form 6, *Business Names Act* (Limited Liability Partnership)
  - Form 3, *Limited Partnerships Act*
  - Case Analysis
- Appendix:
  - *Partnerships Act*
  - Partnership Agreement Checklist

1. General Partnerships

Many clients do not want to start a business on their own, but instead prefer to share risk and resources with others. One way to structure a business that is operated by more than one person is to create a partnership. Essentially, a partnership is a business enterprise operated by two or more persons, for a profit. A business that is operated as a partnership is referred to as a "firm".[1]

The *Partnerships Act*[2] is the statute that governs the creation and operation of partnerships in Ontario. It is divided into five main parts:

1. The nature of a partnership

2. The relationship between partners and others who deal with them

3. The relationship between partners to one another

4. Dissolution of a partnership

5. Limited liability partnerships

A copy of the *Partnerships Act* is provided in the Appendix to this chapter, for your reference. A current copy can be obtained online from the e-Laws website.

Note that Form 1 under the *Business Names Act* (discussed in Chapter 2) must be filed to register a partnership name. (This is the same form that is used to register the business name of a sole proprietorship.) Form 5 of the *Business Names Act* is used to register, renew, change or cease a business name that is different from the firm name of a registered general partnership, or an existing limited partnership.

(a) The Nature of a Partnership

Section 2 of the *Partnerships Act* defines a partnership in the following way:

Partnership is the relation that subsists between persons carrying on a business in common with a view to profit, but the relation between the members of a company or association that is incorporated by or under the authority of any special or general Act in force in Ontario or elsewhere, or registered as a corporation under any such Act, is not a partnership within the meaning of this Act.[3]

Many individuals who start a business together do not actually discuss the form of business organization that their business will take; they simply agree to work together to make money. However, the type of business organization affects legal rights and obligations. For this reason, the Act also provides some guidelines to help the court determine whether or not a business relationship qualifies as a "partnership". Generally, the receipt of profits from the business, in the absence of evidence to the contrary, is an indicator of a partnership. Section 3 of the Act also provides a list of factors that do <u>not</u> automatically indicate the presence of a partnership, such as:

---

1 *Partnerships Act*, R.S.O. 1990, c. P.5, s. 5.

2 R.S.O. 1990, c. P.5.

3 *Partnerships Act*, R.S.O. 1990, c. P.5, s. 2.

1. Ownership of property

2. Sharing of gross returns

3. Receipt of debts

4. Remuneration paid by a share of profits

5. Receipt of an annuity by a spouse or child of a deceased partner

6. Loans to a person engaged in the business, with a term that the lender shall receive a share of profits or an interest rate that varies with profits

7. Receipt of goodwill payments that vary with profits.[4]

Please refer to the *Partnerships Act* for details on each of these factors.

In some circumstances, the courts may have to determine whether or not a partnership exists in order to determine the financial or legal consequences for the parties involved. Sometimes, a plaintiff or defendant will argue that a business relationship was a partnership, so that he/she can receive tax or other benefits. At other times, a client may argue that no partnership existed so that he/she is not liable for damages claimed by another party against the partnership. In these (and other) circumstances, the courts will refer to sections 2 and 3 of the *Partnerships Act* to determine whether a partnership exists. The consequences of this determination can be very significant, as you will see from the cases summarized in this chapter.

Continental Bank of Canada v. R., (*sub nom.* Continental Bank Leasing Corp. v. Canada) [1998] 2 S.C.R. 298 (S.C.C.)

A bank sold its wholly owned subsidiary, a leasing company, to Central Capital Leasing ("Central"). On December 24, 1986, a partnership was formed between the leasing company and Central's subsidiaries in order to carry on the leasing company's business. On December 27, 1986, the leasing company transferred its assets, tax free, to the partnership, and then dissolved. The bank then sold its partnership interest to Central's subsidiaries. The tax authorities challenged this transaction, with the view that the leasing company was essentially disposing of its assets and should pay tax on that disposition. While the Minister was successful in lower courts, the leasing company ultimately appealed to the Supreme Court of Canada.

A key issue in this case was whether a true partnership existed between the leasing company and Central, under s. 2 of the *Partnerships Act* of Ontario. In its analysis of this issue, the court stated:

> Section 2 of the *Partnerships Act* defines partnership as "the relation that subsists between persons carrying on a business in common with a view to profit". This wording, which is common to the majority of partnership statutes in the common law world, discloses three essential ingredients: (1) a business, (2) carried on in common, (3) with a view to profit.

---

4 *Ibid.*, s. 3.

The court relied on the Partnership Agreement, as well as other facts relevant to this case, to determine that the leasing company and Central were, in fact, engaged in a business, carried on in common, with a view to profit. The parties were continuing an existing business that they did believe would generate a profit. The duration of the partnership (3 days) was irrelevant, as was the fact that the primary motive may have been a tax related one. As long as the enterprise had the three elements discussed above, it was a partnership under s. 2 of the *Partnerships Act.*

The appeal by the leasing company was allowed with costs, and the transaction which allowed it to transfer assets tax free was found to be valid.

Backman v. R., [2001] 1 S.C.R. 367 (S.C.C.)

A U.S. partnership owned an apartment complex whose value was less than its cost. A Canadian taxpayer bought an interest in this partnership, and on the same day, sold its main asset – thereby incurring a loss that the taxpayer could claim on his Canadian income tax. As part of the same transaction, the taxpayer also acquired a 1% interest in an oil and gas property, which did not produce a profit and was shut down within a short time due to flooding. The tax authorities denied the taxpayer's deduction of partnership loss when calculating its income tax, and the taxpayer appealed all the way to the Supreme Court of Canada.

In analyzing whether or not there was a true partnership in this case, the court referred to its decision in *Continental Bank of Canada v. R.*, 1998 CarswellNat 1496, 1998 CarswellNat 1497, (*sub nom.* Continental Bank Leasing Corp. v. Canada) [1998] 2 S.C.R. 298 (S.C.C.). The court reiterated that there are 3 elements that must be satisfied to show that a partnership exists, namely: a business, carried on in common, with a view to profit. The court clarified that a partnership can be formed for a single transaction, and that it can be formed for a tax related motive. In addition, a partnership does not require the formation of a new business – it can be created to continue operating an existing business. A business can even involve the passive receipt of rent. Provincial partnership acts usually define "business" in a very broad manner, including every trade, occupation and profession.

To find evidence that the business was carried on in common, the courts rely primarily on the terms of a partnership agreement (if there is one.) "Other evidence consistent with an intention to carry on business in common includes: the contribution of skill, knowledge or assets to a common undertaking, a joint property interest in the subject-matter of the adventure, the sharing of profits and losses, the filing of income tax returns as a partnership, financial statements and joint bank accounts, as well as correspondence with third parties: see *Continental Bank, supra*, at paras. 24 and 36."

To find that a venture was entered into "with a view to profit", there must be some intention that profits would be generated, even if that is not the primary motive for the transaction or relationship. Even if the primary motive is to reduce taxes, there must be some intention that the venture will generate profit at some point in the future. The court ultimately found that the parties never intended for the apartment complex or the oil and gas property to generate a profit, and as such, there was no partnership in this case.

The appeal was dismissed with costs.

(b) Advantages & Disadvantages

There are many advantages and disadvantages to operating a business as a partnership. Some of the key advantages include:

- a potentially larger pool of investment capital (assuming that each one of the partners contributes to the initial investment)

- sharing of financial and legal risk with other partners

- each partner can contribute different skills, experiences and contacts

- distribution of work load amongst the partners

- there may be tax advantages, depending on the tax position of each partner (as partnership income is divided and treated as the personal income of each partner)

Some of the key disadvantages include:

- vicarious liability for the acts and omissions of other partners

- each partner can bind the partnership in contract (unless suppliers/customers have been made aware that this is not the case)

- sharing of profits amongst the partners

- some loss of control, as decisions must be made after consulting with the other partners

(c) The Relationship between Partners and Others

Sections 6 through 19 of the *Partnerships Act* address how others are affected by the existence of a partnership. The fundamental principle is that each partner is an agent of the firm and of the other partners. Therefore, each partner can bind the other partners and the firm in a contract, even if the other partners know nothing about it.[5] A firm *can* limit the power of any partner to bind the firm, but that power is only effective against a third party that is given notice of this limitation.[6]

Partners in a firm have joint and several liability for the debts and obligations of the firm. This is a critical feature of a partnership, and one that legal professionals should discuss with their clients. The liability of partners is addressed in section 10 of the Act, which states:

> Except as provided in subsection (2), every partner in a firm is liable jointly with the other partners for all the debts and obligations of the firm incurred while the person is a partner, and after the partner's death the partner's estate is also severally liable in a due course of administration for such debts and obligations so far as they remain unsatisfied, but subject to the prior payment of his or her separate debts.[7]

(Subsection 10(2) refers to limited liability partnerships, which will be discussed later in this chapter.) In addition, section 13 states:

---

5 *Ibid.*, ss. 6 – 7.
6 *Ibid.*, s. 9.
7 *Ibid.*, s. 10.

Except as provided in subsection 10(2), every partner is liable jointly with the co-partners and also severally for everything for which the firm, while the person is a partner therein, becomes liable under section 11 or 12.[8]

> Assume that Javid, Helena and Mike enter into a partnership to start Nirvana Nightclub. The partnership owes a supplier $10,000, which the partnership cannot pay. The principle of joint and several liability means that, if the supplier sues for recovery of the $10,000, Javid, Helena and Mike will each be named as defendants, and all three are responsible for the debt of $10,000. In addition, if judgment is obtained against all three defendants, the supplier can enforce the full amount of the judgment – that is, the full $10,000 – against any one of the defendants. Since Javid is the only defendant with significant personal assets, the supplier will likely go after Javid to recover the full $10,000. The supplier does not have to get 1/3 of the amount from each of the three defendants. It will then be up to Javid to try to recover some money from Helena and Mike (which will be unlikely, in the circumstances, since both Helena and Mike have minimal assets.)

> *Fedirchuk v. Levitz*, 1998 CarswellOnt 843, [1998] O.J. No. 831 (Ont. Gen. Div.), affirmed 1999 CarswellOnt 2528 (Ont. C.A.)
>
> The defendant, Fage, was a partner in an accounting firm called Ginsberg, Gluzman, Fage and Levitz. The accounting firm was affiliated with an office management company ("Electrodata") that provided IT services to the accounting firm's clients. Fage was the Chairman of the Board for Electrodata, and as the accounting partner responsible for technology, Fage was also the key partner (in the accounting firm) responsible for the direction of Electrodata.
>
> The plaintiff hired Fage as his advisor in valuing companies that he was interested in purchasing. The plaintiff told Fage that he was looking for a stable, established company with ongoing profitability. Fage reviewed several business proposals and advised against them. He then suggested that the plaintiff acquire an interest in Electrodata, particularly since the plaintiff had a background in the same industry. The plaintiff relied on Fage's advice, believing that Electrodata fit his criteria of a stable, established, profitable company. Fage did not advise the plaintiff that he should seek independent advice from another financial advisor, given Fage's connection and the accounting firm's affiliation with Electrodata. The investment was not profitable. The plaintiff sued the defendant and his partners for return of his investment and damages, due to a breach of fiduciary duty.
>
> The court held that the defendant had breached his fiduciary duty to the plaintiff in the circumstances. It referred to section 11 of the *Partnerships Act*, which states:
>
> "Where by any wrongful act or omission of a partner acting in the ordinary course of the business of the firm, or with the authority of the co-partners, loss or injury is caused to a person not being a partner of the firm, or any penalty is incurred, the firm is liable therefore to the same extent as the partner so acting or omitting to act."

---

8 *Ibid.*, s. 13.

The court held that section 11 was clearly broad enough to include a breach of fiduciary duty which occurred in the ordinary course of the firm's business. In this case, the partners had authorized the transaction. It was irrelevant that the partners did not know at that time that the plaintiff was a client of their firm, and that he had an ongoing professional relationship with Fage. The impugned conduct of one partner was vicariously attributed to all of the other partners.

The action was allowed, with damages awarded against all of the partners in the accounting firm in the amount of approximately $198,885.00 for the plaintiff's initial investment, the plaintiff's loan to Electrodata, salary foregone by the plaintiff, and for interest and bank charges paid by the plaintiff to finance his initial investment.

Sometimes, the courts will also attribute liability to individuals if they acted as if they were part of a partnership. This is referred to as "holding out".

Section 15 of the *Partnerships Act* states:

Every person, who by words spoken or written or by conduct represents himself or herself or who knowingly suffers himself or herself to be represented as a partner in a particular firm, is liable as a partner to any person who has on the faith of any such representation given credit to the firm, whether the representation has or has not been made or communicated to the persons so giving credit by or with the knowledge of the apparent partner making the representation or suffering it to be made.[9]

Essentially, this means that, if someone acts as if he/she is a partner in a firm, and the other individuals allow this to happen, all of the individuals that are involved will have joint and several liability for damages incurred by others who rely on the fact that these individuals were working together as a firm. However, the plaintiff must first prove that he/she relied on the fact that the individuals held themselves out to be partners in a firm – in other words, the plaintiff entered into the transaction because he/she thought that he was dealing with a group of partners in a firm. The next case illustrates how the court analyzes these types of situations.

Bet-Mur Investments Ltd. v. Spring (1994), 20 O.R. (3d) 417, 17 B.L.R. (2d) 55 (Ont. Gen. Div.), affirmed 1999 CarswellOnt 390 (Ont. C.A.)

The plaintiff sued Spring and Alexandor, two lawyers who appeared to be working in partnership. Default judgment was obtained against Spring, who was disbarred and serving jail time for the fraud committed in this case. The plaintiff was suing Alexandor, because Alexandor and Spring held themselves out to be in partnership.

The plaintiff hired Spring to represent it in a mortgage transaction. Spring was a friend of Murray Schwartz, the controlling mind of Bet-Mur Investments Ltd. (the plaintiff), and had also acted as Schwartz's lawyer from time to time over 10 years prior to this transaction. Spring introduced the plaintiff to this mortgage deal, and then stole the money advanced to him by Bet-Mur.

The court stated that there was no real partnership between Spring and Alexandor. There was no sharing of profits or expenses, and no intention by the parties to enter

9 *Ibid.*, s. 15(1).

into a partnership. Alexandor was an employee hired by Spring. However, Spring and Alexandor held themselves out to be partners.

> Their letterhead, Spring, Alexandor, and a similar sign on the door was sufficient to establish that "holding-out." In addition, a bank account in the firm name was opened and, in fact, the $250,000 cheque from the plaintiff was paid to "Spring, Alexandor, in trust." In such circumstances, the onus is on the solicitors to show that they had clearly conveyed to the public that they were not partners if those solicitors wished to avoid the ramifications of s. 15(1) of the *Partnerships Act*.

The court held that Spring and Alexandor had held themselves out to be partners. However, "[t]his finding is not, by itself, sufficient to find Alexandor liable to the plaintiff. The plaintiff must show that it has "given credit" to the firm on the faith of such holding-out or representation."

In this case, the plaintiff hired Spring because Schwartz and Spring were friends prior to the mortgage transaction, and because Spring introduced Schwartz to the mortgage deal.

> [T]he holding-out by Harold Spring and David Alexandor of themselves as partners had nothing to do with the extending of "credit to the firm" by the plaintiff. The plaintiff, through its directing mind, Murray Schwartz, clearly on the facts of this case, was dealing with Harold Spring and Harold Spring alone.

As a result, the plaintiff's action against Alexandor was dismissed with costs.

(d) The Relationship of Partners to One Another

The rules that govern a partnership are defined by the *Partnerships Act*, but can be varied by a partnership agreement.[10] It is always prudent to enter into a partnership agreement when two or more individuals decide to start a business as partners. The partnership agreement is a contract that allows the partners to specify rules about their rights, duties and responsibilities. If there is no partnership agreement between the parties, the rules established by the *Partnerships Act* will apply.

> Do you think Javid, Helena and Mike should start their nightclub business as partners? Who has the most to gain in a partnership arrangement? Who has the most to lose? What kinds of things would you suggest should be in a partnership agreement between Javid, Helena and Mike?

A "Partnership Agreement Checklist" is provided in the Appendix to this chapter. It highlights issues that are commonly addressed in a partnership agreement. Of course, each agreement must be tailored to a client's circumstances; in some cases, it may be appropriate to have a very simple agreement, and in other situations, it may be prudent to make the agreement more complex. If, however, there are issues in the checklist that will not be included in a partnership agreement, a lawyer should explain those issues to the client and make them aware of the consequences of leaving them out of the agreement. Finally, the checklist can be given to a client before the partnership agreement is drafted,

---

10 *Partnerships Act*, R.S.O. 1990, c. P.5, s. 20.

in order to prepare the client for the type of information that will be required from the client.

As indicated above, if there is no partnership agreement in place, the rules in the *Partnership Act* will be applied to a business that is run as a partnership. Generally, all of the property that has been contributed to the partnership by the partners, or has been bought by the partnership, becomes "partnership property".[11] The partners can only use this property for the purposes of the partnership. The *Partnerships Act* specifies how partners must handle property – such as land – in different circumstances.[12] Unless otherwise agreed in a partnership agreement, partners share equally in the capital and profits of a business, and must contribute equally towards the losses. In addition, the firm must indemnify every partner for payments made and personal liabilities incurred by the partner in the ordinary and proper course of business, or in relation to the preservation of the business or property of the firm.

A key element of a partnership is trust. Partners owe a fiduciary duty to the partnership, and to one another. Generally, a fiduciary duty is a duty of utmost good faith to another person. It includes, but is not limited to, the duty of loyalty and the duty to avoid conflicts of interest. The next case discusses the concept of fiduciary duty.

Moffat v. Wetstein (1996), 29 O.R. (3d) 371, 135 D.L.R. (4th) 298 (Ont. Gen. Div.), leave to appeal refused 1997 CarswellOnt 633 (Ont. Gen. Div.)

David Thompson was a partner in an accounting firm, and later became a lawyer in a national law firm. While he was a lawyer at that firm, he advised a client that he, and others, had lost a significant amount of money due to the misrepresentations of a partner at the accounting firm where Thompson used to be a partner. The alleged misrepresentations occurred at the time that Thompson was a partner at that accounting firm.

One of the issues in the case was whether Thompson had breached his fiduciary duty to his former partners at the accounting firm, by representing this client.

A fiduciary is subject to a strict ethic to provide, among other things, the utmost good faith and loyalty to those to whom he acts in the capacity of fiduciary. Subsumed in the fiduciary's duties of good faith and loyalty is the duty to avoid a conflict of interest. The fiduciary must not only avoid a direct conflict of interest but must also avoid the appearance of a possible or potential conflict. The fiduciary is barred from dividing loyalties between competing interests, including self interest.

Although the partnership relationship is contractual in nature and origin, the guise under which a partner operates vis-a-vis other partners is that of fiduciary. The individual partner owes a fiduciary duty to the partnership in general, as well, as his fellow partners.

The court held, amongst other things, that the fiduciary duty of a partner may extend beyond the date of the partner's departure from the partnership. In this case, Thompson's representation of the client posed a conflict of interest with his former partners at the accounting firm, which amounted to a breach of fiduciary duty towards his former partners. Thompson was removed as the solicitor for the client in this case.

---

11   *Ibid.*, s. 21.
12   *Ibid.*, ss. 21 – 24.

Although the concept of fiduciary duty is quite broad, the *Partnerships Act* mentions the following specific duties of partners:

- the duty to render true accounts and full information of everything relating to the partnership to any partner (or his/her legal representative)[13]

- the duty not to compete with the firm[14]

In addition, the partner must account to the firm for any benefit derived by the partner without the consent of the other partners from a transaction related to the partnership, or from the use of partnership property, the firm's name or the firm's business connections.[15]

(e) Dissolution of the Partnership

A partnership may be dissolved by any one of the following circumstances:

- expiration of the term of the partnership, if an expiration date was established when the partnership was created

- completion of a transaction or undertaking, if the partnership was created for a specific transaction or undertaking

- upon notice given by any partner, if the partnership was created for an indefinite amount of time

- upon the death or insolvency of a partner

- upon the occurrence of any event that makes it illegal for the business of the firm to be carried out, or for the members to continue the partnership

- by court order, in certain circumstances[16]

Sections 36 through 44 of the *Partnerships Act* discuss how a partnership is dissolved, and how assets, debts and other obligations are handled upon dissolution of a partnership.

2. Limited Liability Partnerships

Limited liability partnerships are a special kind of partnership that applies to certain professions, such as the legal and accounting professions. As firms in these professions grew larger and larger over time – sometimes, with more than a thousand partners – the issue of liability for the acts or omissions of other partners became more problematic. Lawyers, for example, have been prohibited from incorporating because the overarching burden of joint and several liability in a partnership was thought to keep lawyers vigilant about what their partners were doing. In other words, if you are a partner in a law firm and you know that you have joint and several liability for what other partners do or do not do, you will be very careful to keep an eye on how your partners operate. This becomes problematic, and perhaps unfair, as partnerships grow in size. How can a partner

---

13 *Partnerships Act*, R.S.O. 1990, c. P.5, s.28.

14 Ibid., s.30.

15 Ibid., s.29.

16 *Partnerships Act*, R.S.O. 1990, c. P.5, ss. 32 – 35.

in the Toronto office of a law firm, for example, be expected to oversee the actions of a partner in the Vancouver office?

The concept of a limited liability partnership addresses these concerns, in part, but keeps most of the concepts that have been discussed about partnership intact. A limited liability partnership is formed when two or more persons enter into a written agreement that:

- designates the partnership as a limited liability partnership, and

- states that the *Partnerships Act* governs the agreement.[17]

A limited liability partnership can only be formed for the purpose of practising a profession that is governed by an Act that specifically allows the formation of a limited liability partnership. In addition, the governing body for that profession must require the partnership to maintain a minimum amount of liability insurance[18], and the firm must register its name under the *Business Names Act*. The firm's name must contain the words "limited liability partnership" or the abbreviation "LLP" (or their French equivalents) as the first or last words of the name.[19] The form used for this purpose is Form 6 under the *Business Names Act*. (Please refer to the Workbook for a copy of Form 6.)

The most critical aspect of the formation of a limited liability partnership is found in s. 10(2):

Subject to subsections (3) and (3.1), a partner in a limited liability partnership is not liable, by means or indemnification, contribution or otherwise, for,

(a) the debts, liabilities or obligations of the partnership or any partner arising from the negligent or wrongful acts or omissions that another partner or an employee, agent or representative of the partnership commits in the course of the partnership business while the partnership is a limited liability partnership; or

(b) any other debts or obligations of the partnership that are incurred while the partnership is a limited liability partnership. 2006, c. 34. s. 19

(3) Subsection (2) does not relieve a partner in a limited liability partnership from liability for,

(a) the partner's own negligent or wrongful act or omission;

(b) the negligent or wrongful act or omission of a person under the partner's direct supervision; or

(c) the negligent or wrongful act or omission of another partner or an employee of the partnership not under the partner's direct supervision, if,

(i) the act or omission was criminal or constituted fraud, even if there was no criminal act or omission, or

(ii) the partner knew or ought to have known of the act or omission and did not take the actions that a reasonable person would have taken to prevent it. 2006, c. 34, s.19

---

17 *Ibid.*, s. 44.1.

18 *Ibid.*, s. 44.2.

19 *Ibid.*, s. 44.3.

(3.1) Subsection (2) does not protect a partner's interest in the partnership property from claims against the partnership respecting a partnership obligation.

> Javid's uncle, Sam, has several nightclubs in Montreal, Quebec. He is excited about his nephew's new business venture, and wants to help him out financially. However, he does not want to take on any liabilities (other than the money that he will lend to Javid) and, since he lives and works in Quebec, he cannot take an active role in the business. Essentially, he wants to be a "silent partner". How can Javid, Helena, Mike and Sam structure a business arrangement that will allow Sam to invest in this partnership, without becoming an active partner?

3. Limited Partnerships

(a) What is a Limited Partnership?

The type of partnership that we have been discussing so far in this chapter is referred to as a general partnership – that is, a partnership where all partners are involved in the business, and all partners are jointly and severally liable for the acts and omissions of other partners, as they relate to partnership business. Someone who wants to be a "silent partner" does not want to be involved in the business, and most importantly, does not want joint and several liability.

The *Limited Partnerships Act*[20] relates to a different type of partnership – a limited partnership. A limited partnership, as defined in the Act, is a partnership which consists of at least one general partner and at least one limited partner. It can carry on any type of business that a general partnership can carry on.[21] The Act does not actually define the terms "general partner" and "limited partner", but instead, talks about the rights, powers and liabilities of general and limited partners. Essentially, a general partner in a limited partnership has all the rights, powers, restrictions and liabilities discussed in the *Partnerships Act*[22], except that the general partner must obtain the permission of limited partners to:

- do anything that contravenes the partnership agreement

- do anything that makes it impossible to carry on business

- consent to a judgment against the limited partnership

- possess or assign the property of the limited partnership, for other than a partnership purpose

- admit a person as a general partner

- admit a person as a limited partner, unless that right is conferred by the partnership agreement

- continue the business of the limited partnership if a general partner dies (or is

---

20 R.S.O. 1990, c. L.16.
21 *Ibid.*, s. 2.
22 R.S.O. 1990, c. P.5.

dissolved in the case of a corporation,) retires or becomes incapable as defined in the *Substitute Decisions Act, 1992*.[23]

Unlike a general partner, a limited partner can only contribute money or property to the limited partnership. A limited partner cannot provide any services for the partnership,[24] and significantly, must take care not to be involved in the operation of the business. Although a limited partner gives up the ability to control the business, a limited partner benefits from limited liability. Specifically, a limited partner is not liable for the obligations of the limited partnership, and is only responsible for providing the money and other property that the limited partner agreed to contribute to the limited partnership.[25] In order to ensure that the public is not deceived into thinking that a limited partner is a general partner (who has joint and several liability,) a limited partner's name cannot be used in the name of the limited partnership.[26]

Sam, Javid's uncle, becomes a limited partner in a partnership created with Javid, Helena and Mike. Because of Sam's experience in the nightclub business, he can't help enquiring about the general partners' plans, and tries to convince them to follow his marketing strategy. He starts to take trips to Toronto once a week, and even helps out at the nightclub when it first opens. On opening night, a patron becomes ill from a tainted drink that is served at the bar, and sues Javid, Helena, Mike and Sam. Is Sam liable for any damages that the plaintiff may be awarded?

A limited partner must be very careful to preserve the status of a limited partnership, if he/she wants to avoid sharing joint and several liability with his partners. Specifically, a limited partner must ensure that:

1. the limited partnership is properly registered, which means ensuring that the general partners have filed a declaration under the Act[27]

2. the limited partner does not offer services to the partnership, and does not get involved in control of the partnership business[28]

3. the firm's name does not include the limited partner's name, unless that name is the same as a general partner's name[29]

---

23 *Limited Partnerships Act*, R.S.O. 1990, c. L.16, s. 8.
24 Ibid., s.7.
25 Ibid. s. 9.
26 Ibid., s. 6.
27 Ibid., s. 3.
28 Ibid., ss. 7, 13.
29 Ibid., s. 6.

Haughton Graphic (Graphics) Ltd. v. Zivot, 1986 CarswellOnt 153 (Ont. H.C.), affirmed (1988), 38 B.L.R. xxxiii (Ont. C.A.), leave to appeal refused (1988), 38 B.L.R. xxxiii (S.C.C.)

Printcast Publishing Network ("Printcast") was established as an Alberta limited partnership to publish a magazine. The general partner was a corporation called Lifestyle Magazine Inc. ("L Inc.") and the two limited partners were individuals named Zivot and Marshall. The plaintiff provided printing services for Printcast in Toronto, and was ultimately not paid $128,251.79 for those services. Although the plaintiff obtained judgment against Printcast, the debt was still outstanding. The plaintiff sued the two limited partners, arguing that they both took control of the business of the limited partnership and should, therefore, be liable as general partners.

Section 63 of the *Alberta Partnership Act*, R.S.A., 1980, c. P-2, as amended by R.S.A. 1980 (supp.), c. 2; S.A. 1981 c. 28 states:

Liability to creditors. – A limited partner does not become liable as a general partner unless, in addition to exercising his rights and powers as a limited partner, he takes part in the control of the business.

There is a surprising absence of authority in Canada on the issues raised in this case. The only recent case to which I was referred is *Elevated Construction Ltd. v. Nixon et al.*, [1970] 1 O.R. 650 ...

In his decision, Osler J. really dealt with different aspects of the *Ontario Limited Partnerships Act*, but at p. 655, in obiter he touched upon the question of the degree of control of the business that must be exercised by a limited partner in order to make him liable as a general partner. He pointed out that the cases are far from exhaustive, referring only to three cases from 1857 and one from 1877, all of which refer to the same limited partnership. He concluded by saying:

The cases are of little assistance in determining where the line is to be drawn beyond which a limited partner is deemed to be taking part in the control of the business and each case will presumably have to be decided upon its own facts.

In this case, Zivot was clearly the controlling mind of Printcast. His business card indicated that he was the "President" of Printcast, and Marshall's business card indicated that he was the "Vice President". Zivot agreed that he was responsible for all managerial decisions for Printcast. Marshall made many of the decisions about sales and administration, and both Zivot and Marshall had authority to sign cheques for Printcast. Zivot and Marshall were in complete control of Printcast.

The action was allowed by the court, and the defendants were found liable as general partners. The defendants appealed this decision to the Ontario Court of Appeal, where the appeal was dismissed.

A limited partner has the right to demand the return of his/her contribution and is entitled to have the limited partnership dissolved, in certain circumstances.[30] A limited partnership is automatically dissolved when a general partner dies, retires or is incapable of managing property (or a corporate partner is dissolved,) unless the remaining general

---

30 Ibid., s. 15.

partners continue the business pursuant to a right to do so in a partnership agreement and with the consent of all of the remaining partners.[31]

(b) Filing a Declaration

Filing a declaration is a requirement of the Act, and moreover, is essential to guarantee that a limited partner only has "limited" liability. Clients may feel that they do not need any formal documentation to enter into a transaction where they are "silent partners" and there is no doubt that this occurs in day-to-day business transactions. However, in addition to accepting greater liability than they bargained for, failure to file a declaration under the Act is an offence. In fact, any contravention of the *Limited Partnerships Act* – including providing false or misleading information - is an offence which can result in a fine of $2,000, or if the person is a corporation, to a fine of not more than $20,000.[32] Moreover, a limited partnership that has not filed a declaration (or has unpaid fees or penalties as a result of not filing a declaration) cannot sue another party in an Ontario court except with leave of the court. The court will only grant permission to sue if the limited partnership can prove that it failed file the declaration or pay fees/penalties by mistake, that the public has not been deceived or misled as a result, and that the limited partnership has since filed the declaration and paid all outstanding fees and/or penalties.[33]

The declaration that a limited partnership must file is referred to as Form 3 under the *Limited Partnerships Act*. This form can be accessed through the Ontario Central Forms Repository website at <www.forms.ssb.gov.on.ca> Please refer to the Workbook for a copy of Form 3.

---

31 Ibid., s.21.
32 Ibid., s. 35.
33 Ibid., s. 20.

HOME | NEWSROOM | SERVICES | YOUR GOVERNMENT | ABOUT ONTAR

Central Forms Repository

Location: Forms Home > Quick Search > Quick Search Results > Form Details

Form Details

Format	Form Link Address	Functionality	Size
Adobe PDF	Declaration - Form 3 under Limited Partnerships Act	Fill & Print	370.0 kb

Form Classification / Identification:

Form Number:	007-07191	Edition date:	2011/04
Title:	Declaration - Form 3 under Limited Partnerships Act		
Ministry:	Government Services		
Branch/ABC:	ServiceOntario		
Program:	Central Production and Verification Services Branch		

Purpose of Form: This form must be completed and submitted to the Companies and Personal Property Security Branch to form, renew, dissolve or make a change to an Ontario limited partnership.. It must also be completed by an extra-provincial limited partnership before it carries on business in Ontario, and once it ceases carrying on business in Ontario.

Ordering Information: 393 University Ave., 2nd floor, Toronto ON M5G 2M2

(c) Extra-Provincial Limited Partnerships

The *Limited Partnerships Act* also refers to an "extra-provincial limited partnership" and defines it as "a limited partnership organized under the laws of a jurisdiction other than Ontario".[34]

> Assume that Sam decides to register the limited partnership in Quebec, since he has experience with both business and legal matters, and he wants to ensure that the limited partnership is actually registered. Before the limited partnership can open Nirvana Nightclub in Ontario, the limited partnership must be registered in Ontario in accordance with the *Limited Partnerships Act*. In Ontario, the business entity will now be referred to as an "extra-provincial limited partnership" – that is, a limited partnership that was created outside of Ontario, but now wants to operate a business in Ontario. (Note the term *"extra"* means "outside" in Latin.)

Just like a limited partnership created in Ontario, an extra-provincial limited partnership must file a declaration (Form 3 under the *Limited Partnerships Act*) – this is how the extra-provincial limited partnership "registers" itself in Ontario. Section 25(1) of the *Limited Partnerships Act* provides that:

---

34 *Ibid.*, s. 1.

No extra-provincial limited partnership shall carry on business in Ontario unless it has filed a declaration with the Registrar that sets forth the information required by subsection 3(2) and states the jurisdiction in which the extra-provincial limited partnership is organized.[35]

An extra-provincial limited partnership carries on business in Ontario if it:

- solicits business in Ontario

- lists its name in a telephone directory in any part of Ontario

- advertises an Ontario address for the business

- has a resident agent, representative, warehouse, office or other place of business in Ontario

- owns real property in Ontario

- distributes securities in Ontario in compliance with the *Securities Act*[36] (for public companies), or

- otherwise carries on business in Ontario.[37]

As you can see, the list of things which qualify as "carrying on business in Ontario" is quite broad, and as such, a legal professional should make relevant enquiries of a client that has a limited partnership in another province to determine whether or not a declaration must be filed in Ontario (as an extra-provincial limited partnership).

The declaration filed by an extra-provincial limited partnership must be signed by all of the general partners.[38] If there are changes to the information provided in this declaration, other than a change in the firm's name, a declaration of change must be filed; for a change in the firm's name, a new declaration is required.[39] In addition, the extra-provincial limited partnership must appoint a person who is resident in Ontario (or a corporation with its head or registered office in Ontario) as its attorney or representative in Ontario. Note, however, that the requirement to execute a power of attorney does not apply to an extra-provincial limited partnership that was:

(a) formed in another Canadian jurisdiction (that is, another province or territory), and

(b) has an office or other place of business in Ontario.[40]

> Assume that Sam registers a limited partnership in Quebec, and arranges for a declaration to be filed in Ontario so that the limited partnership can start Nirvana Nightclub in Ontario. Who needs to sign the declaration? Will it be necessary for the extra-provincial limited partnership to give a power of attorney to a resident of Ontario?

---

35 *Ibid.*, s. 25(1).
36 R.S.O. 1990, c. S.5.
37 *Limited Partnerships Act*, R.S.O. 1990, c. L.16, s. 25(2).
38 *Ibid.*, s. 25(3).
39 *Ibid.*, ss. 6.1 & 7.
40 *Ibid.* ss. 25(4)–(6.2).

If a limited partnership was created in Alberta and has registered as an extra-provincial partnership in Ontario, does it have to follow Alberta law or Ontario law? Subsection 27(2) of the *Limited Partnerships Act* clarifies this issue by stating that the laws of the jurisdiction in which the limited partnership was created govern its organization and internal affairs. In other words, in the example provided, Alberta law would apply to the organization and internal affairs of the limited partnership.[41]

> Javid is anxious to start Nirvana Nightclub and assumes that, since Sam registered the limited partnership in Quebec, they have fulfilled the legal requirements. What happens if the limited partnership fails to register a declaration in Ontario as an extra-provincial limited partnership?

Section 28 of the *Limited Partnership Act* provides serious consequences for failure to register an extra-provincial limited partnership in the correct way:

(1) No extra-provincial limited partnership that has unpaid fees or penalties or in respect of which a declaration or power of attorney has not been filed as required by this Act and no member thereof is capable of maintaining a proceeding in a court in Ontario in respect of the business carried on by the extra-provincial limited partnership except with leave of the court. R.S.O. 1990, c. L.16, s. 28 (1).

(2) The court shall grant leave if the court is satisfied that,

(a) the failure to pay the fees or penalties or file the declaration or power of attorney was inadvertent;

(b) there is no evidence that the public has been deceived or misled; and

(c) at the time of the application to the court, the extra-provincial limited partnership has no unpaid fees or penalties and has filed all declarations and powers of attorney required by this Act. R.S.O. 1990, c. L.16, s. 28 (2).

(3) No contract is void or voidable by reason only that it was entered into by an extra-provincial limited partnership that was in contravention of this Act or the regulations at the time the contract was made.[42]

4. Other Considerations

Once a client has decided to start a business as a general or limited partnership and the legal requirements for doing so have been fulfilled, the legal professional should consider whether there are any licenses or other special requirements related to the business that the clients are starting. For example, it may be necessary to apply for a liquor license under the *Liquor Licence Act*[43]. In addition, the business will need to open up a bank account, and will also have to register with the appropriate government authorities for tax purposes. The business may also need to register with the Workplace Safety and Insurance Board (WSIB), amongst other requirements. A discussion of these processes

---

41 *Ibid.*, s. 27(2).
42 *Ibid.*, s. 28.
43 R.S.O. 1990, c. L.19.

is beyond the scope of this textbook, but should be investigated by a legal professional advising a client.

5. Other Types of Business Associations

(a) Joint Ventures

Sometimes, persons – individuals or corporations – want to work together for a specific purpose, project or period of time. They do not intend to have a long-term working relationship. For example, a construction company may want to work with a particular architect to design and build a specific project, because they both have special expertise or resources that are necessary for this particular project. They do not want to work together beyond the project.

In this case, the parties may decide to form a joint venture, instead of a partnership. A joint venture is a type of business association between persons (individuals, partnerships or corporations) for a limited purpose or time, with the intention to generate a profit. The parties in a joint venture contribute knowledge, skills, resources such as capital and property, contacts and other factors for the benefit of all parties involved. The relationship is contractual in nature – and as such, the parties should negotiate and sign a joint venture agreement to outline each party's responsibilities, duties, contributions and entitlements.[44]

Parties in a joint venture owe a fiduciary duty to one another, similar to the fiduciary duty that partners owe to one another.[45] This includes the "reciprocal obligations of good faith and loyalty as regards the common interest in the common venture."[46] Specifically, parties in a joint venture have the duty:

- to make full disclosure with respect to the joint venture

- not to make secret profits, and

- not to compete with the business created through the joint venture.[47]

(b) Franchises

Some individuals prefer to start a business that already has a recognized name, a strong marketing strategy, an established business model, and training and other assistance provided to a new business owner. A franchise organization is a business model in which the parent company (the "franchisor") creates a recognized business unit that

---

44 *Central Mortgage & Housing Corp. v. Graham*, 1973 CarswellNS 192, 43 D.L.R. (3d) 686 (N.S. T.D.); *Bradley v. Egan*, 1908 CarswellOnt 253, 11 O.W.R. 944 (Ont. C.P.), affirmed 1908 CarswellOnt 504, 12 O.W.R. 67 (Ont. Div. Ct.); *Sutton v. Forst* (1924), 55 O.L.R. 281 (Ont. C.A.); *Lewis v. Iron & Metal Exporters Ltd.* (1931), 39 O.W.N. 504.

45 *Hogar Estates Ltd. v. Shebron Holdings Ltd.*, 1979 CarswellOnt 1499, 25 O.R. (2d) 543 (Ont. H.C.).

46 *Hitchcock v. Sykes*, 1914 CarswellOnt 422, 23 D.L.R. 518 (S.C.C.), at p. 521 [D.L.R], per Duff J.

47 *Wonsch Construction Co. v. National Bank of Canada*, 1990 CarswellOnt 135, 1 O.R. (3d) 382 (Ont. C.A.), additional reasons 1994 CarswellOnt 2442 (Ont. C.A.); *Meinhard v. Salmon* (1928), 164 N.E. 545 (U.S. N.Y. Ct. App.).

it can sell to someone else (the "franchisee") to operate. The franchisor typically controls the business model – everything from the construction and design of the business, selection of the location, supply of all materials and goods, training, marketing, pricing, amongst other factors. In addition to an initial franchise fee, the franchisor will require ongoing payment of fees and royalties from the franchisee.

What does the franchisee get in return? The franchisee can walk into a business that has been set up for him/her, with training and marketing support. Someone who wants to start a coffee shop, for example, may consider it worthwhile to purchase a Tim Hortons franchise, as opposed to starting his/her own coffee shop. The franchisee's assumption is that he/she can operate the franchise more profitably than a business created on his/her own.

The franchise relationship is also a contractual one. Special attention must be paid to the terms of a franchise agreement, which establish the rights and obligations of both the franchisor and the franchisee. There is caselaw that indicates that a franchisor and franchisee owe each other a duty to negotiate in good faith. Moreover, a franchisor – which is typically the stronger party – owes a franchisee a duty to deal honestly and reasonably, taking in consideration the franchisee's interests before making decisions which affect the franchisee. Whether or not a franchisor has breached the duty of good faith will depend on the facts of each case.[48]

(c) Licence

Under a licensing agreement, the licensor grants the licensee the right to use the licensor's property, in order to produce and distribute patented goods. The licensor will provide technical assistance to the licensee and will monitor sales, but will otherwise exercise little control over the licensee's business. Conversely, the licensee will manufacture and distribute the product, pay for all the costs of the manufacturing process, and pay a royalty fee on each unit sold. Licensing arrangements are common for many consumer goods, such as clothing and sporting goods.

(d) Co-ownership

In this situation, the parties do not intend to run a business together – they simply own a property together. For real estate, the form of ownership would be as tenants in common. The income or losses from the property would be allocated based on the proportional ownership. Co-ownership may be motivated by tax or other considerations. Co-owners avoid the vicarious, contractual and tort liability that can arise from a partnership, and can also transfer or assign their rights to the property, subject to the terms of a co-ownership agreement.

(e) Business Trusts

In this arrangement, property is transferred to a trustee who holds the property in trust for the benefit of others. The trustee may be an individual, partnership or corpora-

---

48 *Shelanu Inc. v. Print Three Franchising Corp.*, 2003 CarswellOnt 2038, 64 O.R. (3d) 533 (Ont. C.A.), additional reasons 2006 CarswellOnt 2627 (Ont. C.A.); *Country Style Food Services Inc. v. 1304271 Ontario Ltd.*, 2005 CarswellOnt 2744, 200 O.A.C. 172 (Ont. C.A.).

tion. With income trusts, an asset or property that generates income is held in trust for the benefit of individuals who are referred to as "unit holders" of the trust. In this way, investors hold the investment indirectly as beneficiaries under the trust.

(f) Not-for-Profit Organizations

This textbook focuses on businesses that intend to make a profit, and as such, it will not explore not-for-profit organizations in any level of detail. However, a legal professional should be aware that there are laws that pertain specifically to organizations whose primary purpose is social or charitable, and who do not seek to generate a profit for their "owners". There are many variations in the way that charitable organizations can be established, including the formation of a not-for-profit corporation.

Partnerships Act, R.S.O. 1990, c. P.5

Consolidation Period: From December 15, 2009 to the e-Laws currency date (Thursday, February 23, 2012)

PARTNERSHIPS ACT

R.S.O. 1990, c. P.5 as am. **S.O. 1998, c. 2, ss. 1–8;** 1999, c. 6, s. 52; 2005, c. 5, s. 55; 2006, c. 19, Sched. G, s. 7; 2006, c. 34, s. 19; 2009, c. 33, Sched. 2, s. 57

Definitions

1. (1) — In this Act,

"business" includes every trade, occupation and profession;

"court" includes every court and judge having jurisdiction in the case.

"extra-provincial limited liability partnership" means a limited liability partnership formed under the laws of another jurisdiction but does not include an extra-provincial limited partnership with the meaning of the *Limited Partnerships Act*;

"limited liability partnership" means a partnership, other than a limited partnership, that is formed or continued as a limited liability partnership under section 44.1 or that is an extra-provincial limited liability partnership.

Idem

(2) — A person is deemed to be "insolvent" within the meaning of this Act if the person is adjudged a bankrupt under the *Bankruptcy Act* (Canada) or if the person makes an assignment for the general benefit of his or her creditors, and "insolvency" has a meaning corresponding with "insolvent".

1998, c. 2, s. 1

NATURE OF PARTNERSHIP

Partnership

2. — Partnership is the relation that subsists between persons carrying on a business in common with a view to profit, but the relation between the members of a company or association that is incorporated by or under the authority of any special or general Act in force in Ontario or elsewhere, or registered as a corporation under any such Act, is not a partnership within the meaning of this Act.

Rules for determining existence of partnership

3. — In determining whether a partnership does or does not exist, regard shall be had to the following rules:

1. Joint tenancy, tenancy in common, joint property, common property, or part

ownership does not of itself create a partnership as to anything so held or owned, whether the tenants or owners do or do not share any profits made by the use thereof.

2. The sharing of gross returns does not of itself create a partnership, whether the persons sharing such returns have or have not a joint or common right or interest in any property from which or from the use of which the returns are derived.

3. The receipt by a person of a share of the profits of a business is proof, in the absence of evidence to the contrary, that the person is a partner in the business, but the receipt of such a share or payment, contingent on or varying with the profits of a business, does not of itself make him or her a partner in the business, and in particular,

(a) the receipt by a person of a debt or other liquidated amount by instalments or otherwise out of the accruing profits of a business does not of itself make him or her a partner in the business or liable as such;

(b) a contract for the remuneration of a servant or agent or a person engaged in a business by a share of the profits of the business does not of itself make the servant or agent a partner in the business or liable as such;

(c) a person who,

(i) was married to a deceased partner immediately before the deceased partner died,

(ii) was living with a deceased partner in a conjugal relationship outside marriage immediately before the deceased partner died, or

(iii) is a child of a deceased partner,

and who receives by way of annuity a portion of the profits made in the business in which the deceased partner was a partner is not by reason only of such receipt a partner in the business or liable as such;

(d) the advance of money by way of loan to a person engaged or about to engage in a business on a contract with that person that the lender is to receive a rate of interest varying with the profits, or is to receive a share of the profits arising from carrying on the business, does not of itself make the lender a partner with the person or persons carrying on the business or liable as such, provided that the contract is in writing and signed by or on behalf of all parties thereto;

(e) a person receiving by way of annuity or otherwise a portion of the profits of a business in consideration of the sale by him or her of the goodwill of the business, is not by reason only of such receipt a partner in the business or liable as such.

1999, c. 6, s. 52; 2005, c. 5, s. 55

Insolvency

4. — In the event of a person to whom money has been advanced by way of loan upon such a contract as is mentioned in section 3, or of a buyer of the goodwill in consideration of a share of the profits of the business, becoming insolvent or entering into an arrangement to pay his or her creditors less than 100 cents on the dollar or dying in insolvent circumstances, the lender of the loan is not entitled to recover anything in respect of the loan, and the seller of the goodwill is not entitled to recover anything in respect of the share of profits contracted for, until the claims of the other creditors of the borrower or buyer, for valuable consideration in money or money's worth, are satisfied.

Meaning of "firm"

5. — Persons who have entered into partnership with one another are, for the purposes of this Act, called collectively a firm, and the name under which their business is carried on is called the firm name.

RELATION OF PARTNERS TO PERSONS DEALING WITH THEM

Power of partner to bind firm

6. — Every partner is an agent of the firm and of the other partners for the purpose of the business of the partnership, and the acts of every partner who does any act for carrying on in the usual way business of the kind carried on by the firm of which he or she is a member, bind the firm and the other partners unless the partner so acting has in fact no authority to act for the firm in the particular matter and the person with whom the partner is dealing either knows that the partner has no authority, or does not know or believe him or her to be a partner.

Partners bound by acts on behalf of firm

7. — An act or instrument relating to the business of the firm and done or executed in the firm name, or in any other manner showing an intention to bind the firm by a person thereto authorized, whether a partner or not, is binding on the firm and all the partners, but this section does not affect any general rule of law relating to the execution of deeds or negotiable instruments.

Partner using credit of firm for private purposes

8. — Where one partner pledges the credit of the firm for a purpose apparently not connected with the firm's ordinary course of business, the firm is not bound, unless he or she is in fact specially authorized by the other partners, but this section does not affect any personal liability incurred by an individual partner.

Effect of notice that firm not bound by act of partner

9. — If it is agreed between the partners to restrict the power of any one or more of them to bind the firm, no act done in contravention of the agreement is binding on the firm with respect to persons having notice of the agreement.

Liability of partners

10. (1) — Except as provided in subsection (2) every partner in a firm is liable jointly with the other partners for all debts and obligations of the firm incurred while the person is a partner, and after the partner's death the partner's estate is also severally liable in a due course of administration for such debts and obligations so far as they remain unsatisfied, but subject to the prior payment of his or her separate debts.

Limited liability partnerships

(2) — Subject to subsections (3) and (3.1), a partner in a limited liability partnership is not liable, by means of indemnification, contribution or otherwise, for,

    (a) the debts, liabilities or obligations of the partnership or any partner arising from the negligent or wrongful acts or omissions that another partner or an employee, agent or representative of the partnership commits in the course of the partnership business while the partnership is a limited liability partnership; or

    (b) any other debts or obligations of the partnership that are incurred while the partnership is a limited liability partnership.

Limitations

(3) — Subsection (2) does not relieve a partner in a limited liability partnership from liability for,

    (a) the partner's own negligent or wrongful act or omission;

    (b) the negligent or wrongful act or omission of a person under the partner's direct supervision; or

    (c) the negligent or wrongful act or omission of another partner or an employee of the partnership not under the partner's direct supervision, if,

        (i) the act or omission was criminal or constituted fraud, even if there was no criminal act or omission, or

        (ii) the partner knew or ought to have known of the act or omission and did not take the actions that a reasonable person would have taken to prevent it.

Same

(3.1) — Subsection (2) does not protect a partner's interest in the partnership property from claims against the partnership respecting a partnership obligation.

Partner not proper party to action

(4) — A partner in a limited liability partnership is not a proper party to a proceeding by or against the limited liability partnership for the purpose of recovering damages or enforcing obligations arising out of the negligent acts or omissions described in subsection (2).

Extra-provincial limited liability partnerships

(5) — This section does not apply to an extra-provincial limited liability partnership.

1998, c. 2, s. 2; 2006, c. 34, s. 19

Liability of firm for wrongs

11. — Where by any wrongful act or omission of a partner acting in the ordinary course of the business of the firm, or with the authority of the co-partners, loss or injury is caused to a person not being a partner of the firm, or any penalty is incurred, the firm is liable therefor to the same extent as the partner so acting or omitting to act.

Misapplication of money or property received for or in custody of the firm

12. — In the following cases, namely,

(a) where one partner, acting within the scope of the partner's apparent authority, receives the money or property of a third person and misapplies it; and

(b) where a firm in the course of its business receives money or property of a third person, and the money or property so received is misapplied by one or more of the partners while it is in the custody of the firm,

the firm is liable to make good the loss.

Liability for wrongs joint and several

13. — Except as provided in subsection 10(2) every partner is liable jointly with the co-partners and also severally for everything for which the firm, while the person is a partner therein, becomes liable under section 11 or 12.

1998, c. 2, s. 3

Improper employment of trust property for partnership purposes

14. — If a partner, being a trustee, improperly employs trust property in the business or on the account of the partnership, no other partner is liable for the trust property to the persons beneficially interested therein, but,

(a) this section does not affect any liability incurred by any partner by reason of the partner having notice of a breach of trust; and

(b) nothing in this section prevents trust money from being followed and recovered from the firm if still in its possession or under its control.

Persons liable by "holding out"

15. (1) — Every person, who by words spoken or written or by conduct represents himself or herself or who knowingly suffers himself or herself to be represented as a partner in a particular firm, is liable as a partner to any person who has on the faith of any such representation given credit to the firm, whether the representation has or has not been made or communicated to the persons so giving credit by or with the knowledge of the apparent partner making the representation or suffering it to be made.

Continuing business after death of partner

(2) — Where after a partner's death the partnership business is continued in the old firm name, the continued use of that name or of the deceased partner's name as part thereof does not of itself make his or her executor's or administrator's estate or effects liable for any partnership debts contracted after his or her death.

Admissions and representations of partners

16. — An admission or representation made by a partner concerning the partnership affairs and in the ordinary course of its business is evidence against the firm.

Notice to acting partner to be notice to the firm

17. — Notice to a partner who habitually acts in the partnership business of any matter relating to partnership affairs operates as notice to the firm, except in the case of a fraud on the firm committed by or with the consent of that partner.

Liability commences with admission to firm

18. (1) — A person who is admitted as a partner into an existing firm does not thereby become liable to the creditors of the firm for anything done before the person became a partner.

Liability for debts, etc., incurred before retirement

(2) — A partner who retires from a firm does not thereby cease to be liable for partnership debts or obligations incurred before the partner's retirement.

Agreement discharging retiring partner

(3) — A retiring partner may be discharged from any existing liabilities by an agreement to that effect between the partner and the members of the firm as newly constituted and the creditors, and this agreement may be either express or inferred as a fact from the course of dealing between the creditors and the firm as newly constituted.

Revocation of continuing guaranty by change in firm

19. — A continuing guaranty or cautionary obligation given either to a firm or to a third person in respect of the transactions of a firm is, in the absence of agreement to the contrary, revoked as to future transactions by any change in the constitution of the firm to which, or of the firm in respect of the transaction of which, the guaranty or obligation was given.

RELATION OF PARTNERS TO ONE ANOTHER

Variation by consent of terms of partnership

20. — The mutual rights and duties of partners, whether ascertained by agreement or defined by this Act, may be varied by the consent of all the partners, and such consent may be either expressed or inferred from a course of dealing.

Partnership property

21. (1) — All property and rights and interests in property originally brought into the partnership stock or acquired, whether by purchase or otherwise, on account of the firm, or for the purposes and in the course of the partnership business, are called in this Act "partnership property", and must be held and applied by the partners exclusively for the purposes of the partnership and in accordance with the partnership agreement.

Devolution of land

(2) — The legal estate or interest in land that belongs to a partnership devolves according to the nature and tenure thereof and the general rules of law thereto applicable, but in trust, so far as necessary, for the persons beneficially interested in the land under this section.

Co-owners of land

(3) — Where co-owners of an estate or interest in land, not being itself partnership property, are partners as to profits made by the use of that land or estate, and purchase other land or estate out of the profits to be used in like manner, the land or estate so purchased belongs to them, in the absence of an agreement to the contrary, not as partners, but as co-owners for the same respective estates and interests as are held by them in the land or estate first mentioned at the date of purchase.

Property bought with partnership money

22. — Unless the contrary intention appears, property bought with money belonging to the firm shall be deemed to have been bought on the account of the firm.

Conversion of land bought with partnership money into personalty

23. — Where land or any heritable interest therein becomes partnership property, unless the contrary intention appears, it is to be treated as between the partners, including the representatives of a deceased partner, and also as between the heirs of a deceased partner and his or her executors or administrators as personal or movable and not real or heritable estate.

Rules as to interests and duties of partners

24. — The interests of partners in the partnership property and their rights and duties in relation to the partnership shall be determined, subject to any agreement express or implied between the partners, by the following rules:

1. All the partners are entitled to share equally in the capital and profits of the business, and must contribute equally towards the losses, whether of capital or otherwise, sustained by the firm, but a partner shall not be liable to contribute toward losses arising from a liability for which the partner is not liable under subsection 10(2).

2. The firm must indemnify every partner in respect of payments made and personal liabilities incurred by him or her,

   (a) in the ordinary and proper conduct of the business of the firm; or

   (b) in or about anything necessarily done for the preservation of the business or property of the firm.

2.1 A partner is not required to indemnify the firm or other partners in respect of debts or obligations of the partnership for which a partner is not liable under subsection 10(2).

3. A partner making, for the purpose of the partnership, any actual payment or advance beyond the amount of capital that he or she has agreed to subscribe is entitled to interest at the rate of 5 per cent per annum from the date of the payment or advance.

4. A partner is not entitled, before the ascertainment of profits, to interest on the capital subscribed by the partner.

5. Every partner may take part in the management of the partnership business.

6. No partner is entitled to remuneration for acting in the partnership business.

7. No person may be introduced as a partner without the consent of all existing partners.

8. Any difference arising as to ordinary matters connected with the partnership business may be decided by a majority of the partners, but no change may be made in the nature of the partnership business without the consent of all existing partners.

9. The partnership books are to be kept at the place of business of the partnership, or the principal place, if there is more than one, and every partner may, when he or she thinks fit, have access to and inspect and copy any of them.

1998, c. 2, s. 4

Expulsion of partner

25. — No majority of the partners can expel any partner unless a power to do so has been conferred by express agreement between the partners.

Retirement from partnership at will

26. (1) — Where no fixed term is agreed upon for the duration of the partnership, any partner may determine the partnership at any time on giving notice of his or her intention to do so to all the other partners.

Notice of retirement

(2) — Where the partnership was originally constituted by deed, a notice in writing, signed by the partner giving it, is sufficient for that purpose.

Presumption of continuance after expiry of term

27. (1) — Where a partnership entered into for a fixed term is continued after the term has expired and without any express new agreement, the rights and duties of the partners remain the same as they were at the expiration of the term, so far as is consistent with the incidents of a partnership at will.

Arises from continuance of business

(2) — A continuance of the business by the partners or such of them as habitually acted therein during the term without any settlement or liquidation of the partnership affairs shall be presumed to be a continuance of the partnership.

Duty as to rendering accounts

28. — Partners are bound to render true accounts and full information of all things affecting the partnership to any partner or the partner's legal representatives.

Accountability for private profits

29. (1) — Every partner must account to the firm for any benefit derived by the partner without the consent of the other partners from any transaction concerning the partnership or from any use by the partner of the partnership property, name or business connection.

Extends to survivors and representatives of deceased

(2) — This section applies also to transactions undertaken after a partnership has been dissolved by the death of a partner and before its affairs have been completely wound up, either by a surviving partner or by the representatives of the deceased partner.

Duty of partner not to compete with firm

30. — If a partner, without the consent of the other partners, carries on a business of the same nature as and competing with that of the firm, the partner must account for and pay over to the firm all profits made by the partner in that business.

Rights of assignee of share in partnership

31. (1) — An assignment by a partner of the partner's share in the partnership, either absolute or by way of mortgage or redeemable charge, does not, as against the other partners, entitle the assignee, during the continuance of the partnership, to interfere in the management or administration of the partnership business or affairs, or to require any accounts of the partnership transactions, or to inspect the partnership books, but entitles the assignee only to receive the share of profits to which the assigning partner

would otherwise be entitled, and the assignee must accept the account of profits agreed to by the partners.

On dissolution

(2) — In the case of a dissolution of the partnership, whether as respects all the partners or as respects the assigning partner, the assignee is entitled to receive the share of the partnership assets to which the assigning partner is entitled as between the assigning partner and the other partners, and, for the purpose of ascertaining that share, to an account as from the date of the dissolution.

DISSOLUTION OF PARTNERSHIP

Dissolution by expiry of term or notice

32. — Subject to any agreement between the partners, a partnership is dissolved,

(a) if entered into for a fixed term, by the expiration of that term;

(b) if entered into for a single adventure or undertaking, by the termination of that adventure or undertaking; or

(c) if entered into for an undefined time, by a partner giving notice to the other or others of his or her intention to dissolve the partnership, in which case the partnership is dissolved as from the date mentioned in the notice as the date of dissolution, or, if no date is so mentioned, as from the date of the communication of the notice.

Dissolution by death or insolvency of partner

33. (1) — Subject to any agreement between the partners, every partnership is dissolved as regards all the partners by the death or insolvency of a partner.

Where partner's share charged for separate debt

(2) — A partnership may, at the option of the other partners, be dissolved if any partner suffers that partner's share of the partnership property to be charged under this Act for that partner's separate debt.

By illegality of business

34. — A partnership is in every case dissolved by the happening of any event that makes it unlawful for the business of the firm to be carried on or for the members of the firm to carry it on in partnership.

By the court

35. (1) — On application by a partner, the court may order a dissolution of the partnership,

(a) when a partner is found to be incapable as defined in the Substitute Decisions Act, 1992;

(b) when a partner, other than the partner suing, becomes in any other way permanently incapable of performing the partner's part of the partnership contract;

(c) when a partner, other than the partner suing, has been guilty of such conduct as, in the opinion of the court, regard being had to the nature of the business, is calculated to prejudicially affect the carrying on of the business;

(d) when a partner, other than the partner suing, wilfully or persistently commits a breach of the partnership agreement, or otherwise so conducts himself or herself in matters relating to the partnership business that it is not reasonably practicable for the other partner or partners to carry on the business in partnership with the partner;

(e) when the business of the partnership can only be carried on at a loss; or

(f) when in any case circumstances have arisen that in the opinion of the court render it just and equitable that the partnership be dissolved.

Application where incapacity

(2) — In the case of an application under clause (1)(a), the application may be made by the litigation guardian of the partner found to be incapable, on the partner's behalf.

2009, c. 33, Sched. 2, s. 57

Rights of persons dealing with firm against apparent members

36. (1) — Where a person deals with a firm after a change in its constitution, the person is entitled to treat all apparent members of the old firm as still being members of the firm until the person has notice of the change.

Notice

(2) — An advertisement in The Ontario Gazette shall be notice as to persons who had not dealings with the firm before the dissolution or change so advertised.

Estate of dead or insolvent partner, how far liable

(3) — The estate of a partner who dies, or who becomes insolvent, or of a partner who, not having been known to the person dealing with the firm to be a partner, retires from the firm, is not liable for partnership debts contracted after the date of the death, insolvency, or retirement.

Right to give notice of dissolution

37. — On the dissolution of a partnership or retirement of a partner, any partner may publicly given notice of the same, and may require the other partner or partners to concur for that purpose in all necessary or proper acts, if any, that cannot be done without his, her or their concurrence.

Continuing authority of partners for purposes of winding up

38. — After the dissolution of a partnership, the authority of each partner to bind the firm and the other rights and obligations of the partners continue despite the dissolution so far as is necessary to wind up the affairs of the partnership and to complete transactions begun but unfinished at the time of the dissolution, but not otherwise; provided that the firm is in no case bound by the acts of a partner who has become insolvent; but this proviso does not affect the liability of a person who has, after the insolvency, represented himself or herself or knowingly suffered himself or herself to be represented as a partner of the insolvent.

Rights of partners as to application of partnership property

39. — On the dissolution of a partnership every partner is entitled, as against the other partners in the firm and all persons claiming through them in respect of their interests as partners, to have the property of the partnership applied in payment of the debts and liabilities of the firm and to have the surplus assets after such payment applied in payment of what may be due to the partners respectively after deducting what may be due from them as partners to the firm, and for that purpose any partner or the partner's representative may, on the termination of the partnership, apply to the court to wind up the business and affairs of the firm.

Apportionment of premium on premature dissolution

40. — Where one partner paid a premium to another on entering into a partnership for a fixed term and the partnership is dissolved before the expiration of that term otherwise than by the death of a partner, the court may order the repayment of the premium, or of such part thereof as it thinks just, having regard to the terms of the partnership contract and to the length of time during which the partnership has continued, unless,

(a) the dissolution is, in the judgment of the court, wholly or chiefly due to the misconduct of the partner who paid the premium; or

(b) the partnership has been dissolved by an agreement containing no provision for a return of a part of the premium.

Rights where partnership dissolved for fraud or misrepresentation

41. — Where a partnership contract is rescinded on the ground of fraud or misrepresentation of one of the parties thereto, the party entitled to rescind is, without prejudice to any other right, entitled,

(a) to a lien on, or right of retention of, the surplus of the partnership assets, after satisfying the partnership liabilities, for any sum of money paid by the party for the purchase of a share in the partnership and for any capital contributed by him or her; and

(b) to stand in the place of the creditors of the firm for any payments made by the party in respect of the partnership liabilities; and

(c) to be indemnified by the person guilty of the fraud or making the representation against all the debts and liabilities of the firm.

Right of outgoing partner as to share in profits after dissolution

42. (1) — Where any member of a firm dies or otherwise ceases to be a partner and the surviving or continuing partners carry on the business of the firm with its capital or assets without any final settlement of accounts as between the firm and the outgoing partner or his or her estate, then, in the absence of an agreement to the contrary, the outgoing partner or his or her estate is entitled, at the option of the outgoing partner or his or her representatives, to such share of the profits made since the dissolution as the court finds to be attributable to the use of the outgoing partner's share of the partnership assets, or to interest at the rate of 5 per cent per annum on the amount of his or her share of the partnership assets.

Proviso as to option of remaining partners to purchase share

(2) — Where by the partnership contract an option is given to surviving or continuing partners to purchase the interest of a deceased or outgoing partner and that option is duly exercised, the estate of the deceased partner, or the outgoing partner or his or her estate, as the case may be, is not entitled to any further or other share of profits, but if any partner, assuming to act in exercise of the option, does not in all material respects comply with the terms thereof, he or she is liable to account under the foregoing provisions of this section.

Retiring or deceased partner's share to be a debt

43. — Subject to any agreement between the partners, the amount due from surviving or continuing partners to an outgoing partner or the representatives of a deceased partner in respect of the outgoing or deceased partner's share, is a debt accruing at the date of the dissolution or death.

Rules for distribution of assets on final settlement of accounts

44. — In settling accounts between the partners after a dissolution of partnership, the following rules shall, subject to any agreement, be observed:

1. Losses, including losses and deficiencies of capital, are to be paid first out of profits, next out of capital, and lastly, if necessary, by the partners individually in the proportion in which they were entitled to share profits, but a partner is not required to pay any loss arising from a liability for which the partner is not liable under subsection 10(2).

2. The assets of the firm, including the sums, if any, contributed by the partners to make up losses or deficiencies of capital, are to be applied in the following manner and order,

    (a) in paying the debts and liabilities of the firm to persons who are not partners therein;

    (b) in paying to each partner rateably what is due from the firm to him or her for advances as distinguished from capital;

    (c) in paying to each partner rateably what is due from the firm to him or her in respect of capital.

3.   After making the payments required by paragraph 2, the ultimate residue, if any, is to be divided among the partners in the proportion in which profits are divisible.

1998, c. 2, s. 5

LIMITED LIABILITY PARTNERSHIPS

Formation

44.1 (1) — A limited liability partnership that is not an extra-provincial limited liability partnership is formed when two or more persons enter into a written agreement that,

    (a) designates the partnership as a limited liability partnership; and

    (b) states that this Act governs the agreement.

Continuance

(2) — A partnership may be continued as a limited liability partnership that is not an extra-provincial limited liability partnership if all of the partners,

    (a) enter into an agreement that continues the partnership as a limited liability partnership and states that this Act governs the agreement; or

    (b) if there is an existing agreement between the partners that forms the partnership, amend the agreement to designate the partnership as a limited liability partnership and to state that this Act governs the agreement.

Effect of continuance

(3) — Upon the continuance of a partnership as a limited liability partnership under subsection (2),

    (a) the limited liability partnership possesses all the property, rights, privileges and franchises and is subject to all liabilities, including civil, criminal and quasi-criminal, and all contracts, disabilities and debts of the partnership which were in existence immediately before the continuance; and

    (b) all persons who were partners immediately before the continuance remain liable for all debts, obligations and liabilities of the partnership or all partners with respect to the other partners that arose before the continuance.

1998, c. 2, s. 6

Limitation on business activity

44.2 — A limited liability partnership may carry on business in Ontario only for the purpose of practising a profession governed by an Act and only if,

(a) that Act expressly permits a limited liability partnership to practise the profession;

(b) the governing body of the profession requires the partnership to maintain a minimum amount of liability insurance; and

(c) the partnership complies with section 44.3 if it is not an extra-provincial limited liability partnership or section 44.4 if it is an extra-provincial limited liability partnership.

1998, c. 2, s. 6

Business name

44.3 (1) — No limited liability partnership formed or continued by an agreement governed by this Act shall carry on business unless it has registered its firm name under the *Business Names Act*.

Amendments, cancellations and renewals

(2) — To amend, renew or cancel a registration of its firm name, a limited liability partnership mentioned in subsection (1) shall register an amendment, renewal or cancellation of a registration in accordance with the requirements of the *Business Names Act*.

Firm name

(3) — The firm name of a limited liability partnership mentioned in subsection (1) shall contain the words "limited liability partnership" or "société à responsabilité limitée" or the abbreviations "LLP", "L.L.P." or "s.r.l." as the last words or letters of the firm name.

Same

(3.1) — A limited liability partnership mentioned in subsection (1) may have a firm name that is in,

(a) an English form only;

(b) a French form only;

(c) a French and English form, where the French and English are used together in a combined form; or

(d) a French form and an English form, where the French and English forms are equivalent but are used separately.

Same

(3.2) — A limited liability partnership mentioned in subsection (1) that has a firm name described in clause (3.1)(d) may be legally designated by the French or English version of its firm name.

Use of registered name only

(4) — No limited liability partnership mentioned in subsection (1) shall carry on business under a name other than its registered firm name.

Right to carry on business outside of Ontario

(5) — Nothing in this Act prevents a limited liability partnership mentioned in subsection (1) from carrying on its business and exercising its powers in any province or territory of Canada or any other country.

1998, c. 2, s. 6; 2006, c. 19, Sched. G, s. 7(1), (2)

Extra-provincial limited liability partnerships

44.4 (1) — No extra-provincial limited liability partnership shall carry on business in Ontario unless it has registered its firm name under the *Business Names Act*.

Amendments, cancellations and renewals

(2) — To amend, renew or cancel a registration of its firm name, an extra-provincial limited liability partnership shall register an amendment, renewal or cancellation of a registration in accordance with the requirements of the *Business Names Act*.

Use of registered name only

(3) — No extra-provincial limited liability partnership shall carry on business under a name other than its registered firm name.

Laws of other jurisdiction

(4) — The laws of the jurisdiction under which an extra-provincial limited liability partnership is formed shall govern,

  (a) its organization and internal affairs; and

  (b) the liability of its partners for debts, obligations and liabilities of or chargeable to the partnership or any of its partners.

Service

(5) — A person may serve a notice or document on an extra-provincial limited liability partnership at its Ontario place of business, if any, or its address required to be maintained under the laws of the jurisdiction of formation or its principal office address.

1998, c. 2, s. 7; 2006, c. 19, Sched. G, s. 7(3)

GENERAL

Saving as to rules of equity and common law

45. — The rules of equity and of common law applicable to partnership continue in force, except so far as they are inconsistent with the express provisions of this Act.

Construction

46. — This Act is to be read and construed as subject to the *Limited Partnerships Act* and the *Business Names Act*.

Last amendment: 2009, c. 33, Sched. 2, s. 57.

Appendix B: Partnership Agreement Checklist

Item	Details	Included/ Considered (✔)	Not Applicable (✔)
1. Date	• Date of agreement		
2. Parties	• Designate all parties precisely • Can be corporations • Individuals must be more than 18 years old • Confirm that each partner is acquiring the interest for its own account (recommended)		
3. Definitions	• Define all terms as required		
4. Partnership Name	• Confirm that business will be carried out under this name • Consider conflict with the name of another, existing business • Consider conducting name search • Consider registration under *Trade-Marks Act (Canada)*, R.S.C. 1985, c. T-13 • Corporate partner must register under *Business Names Act* or comparable legislation		
5. Term	• Insert date of commencement (otherwise, signing date governs) • Unless a specific term is provided, the partnership can be terminated at the will of all partners		
6. Place of Business	• Not required if there is no desire to restrict geographical limits • Consider designating a principal place of business or head office		

7. Description of Business	• Define the scope of agency of each partner • No changes without unanimous consent • Description will set the parameters governing the scope of prohibited competition and other restrictive covenants • Ensure description is not overly broad or narrow		
8. Capital Contributions	• Specify obligations to make future contributions (could include a percentage of profits, or that a percentage of profits be retained as a reserve) • If a limited partnership, a change in contributed capital (as opposed to additional advances) requires a new declaration • In absence of agreement, partners must contribute equally • Attach a form of subscription for limited partners		
9. Division of Net Profits	In absence of agreement, partners must share equally • Include provision for periodic review and criteria or basis for revising interests		
10. Accounting and Other Records	Describe the nature of records kept and nature of statements to be given to partners • Records should be sufficient for tax and legal purposes (auditor/accountant can advise) • In absence of agreement, every partner is entitled to access partnership books and records		
11. Auditor or Accountant	Name of auditor or accountant		
12. Fiscal Year	Designate year end or partnership • (seek advice from auditor/accountant)		

13. Accounting Principles	• Valuation of assets (cost, market, depreciated value) • Valuation of goodwill • Capital vs. income • Depreciation policy • Interest on advances and capital • Write-offs • Reserves for working capital (receivables, overvalued inventory, etc.) • Partnership vs. personal expenses • Calculation of profit		
14. Banking Arrangements	• Designate banker • Designate types of accounts and who has signing authority • Consider requiring two or more signatures on large amounts		
15. Encumbering Partnership Interest	• Restrict partners from charging partnership interest to secure personal debts • A partner's liability for personal obligations exigible out of his share of partnership assets (so a partner's personal creditors may be able to dissolve the partnership)		
16. Full Time and Attention	• Partnership legislation provides that partners are liable to account for certain outside income • State all income/remuneration, etc. to be included in partnership income (i.e. directors' fees, royalties) • Consider a "no moonlighting" clause • Where one partner is part-time, consider providing salary for full-time partners (and for the general partner in a limited partnership)		

17. Management	• Describe the business/management roles of partners and others • Describe meetings (frequency, notice, procedure, voting, etc.) • Unless there is agreement to the contrary, a simple majority governs (except for changes in partners, changes in the nature of the business and changes in this agreement) • If limited partnership, only general partner may manage • Include specific powers of general partner (i.e. no major borrowing or sale or encumbrance of assets out of the ordinary course of business, without the consent of a specified majority of limited partners)		
18. Partnership Contracts	• Who signs what contracts • If limited partnership, only general partner can sign		
19. Drawing Arrangements	• How often, and how much can partners withdraw from the business (should not exceed specified percentage of anticipated share of profit for the year)		
20. Retirement, Bankruptcy or Death of a Partner	• Unless partners agree otherwise, retirement, bankruptcy or death of a partner results in dissolution • Provide notice period and agreement by which remaining partners to buy retiring, bankrupt or deceased partner's interest • Method of valuation of former partner's interest, and payment • Obligation to purchase by the continuing partners on retirement, expulsion or death of a partner • Option to purchase by successors from continuing founder		

	• Mandatory retirement at a specified age, with right of younger partners to purchase 20% of older partners' interest in each of the 5 years prior to retirement date		
21. Valuation of Partnership Interest	• How is amount to be calculated and paid • If goodwill is to be included, price could be based on a reasonable multiple of book value at cost or depreciated value or at a figure to be agreed upon periodically by all partners • If goodwill is not included, price would be equal to advances or loans, plus share of capital assets, including amounts contributed by partners, plus undrawn share of profits • Review income tax consequences to valuation (auditor/accountant to advise) • Make sure price is not based on future profits, since retiring partner may be considered a continuing partner		
22. Non-Competition	• Restrictive covenant to prevent partners from competing after leaving the firm – must be reasonable in time, activity and geographic area		
23. Sale of Partnership Interest to Third Parties	• Prohibited, unless agreed upon by all partners • Could allow for it if remaining partners refuse to buy out the interest of a retiring partner		
24. Expulsion of Partner	• Partner cannot be expelled, unless there is an agreement to the contrary • Could allow in certain circumstances (e.g. on grounds of insolvency or other grounds for court order in partnership legislation)		

25. Dissolution of Partnership	• Death, insolvency and notice of partner dissolve a partnership, unless there is an agreement to the contrary; dissolution is automatic, making it unlawful to continue the partnership • Partners may dissolve if there is any charge made to the partnership for personal debts		
26. Admission of New Partners	• Cannot admit new partners without unanimous approval, unless there is an agreement to the contrary • Provide for majority vote • Contribution to be made to capital • Allocate new partners' interest in capital and profits *pro rata* from others, and provide method of payment		
27. Partnership Property	• Registered in firm name • If registered in the name of one or more partners, then define the property		
28. Liability	• Consider limiting the liability of general partner to limited partners		
29. Insurance	• Kinds, limits and deductibles for insurance required for the partnership • Obligation on each partner to buy term insurance (in certain amount) on life of other partners, to fund in whole or in part the partner's obligation to purchaser the interest of the deceased partner		
30. Arbitration	• Consider naming an arbitrator – possibly the auditor/accountant on financial matters, and another named person on other matters • One or three arbitrators, under *Arbitration Act*,[49] whose decision is final and not appealable (expensive)		

---

49 S.O. 1991, c. 17.

31. Registration	• Provide for registration under the *Limited Partnerships Act* & undertakings by partners to facilitate registration of any change made in accordance with the partnership agreement • Attach power of attorney making each partner attorney for the other (surviving death or any assignment of interest) for the purpose of registration requirements • Attach limited partnership declaration to be signed and registered • Provide for less than unanimous vote to change such terms of the partnership agreement as partners agree will not require unanimous consent • Consider need, pursuant to *Personal Information Protection and Electronic Documents Act*,[50] for consents with respect to disclosure of information concerning employees, customers or any other individual • Consider need for a clause regarding confidentiality for information disclosed during the due diligence process (about employees, customers, etc.) with all copies of information to be returned or destroyed if the transaction does not go through		

---

50 R.S.O. 2000, c. 5.

32. General Contract Provisions	• Term • Notice procedure • Additional documents • Counterparts • Time of the essence • Entire agreement • Enurement • Currency • Headings for convenience only • Governing law • Gender • Calculation of time • Legislation references • Extended meaning of units • Severability • Termination of prior agreements • Assignability • Facsimile clause		
33. Signatures	• Who has signing authority • Corporate seal		
34. Schedules	• Include all required Schedules		

CHAPTER 4: CORPORATIONS

Overview:

- Corporate law
- *Business Corporations Act*
- "Separate legal entity"
- Advantages & disadvantages of incorporation
- Corporate name
- Numbered company
- Types of corporations
  - Provincial and federal corporations
  - Offering and non-offering corporations
  - Professional corporation
  - Extra-provincial corporation
- Workbook:
  - Incorporation questionnaire
  - Form 2, *Business Names Act*

1. Corporate Law

Corporate law is, simply, the law that relates to corporations, and a corporation is one way that a person or persons may choose to operate a business. Generally, a corporation is formed to carry on a business, by one or more persons, with a view to making a profit. When a person wants to start and operate a business, the law imposes certain rules, in order to protect individuals who deal with that business and the public at large. So far, we have discussed sole proprietorships and partnerships, and we have examined the law – statutes, regulations and cases – that pertain to these two forms of business association.

One of the main disadvantages with operating a sole proprietorship or a partnership is unlimited, personal liability for the owner(s). With a partnership, that liability goes further – there is joint and several liability, which means that one partner will be responsible for the acts and omissions of other partners, as long as those acts and omissions relate to the business. It is one thing to be responsible for one's own mistakes – as in a sole proprietorship – and quite another to be responsible for someone else's mistakes (whether or not you knew about them) – as in a partnership.

For this reason, the law has created a separate form of business association, which addresses the problem of unlimited, personal liability. That form of business association is the corporation. In Ontario, corporations are governed primarily by the *Business Corporations Act*,[1] hereinafter referred to as the "*BCA*". A corporation incorporated (or created) under the *BCA* is called an "Ontario corporation".

2. *Business Corporations Act*

The *BCA* is the main statute that a legal professional should be familiar with, if he/she is dealing with an Ontario corporation. Please refer to a current copy of this statute through the e-Laws website. The Act defines "corporation" as "a body corporate with share capital to which this Act applies."[2] A "body corporate" is defined as "any body corporate with or without share capital and whether or not it is a corporation to which this Act applies".[3] Not surprisingly, someone who reads the *BCA* may have difficulty understanding what a corporation really is.

Javid does not feel that he has enough experience in the nightclub business to start "Nirvana Nightclub" on his own. He knows that Helena has worked in a nightclub for several years, and that Mike has significant connections in the entertainment business. However, neither Helena nor Mike have any capital to contribute to the business. Moreover, Javid does not want his investment to be at risk if Helena or Mike are negligent in any way. Javid certainly does not want joint and several liability with Helena and Mike. How can Javid work with Mike and Helena, without assuming personal liability?

---

1 R.S.O. 1990, c. B.16.
2 *Ibid.*, s. 1(1).
3 *Ibid.*

In the scenario described above, imagine that Javid, Mike and Helena could create an imaginary person who would run "Nirvana Nightclub". The imaginary person would be fully responsible for the business, and would have complete liability – just like a sole proprietor. The only difference would be that Javid, Mike and Helena would control that imaginary person, telling the imaginary person exactly what to do and how to do it. In addition, Javid, Mike and Helena would give this imaginary person the money and other resources to start the business – so the risk that Javid, Mike and Helena still take is that the money and resources that they invest in the business may be lost if the business is not successful. In legal terminology, Javid, Helena and Mike can "incorporate" – that is, they can create a corporation under the relevant statute. The corporation is the "imaginary person" described above.

3. Separate Legal Entity

In the example given above, the "imaginary person" that started and operated the business was a different person than Javid, Helena or Mike. When a person incorporates, the corporation is treated as a separate (imaginary) person. For example, if Javid, Mike and Helena create a corporation called "Nirvana Nightclub Ltd.", then Nirvana Nightclub Ltd. is treated by the law as a separate person that runs and operates that nightclub. Nirvana Nightclub Ltd. may be controlled by Javid, Helena and Mike, but it is still treated as a separate person in the law.

Brewer v. Sarangio Investments Inc. (1993), 12 C.L.R. (2d) 119 (Ont. Gen. Div.), affirmed 1996 CarswellOnt 5022 (Ont. C.A.)

The plaintiff hired Ren Home Consulting Inc. ("Ren Home") to perform a home inspection, which the plaintiff relied upon when purchasing a property. The plaintiff claimed that the inspection was performed negligently, as problems arose with the property after he purchased it. The plaintiff sued Ren Molnar, who was his main contact, as well as several corporate defendants. The defendant, Ren Molnar, was the sole director and shareholder of Ren Home, and acted as its employee. The inspection report and invoice provided to the plaintiff were all on corporate letterhead, and the cheque written by the plaintiff was made out to Ren Home. Ren Molnar brought a motion to dismiss the plaintiff's claim against him personally.

The court held that Ren Molnar had done everything he could do to make it clear that the plaintiff was dealing with a corporation; the plaintiff, therefore, could not sue Ren Molnar in contract since there was no privity of contract between them. With respect to the plaintiff's ability to sue Ren Molnar in negligence, the court stated:

. . .

A party can choose to limit his or her tortious liability by means of express or implied terms in a contract. So long as the limitation is clear, it will be effective. Mr. Ren Molnar's intention to limit his personal tortious liability can be implied by the fact that he chose to operate through a limited corporation. He made his intention known quite clearly and the plaintiff, in forming a contract with Ren Home Consultation Inc. for the preparation of the building inspection report must be taken to have accepted this. It has long been established that a one person corporation, like any validly set up corporation, has a separate legal existence and is an independent person in law: *Salomon v. Salomon & Co.* (1896), [1897] A.C. 22, 13 T.L.R. 46 (U.K. H.L.). While the corporate veil can be lifted where the corporate

> vehicle is used to perpetrate a fraud or to effect an unlawful purpose . . . there is nothing improper in using a corporation as a means of limiting liability or avoiding bearing business losses.
>
> The court dismissed the action against Ren Molnar, with costs fixed at $2,500. (Motion allowed.)

From a customer's point of view, the fact that a business operates as a sole proprietorship, partnership or corporation makes little difference in the provision of goods and services. For example, in the *Brewer* case,[4] the plaintiff contacted Ren Molnar to perform a home inspection. The actual home inspection report would have been exactly the same if it had been provided by Ren Molnar as a sole proprietor, as a partner in a firm, or as an employee of a corporation. Similarly, if you buy an item at a coffee shop, it makes no difference – in terms of the product you are buying – if that coffee shop is operated as a sole proprietorship, a partnership or a corporation. The significance of the type of business association lies in the customer's ability to sue the owner.

> Assume that Javid, Helena and Mike have incorporated "Nirvana Nightclub Ltd.", an Ontario corporation. Someone attends the opening night of the nightclub, and starts to get rowdy. The bouncer evicts the individual, but in doing so, breaks his arm. The individual wants to sue to recover damages from lost wages, medical expenses and other costs resulting from the injury. Who can the plaintiff sue, and why?

Unlike a sole proprietor or a partner, shareholders of a corporation have "limited liability".

We will discuss shareholders in greater detail in Chapter 7, but essentially, shareholders are the owners of a corporation – just like a sole proprietor is the owner of a sole proprietorship, and a partner is an owner in a firm. While sole proprietors and partners (at least, general partners) have unlimited, personal liability, a shareholder has *limited* liability. Section 92 (1) of the *BCA* states:

> The shareholders of a corporation are not, as shareholders, liable for any act, default, obligation or liability of the corporation except under section 34(5), subsection 108(5) and section 243.[5]

In other words, shareholders – the owners of the corporation – have limited liability because they cannot be held responsible for the debts, obligations, acts, omissions or other liabilities of the corporation, except in certain circumstances. This is a key advantage of incorporating to run a business. In other words, if Nirvana Nightclub Ltd. takes out a loan from the bank and fails to pay it, the bank cannot sue Javid, Helena and Mike personally to recover the amount of the loan; the bank can only sue Nirvana Nightclub Ltd. (To deal with this problem, banks will often ask shareholders or others to give personal guarantees on a loan taken out by a corporation, with the result being that the bank has a separate contract, that is the guarantee, under which to sue the shareholders.)

---

4   *Brewer v. Sarangio Investments Inc.*, 1993 CarswellOnt 831, 12 C.L.R. (2d) 119 (Ont. Gen. Div.), affirmed 1996 CarswellOnt 5022 (Ont. C.A.).
5   *Business Corporations Act*, R.S.O. 1990, c. B.16, s. 92(1).

Similarly, if Nirvana Nightclub Ltd. purchases furniture for its nightclub from a furniture supplier, that furniture supplier can only demand payment from Nirvana Nightclub Ltd., not from Javid, Helena and Mike personally. This is how the corporation protects its owners from personal liability.

In certain circumstances, however, a shareholder can lose this "limited liability" status. First, it is critical that a shareholder in a corporation makes it clear to third parties that they are dealing with a corporation, and not the shareholder as an individual. This can be done by ensuring that all correspondence, contracts, invoices, cheques and other documents are in the name of the corporation (on corporate letterhead,) and not in the shareholder's personal name. In addition, assuming that a shareholder is the key contact for third parties, he/she should ensure that any contracts or other documents are signed by the shareholder as agent for the corporation (and not in the shareholder's personal capacity.) Failure to clearly indicate that the third party is dealing with a corporation can be disastrous for the shareholder.

Pax-All Manufacturing Inc. v. Provit Canada Ltd., 2010 CarswellOnt 2095, [2010] O.J. No. 1447 (Ont. C.A.)

Mr. Khan was the principal owner of the corporate defendant, Provit Canada Ltd. ("Provit"). In the Superior Court of Justice, the judge found that amounts owed to the plaintiff were owed by Provit, since Mr. Khan was acting in his corporate capacity when he was dealing with the plaintiff. The plaintiff appealed, and the Court of Appeal allowed the appeal. The court pointed out that a quotation made by the plaintiff to Mr. Khan was in his personal name. Moreover, a purchaser order that was sent to Provit and Mr. Khan was returned and signed by Mr. Khan, and there was no indication at all that he was signing on behalf of the corporation. The court found Mr. Khan personally liable for damages of approximately $90,000 plus pre-judgment interest, with costs of $3,000 awarded to the plaintiff.

In rare circumstances, the courts will also "pierce the corporate veil"; in other words, the courts will sometimes ignore the existence of a corporation, and will hold the individuals that control the corporation personally liable. Since this negates a key reason for creating a corporation, the courts will exercise this option very carefully – usually in circumstances involving fraud or other criminal activity, activities that are otherwise against public policy, or where it would be "flagrantly unjust" to allow the principals of a corporation to hide behind the corporate veil.[6] The court stated the guiding principle in the following way in the 1996 case of *Transamerica Life Insurance Co. of Canada v. Canada Life Assurance Co.*:

---

6 *642947 Ontario Ltd. v. Fleischer*, 2001 CarswellOnt 4296, 56 O.R. (3d) 417 (Ont. C.A.); *Clarkson Co. v. Zhelka*, 1967 CarswellOnt 144, [1967] 2 O.R. 565 (Ont. H.C.); *Kosmopoulos v. Constitution Insurance Co. of Canada*, 1987 CarswellOnt 132, 1987 CarswellOnt 1054, [1987] 1 S.C.R. 2 (S.C.C.).

the courts will disregard the separate legal personality of a corporate entity where it is completely dominated and controlled and being used as a shield for fraudulent or improper conduct. [7]

Joy Estate v. 1156653 Ontario Ltd., 2007 CarswellOnt 3762 (Ont. S.C.J.), additional reasons 2007 CarswellOnt 7323 (Ont. S.C.J.), additional reasons 2007 CarswellOnt 7739 (Ont. S.C.J.)

B. Thomas Joy was the majority shareholder and director of a racetrack, Windsor Raceway Inc. ("WRI"). He obtained a personal loan from certain corporate and individual lenders, with the loan being guaranteed by WRI. Mr. Bharat and Mr. Fanelli were representatives of the corporate lenders, and signed the loan agreement on behalf of the respective corporations.

One of the issues that the court had to decide was whether Bharat and Fanelli should have personal liability because the corporate lenders allegedly charged a criminal rate of interest on the loan. The court ultimately found that the rate of interest was not criminal, but it addressed the issue of "piercing the corporate veil" and made important statements on this issue.

First, the court reiterated that a corporation is a separate legal entity, and the corporate form should only be disregarded where it would be "flagrantly unjust" to protect the principals of the corporation from personal liability. Second, the corporate veil should only be disregarded in rare circumstances.

> Typically, the corporate veil is pierced when the company is incorporated for an illegal, fraudulent or improper purpose. But it can also be pierced if when incorporated "those in control expressly direct a wrongful thing to be done."

In addition,

> the courts will disregard the separate legal personality of a corporate entity *where it is completely dominated and controlled and being used as a shield for fraudulent or improper conduct* [emphasis added]. "Complete control" over a corporation requires more than simply ownership. Complete domination such that the subsidiary cannot function independently must be demonstrated.

In this case, Bharat and Fanelli did not have complete control over the corporate lenders because there were other individuals who were active in the businesses and who served as directors or had significant holdings as shareholders. In addition, the corporations that were involved in the loan agreement had been in existence long before the loan agreement was entered into, and had been involved in other legitimate transactions. While the court held that there was no criminal rate of interest charged in this case, it did comment that the fact that a criminal rate of interest was charged in a loan would not, in and of itself, be sufficient to pierce the veil.

The action against Bharat and Fanelli was dismissed.

---

7 *Transamerica Life Insurance Co. of Canada v. Canada Life Assurance Co.*, 1996 CarswellOnt 1699, 28 O.R. (3d) 423 (Ont. Gen. Div.), affirmed 1997 CarswellOnt 3496, [1997] O.J. No. 3754 (Ont. C.A.).

1005633 Ontario Inc. v. Winchester Arms Ltd. (2000), 8 B.L.R. (3d) 176 (Ont. S.C.J.), additional reasons 2000 CarswellOnt 4298 (Ont. S.C.J.), affirmed 2000 CarswellOnt 4748 (Ont. C.A.)

The plaintiff company entered into a franchise agreement with the defendant ("WAL") and an agreement with Winchester Construction Company Limited ("WCCL"), to build and operate a pub. Pauline and John Lee were the shareholders and officers of WAL, and John was a shareholder and officer of WCCL. The court found that the defendants made misrepresentations to the plaintiffs about providing them with a turnkey operation, and about other matters. By the time this case went to court, the corporate defendants were either bankrupt or inactive, making them judgment proof.

In this case, the court did pierce the corporate veil and found all of the defendants, including the Lees, jointly and severally liable. The court stated:

> Pauline and John were the guiding minds of the corporate Defendants. Each personally dealt with the Plaintiffs and made misrepresentations, which were acted upon by the Plaintiffs. John knowingly swore a false statement to the LLBO in the Application for transfer of license. Neither produced any proper financial records on which the Court could rely, thereby directing the corporations not to reveal what ought to have been revealed about the operations of #945 and their franchise system under WAL. All of these corporate Defendants were closely related and co-mingled funds, including the monies received for the first six operational days of the pub. No one else sat on the Boards of the companies other than the Lees during the time in question. See: *Manley Inc. v. Fallis* (1977), 2 B.L.R. 277 (Ont. C.A.) at p.279 . . .The Defendant companies were mere puppets of the Lees which John, in particular, manipulated to suit his own purposes.

The plaintiffs were awarded damages for breach of contract, misrepresentation and acting in bad faith, in the amount of $138,780.12 plus interest.

4. Advantages & Disadvantages of Incorporation

The main advantages of incorporating when a person wants to start a business include:

- the owners have limited liability

- a corporation never dies, even if its shareholders die; as long as its life is not terminated by its shareholders, a court or a governmental body (as provided for in its governing statute,) the corporation continues to exist. This means that death of one owner (a shareholder) does not cease operation of the business.

- there may be some tax advantages to the owners, depending on the owners' personal tax situations

The main disadvantages of incorporating include:

- the cost of incorporating is greater than starting a sole proprietorship or partnership

- the process for incorporation is more involved than the process for starting a sole proprietorship or partnership

- there may be tax *dis*advantages to the owners, depending on the owners' personal tax situations

- in addition to legal requirements, a corporation must maintain separate accounting and tax records, resulting in additional cost

5. Corporate Name

Like any other form of business association, a corporation must have a name that is registered with the government. A corporate name has three elements:

1. a distinctive or unique element (such as a surname or unique term)

2. a descriptive element that tells the public what the business is about (such as "Manufacturing")

3. a mandatory, legal element (such as Limited, Incorporated, Corporation or their abbreviations or French equivalents)

For example, the corporate name "Jonas Consulting Inc." has all three elements of a corporate name – a unique element (Jonas), a descriptive element (Consulting) and a legal element (Inc.)[8]

However, not any corporate name will be acceptable. The *BCA* provides certain restrictions on the names that can be chosen. Specifically:

- the corporation's name must include the word "Limited", "Incorporated" or "Corporation", or their abbreviations or French language equivalents[9]

- the corporation may have an English or French name, or a name that has a combination of English and French[10]

- the corporation cannot have a name that contains a word or expression that is not allowed by the regulations to the *BCA*, a name that is the same or similar to the name of a known corporation, trust, association, partnership, sole proprietorship or individual (whether in existence or not) if that name would like deceive the public, or a name that otherwise does not meet the requirements specified in the regulations to the *BCA*.[11]

By including the words "Limited", "Incorporated" or "Corporation" in the name of a corporation, the public is given notice that it is dealing with an entity whose owners have limited liability.

The following regulation to the *BCA* provides additional details about a corporate name: *General*, R.R.O. 1990, Reg. 62.

---

8   *Guide to Federal Incorporation*, March 2011, Corporations Canada, Industry Canada, p. 8.
9   *Business Corporations Act*, R.S.O. 1990, c. B.16, s. 10(1).
10   *Ibid.*, s. 10(2).
11   *Ibid.*, s. 9.

This regulation provides important clarifications, such as explaining what terms such as "likely to deceive"[12] mean, and what criteria the Director will use to determine if a corporation has violated section 9 of the *BCA* in selecting an inappropriate name.[13] The regulation also provides exceptions to the prohibition for using similar names for corporations that are affiliated,[14] and explains circumstances in which the use of a name similar to another body will be allowed.[15] If a corporation is formed by two or more amalgamating corporations, the new corporation may use the name of one of the amalgamating corporations.[16] Finally, the regulation also provides additional details on what can and cannot be used as part of a corporate name, including (but not limited to):

- a corporate name cannot be too general or formed primarily of punctuation marks[17]

- a corporate name cannot include a person's name, except where he/she has given permission[18]

- a corporate name cannot be immoral, obscene, scandalous or otherwise objectionable on public grounds[19]

- certain words such as "amalgamated" may only be used in certain circumstances[20]

- certain words, such as "college", may only be used if permission is obtained from the requisite body[21]

- certain words, such as "condominium", "cooperative" and "council", cannot be used[22]

- no word can be used that suggests that the corporation is affiliated with the Crown or any level of government[23]

- words cannot be used that suggest that the corporation is controlled or associated with a professional association,[24] or a political party[25]

- no words can be used that suggests that the corporation operates as a bank, trust company or other financial institution[26]

---

12 *General*, R.R.O. 1990, Reg. 62, s. 2.
13 *Ibid.*, s. 3.
14 *Ibid.*, ss. 4 – 5.
15 *Ibid.*, ss. 6, 8 – 9.
16 *Ibid.*, s. 10.
17 *Ibid.*, s. 11.
18 *Ibid.*, s. 12.
19 *Ibid.*, s. 13.
20 *Ibid.*, s. 15.
21 *Ibid.*
22 *Ibid.*
23 *Ibid.*, s. 16(1)(a).
24 *Ibid.*, s. 16(1)(b).
25 *Ibid.*, s. 16(2).
26 *Ibid.*, s. 16(1)(c).

- a corporate name cannot be misleading in the type of goods and services that the corporation will provide, or who produces those goods and services, or where those goods and services come from[27]

- a corporate name cannot exceed 120 characters, including punctuation and spaces[28]

For additional details, refer to sections 1 through 22.1 of the Regulation.[29]

6. Numbered Company

A numbered company is a corporation that chooses not to select a corporate name, but instead, uses a number to identify itself. Section 8 of the *BCA* provides:

> 8. (1) Every corporation shall be assigned a number by the Director and such number shall be specified as the corporation number in the certificate of incorporation and in any other certificate relating to the corporation endorsed or issued by the Director . . .

> (2) Where no name is specified in the articles that are delivered to the Director, the corporation shall be assigned a number name.

Sometimes, a business is incorporated for a specific purpose – such as a tax-related purpose, or for a joint venture – and there is no need to assign the corporation a name because the corporation will not be presenting that name to the public. In other words, the corporation will not have a store front with a sign that has its name on it, and it will not have any advertisements with its name on it. In this case, it will be quicker and less expensive to incorporate a "numbered company." In Chapter 5, we will explore the incorporation process in detail.

If the corporation is incorporated under the *BCA*, it is referred to as an Ontario corporation, and its numbered company name will be the corporation number, followed by "Ontario", and then the legal element of the name, which is "Limited", "Incorporated" or "Corporation" (or their abbreviations.) In a case reviewed earlier in this chapter, for example, the name of the plaintiff corporation was 1005633 Ontario Inc. Similarly, many numbered companies are referred to as the corporation number, followed by "Ontario Ltd." – for example, 642947 Ontario Ltd.

A numbered company incorporated under the *Canada Business Corporations Act*[30] (hereinafter referred to as the "*CBCA*") will also be referred to by a number that is assigned to it by the Director of the *CBCA*, followed by "Canada" and then the legal element of the name – that is, "Limited", "Incorporated", "Corporation" or French equivalents or abbreviations. The *CBCA* provides:

> 10. (1) The word or expression "Limited", "Limitée", "Incorporated", "Incorporée", "Corporation" or "Société par actions de régime fédéral" or the corresponding abbreviation "Ltd.", "Ltée", "Inc.", "Corp." or "S.A.R.F." shall be part, other than only in a figurative or descriptive sense, of the name of every corporation, but a corporation may use and be legally designated by either the full or the corresponding abbreviated form.

---

27 *Ibid.*, s. 17.
28 *Ibid.*, s. 21(1).
29 *General*, R.R.O. 1990, Reg. 62.
30 *Canada Business Corporations Act*, R.S.C. 1985, c. C-44.

. . .

11(2) If requested to do so by the incorporators or a corporation, the Director shall assign to the corporation as its name a designating number followed by the word "Canada" and a word or expression, or the corresponding abbreviation, referred to in subsection 10(1).

An example of a numbered company incorporated under the CBCA is 4178963 Canada Inc.

4178963 Canada Inc. carries on business as Canadian Tire, and you will sometimes see the notation "4178963 Canada Inc. o/a Canadian Tire" or "4178963 Canada Inc. (c.o.b. Canadian Tire)" in caselaw. The notation "o/a" refers to "operating as", and the notation "c.o.b." refers to "carrying on business as". This illustrates the point that a numbered company can, once it is established, decide to operate under a business name. That business name must, however, be registered under the *Business Names Act*.[31] Similarly, if a named corporation (such as Entertainment Group Ltd.) decides to operate a business under a different name (such as Nirvana Nightclub,) the business name (Nirvana Nightclub) must be registered under the *Business Names Act*. Section 2(1) of the *Business Names Act* states:

> No corporation shall carry on business or identify itself to the public under a name other than its corporate name unless the name is registered by that corporation.

To register a business or trade name, it is necessary to file Form 2 under the *Business Names Act*. This form is accessible for free from the Ontario Central Forms Repository (introduced in Chapter 2). As always, legal professionals must read the instructions to the form to ensure that there are no unnecessary delays because of minor errors. For example, the form specifies that it must be completed in black ink and in capital letters. You can also complete the form online (which is preferable, as it prompts you if you have omitted required information.) However, the form cannot be saved in the online format – you must complete it and then print it immediately.

Please refer to the Workbook for a copy of Form 2 under the *Business Names Act*.

7. Types of Corporations

(a) Provincial and Federal Corporations

So far, we have been discussing corporations primarily with respect to corporations created pursuant to the *BCA*. The *BCA* is Ontario legislation, and as such, corporations created under this statute are referred to as Ontario corporations. An Ontario numbered company is referred to by a number, followed by "Ontario Ltd." or a similar ending (see "Numbered Companies" above for more details.)

Each jurisdiction in Canada will have a similar statute that allows a corporation to be created in each of those jurisdictions. In addition, a business operating in any part of Canada – including Ontario – can choose to incorporate under the *Canada Business Corporations Act* ("*CBCA*").[32] Fortunately, the *BCA* and *CBCA* are very similar, although there are some differences. However, for most legal practitioners advising businesses in Ontario, most incorporations will be for Ontario companies. For this reason, this textbook

---

31 R.S.O. 1990, c. B.17.
32 R.S.C. 1985, c. C-44.

focuses on the *BCA* and the laws that relate to Ontario corporations, with the view that, once you are familiar with the legal framework for Ontario companies, you will be able to understand and interpret the legal framework relating to federal companies with relative ease. However, this section of Chapter 4 will provide an overview of some of the salient features of the *CBCA*, and the creation of federal corporations.

To view a current version of the *CBCA*, go to the website for the Department of Justice Canada, and refer to the menu under "Laws". To access the site in general, go to <www.justice.gc.ca>, and to go directly to the Justice Laws Website, go to <www.laws.justice.gc.ca>.

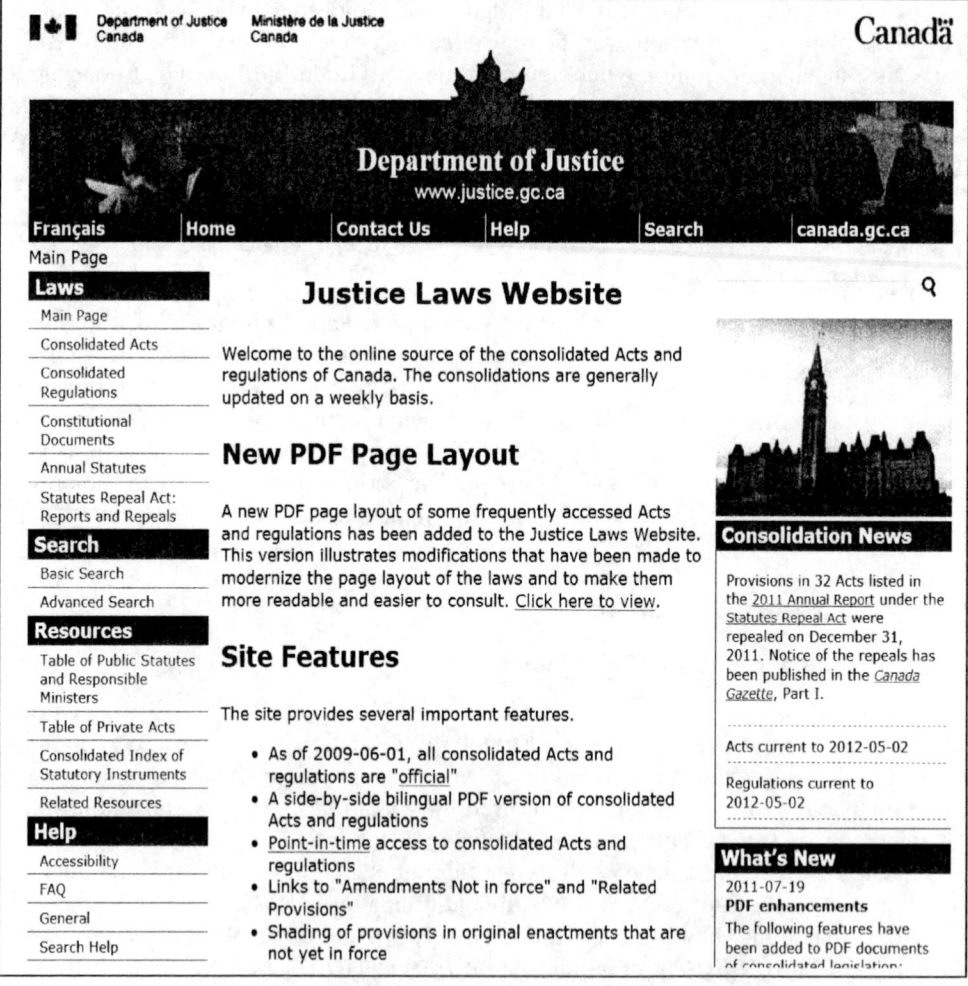

Like the e-Laws website for Ontario legislation, the Justice Laws Website provides official versions of all consolidated acts and regulations. However, the Justice Laws Website only provides federal statutes and regulations. Official versions of the legislation are versions that can be used for evidentiary purposes – meaning that they can be submitted in court. Statutes and regulations are generally updated weekly on this site (as of the date of writing.)

Click on "Consolidated Acts" on the left side of the screen, and then on "C" to access the *CBCA*. You will be able to access an online version of the Act, as well as a PDF version for printing. To access the regulations to the Act, click on the yellow box with an "R" on the right side of the screen, across from "*Canada Business Corporations Act*".

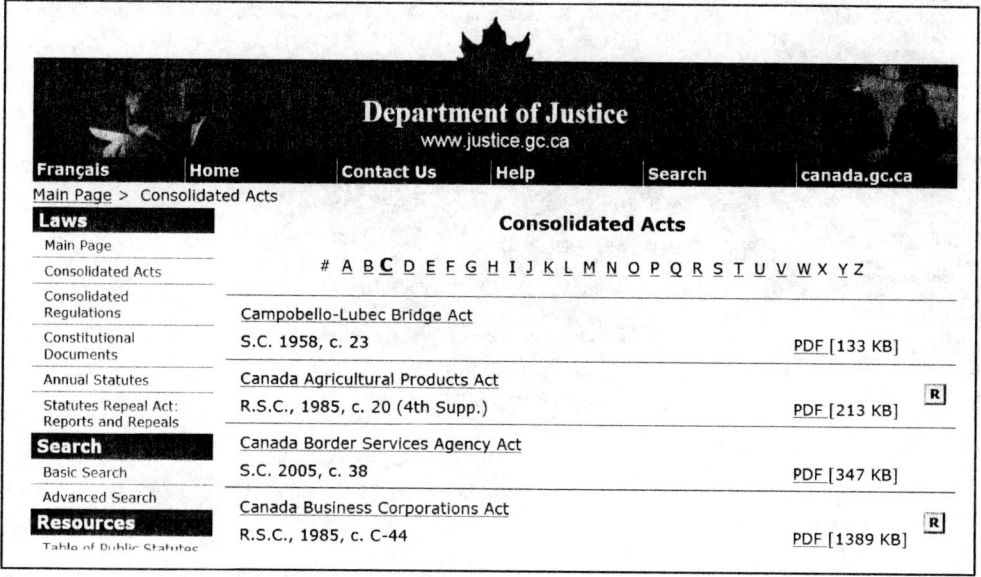

Once you click on the link to the *CBCA*, you will see the following screen:

Note the currency date of the Act near the top of the screen.

The *CBCA* applies to every corporation incorporated under the *CBCA* and every body corporate continued under the *CBCA*.[33] The definition of a "body corporate" is simpler than in the *BCA*, and is provided in section 1 which states: "body corporate" includes a company or other body corporate wherever or however incorporated". Section 3 states:

3. (1) This Act applies to every corporation incorporated and every body corporate continued as a corporation under this Act that has not been discontinued under this Act.

(2) [Repealed, 1991, c. 45, s. 551]

(3) The following do not apply to a corporation:

(*a*) the Canada Corporations Act, chapter C-32 of the Revised Statutes of Canada, 1970;

(*b*) the Winding-up and Restructuring Act; and

(*c*) the provisions of a Special Act, as defined in section 87 of the Canada Transportation Act, that are inconsistent with this Act.

(4) No corporation shall carry on the business of

(*a*) a bank;

---

33 *Canada Business Corporations Act*, R.S.C. 1985, c. C-44, s. 3(1).

(*a.1*) an association to which the Cooperative Credit Associations Act applies;

(*b*) company or society to which the Insurance Companies Act applies; or

(*c*) a company to which the Trust and Loan Companies Act applies.

(5) No corporation shall carry on business as a degree-granting educational institution unless expressly authorized to do so by a federal or provincial agent that by law has the power to confer degree-granting authority on an educational institution.[34]

Unlike the *BCA*, the *CBCA* provides an overall objective for the *CBCA*, stating that its purpose is, amongst other things, to revise the law related to corporations in Canada, and to attempt to make corporate laws more uniform across Canada.[35]

Under the *CBCA*, one or more individuals who are over the age of 18 years, of sound mind and not bankrupt, may incorporate by signing articles of incorporation and complying with the Act. Similarly, one or more corporations may also incorporate a company following the same process. Sections 11 through 13 address the name of a corporation. While most of the principles are the same as in the *BCA*, the *CBCA* allows the Director to reserve a name for 90 days for an intended corporation or a corporation that is going to change its name.[36]

The *CBCA* clearly addresses the capacity and powers of a corporation under that Act:

15. (1) A corporation has the capacity and, subject to this Act, the rights, powers and privileges of a natural person.

(2) A corporation may carry on business throughout Canada.

(3) A corporation has the capacity to carry on its business, conduct its affairs and exercise its powers in any jurisdiction outside Canada to the extent that the laws of such jurisdiction permit.

16. (1) It is not necessary for a by-law to be passed in order to confer any particular power on the corporation or its directors.

(2) A corporation shall not carry on any business or exercise any power that it is restricted by its articles from carrying on or exercising, nor shall the corporation exercise any of its powers in a manner contrary to its articles.

(3) No act of a corporation, including any transfer of property to or by a corporation, is invalid by reason only that the act or transfer is contrary to its articles or this Act.[37]

Note that a corporation incorporated under the *CBCA* is given the power to carry on business anywhere in Canada, as well as outside of Canada (to the extent that the relevant foreign laws allow it to do so).

Finally, just as in the *BCA*, the *CBCA* provides limited liability to shareholders. Section 45(1) states that the "shareholders of a corporation are not, as shareholders, liable

---

34 *Ibid.*, s. 3.
35 *Ibid.*, s. 4.
36 *Ibid.*, s. 11(1).
37 *Ibid.*, ss. 15 – 16.

for any liability, act or default of the corporation except under subsection 38(4), 118(4) or (5), 146(5) or 226(4) or (5)."[38]

> Javid, Helena and Mike have decided to incorporate their business. Should they incorporate it as an Ontario corporation or a federal corporation? Should they select a name for the corporation, or simply opt for a numbered company?

The process for incorporating both an Ontario and a federal company has become easier in recent times, and will be discussed in Chapter 5. Most businesses that plan to operate solely in Ontario will opt for the more common process of incorporating an Ontario company. However, if the business is likely to operate across several provinces in Canada or internationally, there are advantages to incorporating federally. For example, a federal corporation may operate its business anywhere in Canada, although it will have to register its name in each jurisdiction that it operates in. For example, a *CBCA* company that operates in Ontario will have to register its corporate name under the *Business Names Act*.[39] For a company that plans to operate internationally, a "Canada" corporation may be more recognized in some jurisdictions than an "Ontario" corporation – although an Ontario corporation may conduct business internationally if the foreign jurisdiction allows it to do so. Finally, the initial incorporation fee is less expensive for a federal company; however, federal companies have additional fees related to other registrations (such as registration under the *Business Names Act*)[40] that do not apply to Ontario corporations. In the end, the main consideration is likely going to be whether or not the clients intend their business to remain in Ontario, or if the business is likely to expand or operate across Canada and beyond.

(b) Offering and Non-Offering Corporations

The *BCA* makes a distinction between an "offering corporation" and other types of corporations. An "offering corporation" means:

> a corporation that is offering its securities to the public within the meaning of subsection (6) and that is not the subject of an order of the Commission deeming it to have ceased to be offering its securities to the public[41]

It further explains, in section 1(6):

> For the purposes of this Act, a corporation is offering its securities to the public only where,
>
> > (a) in respect of any of its securities a prospectus or statement of material facts has been filed under the Securities Act or any predecessor thereof, or in respect of which a prospectus has been filed under The Corporations Information Act, being chapter 72 of the Revised Statutes of Ontario, 1960, or any predecessor thereof, so long as any of such securities are outstanding or any securities into which such securities are converted are outstanding; or

---

38   *Canada Business Corporations Act*, R.S.C. 1985, c. C-44, s. 45(1).
39   R.S.O. 1990, c. B.17.
40   *Ibid.*
41   *Business Corporations Act*, R.S.O. 1990, c. B.16, s. 1(1).

(b) any of its securities have been at any time since the 1ˢᵗ day of May, 1967, listed and posted for trading on any stock exchange in Ontario recognized by the Commission regardless of when such listing and posting for trading commenced,

except that where, upon the application of a corporation, the Commission is satisfied, in its discretion, that to do so would not be prejudicial to the public interest, the Commission may order, subject to such terms and conditions as the Commission may impose, that the corporation shall be deemed to have ceased to be offering its securities to the public.[42]

Essentially, an offering corporation under the *BCA* is what is often referred to as a public company. Corporations must achieve a certain financial size (in terms of assets, revenues and other financial measures) before they are allowed to list on a stock exchange like the Toronto Stock Exchange (TSX). Listing on a stock exchange usually allows the shareholders (owners) of a corporation to achieve a higher return on their investment, as it allows the corporation to sell its shares to the public. Companies must apply to a stock exchange before they are allowed to list their stocks on it.

Because offering – or public – corporations sell their shares to the public, there is more government regulation for those corporations, in order to ensure that the public is protected from fraudulent, unfair, or otherwise harmful activity. For example, corporations that trade in securities must register under the *Securities Act*[43] and comply with its registration, disclosure and other requirements. Securities legislation is a specialized area of the law, and goes beyond the scope of this corporate law textbook.

> What are some examples of public corporations that you are familiar with? What makes them public corporations? One example is WestJet Airlines Ltd., which is a public company listed on the Toronto Stock Exchange (TSX). It is known by the ticker symbol "WJA". Any member of the public can become an owner of WestJet Airlines Ltd. if he/she buys shares of WJA on the TSX at the current market price.

The term "non-offering corporation" is not specifically defined in the *BCA*; however, a "non-offering corporation" is essentially a corporation that is not an "offering corporation" under the *BCA*. In other words, it is a corporation that does not offer its shares for sale to the public. We often refer to this type of corporation as a private company. Most of the businesses that are incorporated in Ontario will be non-offering corporations, or private companies.

While the term "private company" is not part of the *BCA*, it is found in the *Securities Act* and is defined as follows:

private company" means a company in whose constating document,

(a) the right to transfer its shares is restricted,

(b) the number of its shareholders, exclusive of persons who are in its employment and exclusive of persons who, having been formerly in the employment of the company, were, while in that employment, and have continued after termination of that employment to be, shareholders of the company, is limited to not more than fifty, two or more persons

---

42 *Ibid.*, s. 1(6).
43 R.S.O. 1990, c. S.5.

who are the joint registered owners of one or more shares being counted as one share-holder, and

(c) many invitation to the public to subscribe for its securities is prohibited[44]

Basically, these "private company restrictions" state that, in a private company:

- shareholders cannot freely transfer shares

- there cannot be more than 50 shareholders

- shares cannot be offered for sale to the public

The *CBCA* does not use the terms "offering" or "non-offering" corporation.

(c) Professional Corporation

The *BCA* allows for the creation of a "professional corporation", which is: "a corporation incorporated or continued under this Act that holds a valid certificate of authorization or other authorizing document issued under an Act governing a profession."[45] A "member" is defined as "a member of a profession governed by an Act that permits the profession to be practiced through a professional corporation."

The *BCA* allows for professional corporations to be created, where a statute permits that profession to incorporate.[46] The *BCA* itself mentions the following acts, which relate to the professions referred to in those acts:

- An act named in Schedule 1 of the *Regulated Health Professions Act, 1991*[47] (which includes the *Dental Hygiene Act, 1991*[48], *Massage Therapy Act, 1991*[49], *Pharmacy Act, 1991*[50], amongst many other statutes)

- *Certified General Accountants Act, 2010*[51]

- *Law Society Act*[52]

- *Social Work and Social Service Work Act, 1998*[53]

- *Veterinarians Act*[54]

Like other Ontario corporations, professional corporations must follow the requirements of the *BCA* and its regulations, except where otherwise noted. In addition, a professional corporation must meet all of the following conditions:

---

44   *Ibid.*, s. 1(1).
45   *Business Corporations Act*, R.S.O. 1990, c. B.16, s. 3.1(1).
46   *Ibid.*, ss. 3.1(2)–(3).
47   S.O. 1991, c. 18.
48   S.O. 1991, c. 22.
49   S.O. 1991, c. 27.
50   S.O. 1991, c. 36.
51   S.O. 2010, c. 6, Sched. A.
52   R.S.O. 1990, c. L.8.
53   S.O. 1998, c. 31.
54   R.S.O. 1990, c. V.3.

- all of the corporation's shares must be owned by one or more members of the same profession

- all of the officers and directors of the corporations must also be shareholders of the corporation

- the name of the corporation must include the words "Professional Corporation" or its French equivalent, and must comply with any rules related to the names of professional corporations that are established by regulations to the *BCA*, or by the Act governing the profession

- the corporation cannot have a number name

- the articles of incorporation for a professional corporation must state that the corporation cannot carry any business other than the practice of the profession, but it may carry on activities that are ancillary to the practice of that profession (including investment of surplus funds earned by the corporation)[55]

Health profession corporations may be exempted from these requirements.[56]

A critical feature, however, of the professional corporation is addressed by section 3.4 of the *BCA*, which states:

3.4(1) Subsection 92(1) shall not be construed as limiting the professional liability of a shareholder of a professional corporation under an Act governing the profession for acts of the shareholder or acts of employees or agents of the corporation.

(2) For the purposes of professional liability, the acts of a professional corporation shall be deemed to be the acts of the shareholders, employees or agents of the corporation, as the case may be.

(3) The liability of a member for a professional liability claim is not affected by the fact that the member is practicing the profession through a professional corporation.[57]

Subsection 92(1) states:

The shareholders of a corporation are not, as shareholders, liable for any act, default, obligation or liability of the corporation except under subsection 34(5), subsection 108(5) and section 243.[58]

This means that, unlike other corporations, a professional corporation (as defined in the *BCA*) does not provide its shareholders with limited liability. Limited liability was one of the primary reasons for incorporating, so why would members of a profession incorporate if they cannot benefit from limited liability? There may be some tax benefits to incorporation, but at the moment, the liability of a professional that practices through a professional corporation appears to be the same as the liability of a professional that practices through a traditional partnership model.

The following regulation under the *BCA* addresses health profession corporations: *Health Profession Corporations*, O. Reg. 665/05. This regulation specifically addresses

---

55 *Business Corporations Act*, R.S.O. 1990, c. B.16, s. 3.2.
56 *Ibid.*, s. 3.2(6).
57 *Ibid.*, s. 3.4.
58 *Ibid.*, s. 92(1).

Physician Corporations and Dentist Corporations, and makes them exempt from the conditions specified in section 3.2(2) of the *BCA*. Instead, the regulation provides a different set of requirements that must be met by these two types of health profession corporations.

(d) Extra-Provincial Corporations

Extra-provincial corporations are, in simple terms, companies that are incorporated in a jurisdiction other than Ontario, but want to do business in Ontario. The *Extra-Provincial Corporations Act*[59] divides these types of corporations into three groups:

- Class 1 corporations are corporations that have been incorporated or continued in another province (other than Ontario)

- Class 2 corporations are federal corporations, or corporations incorporated in a territory of Canada (that is, in the Northwest Territories or Nunavut)

- Class 3 corporations are corporations from outside of Canada[60]

(Corporations that are incorporated in the territories, but are governed by the laws of a province, are included in Class 1.)[61]

An extra-provincial corporation that carries on business in Ontario must meet the requirements of the *Extra-Provincial Corporations Act*. "Carrying on business in Ontario" is defined as:

- having a resident agent, representative, warehouse, office or place of business in Ontario

- holding an interest (other than a security interest) in real property that is in Ontario, or

- otherwise carrying on business in Ontario.[62]

Note, however, that:

1(3) An extra-provincial corporation does not carry on its business in Ontario by reason only that,

(a) it takes orders for or buys or sells goods, wares and merchandise; or

(b) offers or sells services of any type,

by use of travellers or through advertising or correspondence.[63]

The key provisions of the Act include that Class 1 and Class 2 corporations do not require a license to carry on business in Ontario; however, a Class 3 corporation does require a license to carry on business in Ontario.[64] The Act specifies details about this license, and also indicates that the license to do business in Ontario may have restrictions,

---

59 R.S.O. 1990, c. E.27.
60 *Extra-Provincial Corporations Act*, R.S.O. 1990, c. E.27, s. 2.
61 *Ibid.*, s. 2(2).
62 *Ibid.*, s. 1(2).
63 *Ibid.*, s. 1(3).
64 *Ibid.*, s. 4.

and can be cancelled in certain circumstances.[65] In addition, all extra-provincial corporations must comply with the requirements of the *Corporations Information Act*[66], including filing returns. (The requirements of the *Corporations Information Act* will be discussed in Chapter 11.) The *Extra-Provincial Corporations Act* also indicates whether or not a Class 1 or Class 3 corporation can use its name in Ontario. Generally speaking, Class 2 (federal) corporations may use their name in Ontario, but Class 1 or Class 3 corporations may only use their name if, after conducting a NUANS search, it is clear that the name is not being used already by another corporation.[67] (NUANS searches will be discussed in Chapter 5.) Class 3 corporations must have an agent that is resident in Ontario on whom service of process (for legal matters) can be made.[68] Finally, the Act specifically confers upon all extra-provincial corporations who comply with the Act with the power to "acquire, hold and convey land or interest therein in Ontario necessary for its actual use and occupation or for carrying on its undertaking."[69]

Non-compliance with the *Extra-Provincial Corporations Act* can have serious consequences. Individuals may be fined up to $2,000, and a corporation can be fined up to $25,000. Moreover, directors, officers and agents of the corporation may also be fined up to $2,000 personally.[70] Finally, a Class 3 corporation that does not have a license to operate in Ontario or does not have an agent resident in Ontario "is not capable of maintaining any action or any other proceeding in any court or tribunal in Ontario in respect of any contract made by it,"[71] unless the default has been corrected.[72]

> Javid, Helena and Mike have decided to incorporate a company called "Nirvana Nightclub Ltd." What kind of corporation should they incorporate?

(e) Incorporation Questionnaire

A very useful tool for a legal professional to use is an incorporation questionnaire that clients can complete prior to the incorporation process. This allows the legal professional to obtain the information necessary to complete the incorporation process, but also provides an opportunity to discuss options and legal requirements. A copy of a sample incorporation questionnaire is provided in the Workbook.

---

65 *Ibid.*, ss. 5 – 7.
66 R.S.O. 1990, c. C.39.
67 *Ibid.*, ss. 9 – 10; refer to the full text of these provisions for all the requirements regarding use of a corporate name in Ontario.
68 *Extra-Provincial Corporations Act*, R.S.O. 1990, c. E.27, s. 19.
69 *Ibid.*, s. 22.
70 *Ibid.*, s. 20.
71 *Ibid.*, s. 21(1).
72 *Ibid.*, s. 21(2).

CHAPTER 5: THE INCORPORATION PROCESS

Overview:

- Ontario government structure and resources
- Federal government structure and resources
- Incorporating an Ontario company
- Incorporating a federal company
- NUANS search
  - NUANS report for an Ontario company
  - NUANS report for a federal company
- Articles of Incorporation
  - Articles of Incorporation for an Ontario company
  - Articles of Incorporation for a federal company
- Corporate Name Information Form (federal company)
- Other Registrations for a federal company
- Workbook:
  - Form 1, *BCA* (Articles of Incorporation)
  - Form 2, *BCA* (Consent to Act as First Director)
  - Form 1, *CBCA* (Articles of Incorporation)
  - Form 2, *CBCA* (Initial Registered Office and Board of Directors)
  - Corporate Name Information Form

1. Ontario Government Structure and Resources

Obtaining information about incorporation and other corporate requirements has become much easier in recent times. The Ministry of Government and Consumer Services oversees matters that relate to corporations. The specific Branch that deals with these matters is the Companies and Personal Property Security Branch. The mailing address for the Companies and Personal Property Security Branch is 393 University Avenue, Suite 200, Toronto ON M5G 2M2, and its actual address is at 375 University Avenue, on the 2nd floor. In addition, there are a number of online resources available to the public, and to legal professionals. ServiceOntario provides access to information about Ontario government services in person, on the phone, at kiosks and online. It can be accessed at <http://www.serviceontario.ca>.

ServiceOntario now has a site called ONe-Source for Business, which provides a variety of business related information in one place.

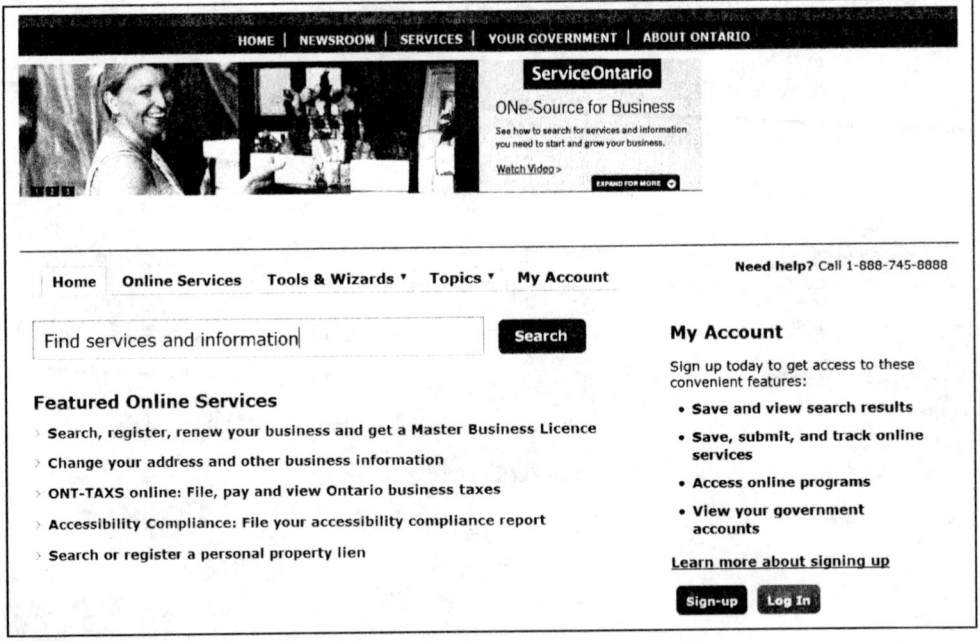

ONe-Source for Business is a portal that provides access to government services, forms and information related to doing business in Ontario. Among other features, it allows clients to search for information related to starting a business and operating a business. For a client who is thinking about starting a business, the site provides information on planning a business, understanding the marketplace, registering a business, obtaining financing, obtaining necessary permits and licensing, hiring and managing staff, and developing facilities and property. Once a client is operating his/her business, the site provides information on incorporating the business, filing taxes and tax-related information, marketing and sales, selling to government, research and innovation, finding legal services and even exiting the business. Online services that can be performed through this website include:

- registering or renewing a business registration

- filing tax information, paying taxes and viewing records related to Ontario business taxes

- searching or registering a personal property lien under the *Personal Property Security Act* (*PPSA*) or the *Repair and Storage Liens Act* (*RSLA*)

- updating business information with several Ontario and federal government programs

- finding the appropriate location for a business through Select Ontario (a site selection program)

Clients can sign up for an account with ONe-Source for Business, which will allow them to save and view searches, save, submit and track forms, access online programs and manage government accounts.[1]

The Business Info Line is a service provided in collaboration between ServiceOntario and Industry Canada, and is targeted specifically at small business. It allows clients to call one number and get information on a variety of government-related programs, including programs dealing with (but not limited to):

- tax

- employees/labour issues

- job banks

- licensing

- workplace safety

The Business Info line will also connect clients with business related information provided by Industry Canada. It can be reached toll-free at 1-888-745-8888, or in Toronto at 416-212-8888.[2]

2. Federal Government Structure and Resources

To access information about federal companies, go to the Corporations Canada website at <http://www.ic.gc.ca>. Corporations Canada is an agency of Industry Canada, which is the federal government department responsible for economic development, research and innovation and investment. The Industry Canada website provides a wealth of business information on a number of industries, as well as a wide range of tools that clients can use to assist them in starting a business. For example, BizPal is an online

---

1 "ONe-Source for Business," online: ServiceOntario <https://www.appmybizaccount.gov.on.ca/wps/portal/mba_pub/!ut/p/c4/04_SB8K8xLLM9MSSzPy8xBz9CP3lgsT01JzMvGyr_OIkvYL8opLEHL2C0qSczGS9jPzcVP2CbEdFANyVxZk!/>.

2 "Services for Business," online: ServiceOntario <http://www.ontario.ca/en/services_for_business/ONT06_023541.html>.

service that allows businesses to obtain permits and licenses from various levels of government. It operates in more than 500 jurisdictions across Canada, and allows a business person to obtain all required permits and licenses, without worrying if he/she has missed something from one of the levels of government. The Small Business Research and Statistics portion of Industry Canada's website allows small business clients to obtain valuable market information, before they decide to start a business.[3]

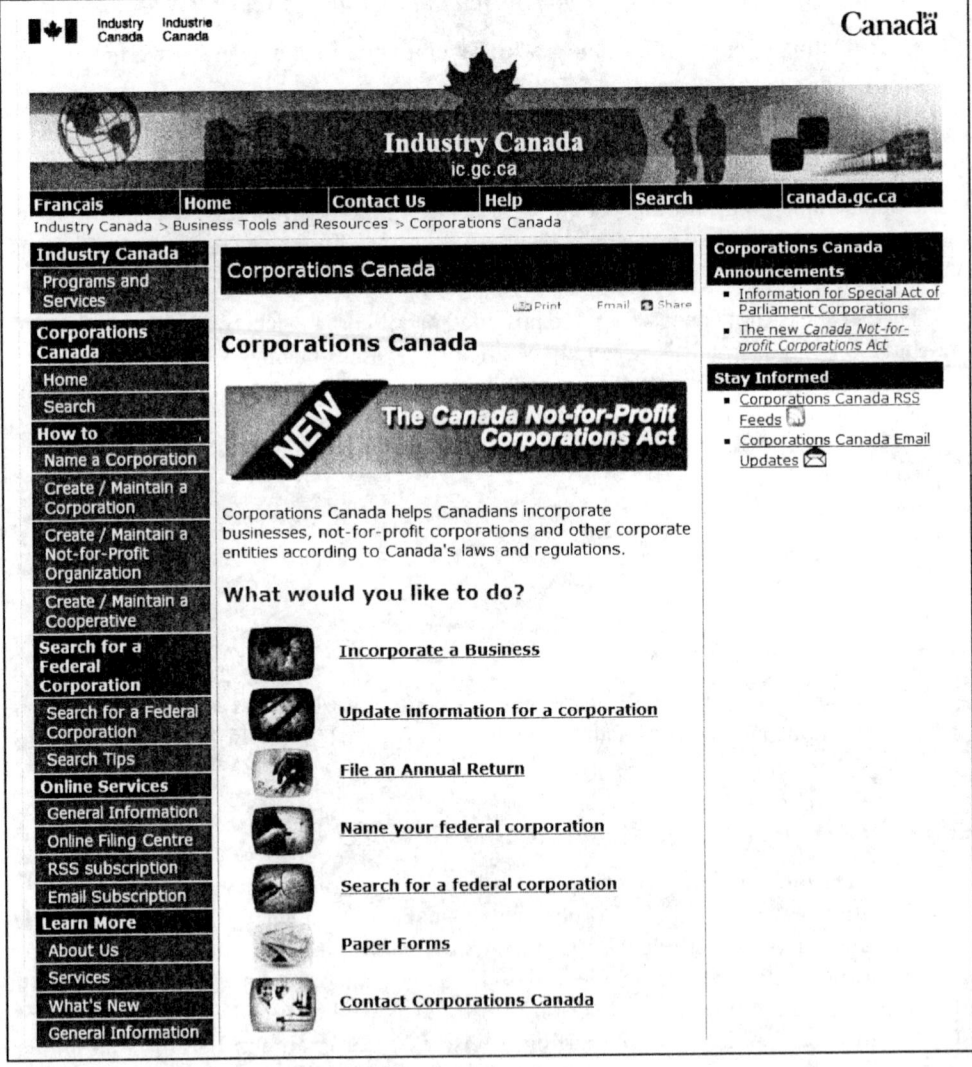

3 "Programs and Services," online: Industry Canada <http://www.ic.gc.ca/eic/site/ic1.nsf/eng/h_00006.html>.

Corporations Canada is the key component of Industry Canada's website, for our purposes. It is the area of the site that is used to incorporate a federal company, and to manage corporate affairs after incorporation. For someone who is looking for information about a federal corporation (perhaps in anticipation of a lawsuit,) Corporations Canada provides a "Search for a Federal Corporation" function, which allows you to search by corporation name, corporation number or business number. The corporate name must be all or part of the legal name of the corporation, not a trade name (that is, not a different name that the corporation operates under.) The corporation number is a seven-digit number that was assigned to the corporation when it was first incorporated, or if it has been continued or amalgamated into federal jurisdiction (more on continuance and amalgamation in Chapter 12.) The Business Number (BN) is a fifteen-digit number assigned to a federal corporation by the Canada Revenue Agency (CRA) for tax purposes. Searches can also be tailored by adding information on the province of the registered head office of the corporation, the corporation status, or the governing legislation for the corporation. Note that the only corporations that can be identified with this online tool are those created under the *CBCA*, *Canada Corporations Act*, Part II (not-for-profit corporations), *Canada Cooperatives Act*, *Boards of Trade Act* and special Act corporations that are also regulated by Corporations Canada. The database does not include financial institutions, insurance companies, or loan and trust companies. Finally, it does not allow you to search for corporations – such as Ontario corporations – incorporated under provincial/territorial legislation, or under corporate legislation from another jurisdiction.

In addition to searching for a federal corporation, a business owner or legal professional can fulfill many corporate requirements through the Corporations Canada website. For example, the site allows you to access the NUANS system (explained later in this chapter) in order to select a name for a federal corporation. Once the corporation's name has been selected and approved, a federal company can be incorporated online through the Corporations Canada website, and an Annual Return can also be filed. (We will address the Annual Return in Chapter 11.) Finally, corporate information can also be easily updated through this website.

Corporations Canada is located in Ottawa, and can be contacted at 1-866-333-5556, or corporationscanada@ic.gc.c or by mail at Jean Edmonds Building, South Tower, 9th Floor, 365 Laurier Avenue West, Ottawa, Ontario K1A 0C8.[4]

3. Incorporating an Ontario Company

There are three ways to incorporate an Ontario company, namely:

- electronically, through one of the service providers contracted by the Ministry of Government Services

- by mail, to the Companies and Personal Property Security Branch, 393 University Avenue, Suite 200, Toronto ON M5G 2M2

- in person, at the Toronto office of the Companies and Personal Property Security Branch at 375 University Avenue, 2nd floor, or at some Land Registry/ServiceOntario offices in Ontario

---

4 "Corporations Canada," online: Industry Canada <http://www.ic.gc.ca/eic/site/cd-dgc.nsf/eng/home>.

(a) Incorporating an Ontario Company Online

At the time of writing, there are three Private Service Providers that have a contract with the Ministry of Government Services to incorporate Ontario companies online. These Private Service Providers also offer additional corporate services, which can provide useful assistance to a legal professional. The Private Service Providers include:

Cyberbahn, a division of Thomson Reuters Canada Limited

Internet address: <www.cyberbahngroup.com>
Telephone: (416) 595-9522
Toll free: 1-800-806-0003

OnCorp Direct Inc.

Internet address: <www.oncorp.com>
Telephone: (416) 964-2677
Toll free: 1-800-461-7772

ESC Corporate Services Ltd.

Internet address: <www.eservicecorp.ca>
Telephone: (416) 595-7177
Toll free: 1-800-668-8208

The government fee for online filing is $300, plus an additional fee (currently ranging from approximately $30 to approximately $100, depending on the services provided) charged by the Private Service Provider. Note that the government fee for filing articles of incorporation by mail or in person is higher.[5]

Before you can file articles of incorporation online, you will be required to obtain a NUANS search with respect to the corporate name. NUANS search reports will be discussed under heading 5 in this Chapter. Note that, when you incorporate online through one of the Private Service Providers indicated above, there is no need to actually submit the NUANS report; instead the NUANS report reference number must be provided. Subsection 18(1.1) of Regulation 62 of the *BCA* addresses this exception:

18. (1) The following documents shall accompany any articles containing a proposed name for a corporation or a change of corporate name:

1. An Ontario biased or weighted computer printed search report for the proposed name from the NUANS automated name search system maintained by the Department of Consumer and Corporate Affairs, Canada dated not more than ninety days prior to the submission of the articles.

2. Any consent or consent and undertaking required under the Act or this Regulation and, if applicable, in the Form prescribed. R.R.O. 1990, Reg. 62, s. 18 (1); O. Reg. 59/07, s. 2 (1).

---

5 "Services for Business," online: ServiceOntario <http://www.ontario.ca/en/services_for_business/STEL02_039947>.

(1.1) Despite paragraph 1 of subsection 18 (1), if articles containing a proposed name for a corporation are filed with the Director electronically under section 24.1, they shall be accompanied by the NUANS report reference number, the date of the report and the proposed name searched, and not the report itself. O. Reg. 288/00, s. 1 (1).[6]

(b) Incorporating an Ontario Company by Mail or in Person

To incorporate by mail or in person, the following documents are required:

- Articles of Incorporation (Form 1 under the *BCA*)

- Ontario-biased NUANS search for the proposed corporate name

- a cheque or money order in the amount of $360, payable to the Minister of Finance (cash, credit card and debit card payments may be acceptable in person at Land Registry or ServiceOntario offices)

- a cover letter providing a contact name, return address and telephone number, and stating a future date of incorporation (up to 30 days ahead) if incorporation is not intended to be immediate

- supporting documents, such as a legal opinion, in specific cases

- consent to Act as First Director (Form 2 under the *BCA*), which is not submitted to the government but must be kept at the corporation's head office, if applicable[7]

Both the Articles of Incorporation (Form 1 under the *BCA*) and Consent to Act as First Director (Form 2 under the *BCA*) can be obtained from the Ontario Central Forms Repository website at <http://www.forms.ssb.gov.on.ca>.

---

6 *General*, R.R.O. 1990, Reg. 62, s. 18.
7 "Articles of Incorporation – Incorporating a Business Corporation", pp. 1-2 online: Service-Ontario <http://www.ontario.ca/ontprodconsume/groups/content/@onca/@bundles/@cppsb/documents/document/stel02_167482.htm>.

HOME | NEWSROOM | SERVICES | YOUR GOVERNMENT | ABO

Central Forms Repository

Location: Forms Home > Quick Search > Quick Search Results > Form Details

Form Details

Format	Form Link Address	Functionality	Size
Adobe PDF	Articles of Incorporation - Form 1 - Business Corporations Act	Fill & Print	125.0 kb

Form Classification / Identification:

Form Number:	007-07116	Edition date:	2007/08
Title:	Articles of Incorporation - Form 1 - Business Corporations Act		
Ministry:	Government Services		
Branch/ABC:	ServiceOntario		
Program:	Central Production and Verification Services Branch		
Purpose of Form:	To incorporate a business corporation in Ontario.		
Ordering Information:	393 University Ave., 2nd floor, Toronto ON M5G 2M2		

After incorporation, the Companies and Personal Property Security Branch will assign the corporation an Ontario Corporation Number (OCN), which is unique to that corporation, and will provide a Certificate of Incorporation. The OCN cannot be changed or transferred to another corporation. Even when corporations amalgamate, the amalgamated corporation is assigned a new number. The OCN will be requested in future dealings with the Ontario government, such as other forms that must be filed by the corporation. The Certificate of Incorporation will indicate the date upon which the Articles of Incorporation become effective. This date is referred to as the "incorporation date" or "effective date". If necessary, you may request an "effective date" up to 30 days later than the earliest date the Articles of Incorporation can be endorsed by the Branch. You must indicate this request in a cover letter using bold or highlighted letters, when you submit the Articles of Incorporation. If you are submitting the Articles of Incorporation in person and you require a future effective date, you may bring this to the attention of the clerk who endorses the Articles. [8]

4. Incorporating a Federal Company

There are five ways to incorporate a federal company:

- online, through the Corporations Canada website: <www.corporationscanada. ic.gc.ca>

---

8 *Ibid.*, pp. 5-6.

- by email at corporationscanada@ic.gc.ca

- by fax at 613-941-4803

- by mail at Corporations Canada, Jean Edmonds Building, South Tower, 9th Floor, 365 Laurier Avenue West, Ottawa, ON K1A 0C8

- in person at the mailing address

To incorporate a federal company, you must file the following forms with Corporations Canada:

- Articles of Incorporations (Form 1 under the *CBCA*)

- Initial Registered Office Address and First Board of Directors (Form 2 under the *CBCA*)

- NUANS Report (not more than 90 days prior to the filing date)

- Corporate Name Information Form (optional)

- filing fee - $200 online, or $250 by email, fax or mail

(a) Incorporating a Federal Company Online

To incorporate a federal company online, go to the Corporations Canada website at <www.corporationscanada.ic.gc.ca>. Click on "Incorporate a Business" and then "Online" filing.

The "Online Filing Centre" allows you to incorporate a business, and also perform a number of other functions, such as updating corporate information and filing government forms related to corporate transactions (like dissolving a company).

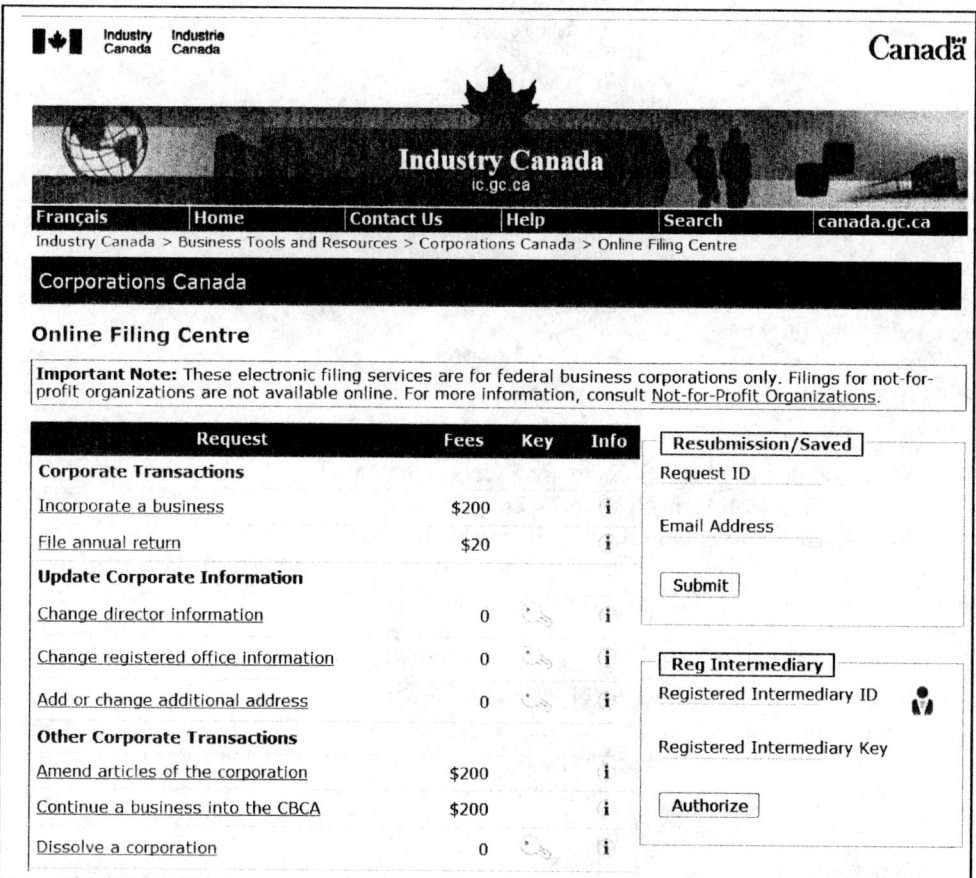

Once you click on "Incorporate a business", you will be asked to complete nine steps. In most of the steps, you will provide information online. In steps 3 and 5, however, you will be asked to print Form 1 under the *CBCA* (Articles of Incorporation) and Form 2 under the *CBCA* (Initial Registered Office Address and First Board of Directors) and have the forms signed. These forms are not sent to Corporations Canada, but must be kept at the corporations' registered office, or at some other location in Canada specified by the directors.

As part of step 1, you will be asked to choose one of the following options:

- incorporating a named company, which will require a NUANS search

- incorporating a company with a name that has been pre-approved by Corporations Canada, or

- incorporating a numbered company

Once you select one of these three options, you will be prompted to complete the required information. Note that preapproval of a corporate name can also be obtained online through the Corporations Canada website. This is an option that some clients may consider if they are not ready to incorporate, but want to reserve a corporate name for 90 days from the date of the NUANS report that is submitted with the pre-approval request.

(b) Incorporating a Federal Company In Person, By Mail, Fax or Email

If you plan to submit the required documents in person, you must do so between 8:30 a.m. and 2:30 p.m. at the Corporations Canada address provided previously. Note that you may only submit four requests for incorporation at one time.

If you are submitting documents by fax, retain the original documents with the corporate records at the corporation's registered office, or at a location in Canada designated by the directors.

(c) After Filing Articles of Incorporation

Once you have filed Articles of Incorporation, Corporations Canada will determine whether the corporation's proposed name is acceptable (unless it has been pre-approved,) and will ensure that all forms have been completed properly. It will then send the client (or his/her legal representative) a Certificate of Incorporation, which will indicate the corporation's name, the corporation number and date of incorporation. The date of incorporation is the date that Corporations Canada receives the Articles of Incorporation and associated fees; however, you can request a later incorporation date when you file the Articles of Incorporation, if necessary. The Certificate of Incorporation will be sent with a copy of the Articles of Incorporation. Corporations Canada will also provide a Corporation Information Sheet which includes a Corporation Key. The Corporation Key is an access code that can be used to perform certain functions online – such as updating corporate information. If the Corporation Key is lost, a new Key may be requested online through the Online Filing Centre.[9]

5. NUANS Search

The following regulation of the *BCA* addresses the requirement for a NUANS search before a company can be incorporated: *General*, R.R.O. 1990, Reg. 62. Section 18 of this regulation states:

18 (1) The following documents shall accompany any articles containing a proposed name for a corporation or a change of corporate name:

1. An Ontario biased or weighted computer printed search report for the proposed name from the NUANS automated name search system maintained by the Department of Consumer and Corporate Affairs, Canada dated not more than ninety days prior to the submission of the articles.

2. Any consent or consent and undertaking required under the Act or this Regulation and, if applicable, in the Form prescribed. R.R.O. 1990, Reg. 62, s. 18 (1); O. Reg. 59/07, s. 2 (1).

(1.1) Despite paragraph 1 of subsection 18 (1), if articles containing a proposed name for a corporation are filed with the Director electronically under section 24.1, they shall be accom-

---

9 "Guide to Federal Incorporation, March 2011," pp. 6 – 7, online: Industry Canada (Corporations Canada) <http://www.ic.gc.ca/eic/site/cd-dgc.nsf/eng/cs04441.html>

panied by the NUANS report reference number, the date of the report and the proposed name searched, and not the report itself. O. Reg. 288/00, s. 1 (1).

(2) If a proposed name is in an English form and a French form, separate computer-printed search reports shall be provided for the English form and the French form of the name, unless the English and French forms of the name are identical and the legal element required under subsection 10 (1) of the Act that is used in the French form of the name is the French version of the legal element used in the English form of the name. O. Reg. 59/07, s. 2 (2).

(3) Subsections (1) and (2) apply to an application for revival under section 241 of the Act if the articles change the name of the corporation or at least 10 years have elapsed since the corporation was dissolved. O. Reg. 400/95, s. 1.

(4) No name that is identified in a computer printed search report as proposed or otherwise where a computer printed search report is not submitted shall be used as a corporate name by a person other than the one who proposed the name unless a consent in writing has been obtained from the person who first proposed the name. O. Reg. 627/93, s. 5; O. Reg. 288/00, s. 1 (2).[10]

As a result, a NUANS report must be obtained and submitted with the Articles of Incorporation for an Ontario or federal company, as long as that company is a named company. In other words, a numbered company does not require a NUANS search – which means that a client can save some expense and time if the client does not require a named corporation. A NUANS search is also required when a corporation wishes to change its name, an extra-provincial corporation wishes to operate in Ontario, and in other circumstances specified by the *BCA*, *CBCA* or other corporate statutes.

NUANS – which stands for Newly Upgraded Automated Name Search – is a computer database that compares a proposed corporate name or trademark with existing corporate names and trademarks. It will then produce a report of all names that are similar to the proposed name. The purpose of this process is to ensure that new corporate names do not create confusion in the market place by duplicating existing names. If the system did not exist, there could be several companies with the same name, making it difficult, for example, to sue the right company or to ensure that the right company was obtaining the benefit of a contract. The NUANS system can be accessed at <www.nuans.com>. NUANS is a registered trademark of the government of Canada, and the computer system is owned by Industry Canada. Hewlett Packard (HP) has been awarded the licence to operate, maintain, update and market the NUANS system since 1996.[11]

---

10 *General*, R.R.O. 1990, Reg. 62, s. 18; see also *Canada Business Corporations Regulations*, 2001, SOR/2001-512 for federal corporations.
11 "Frequently Asked Questions," online: NUANS Corporate Name Search <http://www.nuans.com/nuansinfo_en/faq_en.htm>.

(a) NUANS Report for an Ontario Company

If you are incorporating a company with a name instead of a numbered company, you will require an Ontario-biased NUANS search report to accompany the Articles of Incorporation for the corporation. (Articles of Incorporation will be discussed later in this chapter.) The NUANS report must be less than 90 days old at the time that it is submitted with the Articles of Incorporation. For example, "articles submitted on November 28th could be accompanied by a NUANS name search report dated as early as August 30th, but not dated earlier."[12]

If the company you are incorporating is likely to do business in the province of Quebec or internationally, the client should consider incorporating a company with both an English and a French name. Section 10(2) of the *BCA* provides that:

(2) Subject to this Act and the regulations, a corporation may have a name that is,

(a) English only;

(b) French only;

(c) one name that is a combination of English and French; or

(d) one name in English and one name in French that are equivalent but are used separately.[13]

However, if the proposed corporate name is in an English form and a French form, separate NUANS search reports will have to be provided with the Articles of Incorporation for both the English form and the French form of the name. The only exception

---

12 Form 1, *Business Corporations Act* (Articles of Incorporation), p. 1.
13 *Business Corporations Act*, R.S.O. 1990, c. B.16, s. 10(2).

is if the English and French forms of the name are identical, with the only difference being in the legal element of the name – that is, the only difference is in the words "Limited", "Limitee", "Incorporated", Incorporee", Corporation, or their corresponding abbreviations. In this case only, separate NUANS search reports will not be required for the English and French forms of the name.[14]

To obtain a NUANS search report for an **Ontario** corporation, you must order the NUANS report through a third party. In other words, you cannot order the report yourself through the NUANS website.

The first, and perhaps the simplest option, is to order the NUANS report from one of the three Private Service Providers that can also incorporate the company:

- Cyberbahn, a division of Thomson Reuters Canada Limited

- OnCorp Direct Inc.

- ESC Corporate Services Ltd.

Some of these service providers will give you the option to purchase a report with recommendations on whether or not to select a proposed corporate name – however, that decision is ultimately the decision of the legal professional advising the client. The price range for a NUANS report through one of these providers is approximately \$50 – 60 or higher, depending upon the services requested.

Alternatively, a NUANS search can be obtained from a number of other NUANS Members. A list of NUANS Members can be obtained – and searched – online at <www.nuans.com>. For example, if you prefer to obtain a NUANS report online, you can obtain a list of all NUANS members with online services. Alternatively, you can obtain a list of NUANS members by province, or by city (within that province.) Even if you plan to incorporate online through one of the three Private Service Providers named above, you may be able to obtain a NUANS report through another, less expensive source. (Check with the Private Service Provider first to determine whether it will allow you to obtain a NUANS report elsewhere.)

---

14 *Ibid.*, s. 18(2)

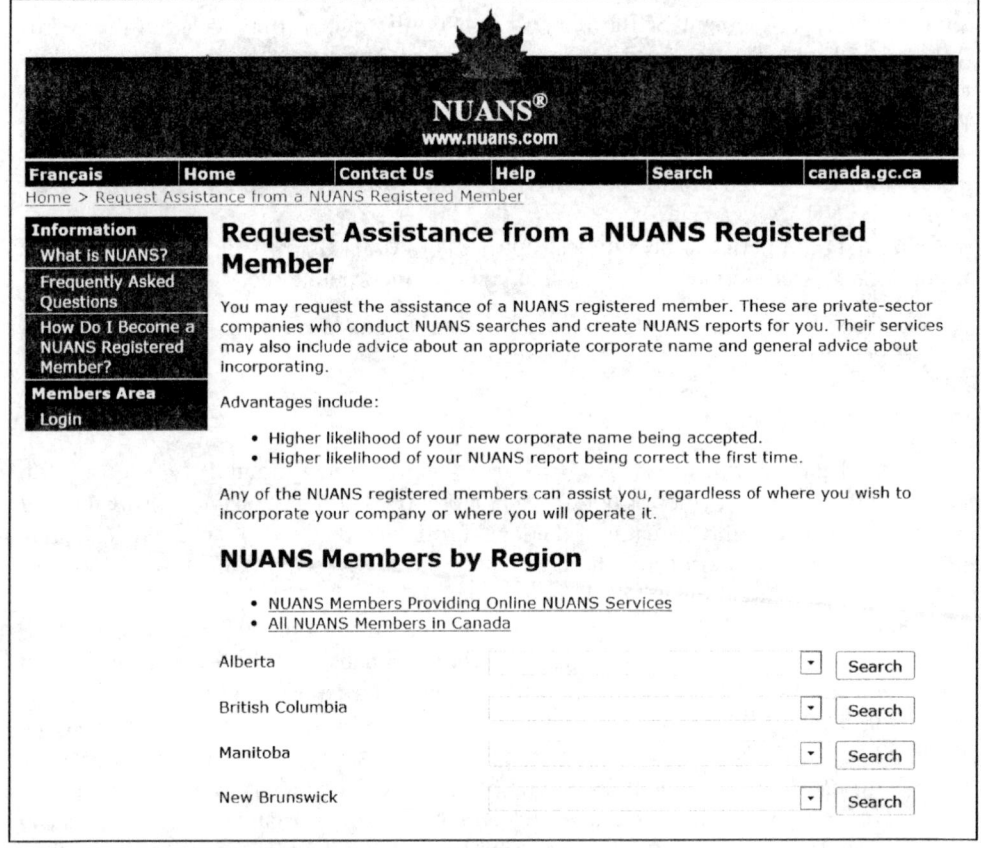

Note that it is the applicant's responsibility to ensure that the name that is being proposed is not identical or similar to existing names, and if any consents to use the name are required, to ensure that those consents have been obtained. The Ministry of Government Services will not grant a name to an Ontario corporation that is the same as the current or former name of another Ontario corporation, whether that corporation is active or not, unless more than 10 years have passed since that other corporation was dissolved or changed its name. There is an exception to this general rule, found in section 6 of Regulation 62 of the *BCA*:

6. (1) Except as provided in subsection (2) and section 10, no corporation may acquire a name identical to the name or former name of another body corporate, whether in existence or not, unless,

(a) the body corporate was incorporated under the laws of a jurisdiction outside Ontario and has never carried on any activities or identified itself in Ontario; or

(b) at least ten years have elapsed since the body corporate was dissolved or changed its name. O. Reg. 627/93, s. 1.

(2) A corporation may acquire a name identical to that of another corporation if a person who is authorized to practise law in Ontario provides a legal opinion stating that,

(a) neither corporation is an offering corporation;

(b) the corporations are affiliated or associated with one another or are controlled by related persons;

(c) the corporation that acquires the name is a successor to the business of the other corporation; and

(d) the other corporation has been dissolved or has changed its name.

O. Reg. 627/93, s. 1; O. Reg. 59/07, s. 1.[15]

Note that the exception provided in subsection 6(2) requires that a legal opinion be filed with the Articles of Incorporation. This legal opinion must be on firm letterhead, must be signed by an individual lawyer (not a law clerk or law firm) and must clearly indicate compliance with subsection 6(2) of Regulation 62 by referring to each clause specifically.[16]

(b) NUANS Report for a Federal Company

If you are incorporating a company under the *CBCA* – that is, incorporating a federal company – then you have several options for obtaining the mandatory NUANS search report. First, you can obtain a NUANS report from one of the three Private Service Providers or the NUANS Members referred to previously. Second, you can obtain a NUANS report from a number of NUANS Members in your area – and these are easily identified by province and city in the website referred to above. Finally, for **federal** incorporations, you can also obtain a NUANS report directly through the NUANS website. The cost for obtaining a NUANS report through the NUANS website is currently $20.48 plus applicable taxes.

---

15 *General*, R.R.O. 1990, Reg. 62, s. 6.
16 Form 1, *Business Corporations Act* (Articles of Incorporation), p. 1.

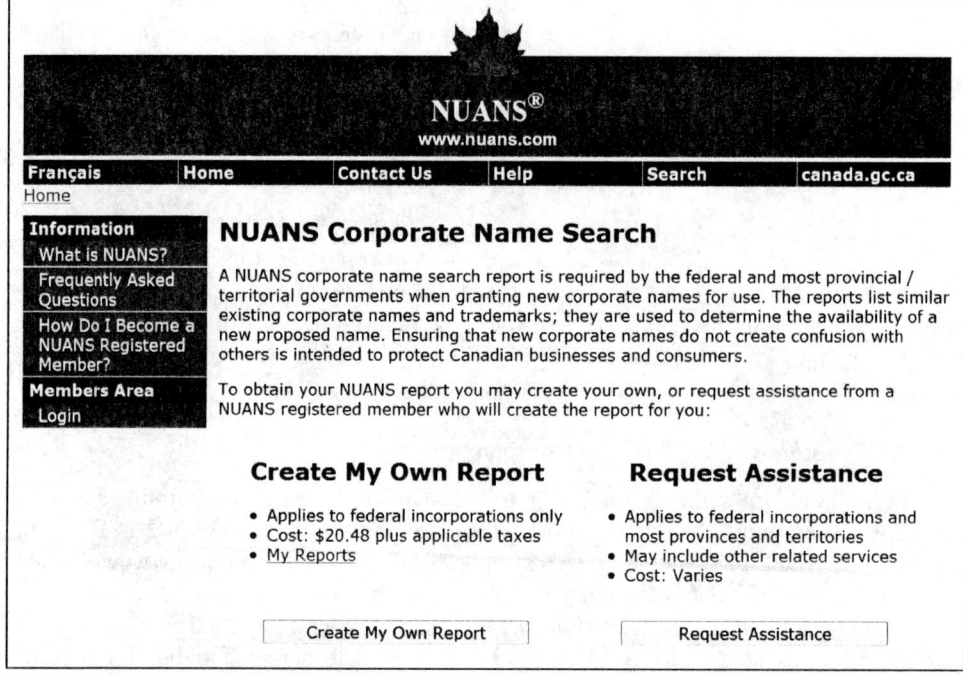

To create your own NUANS report, you must provide your email address and obtain an access key, which can be done simply by following the instructions when you click on "Create My Own Report" in the screen page shown above. Once you have received access to the system, simply follow the instructions provided to you. Note that you can only obtain a NUANS report directly from the NUANS website for federal incorporations.

What are the advantages and disadvantages of conducting the NUANS search yourself? Once you become familiar with the process, it is usually less expensive to obtain the NUANS search yourself through the NUANS website. However, there can be advantages to obtaining the NUANS search through a NUANS Member or one of the three Private Service Providers referred to under the heading "NUANS Report for an Ontario Company". While it may be more expensive, the benefits include the expertise that these third parties have in conducting NUANS searches – which not only means that they know how to conduct a NUANS search, but that they will know what variations of the corporate name to search (in addition to the name the client has provided to the legal professional.) In addition, it may be simpler for billing purposes and convenience to work with the same third party that may also be providing additional legal services – such as minute books and other corporate documents that we will refer to later in this textbook.

Note that the federal government provides a service that is not available through the Ontario government – you can obtain pre-approval of a corporate name before you file Articles of Incorporation. If a client is considering incorporation at a later date, this option should be considered so that the corporate name can be reserved for the client; however, the corporate name is not reserved indefinitely – it is only reserved for 90 days from the date of the NUANS Name Search Report.

The process for obtaining pre-approval of a corporate name can be done online, by mail or by fax. The simplest and quickest option is to go to the Corporations Canada website and access the Online Filing Centre. Click on "Pre-approve a corporate name" and input the information requested. There is no cost for the pre-approval process; however, you will need to have ordered a NUANS Name Search Report before you start the pre-approval process, and there is a cost associated with obtaining that report. Once you have provided all the information requested through the Online Filing Centre, you will receive an email acknowledging receipt of your request to pre-approve the corporate name. Once the request has been processed and approved, you will receive another email containing a Request ID number and confirmation number; note that you will need these numbers to complete the incorporation process.

If you are requesting pre-approval of a corporate name by email, mail or fax, provide a written request to pre-approve the corporate name to Corporations Canada (see contact information provided earlier in this chapter,) along with a NUANS Name Search Report and, if you choose to do so, a completed Corporate Name Information Form. While the Corporate Name Information Form is not mandatory, it is strongly recommended by Corporations Canada. Once the name is pre-approved, you will receive a letter with the Request ID and confirmation numbers, which you will need during the incorporation process.[17]

Note that Corporations Canada may not approve a name, even if the NUANS Name Search Report indicates that there are no similar corporate names currently in existence. This may occur because Corporations Canada does not have sufficient information on which to base its decision. It may request additional information, or may suggest that a different name be proposed (which will require additional time and expense, including a new NUANS Name Search Report.) For this reason, it may be advisable to submit the Corporate Name Information Form with the initial pre-approval request.[18]

6. Articles of Incorporation

(a) Articles of Incorporation for an Ontario Company

"Articles of Incorporation" is the name given to the document that creates a corporation. Recall that a corporation is essentially a legal structure – a form of business organization – that allows the owners of the business to shield themselves from personal liability. It is, essentially, an imaginary thing. In terms of goods and services supplied by the business, it makes no difference to customers whether a business is operated as a sole proprietorship, a partnership or a corporation. For example, if a customer regularly buys coffee from a coffee shop, it makes no difference if the business is a sole proprietorship, partnership or corporation; in either case, the coffee shop will look the same, and the customer's coffee will be the same. However, it makes a great deal of difference to the customer and the owner if there is a lawsuit against the business. If the business is operated as a corporation, then the corporation is treated as an "imaginary" person in

---

17 *Guide to Federal Incorporation*, March 2011, Corporations Canada, Industry Canada, p. 9.
18 *Ibid.*

the law – someone separate from the actual owner. The actual owner is not legally responsible for the debts and other obligations of that imaginary person.

The way that an owner of a business structures his/her business as a corporation in Canada is by filing Articles of Incorporation with the relevant level of government. It does not matter if the business is a small convenience store, or a complex business operating across Canada or even internationally; in either case, the business must file Articles of Incorporation in order to incorporate – that is, in order to create a corporation. Articles of Incorporation are like a "birth certificate" for the corporation. If the corporation is going to be an Ontario corporation, the Articles of Incorporation must be completed according to the requirements of the Ontario government, and must be submitted to the Ontario government. Similarly, if the corporation is going to be a federal corporation, the form to complete is a different one – although it is also called "Articles of Incorporation" – and must be submitted to the federal government. Once submitted to the appropriate level of government, the corporation will be issued a Certificate of Incorporation, which will indicate the date of incorporation.

Section 6 of the *BCA* states:

> An incorporator shall send to the Director Articles of Incorporation and, upon receipt of the articles, the Director shall endorse thereon, in accordance with section 273, a certificate which shall constitute the certificate of incorporation.[19]

The "incorporator" is defined as the "person who signs Articles of Incorporation", and is essentially the person who is requesting the government to create a corporation.[20]

You can obtain a copy of the Articles of Incorporation for an Ontario company from the Ontario Central Forms Repository, which is available online (at no expense) at <www.forms.ssb.gov.on.ca>. Simply type "Articles of Incorporation" in the search window, and you will see the following screen:

---

19 *Business Corporations Act*, R.S.O. 1990, c. B.16, s. 6.
20 *Ibid.*, s. 1.

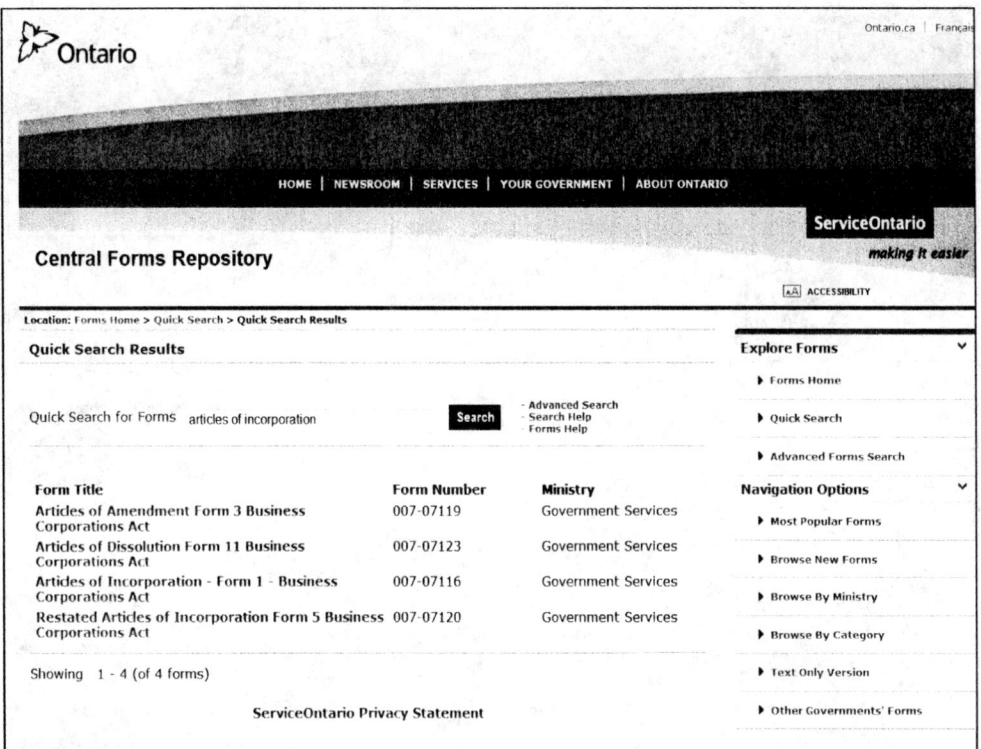

Click on "Articles of Incorporation – Form 1 – Business Corporations Act", and you will be provided with important information about this form.

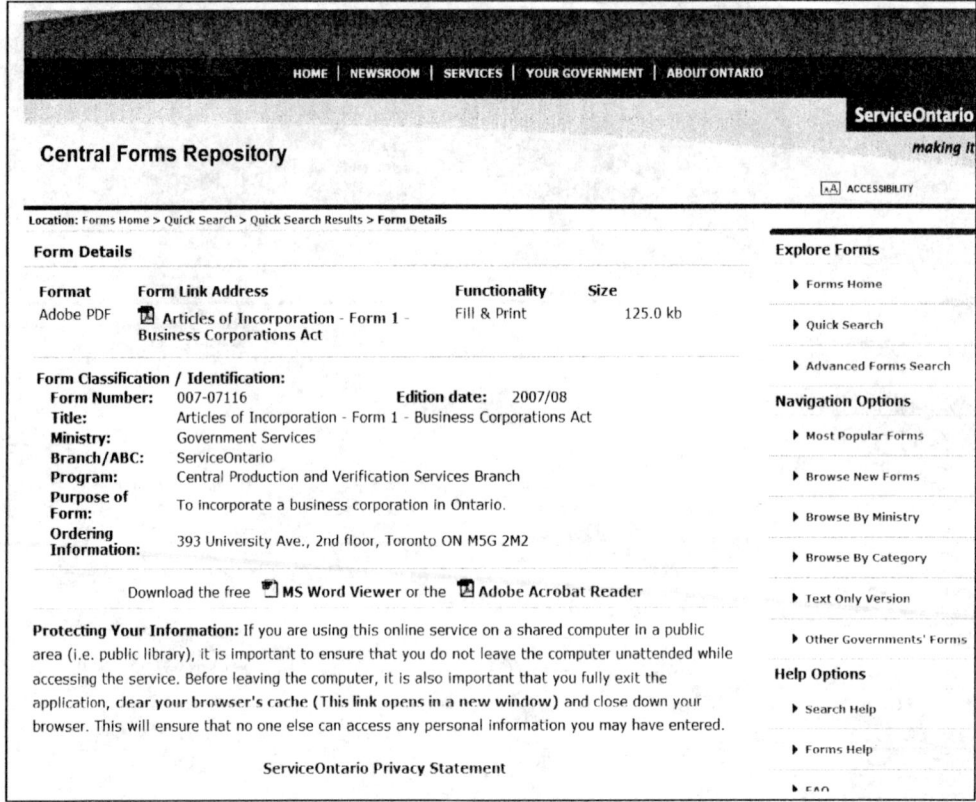

For example, the screen shows you that Articles of Incorporation for an Ontario company are referred to as "Form 1" under the *BCA*, and the relevant ministry to submit the form to is the Ministry of Government Services, through ServiceOntario. Once you click on the link to the PDF version of the Articles of Incorporation (at the top of the screen shown above,) you will be able to access the form itself. This form is a "fill and print" form, which means that you can complete the form online and print a copy when you are done. At the present time, you cannot save the document – you can only print it. It is advisable to complete the form online, as the system will prompt you or automatically complete certain fields where indicated, thereby preventing errors. However, you may also choose to print the form and complete it by hand. It is critical, whether you complete the form online or by hand, that you read the instructions carefully in order to avoid any errors.

Note that this process is relevant if you are planning to submit Articles of Incorporation by mail or in person. If you are planning to file the Articles of Incorporation online through a Private Service Provider, you do not need to fill and print Form 1 under the *BCA* – the Private Service Provider will do this for you (for a fee.) However, you will still have to supply the Private Service Provider with the information required for the form, which we will discuss below.

Note the following instructions to Form 1 under the *BCA* (Articles of Incorporation):

- Forms must be completed in duplicate, and must be submitted with the required fee, an Ontario biased NUANS report, and a covering letter (with the information specified in the instructions to Form 1.)

- The fee (currently $360) can only be paid in the manner specified in the instructions to Form 1; currently, it can be paid by cheque or money order payable to the Minister of Finance, or if the documents are being dropped off in person, also by cash, debit or certain credit cards.

- Offices where you can submit the documents in person can be found online by searching ServiceOntario locations from <www.serviceontario.ca>; click on "Services for Business", which will link you to the "ONe-Source for Business" portion of the website. Go to the bottom of the screen under "Contact Us" and click on "Get In-Person Advice and Support" and then type in your postal code to use the "Service Location Finder" to identify an office in your community. (Call ahead to verify that a particular location accepts Articles of Incorporation.)[21]

- All documents must be completed in block capital letters.

- Each section in the form is referred to as an "article." Articles 1 through 10 must be completed, and must remain in that order. If an article does not apply, you must type in "nil" or "not applicable" – you cannot leave the space blank.

Failure to follow instructions exactly can create a delay in the incorporation process.

Checklist for Completing Articles of Incorporation– Ontario Company

Ontario Corporation Number	Leave this box blank – the corporation number will be provided by the Ministry of Government Services, after the Articles of Incorporation are filed.
Article 1 - Name	Type the name of the corporation in BLOCK LETTERS, with one letter per box, one box for each punctuation mark, and a box for each empty space. If using the "fill and print" form through the Ontario Central Forms Repository, the system will do this automatically for you, as you type. The name entered must be the same as in the attached NUANS report. If you are proposing an English and a French name, insert a "/" (forward slash) between the English and French versions of the name.
Article 2 – Address of Registered Office	The registered office of the corporation must be in Ontario. A post office box address (alone) is not acceptable.

---

21 ServiceOntario website, <https://www.services.gov.on.ca/services/specifyCity.do?action=show_map#scrolltomap>.

Article 3 – Number of Directors	Provide either a fixed number of directors for the corporation, OR a minimum and maximum number of directors. Do not complete both boxes. The disadvantage of providing a fixed number of directors is that the Articles of Incorporation will have to be amended if that number changes (because a director resigns or dies, for example.) A realistic range (minimum and maximum number) provides more flexibility. A non-offering (private) corporation must have at least one director.[22]
Article 4 – First Directors	Provide the full, legal name and address for service for each of the first directors of the corporation. Indicate if the directors are resident Canadians. Directors must be individuals, not corporations, and at least 25% of the directors must be resident Canadians. (When calculating the percentage of directors that are resident Canadians, if the number is not a whole number, round up to the next whole number.) If there are less than four directors, at least one must be a resident Canadian. First directors must hold office from the date of endorsement of the Certificate of Incorporation until the first meeting of shareholders (when they can resign, if they wish.)[23] See Chapter 6 of this book for more details on directors.
Article 5 – Restrictions	Specify any restrictions on the business that the corporation may engage in, or any restrictions on the powers that the corporation may exercise. Generally, it is preferable to place no restrictions on the corporation, unless required by law. If there are no restrictions (which is the most common approach,) complete this box by simply typing "None."

---

22 *Business Corporations Act*, R.S.O. 1990, c. B.16, s. 15(2)(a).
23 *Ibid.*, ss. 118 – 119

Article 6 – Classes/ Number of Shares	Give details about the class and number of shares that the corporation will have. Some corporations may wish to have different types of shares, allowing them to give different rights to different shareholders. (See Chapter 8 for more details on shares.) A typical approach is to provide for common shares only. Type in "Unlimited number of common shares" if this is the approach you are taking. You may also wish to state a specific number of shares – in this case, make the number large enough to allow flexibility (for example, 100,000 common shares.) In a non-offering corporation, the number of shares is less critical than in an offering corporation, because there can only be a maximum of 50 shareholders – so as long as there are at least 50 shares, each shareholder's interest in the corporation can be calculated accordingly.[24] For ease of calculation, however, it is best to indicate an "unlimited number" of shares, or a fixed number that is large enough to avoid calculations with fractions (i.e. fractional shares.) (Details on shareholders and shares will be provided in Chapters 7 and 8.)
Article 7 – Rights/ Restrictions on each Class of Shares	If the corporation has more than one class (that is, more than one kind) of shares, state the rights and restrictions that apply to each class of shares. For example, a corporation may have common and preferred shares, or voting preferred and non-voting preferred shares. (Details on shares will be provided in Chapter 7.) If you indicated in Article 6 that the corporation has an "unlimited number of common shares", simply type "Not applicable" for Article 7.

---

24 *Securities Act*, R.S.O. 1990, c. S.5, s. 1.

Article 8 - Other Provisions	On September 14, 2005, the Canadian Securities Administrator's (CSA) National Instrument 45-106 (NI 45-106) – called "Prospectus and Registration Exemptions" – became effective across Canada. Amongst other things, it replaced the private company restrictions in the *Securities Act* with a new "private issuer" exemption.[25] In the past, the private company restrictions were included in Articles 8 and 9 of the Articles of Incorporation of an Ontario company, in order to exempt the corporation from registration, filing and other requirements of the *Securities Act*.

(The private company restrictions are found in the definition of "private company" in the *Securities Act*, namely:

(a) the right to transfer its shares is restricted,

(b) the number of its shareholders, exclusive of persons who are in its employment and exclusive of persons who, having been formerly in the employment of the company, were, while in that employment, and have continued after termination of that employment to be, shareholders of the company, is limited to not more than fifty, two or more persons who are the joint registered owners of one or more shares being counted as one shareholder, and

(c) any invitation to the public to subscribe for its securities is prohibited[26]

In order to comply with NI 45-106, the following paragraph can be included in Article 8:

The transfer of shares of the Corporation shall be restricted in that no shareholder shall be entitled to transfer any share or shares without either:

(a) the approval of the directors of the Corporation expressed by a resolution passed at a meeting of the board of directors or by an instrument or instruments in writing signed by a majority of the directors; or

---

25 "ARCHIVED – Effect of National Instrument 45-106 on Canada Business Corporation Act Corporations", online: Corporations Canada <http://www.ic.gc.ca/eic/site/cd-dgc.nsf/eng/cs03216.html>.

26 *Ibid.*

	(b) the approval of the holders of at least a majority of the shares of the Corporation entitling the holders thereof to vote in all circumstances (other than a separate class vote of the holders of another class of shares of the Corporation) for the time being outstanding expressed by a resolution passed at a meeting of the holders of such shares or by an instrument or instruments in writing signed by the holders of a majority of such shares.[27]

Article 9 – Other Provisions	Section 2.4 of NI 45-106 defines a "private issuer" as an issuer:
	
	 • that is not a reporting issuer;
	
	 • whose securities are subject to restrictions on transfer that are contained in the issuer's constating documents (such as Articles of Incorporation) or security holders' agreements (such as a Shareholder Agreement);
	
	 • whose securities are beneficially owned, directly or indirectly, by not more than 50 persons; and
	
	 • that has distributed securities only to persons who purchase the security as principal and are:
	
	     • directors, officers, employees, founders, control persons of the issuer (that is, a person who owns more than 20% of the outstanding voting securities), or
	
	     • close relatives, close personal friends or close business associates.[28]
	
	 (A "reporting issuer" is a public company – that is, a company that has issued securities which require filing a prospectus with the Ontario Securities Commission and/or whose securities have been listed and traded on a stock exchange).[29]
	
	 In order to comply with NI 45-106, type the following in Article 9:

---

27 "Appendix 'D': Private Company Provisions", online: Law Society of Upper Canada <http://rc.lsuc.on.ca/pdf/ht/busAppendixD.pdf>

28 "How to Structure the Share Provisions of a Corporation", online: Law Society of Upper Canada <http://rc.lsuc.on.ca/jsp/ht/structureShareProvisionsCorporation.jsp>

29 *Ibid.*

(a) The Corporation shall be a private issuer within the meaning of section 2.4 of National Instrument 45-106 under the *Securities Act* (Ontario).

(b) The Corporation shall not at any time have outstanding securities of the Corporation that are beneficially owned, directly or indirectly, by more than 50 persons or companies that have purchased as principals, not including employees and former employees of the Corporation or its affiliates (provided that each person is counted as one beneficial owner unless the person is created or used solely to purchase or hold securities of the Corporation in which case each beneficial owner or beneficiary of the person, as the case may be, must be counted as a separate beneficial owner) and is:

(i) a director, officer, employee, founder or control person of the Corporation,

(ii) a spouse, parent, grandparent, brother, sister or child of a director, executive officer, founder or control person of the Corporation,

(iii) a parent, grandparent, brother, sister or child of the spouse of a director, executive officer, founder or control person of the Corporation,

(iv) a close personal friend of a director, executive officer, founder or control person of the Corporation,

(v) a close business associate of a director, executive officer, founder or control person of the Corporation,

(vi) a spouse, parent, grandparent, brother, sister or child of the selling security holder or of the selling security holder's spouse,

(vii) a security holder of the Corporation,

(viii) an accredited investor,

(ix) a person of which a majority of the voting securities are beneficially owned by, or a majority of the directors are, persons described in paragraphs (i) to (ix),

	(x) a trust or estate of which all of the beneficiaries or a majority of the trustees or executors are persons described in paragraphs (i) to (ix), or (xi) a person that is not the public, all within the meaning of section 2.4 of National Instrument 45-106 under the *Securities Act* (Ontario).[30]
Article 10 - Incorporators	Normally, the first directors will also sign Article 10 as incorporators. However, if a first director is not available to sign as an incorporator, then that first director must also complete Form 2 under the *BCA* (Consent to Act as First Director). Form 2 does not need to be submitted with the Articles of Incorporation, but must be kept available for inspection at the registered office of the corporation. (See below for a discussion of "office incorporators.") A corporation can also be an incorporator. Note that incorporators must sign both copies of the Articles of Incorporation (which must be submitted in duplicate if they are being filed in person or by mail.)
Form 2, *BCA* (Consent to Act as First Director)	Form 2 must be completed by any first director who was not available to sign the Articles of Incorporation as an incorporator, and should be kept at the registered office of the corporation.

Prior to the introduction of online filing of Articles of Incorporation, a common practice among law firms was to have an "office incorporator" who signed the Articles of Incorporation (and other corporate documents) as first director. This individual was typically a legal professional (lawyer or law clerk) who represented the client. This approach allowed the client to avoid having to sign multiple documents during the incorporation process, and allowed for quicker incorporations. During the first shareholders' meeting, the office incorporator would resign and permanent directors – that is, the "real directors" of the corporation – would be elected.

Today, the use of an "office incorporator" has become much less popular, for several reasons. First, first directors have all the liabilities of directors, during the time that they are acting as first directors.[31] Second, from a practical perspective, the legal professional may not want to receive mail or notices for the corporation – something that can occur even years after the legal professional is no longer representing the client. Finally, and perhaps most significantly, online filing of Articles of Incorporation has made the use of an "office incorporator" unnecessary. Online filing can be done by simply typing in the first directors' names, and the process is both quick and relatively easy. The first directors' signatures can be obtained after the online filing process is complete, on a printed copy of the Articles of Incorporation. Legal professionals should ensure that they

---

30 *Ibid.*
31 *Business Corporations Act*, R.S.O. 1990, c. B.16, s. 119(3).

obtain these signatures in due course, and keep a signed copy of the Articles of Incorporation in the minute book of the corporation (discussed in Chapters 9 and 10.)

However, if Articles of Incorporation are being submitted in person or by mail, it will be necessary to complete Form 2 under the *BCA*, and to ensure that it is kept at the registered office of the corporation. A "fill and print" version of Form 2 can be easily accessed online through the Ontario Central Forms Repository at <www.forms.ssb.gov.on.ca>. Complete Form 2 for each first director that did not sign the Articles of Incorporation as first director. To complete the form, you will need the following information about each of those first directors:

- full legal name (first, middle and last names)

- address for service

- name of the corporation (as indicated on the Articles of Incorporation)

- signature of the first director

See below for a current version of Form 2 under the *BCA*.

Form 2 Business Corporations Act Formule 2 Loi sur les sociétés par actions	**CONSENT TO ACT AS A FIRST DIRECTOR** *CONSENTEMENT DU PREMIER ADMINISTRATEUR*

I,/Je soussigné(e), _____

(First name, middle names and surname)
(Prénom, autres Prénoms et nom de famille)

address for service
domicile élu

_____

(Street & No. or R.R. No., Municipality, Province, Country & Postal Code)
(Rue et numéro, ou numéro de la R.R., nom de la municipalité, province, pays et code postal)

hereby consent to act as a first director of
accepte par la présente de devenir premier administrateur de

_____

(Name of Corporation)
(Dénomination sociale de la société)

_____

(Signature of the Consenting Person)
(Signature de l'acceptant)

Please refer to the Workbook for copies of Form 1 (Articles of Incorporation) and Form 2 (Consent to Act as First Director) under the *BCA*.

(b) Articles of Incorporation for a Federal Company

When you are incorporating a federal company, you will need to complete Form 1 under the *CBCA* (Articles of Incorporation), and Form 2 under the *CBCA* (Initial Registered Office Address and First Board of Directors). You may also submit a Corporate Name Information Form, which provides Corporations Canada with additional information with which to consider a corporate name. The Corporate Name Information Form is not mandatory, but is strongly recommended by Corporations Canada. If you are filing these forms by email, fax or mail, you can obtain copies of the forms online through the Industry Canada website at <www.ic.gc.ca>. Once you have selected your language preference (English or French,) click on "Online Forms" on the left side of the screen.

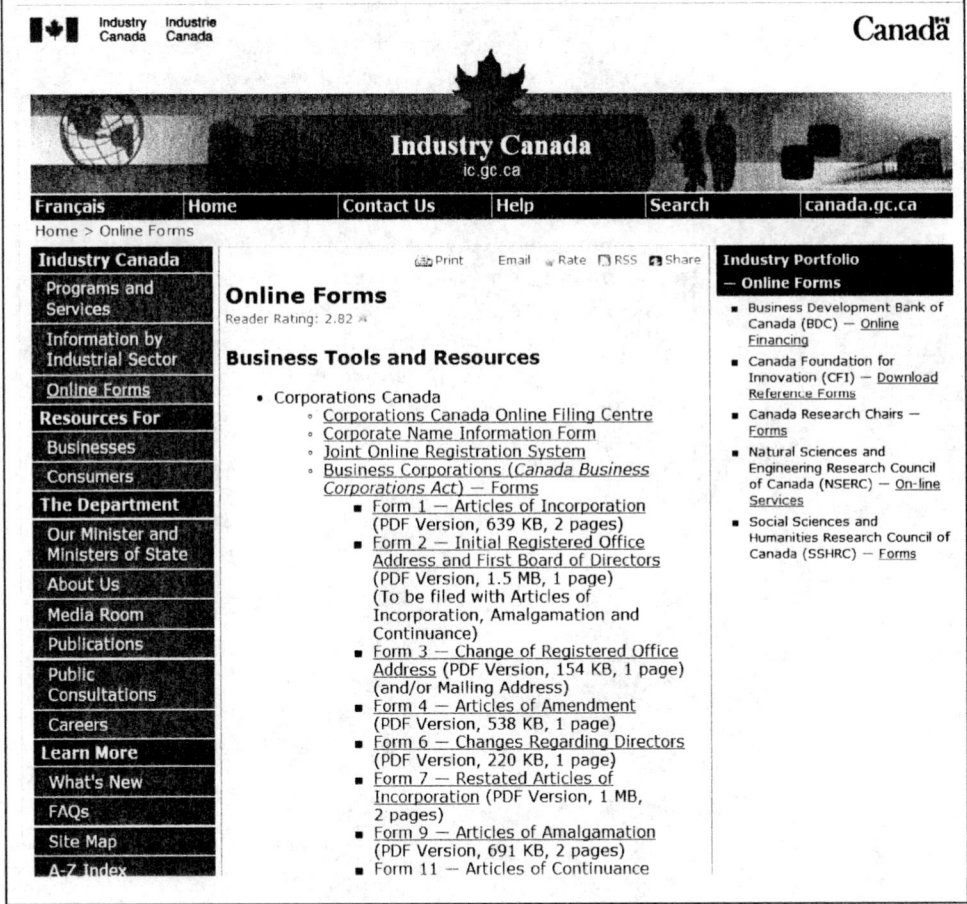

Alternatively, you can file the necessary documents online through Corporations Canada's Online Filing Centre. (See "Incorporating a Federal Company" under heading 4 of this chapter.)

Note that Corporations Canada also provides excellent resources to guide legal professionals and others through the incorporation process. The online "Incorporation Kit" provides guidelines on each step of the process, including suggestions for how to complete the Articles of Incorporation. Some of these suggestions are referred to in the checklist which follows.[32] In addition, the "Guide to Federal Incorporation" is an excellent overview of the incorporation process. This document also provides precedents of completed incorporation documents, which can provide alternatives to the provisions provided in the checklist below.[33]

Checklist for Completing Articles of Incorporation – Federal Company

Article 1 – Corporate Name	Provide the proposed corporate name. If you are requesting a numbered name, leave a blank space and then write in the word "CANADA" followed by the legal element of your choice (such as Ltd., Inc., Corp., etc.)
Article 2 – Province/ Territory	Indicate the province or territory in Canada where the corporation's registered office will be located. A post office box is not acceptable. Note that only the province or territory (not the street address) of the registered office is required on this form.
Article 3 – Classes/ Maximum Number of Shares	Describe the classes (that is, the types) of shares and the maximum number (for each class) that the corporation is authorized to issue. The corporation must issue at least one class of shares – often, it issues "an unlimited number of common shares". However, if there are going to be different classes of shares, you must indicate the rights, privileges, restrictions and conditions for each class of shares. If there is not enough space on the form to do so, simply type "See attached Schedule 1" and provide the information on an attachment titled "Schedule 1".

32 "Incorporation Kit", online: Corporations Canada <http://www.ic.gc.ca/eic/site/cd-dgc.nsf/eng/cs02717.html#s4>.
33 "Guide to Federal Incorporation", online: Corporations Canada <http://www.ic.gc.ca/eic/site/cd-dgc.nsf/eng/h_cs04839.html>.

Article 4 – Restrictions on Share Transfer	In order to comply with NI 45-106, insert the same paragraph included in Article 8 of the Articles of Incorporation for an Ontario company. (See ***Checklist for Completing Articles of Incorporation – Ontario Company,*** provided earlier in this Chapter.)
	Alternatively, the Incorporation Kit provided online by Corporations Canada also suggests including the following paragraphs in Article 4:
	No shares of the capital of the corporation shall be transferred without either (a) the sanction of a majority of the directors of the corporation or alternatively (b) the sanction of the majority of the shareholders of the corporation.
	The corporation's securities, other than non-convertible debt securities, shall not be transferred without either (a) the sanction of a majority of the directors of the corporation, or (b) the sanction of the majority of the shareholders of the corporation, or alternatively (c), if applicable, the restriction contained in security holders' agreements.[34]
Article 5 - Directors	Indicate the minimum and maximum number of directors. If the client chooses to have a fixed number of directors, insert the same number in both boxes. For example, if the corporation will have 3 directors at all times (that is, a fixed number of directors,) type "3" in the box for "Minimum" and "3" in the box for "Maximum". There must be at least one director, and for maximum flexibility, it is best to provide a realistic range (that is, a minimum and maximum number of directors.) By having a range, such as a minimum of 1 director and a maximum of 5 directors, it will not be necessary to file articles of amendment (and incur additional cost) if a director resigns, or the number of directors changes for some other reason.
Article 6 – Restrictions on Business	Most corporations do not provide any restrictions on the business they can conduct, and complete this section simply by typing "None". If there is a reason to restrict the type of business the corporation can conduct (such as a reason prescribed by statute,) then type in: "The business of the corporation shall be limited to the following: . . ." Complete the rest of this sentence accordingly.

---

34 "Incorporation Kit", online: Corporations Canada <http://www.ic.gc.ca/eic/site/cd-dgc.nsf/ eng/cs02717.html#s4>.

Article 7 – Other provisions	In order to comply with NI 45-106, insert the same paragraph included in Article 9 of the Articles of Incorporation for an Ontario company. (See ***Checklist for Completing Articles of Incorporation – Ontario Company,*** provided earlier in this Chapter.)
	Please refer to the Incorporation Kit provided online by Corporations Canada for additional provisions which may be included in Article 7. For example, you may include a provision regarding directors' borrowing powers to limit their authority and/or to satisfy lending institutions. An example of such a provision would be:
	If authorized by a by-law which is duly adopted by the directors and confirmed by ordinary resolution, the directors of the corporation may from time to time:
	i. borrow money on the credit of the corporation;
	ii. issue, reissue, sell or pledge debt obligations of the corporation; and
	iii. mortgage, hypothecate, pledge or otherwise create a security interest in all or any property of the corporation, owned or subsequently acquired, to secure any debt obligation of the corporation.
	Any such by-law may provide for the delegation of such powers by the directors to such officers or directors of the corporation to such extent and in such manner as may be set out in the by-law.
	Nothing herein limits or restricts the borrowing of money by the corporation on bills of exchange or promissory notes made, drawn, accepted or endorsed by or on behalf of the corporation.[35]

---

35 *Ibid.*

| Article 8 – Incorporator's Declaration | Articles of Incorporation must be signed by the incorporator(s), all of whom must be competent, at least 18 years of age and not in a state of bankruptcy. There must be at least one incorporator. Although incorporators may also be directors or shareholders of the corporation, they do not have to be directors or shareholders. The incorporator can also be another corporation, in which case the articles must be signed by a person authorized to sign on behalf of the corporation.[36] Note that for Articles of Incorporation filed online, a copy of the Articles of Incorporation must still be printed and signed by the incorporator(s), and should be kept in the minute book of the corporation. (Minute books will be discussed in Chapters 9 and 10.)[37] |

(c) Form 2, CBCA for Federal Incorporation

When you are incorporating a federal company, you will also need to file Form 2 under the *CBCA*, which is called "Initial Registered Office Address and First Board of Directors". You may notice that the information provided in Form 1 and Form 2 of the *CBCA* are similar to the information provided in Form 1 of the *BCA* (Articles of Incorporation for an Ontario company) – the only difference is that, for a federal company, the information is divided into two forms, instead of one.

Checklist for Completing Form 2, CBCA – Federal Company

Section 1 – Corporate Name	Insert the corporate name exactly as you did in the Articles of Incorporation.
Section 2 –Address of Registered Office	Indicate the street address that will be the registered office of the corporation. A P.O. Box number is not acceptable.
Section 3 – Mailing Address	Provide a mailing address, *if* the mailing address is different from the registered office. (Ask the client if he/she wants to receive government mail at the registered office, or elsewhere.) If the mailing address is the same as the registered office address, simply check the box "Same as Above".

---

36 *Canada Business Corporations Act*, R.S.C. 1985, c. C-44, ss. 5 & 7.
37 *Guide to Federal Incorporation*, March 2011, Corporations Canada, Industry Canada, pp. 10 – 12; *Canada Business Corporations Act*, R.S.C. 1985, c. C-44, s. 6.

Section 4 – Board of Directors	Type the full, legal name and residential address for each of the first directors of the corporation. You must also indicate if each director is a resident Canadian. Generally, at least 25% of the directors of a federal corporation must be resident Canadians; see subsection 105 (3.1) of the *CBCA* for an exception to this general rule. Directors must be at least 18 years of age, of sound mind, not bankrupt, and must be an individual (that is, a corporation cannot be a director.)[38]
Section 5 – Incorporator's Declaration	At least one incorporator must sign in the space provided; a typed name only is not acceptable. (For forms filed online, Form 2 must be printed and signed by one of the incorporators, and kept with the Articles of Incorporation in the minute book. Minute books will be discussed in Chapters 9 and 10.)[39]

Note that the *CBCA* makes it the incorporator's responsibility to file Form 2, which provides a list of the first directors. Those first directors must hold office until the first meeting of shareholders, at which time the shareholders may appoint new directors.[40] Once the incorporation process is complete, the corporation will receive a Certificate of Incorporation. As stated in section 9 of the *CBCA*, "a corporation comes into existence on the date shown in the certificate of incorporation."[41]

Finally, the filing fee to incorporate a business is $200 if you file online through Corporations Canada's Online Filing Centre, or $250 if you file Forms 1 and 2 under the *CBCA* by email, fax or mail. Currently, fees may be paid by credit card if you file online, by email or by fax; fees may be paid by credit card or cheque (made payable to the Receiver General for Canada) if you file Forms 1 and 2 under the *CBCA* by mail.

(d) Corporate Name Information Form for Federal Incorporation

As mentioned previously, it is not mandatory to complete the Corporate Name Information Form when you are incorporating a federal company. Industry Canada does, however, stress on its website that it strongly recommends that the form be completed, as the information on the form helps Industry Canada to make a decision regarding approval of a corporate name. The advantage to completing the form is that it may speed up the process for approving a corporate name, or may prevent the corporate name from being rejected outright. Legal professionals should, as always, discuss the information that is provided in this form with the client, and make the client aware that this information will form part of the government's records.

The Corporate Name Information Form can be obtained from the Corporations Canada website, at <www.ic.gc.ca>. Click on "How to Name a Corporation" in the menu on the left side of the screen, and then click on the links to "Corporate Name Information

---

38 *Canada Business Corporations Act*, R.S.C. 1985, c. C-44, s. 105.
39 *Guide to Federal Incorporation*, March 2011, Corporations Canada, Industry Canada, p. 13.
40 *Ibid.*, s. 106.
41 *Canada Business Corporations Act*, R.S.C. 1985, c. C-44, s. 9.

Form". The form is a "fill and print" form; note that you cannot save it onto your computer, but you can print it after you have completed it.

The following is a checklist which will guide you through the information requested in the Corporate Name Information Form. A copy of the form is provided in the Workbook.

Checklist for Completing Corporate Name Information Form

What is the Proposed Corporate Name?	Provide the corporate name exactly as it appears in the NUANS report (and in the Articles of Incorporation, if you are submitting them all at the same time.)

Information on the Proposed Corporation	You will be asked to:
	    (a) indicate if the corporation is a not-for-profit corporation
	
	    (b) describe the business that the corporation intends to carry on
	
	    (c) indicate the geographic area or areas (city, province, territory) that the business intends to operate in
	
	    (d) describe the type of clients and supplies that the business will likely have
	
	 Completing this part of the form requires careful discussion with the client. It is prudent to provide enough information to allow Corporations Canada to assess the corporate name, but not to be so specific as to remove flexibility. For example, in a form completed for Entertainment Group Ltd., we could state that the company is in the nightclub business but may also provide other food and entertainment services (such as an adjoining restaurant, for example.) Similarly, in part (d) of the form, it would be too restrictive to indicate that the clients of this corporation are going to be fans of a particular vocal artist or a particular type of music. It would be more appropriate to indicate that the clientele are going to be adults over the legal drinking age.

Explain how you came up with the distinctive element of the name	A corporate name is often described as having a distinctive element that sets it apart from other companies, a descriptive element that describes what the company does, and a legal element that indicates that it is a corporation. In the corporate name "Nirvana Nightclub Inc.", "Nirvana" is the distinctive element, "Nightclub" is the descriptive element, and "Inc." is the legal element. In this section, you must describe how your client selected "Nirvana" as the distinctive element. This section will be especially relevant when the distinctive element is a made up word, or a group of initials – possibly from the names of the initial shareholders.
Person's Name	Indicate whether the proposed corporate name includes a person's name, and if so, how that person is connected to the corporation. You may also require that person's consent to use their name, which should be attached to the Corporate Name Information Form, if applicable.
Any other information	(a) Indicate whether you have conducted any other NUANS searches for similar names, and if so, what those names were. (b) Indicate if the client has a trademark or another business registered under the same name. If so, a consent from that other business may be required. (c) Indicate whether you are attaching any consent forms (referred to in the Corporate Name Information Form.) In deciding whether or not a consent form is required, click on the links provided in the form to the Name Granting Compendium.[42]

(e) Other Registrations for a Federal Company

In order to do business in any province or territory of Canada, a federal company will also have to register the corporation in that province or territory. "Doing business" in a province or territory may mean running the business there, or simply having an address, post office box or phone number, or offering services or products there. The corporation must usually be registered in each province or territory where it intends to do business within a few weeks after incorporation – so it is prudent for a legal professional to attend to this matter as soon as possible after incorporation. There may be an additional fee for registration in each province or territory. Note that Corporations Canada has joint registration agreements with Ontario, Saskatchewan, Nova Scotia, and Newfoundland and Labrador, which allow corporations that incorporate online through the

---

42 "Name Granting Compendium, May 3, 2010" online: Industry Canada (Corporations Canada) <http://corporationscanada.ic.gc.ca/eic/site/cd-dgc.nsf/eng/h_cs01407.html>.

Online Filing Centre to apply for provincial registration online. For more information on this process, refer to the Corporations Canada website (<http://www.ic.gc.ca/eic/site/cd-dgc.nsf/eng/home>).

Federal corporations will also receive a Business Number ("BN") which is part of the federal government's way to identify the business and the accounts maintained with the Canada Revenue Agency (CRA). CRA uses the BN for the following tax accounts:

- Goods and Services Tax/Harmonized Sales Tax (GST/HST);

- payroll deductions;

- corporate income tax; and

- import/export duties and taxes.

After Corporations Canada incorporates the business, it provides the required information to CRA; CRA will then issue a BN for the corporation. Note that corporate information is shared between Corporations Canada and CRA. CRA will send the corporation a letter confirming the BN and the accounts registered, along with a summary of information about the corporation. For more information about the BN, please refer to the CRA website (<www.cra-arc.gc.ca>). [43]

---

43 "Guide to Federal Incorporation, March 2011" pp. 14–15, online: Industry Canada (Corporations Canada) <http://www.ic.gc.ca/eic/site/cd-dgc.nsf/eng/cs04441.html>.

Finally, like an Ontario corporation, a federal corporation may have to apply for permits to operate a particular type of business, which may require provincial or municipal permits. For example, a restaurant operating in Toronto will require a liquor permit from the Alcohol & Gaming Commission of Ontario (AGCO).[44] Clients (or their legal representatives) can also use the BizPal website at <www.bizpal.ca>. BizPal was launched in 2005 as a partnership involving federal, provincial, territorial and municipal governments. These levels of government have collaborated to provide one, free online source for information on permits and licenses required to start and operate a business across Canada.[45]

---

44 "Liquor Licence," online: City of Toronto <http://www.toronto.ca/registry-services/liquor_licence.htm>.

45 "Streamlining Your Business Permit and Licensing Experience," online: BizPal website <http://www.bizpal.ca/en/>.

BizPaL *Business starts here*

Home   About Us   Contact   FAQ   Partners   Français

Your are here: Home

Streamlining your business permit and licensing experience

Select your region

Getting started is easy. Just click on the map where you
wish to start or grow your business.

Or launch the BizPaL
application here

Launch BizPaL

Having opened two restaurants over the
span of 6 years, once with the help of BizPaL
and once on my own, I can honestly say
what a difference it made to the red tape
that one normally thinks of when it comes to
regulation requirements during the start up
phase of a new business. I hope all new and
seasoned entrepreneurs are turned onto the

Why BizPaL...

- **It's free** - Search for the permits and licences you may need to start or grow your business.

- **Save time and money** — Spend less time searching for information and more time building your business.

- **Improve business planning** — Know which permits and licences are needed so that you get it right the first time.

Chapter 6: The "Corporate Players"

Overview:

- The "Corporate Players" – directors, officers and shareholders
- Directors
    - Role and power
    - Duties and liability
    - Conflicts of interest
- Officers
    - Roles and responsibilities
    - Duties and liability
- Related issues:
    - Indoor management rule
    - Insider liability
- Workbook:
    - Review exercise

1. The "Corporate Players"

There are three groups of "corporate players" in the economic landscape: directors, officers and shareholders. In the previous chapter, we talked about first directors and shareholders in the context of filing articles of incorporation. In this chapter, we will explore the role that directors and officers play in a corporation. Shareholders will be discussed in Chapter 7.

Recall the scenario introduced in Chapter 1. Assume that Javid, Helena and Mike have incorporated an Ontario corporation to run their new nightclub. The corporation is called Entertainment Group Ltd. All three individuals are listed as first directors in the Articles of Incorporation, and all three are shareholders. What does this mean in terms of who actually runs the business?

There are three roles that individuals can play in a corporation: director, officer and/ or shareholder. One person can play more than one role – just like a person can be a wife, mother and daughter at the same time. The relationship between these three roles can be depicted in a pyramid, such as the one below.

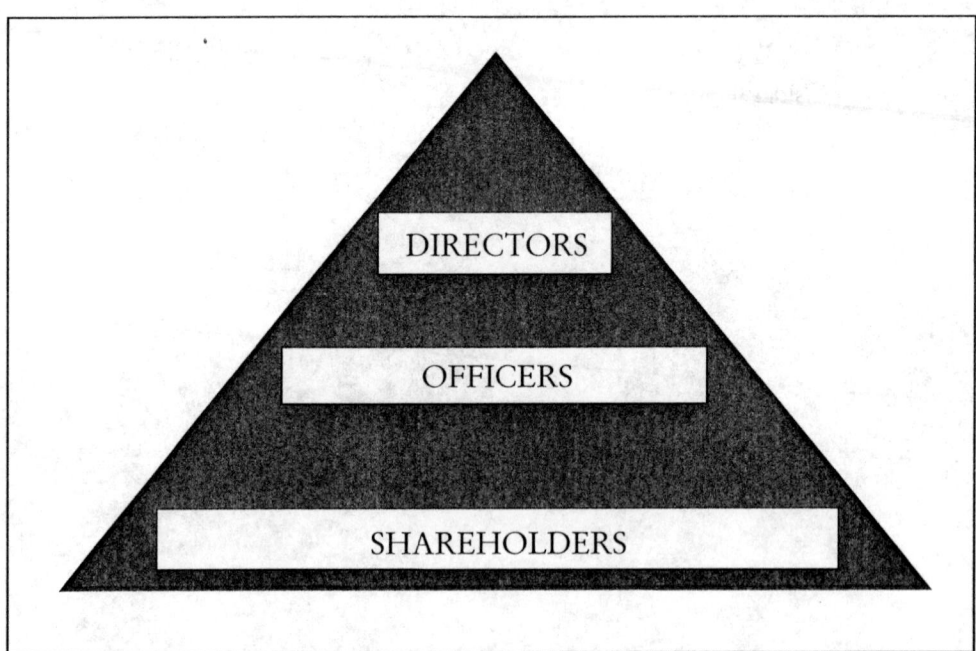

2. Directors

(a) The Role and Power of Directors

Subsection 115(1) of the *BCA* explains the role of directors very succinctly:

> Subject to any unanimous shareholder agreement, the directors shall manage or supervise the management of the business and affairs of a corporation.[1]

---

1 *Business Corporations Act*, R.S.O. 1990, c. B.16, s. 115(1).

(Subsection 102(1) of the *CBCA*, which addresses the same issue, is virtually identical.)[2] Essentially, the directors of an Ontario or federal corporation are the individuals that make all the key, strategic decisions regarding the business. In the case of non-offering corporations like Entertainment Group Ltd., the directors are likely to be one or more of the shareholders. Strategic decisions are decisions that affect the overall business plan, and include (amongst others):

- location of the business

- marketing strategy

- hiring of management

- financial decisions, such as whether or not to take out a loan

- decisions regarding the type of products and/or services to provide

- signing of major contracts, such as a lease for premises

> Who do you think should be a director of Entertainment Group Ltd. – Javid, Helena or Mike? Should all of them be directors? If Javid only wants Helena and himself to be directors, should Mike agree to that arrangement? Why or why not?

According to the *BCA*, an Ontario corporation that is a non-offering corporation must have at least one director, and that director must be an individual (not another corporation.) For an offering corporation, there must be at least 3 individuals who serve as directors.[3] In addition, at least one-third of the directors of an offering corporation cannot be officers or employees of the corporation or any of its affiliates. Sometimes, directors are referred to in the media as "inside directors" or "independent directors". "Inside directors" are directors who are also officers or employees of the corporation, whereas "independent" or "outside" directors are only directors – they do not play any other role in the corporation. In an offering (that is, a public) corporation, the law requires that at least one-third of the directors be "outside directors", so there is some level of objectivity in the decisions made by the directors for the corporation. There is no such requirement for non-offering corporations. In a non-offering (or private) corporation, all the directors can be "inside directors".[4] The *CBCA* has a similar requirement for at least one director in a non-distributing (that is, a private) corporation, and at least three directors in a distributing (that is, a public) corporation; of the three directors in a distributing corporation, at least two directors must not be employees or officers of the company or its affiliates.[5]

Who can be a director of a corporation? The qualifications under the *BCA* and *CBCA* are very similar – a director must be:

1. at least 18 years of age

---

2 *Canada Business Corporations Act*, R.S.C. 1985, c. C-44, s. 102(1).
3 *Business Corporations Act*, R.S.O. 1990, c. B.16, s. 115(2).
4 *Ibid.*, s. 115(3).
5 *Canada Business Corporations Act*, R.S.C. 1985, c. C-44, s. 102(2).

2. someone who is capable of managing property and is of sound mind, and who has not been found incapable or unsound by a court in Canada or elsewhere

3. an individual

4. not bankrupt[6]

In practice, most individuals who are starting a business will be able to satisfy these requirements. However, the decision of who should be a director in a corporation is a critical one, because directors control the corporation. The authority given by subsection 115(1) of the *BCA* and subsection 102(1) of the *CBCA* to manage or supervise the management of the business and affairs of a corporation is a very broad power, and as we will discuss later, shareholders have much less power to affect business decisions.

Both the *BCA* and *CBCA* impose residency requirements on directors. At least 25 per cent of the directors of an Ontario or federal corporation must be resident Canadians. If a corporation has less than four directors, at least one director must be a resident Canadian.[7] However, in a federal corporation, there are some exceptions to the 25 per cent rule, and in some circumstances, a majority of directors will have to be resident Canadians.[8] There are additional exceptions for holding corporations, which in some cases, will only require at least one-third of the directors to be resident Canadians.[9]

In addition to the overall power to manage or supervise the management of the corporation, directors are also given the following specific powers in the *BCA*:

- making, amending or repealing any by-laws that regulate the business or affairs of the corporation (although the shareholders must confirm the by-laws to make them effective)

- adopting forms of security (share) certificates and corporate records

- issuing shares or other securities

- appointing officers

- appointing auditors until the first annual or a special meeting of shareholders

- making banking arrangements

- entering into any other business transactions.[10]

A director is also entitled to receive notice of and to attend and be heard at every shareholders meeting.[11]

When there is only one director in a corporation, that director is usually referred to as the "sole director". Where there are two or more directors, the entire group of directors is called the "board of directors" (or in short, the "board".) Often, a larger board of

---

6 *Business Corporations Act*, R.S.O. 1990, c. B.16, s. 118(1); *Canada Business Corporations Act*, R.S.C. 1985,c. C-44, s. 105(1).

7 *Business Corporations Act*, R.S.O. 1990, c. B. 16, s. 118(3); *Canada Business Corporations Act*, R.S.C. 1985, c. C-44, s. 105(3).

8 *Canada Business Corporations Act*, R.S.C. 1985, c. C-44, s. 105(3.1) – (3.3)

9 *Ibid.*, s. 105(4).

10 *Business Corporations Act*, R.S.O. 1990, c. B.16, ss. 116 – 117.

11 Ibid., s. 123(1); *Canada Business Corporations Act*, R.S.C. 1985, c. C-44, s.110(1).

directors will appoint one of their members to be the "Chairman" or "Chair" of the board. This individual is generally viewed as the leader of the board and is sometimes given additional powers, which are specified in the by-laws of the corporation. (By-laws will be discussed in Chapter 9.)

The *BCA* and *CBCA* give the board of directors the authority to delegate some of their powers and responsibilities to a smaller committee of directors, or to a managing director.[12] Particularly in public companies, the amount of information that the directors must review and be familiar with is large and complex, so it may be advisable to divide responsibilities amongst directors. For example, Walmart is a corporation with 15 directors – ten independent, or outside, directors and five inside directors – at the time of writing.) It has currently has six board committees, namely:

1. Audit Committee

2. Compensation, Nomination and Governance committee

3. Executive Committee

4. Global Compensation Committee

5. Strategic Planning and Finance Committee

6. Technology and eCommerce Committee

Each of the 15 directors (also called "board members") mentioned above will also be a member of one or more of these committees. In this way, the board members can divide their responsibilities to supervise the management of Walmart.[13]

In other (generally, smaller) corporations, there may not be an elaborate committee structure in the board of directors, but the board may delegate some of its responsibilities to a "managing director". Whether there is a committee structure on the board of directors or a managing director, there are some decisions that must be made by the entire board of directors. The *BCA* provides in section 127:

> 127 (1) Subject to the articles or by-laws, directors of a corporation may appoint from their number a managing director or a committee of directors and delegate to such managing director or committee any of the powers of the directors. 2006, c. 34, Sched. B, s. 21 (1). . . .

> (3) Despite subsection (1), no managing director and no committee of directors has authority to,

> (a) submit to the shareholders any question or matter requiring the approval of the shareholders;

> (b) fill a vacancy among the directors or in the office of auditor or appoint or remove any of the chief executive officers, however designated, the chief financial officer, however designated, the chair or the president of the corporation;

> (c) subject to section 184, issue securities except in the manner and on the terms authorized by the directors;

---

12 *Business Corporations Act*, R.S.O. 1990, c. B.16, s.127(1); *Canada Business Corporations Act*, R.S.C. 1985, c. C-44, s.115(1).

13 "Committee Information," online: Walmart Corporate <http://investors.walmartstores.com/phoenix.zhtml?c=112761&p=irol-govcommcomp>.

(d) declare dividends;

(e) purchase, redeem or otherwise acquire shares issued by the corporation;

(f) pay a commission referred to in section 37;

(g) approve a management information circular referred to in Part VIII;

(h) approve a take-over bid circular, directors' circular or issuer bid circular referred to in Part XX of the *Securities Act*;

(i) approve any financial statements referred to in clause 154 (1) (b) of the Act and Part XVIII of the *Securities Act*;

(i.1) approve an amalgamation under section 177 or an amendment to the articles under subsection 168 (2) or (4); or

(j) adopt, amend or repeal by-laws. R.S.O. 1990, c. B.16, s. 127 (3); 1994, c. 27, s. 71 (16).[14]

In other words, the actions specified in subsection 127(3) must be performed by the board of directors as a whole, and cannot be delegated to a managing director or a committee of directors only. The corresponding provision in the *CBCA* is substantially the same.

Directors of an Ontario or federal corporation can be paid for their services. Moreover, it is the directors who have the authority to determine the remuneration that they will receive, in addition to the remuneration received by officers and other employees of the corporation.[15]

It should be clear by now that directors have significant power to control and direct a corporation. As a result, clients must be advised to choose directors very carefully. In most cases, all of the shareholders of a non-offering corporation will want to be directors, so that they will all have a say in the business decisions made for the corporation. This is the most common situation when a small group of individuals are starting a business – all of the shareholders are also officers and directors of the corporation. There are situations, however, where this may not be the case, and the individual who is not a director must understand the consequences. For example, since Javid is the only individual who is able to invest capital in Entertainment Group Ltd., one of his requirements may be that, while Helena and Mike are shareholders (so they will receive a share of the profits of the corporation), only Javid will be a director. A legal professional who is representing either Helena or Mike would have to make them aware of the power that Javid would have as the sole director in the corporation, and consequently, the constraints that Helena and Mike would face.

Sometimes, a corporation may decide to increase the number of directors that it currently has. For example, Entertainment Group Ltd. may have been incorporated with only Javid acting as a director, but as time goes on and the business becomes established, the shareholders may agree that Javid, Helena and Mike should all be directors of the corporation. This – and other – changes to the corporate structure can be made after incorporation. If the Articles of Incorporation provide for a range in the number of

14 *Business Corporations Act*, R.S.O. 1990, c. B.16, s. 127; *Canada Business Corporations Act*, R.S.C. 1985, c. C-44, s.115.

15 *Business Corporations Act*, R.S.O. 1990, c. B.16, s. 137; *Canada Business Corporations Act*, R.S.C. 1985, c. C-44, s.137.

directors (for example, if they state that there can be between 1 and 4 directors) then the change can be made by a special resolution of the shareholders. (Special resolutions will be discussed in greater detail in Chapter 9.) This is a relatively simple process, and as such, it is generally advisable to provide for a range – that is, a minimum and maximum number – of directors in the Articles of Incorporation. That range should, generally, start with a minimum number of one director, and a maximum number that seems reasonable for that specific corporation. If, however, the Articles of Incorporation specify a fixed number of directors – such as one director – and the shareholders decide to add one or more directors, the corporation will first have to file Articles of Amendment in order to allow this change to occur.[16] (Articles of Amendment will be discussed in Chapter 12.)

A director ceases being a director of the corporation when he or she dies, resigns, is removed by the shareholders, or is disqualified pursuant to section 118 of the *BCA* (by declaring bankruptcy or being declared incapable of managing property.)[17] A director who resigns is entitled to submit a written statement to the corporation explaining the reasons for the resignation. Similarly, a director who receives notice of a shareholders meeting in which the shareholders intend to remove him or her as a director, is entitled to submit a statement which explains why he or she opposes this action. In either case (a resignation or opposition to removal), the statement must be provided to every share-holder for consideration.[18]

(b) Directors' Duties & Liability

With power comes responsibility, and as such, both the *BCA* and *CBCA* recognize the necessity to impose duties and liability on directors in certain circumstances. As a starting point, both the *BCA* and the *CBCA* state that:

> Every director and officer of a corporation shall comply with this Act, the regulations, articles, by-laws and any unanimous shareholder agreement.[19]

In addition, directors and officers cannot contract out of liability for a breach of the *BCA* its regulations, except insofar as a unanimous shareholder agreement is put into place.[20] (Please refer to Chapter 7 for more information about unanimous shareholder agreements.)

In addition, directors and officers must exercise their powers in the best interests of the corporation. Subsection 134(1) of the *BCA* states:

> 134. (1) Every director and officer of a corporation in exercising his or her powers and discharging his or her duties to the corporation shall,
>
> (a) act honestly and in good faith with a view to the best interests of the corporation; and

---

16 *Ibid.*, s. 125; *Canada Business Corporations Act*, R.S.C. 1985, c. C-44, s.112.
17 *Business Corporations Act*, R.S.O. 1990, c. B.16, s. 121(1); *Canada Business Corporations Act*, R.S.C. 1985, c. C-44, s.108.
18 *Business Corporations Act*, R.S.O. 1990, c. B.16, s. 123(2) – (3); *Canada Business Corporations Act*, R.S.C. 1985, c. C-44, s. 114.
19 *Business Corporations Act*, R.S.O. 1990, c. B.16, s. 134(2); *Canada Business Corporations Act*, R.S.C. 1985, c. C-44, s.122(2).
20 *Business Corporations Act*, R.S.O. 1990, c. B.16, s. 134(3); *Canada Business Corporations Act*, R.S.C. 1985, c. C-44, s.122(3).

(b) exercise the care, diligence and skill that a reasonably prudent person would exercise in comparable circumstances.[21]

Subsection 122(1) of the *CBCA* is drafted in exactly the same way.[22] Caselaw has elaborated on what is required for officers and directors to meet this standard of care.

Pente Investment Management Ltd. v. Schneider Corp. (1998), 42 O.R. (3d) 177 (Ont. C.A.)

Schneider Corporation ("Schneider") is an Ontario corporation controlled by members of the Schneider Family ("the Family") On November 5, 1997, Maple Leaf Foods Inc. ("M.L.") made an unsolicited take-over bid for Schneider at $19 a share. In response, the Schneider's board of directors ("the Board") established a Special Committee consisting of the independent non-family directors to review the ML offer and to consider other alternatives. Subsequently ML made an offer of $22 a share, but this offer was rejected by the Family. Ultimately, the Family told the Special Committee that the only offer it would accept was an offer made by Smithfield Foods (an American company) that was equal to $25 a share. In order for the Family to accept the Smithfield offer, the Board had to take certain steps which, on the advice of the Special Committee, it took. After the Family had already agreed to the Smithfield offer, on December 22, 1997, Maple Leaf made a further offer of $29 a share to Schneider's shareholders. The appellants include minority shareholders of Scheider and ML, who claim that the board of directors was unduly preferential to the Family shareholders, and did not take into account the best interests of all the shareholders by stopping the auction process and not considering ML's higher bid. One of the grounds of appeal related to whether the directors had breached their duty to act in the best interest of the corporation. (Other grounds of appeal will not be considered in this summary.)

The law as it relates to the general duties of the directors of a company is well known. The directors of a company have an obligation to act honestly and in good faith in the best interests of the corporation: s. 134(1)(a) *Business Corporations Act*, R.S.O. 1990, c. B.16 (the "*OBCA*"). Further, in discharging their obligations, the directors must exercise the care, diligence and skill that a reasonably prudent person would exercise in comparable circumstances: s. 134(1)(b). If the actions of the directors unfairly disregard the interests of a shareholder, unfairly prejudiced those interests, or are oppressive to them, s. 248 of the *OBCA* comes into play and allows the court to grant any remedy it thinks fit.

The court canvassed the caselaw on this issue as follows:

The mandate of the directors is to manage the company according to their best judgment: that judgment must be an informed judgment; it must have a reasonable basis. If there are no reasonable grounds to support an assertion by the directors that they have acted in the best interests of the company, a court will be justified in finding that the directors acted for an improper purpose: *Teck Corp. v. Millar* (1972), 33 D.L.R. (3d) 288 (B.C. S.C.) at 315-316, adopted as the law in Ontario by Montgomery J. in *Olympia & York Enterprises Ltd.*

---

21 *Business Corporations Act*, R.S.O. 1990, c. B.16, s. 134(1).
22 *Canada Business Corporations Act*, R.S.C. 1985, c. C-44, s.122(1).

v. Hiram Walker Resources Ltd. (1986), 59 O.R. (2d) 254 at 255 (Ont. H.C.), affirmed (1986), 59 O.R. (2d) 254 (Ont. Div. Ct.).

One way of determining whether the directors acted in the best interests of the company, according to Farley J., is to ask what was uppermost in the directors' minds after "a reasonable analysis of the situation.": *820099 Ontario Inc. v. Harold E. Ballard Ltd.* (1991), 3 B.L.R. (2d) 113 at 123 (Ont. Gen. Div.), affirmed (1991), 3 B.L.R. (2d) 113 (Ont. Div. Ct.); *CW Shareholdings Inc. v. WIC Western International Communications* (May 17, 1998), Doc. Toronto 98-CL-2821 (Ont. Gen. Div.). . . .

It must be recognized that the directors are not the agents of the shareholders. The directors have absolute power to manage the affairs of the company even if their decisions contravene the express wishes of the majority shareholder: *Teck Corp. v. Millar* (1972), 33 D.L.R. (3d) 288 (B.C. S.C.) at 307. However, acting in the best interests of the company does not necessarily mean that the directors must act in the best interests of one of the groups protected under s. 234. There may be a conflict between the interests of individual groups of shareholders and the best interests of the company: *Brant Investments Ltd. v. KeepRite Inc.* (1987), 60 O.R. (2d) 737 (Ont. H.C.), aff'd (1991), 3 O.R. (3d) 289 (Ont. C.A.) at 301.

Provided that the directors have acted honestly and reasonably, the court ought not to substitute its own business judgment for that of the Board of Directors: *Brant Investments v. KeepRite Inc., supra*, which deals with the analogous section of the *Canadian Business Corporations Act*, R.S.C. 1985, c. C-44. If the directors have unfairly disregarded the rights of a group of shareholders, the directors will not have acted reasonably in the best interests of the corporation and the court will intervene: *820099 Ontario Inc. v. Harold E. Ballard Ltd., supra.*

At paragraph 36, the court continued:

The law as it has evolved in Ontario and Delaware has the common requirements that the court must be satisfied that the directors have acted reasonably and fairly. The court looks to see that the directors made a *reasonable* decision *not a perfect* decision. . . .

Provided the decision taken is within a range of reasonableness, the court ought not to substitute its opinion for that of the board even though subsequent events may have cast doubt on the board's determination. As long as the directors have selected one of several reasonable alternatives, deference is accorded to the board's decision: *Paramount, supra*, at 45: *Brant Investments, supra*, at 320. *Themadel Foundation v. Third Canadian Investment Trust Ltd.* (1998), 38 O.R. (3d) 749 (Ont. C.A.) at 754. This formulation of deference to the decision of the Board is known as the "business judgment rule". The fact that alternative transactions were rejected by the directors is irrelevant unless it can be shown that a particular alternative was definitely available and clearly more beneficial to the company than the chosen transaction: *Brant Investments, supra*, at 314-315.

The court pointed out that a common strategy for addressing a situation where majority shareholders might also be directors was to create a Special Committee comprised of outsiders, who could independently assess the alternatives. The board did create this type of Special Committee, and the court found that the board acted honestly and in good faith. The board was also well informed. In considering ML's final bid, the court found that it was no more advantageous to the company than the Smithfield Foods bid, after tax implications were taken into account. In addition, ML did not address the Family's concerns about Schneider employees, suppliers and customers, which Smithfield was willing to address. The board of directors acted on the advice of the Special Committee, which was reasonable at the time and fair to the non-Family shareholders. Therefore, the directors did act in the best interests of the corporation. The court dismissed this ground of appeal.

As the caselaw demonstrates, directors have an obligation to remain informed about corporate activities, and cannot avoid liability on the basis that they simply were not aware of inappropriate activities occurring in or by the corporation. Each director has a responsibility to ensure that they remain informed about the business, that all the activities of the corporation are legal, and that the decisions that are being made by the board of directors and officers are in the best interest of the corporation.[23] In order to do this, directors must attend meetings regularly and ask officers pertinent questions about business activities. Directors are assumed to agree with any resolution made at a meeting – whether they were present at the meeting or not – unless they take action to record their disagreement in the manner specified by the *BCA* or *CBCA*. This makes it imperative for directors to attend meetings, and when they cannot attend, to follow up afterwards to ensure that they do, in fact, agree with the decisions made at the meeting.[24] When they do not agree with any course of action agreed upon at that meeting, recording their disagreement will help to protect them from liability.

People's Department Stores Ltd. (1992) Inc., Re, [2004] 3 S.C.R. 461 (S.C.C.)

Wise Stores Inc. ("Wise") acquired Peoples Department Stores Inc. ("Peoples") from Marks and Spencer Canada Inc. ("M & S"). Lionel Wise, Harold Wise and Ralph Wise (the "Wise brothers") were majority shareholders, officers and directors of Wise, and the only directors of Peoples. The joint operation of Wise and Peoples did not operate smoothly, eventually requiring the implementation of a new inventory policy. Ultimately, both companies declared bankruptcy. The trustee in bankruptcy for Peoples filed a petition against the Wise brothers, claiming that they had breached their fiduciary duty as directors of Peoples by favouring Wise over Peoples, thereby putting Peoples' creditors at a disadvantage. At trial, the court found against the Wise brothers on this and other grounds. The Court of Appeal set aside the trial judge's decision. The case was then appealed to the Supreme Court of Canada ("SCC").

The SCC explored section 122(1) of the *CBCA*, which "establishes two distinct duties to be discharged by directors and officers in managing, or supervising the management of, the corporation:

122. (1) Every director and officer of a corporation in exercising their powers and discharging their duties shall

    (a) act honestly and in good faith with a view to the best interests of the corporation; and

    (b) exercise the care, diligence and skill that a reasonably prudent person would exercise in comparable circumstances."

The court referred to subparagraph 122(1)(a) as the statutory fiduciary duty of directors.

The statutory fiduciary duty requires directors and officers to act honestly and in good faith vis-à-vis the corporation. They must respect the trust and confidence that have been reposed

---

23 *Guide to Federal Incorporation*, Industry Canada, Corporations Canada, March 2011, p. 33.
24 *Business Corporations Act*, R.S.O. 1990, c. B.16, s. 135(1)–(3); *Canada Business Corporations Act*, R.S.C. 1985, c. C-44, s.123(1)–(3).

in them to manage the assets of the corporation in pursuit of the realization of the objects of the corporation. They must avoid conflicts of interest with the corporation. They must avoid abusing their position to gain personal benefit. They must maintain the confidentiality of information they acquire by virtue of their position. Directors and officers must serve the corporation selflessly, honestly and loyally: see K. P. McGuinness, The Law and Practice of Canadian Business Corporations (1999), at p. 715.

In this case, the court found that there was no personal interest or improper purpose exhibited by the Wise brothers in implementing the new inventory policy, and in fact, they did so to try to improve both companies. As a result, they did not breach their fiduciary duty under subparagraph 122(1)(a) of the CBCA.

The court also commented that

it is clear that the phrase the 'best interests of the corporation' should be read not simply as the 'best interests of the shareholders'. From an economic perspective, the 'best interests of the corporation' means the maximization of the value of the corporation: see E. M. Iacobucci, 'Directors' Duties in Insolvency: Clarifying What Is at Stake' (2003), 39 Can. Bus. L.J. 398, at pp. 400-1. However, the courts have long recognized that various other factors may be relevant in determining what directors should consider in soundly managing with a view to the best interests of the corporation . . .

We accept as an accurate statement of law that in determining whether they are acting with a view to the best interests of the corporation it may be legitimate, given all the circumstances of a given case, for the board of directors to consider, inter alia, the interests of shareholders, employees, suppliers, creditors, consumers, governments and the environment. The court also examined s. 122(1)(b), the director's "duty of care". The court explained that this duty of care must be examined as an objective standard, meaning that it must be considered in light of all of the circumstances of the case, and not in light of the director's intentions. [The director's intentions are relevant to the statutory fiduciary duty in s. 122(1)(a).]

The court held that:

Directors and officers will not be held to be in breach of the duty of care under s. 122(1)(b) of the CBCA if they act prudently and on a reasonably informed basis. The decisions they make must be reasonable business decisions in light of all the circumstances about which the directors or officers knew or ought to have known. In determining whether directors have acted in a manner that breached the duty of care, it is worth repeating that perfection is not demanded. Courts are ill-suited and should be reluctant to second-guess the application of business expertise to the considerations that are involved in corporate decision making, but they are capable, on the facts of any case, of determining whether an appropriate degree of prudence and diligence was brought to bear in reaching what is claimed to be a reasonable business decision at the time it was made.

In this case, the court found that the Wise brothers had not breached their statutory fiduciary duty or their duty of care under s. 122(1) of the CBCA. The appeal was dismissed with costs to the respondents.

The BCA and CBCA specifically address directors' liability in the context of issuing shares for consideration other than money, where that consideration is less than the fair market value of the shares.[25] However, a director is not liable in these circumstances if

---

25 *Business Corporations Act*, R.S.O. 1990, c. B.16, s. 130(1); *Canada Business Corporations Act*, R.S.C. 1985, c. C-44, s.118(1).

he/she did not know *and* could not have reasonably known that the share was issued for less than fair market value.[26] Satisfying this threshold will usually require that the director makes reasonable efforts to determine the value of the shares and the value of the consideration that is being accepted in exchange for the shares. In addition,

130(2) Directors of a corporation who vote for or consent to a resolution authorizing,

(a) Repealed: 2006, c. 34, Sched. B, s. 22 (1).

(b) a purchase, redemption or other acquisition of shares contrary to section 30, 31 or 32;

(c) a commission contrary to section 37;

(d) a payment of a dividend contrary to section 38;

(e) a payment of an indemnity contrary to section 136; or

(f) a payment to a shareholder contrary to section 185 or 248,

are jointly and severally liable to restore to the corporation any amounts so distributed or paid and not otherwise recovered by the corporation. R.S.O. 1990, c. B.16, s. 130 (2); 2006, c. 34, Sched. B, s. 22 (1).[27]

Subsection 118(2) of the *CBCA* is substantially the same as subsection 130(2) of the *BCA*.[28] Where a director is found liable under these provisions, he or she can seek contribution from other directors who voted for or consented to the unlawful act which led to that liability.[29] For this reason, it is critical that a director who disagrees with a decision or votes against a course of action, ensures that the disagreement or "dissent" is recorded. A director who is liable under subsection 130(2) of the *BCA* can apply for a court order compelling a shareholder or other recipient to return any money or other property that was wrongfully paid to that person. Similar provisions are also found in the *CBCA*.[30]

However, both the *BCA* and *CBCA* do provide directors and officers with a defence – often referred to as the "due diligence" defence. The *BCA* provides:

135(4) A director is not liable under section 130 and has complied with his or her duties under subsection 134 (2) if the director exercised the care, diligence and skill that a reasonably prudent person would have exercised in comparable circumstances, including reliance in good faith on,

(a) financial statements of the corporation represented to him or her by an officer of the corporation or in a written report of the auditor of the corporation to present fairly the financial position of the corporation in accordance with generally accepted accounting principles;

(b) an interim or other financial report of the corporation represented to him or her by an officer of the corporation to present fairly the financial position of the corporation in

---

26 *Business Corporations Act*, R.S.O. 1990, c. B.16, s. 130(6); *Canada Business Corporations Act*, R.S.C. 1985, c. C-44, s.118(6).

27 *Business Corporations Act*, R.S.O. 1990, c. B.16, s. 130(2).

28 *Canada Business Corporations Act*, R.S.C. 1985, c. C-44, s.118(2).

29 *Business Corporations Act*, R.S.O. 1990, c. B.16, s. 130(3); *Canada Business Corporations Act*, R.S.C. 1985, c. C-44, s.118(3).

30 *Business Corporations Act*, R.S.O. 1990, c. B. 16, ss. 130(4)–(5); *Canada Business Corporations Act*, R.S.C. 1985, c. C-44, ss.118(4)–(5).

accordance with generally accepted accounting principles;

(c) a report or advice of an officer or employee of the corporation, where it is reasonable in the circumstances to rely on the report or advice; or

(d) a report of a lawyer, accountant, engineer, appraiser or other person whose profession lends credibility to a statement made by any such person. 2006, c. 34, Sched. B, s. 25.[31]

The *CBCA* provides the same type of defence for directors, as follows:

Defence — reasonable diligence

(4) A director is not liable under section 118 or 119, and has complied with his or her duties under subsection 122(2), if the director exercised the care, diligence and skill that a reasonably prudent person would have exercised in comparable circumstances, including reliance in good faith on

(*a*) financial statements of the corporation represented to the director by an officer of the corporation or in a written report of the auditor of the corporation fairly to reflect the financial condition of the corporation; or

(*b*) a report of a person whose profession lends credibility to a statement made by the professional person.

Defence — good faith

(5) A director has complied with his or her duties under subsection 122(1) if the director relied in good faith on

(*a*) financial statements of the corporation represented to the director by an officer of the corporation or in a written report of the auditor of the corporation fairly to reflect the financial condition of the corporation; or

(*b*) a report of a person whose profession lends credibility to a statement made by the professional person.[32]

Directors are also jointly and severally liable to the employees of a corporation for unpaid wages (up to six months' wages) incurred while they were directors (and under the *BCA*, for not more than twelve months' accrued vacation pay while they were directors.) However, the directors are only liable if the corporation is also sued and is unable to satisfy this debt through corporate assets. A director who pays a claim made in this regard is entitled to claim contribution from the other directors who were also liable for the claim.[33]

Finally, others statutes – outside of the *BCA* and *CBCA* – may impose liability on directors of a corporation. For example, in the area of environmental law, the *Environmental Violations Administrative Monetary Penalties Act* states:

8. (1) If a corporation commits a violation, any director, officer, agent or mandatary of the corporation who directed, authorized, assented to, acquiesced in or participated in the commission of the violation is a party to the violation and is liable to an administrative monetary

---

31 *Business Corporations Act*, R.S.O. 1990, c. B.16, s. 135(4).
32 *Canada Business Corporations Act*, R.S.C. 1985, c. C-44, ss.123(4)–(5).
33 *Business Corporations Act*, R.S.O. 1990, c. B.16, s. 131; *Canada Business Corporations Act*, R.S.C. 1985, c. C-44, s. 119.

penalty of an amount to be determined in accordance with the regulations, whether or not the corporation has been proceeded against in accordance with this Act.[34]

Similarly, the *Income Tax Act* provides:

227.1 (1) Where a corporation has failed to deduct or withhold an amount as required by subsection 135(3) or 135.1(7) or section 153 or 215, has failed to remit such an amount or has failed to pay an amount of tax for a taxation year as required under Part VII or VIII, the directors of the corporation at the time the corporation was required to deduct, withhold, remit or pay the amount are jointly and severally, or solidarily, liable, together with the corporation, to pay that amount and any interest or penalties relating to it.[35]

> Javid meets with his legal advisor to discuss his responsibilities and liabilities as a director. He is quite concerned. Unlike Mike and Helena, he has significant personal assets that would be at risk if he was found to be liable as a director. However, it is critical that he becomes a director in order to be able to make significant business decisions. Would you advise him to become a director? Why or why not?

Fortunately, there are ways in which directors can protect themselves from liability. First and foremost, directors must be fully informed about their role and responsibilities, and should ensure that they:

1. attend meetings regularly.

2. follow up on resolutions made at meetings that are not attended.

3. ask officers for reports and explanations of what is in those reports, so that directors are fully informed of business decisions and corporate actions.

4. record dissenting views when a director disagrees with a decision or resolution.

5. ensure that the director is familiar with the "due diligence" defence, and that the director acts accordingly so that the defence will be available to him/her, if necessary.

6. ask officers, at relevant intervals, whether all employee wages have been paid and all government taxes have been remitted (and follow up, if required).

7. obtain an indemnity from the corporation.

8. obtain insurance paid by the corporation.

We have discussed items 1 – 6 in the list provided; we will now explore indemnities and insurance as they relate to directors' and officers' liability.

A corporation can protect its directors and officers by indemnifying them – in other words, by agreeing to pay legal costs reasonably incurred in a civil, criminal, administrative, investigative or other proceeding because of the director's association with the corporation. This indemnity can also extend to former directors and officers. However, the corporation may only indemnify such directors and officers if they acted honestly and in good faith with a view to the best interests of the corporation. In addition, a

---

34 *Environmental Violations Administrative Monetary Penalties Act*, S.C. 2009, c. 14, s. 126.
35 *Income Tax Act*, R.S.C. 1985, c. 1 (5th Supp), s. 227.1.

corporation can only indemnify an individual in a criminal or administrative proceeding if that individual had reasonable grounds for believing that his/her conduct was legal.[36] The limitation of an indemnity from a corporation is that it is only useful for a director if, during the course of litigation, the corporation has sufficient funds to pay the director's legal fees. If the business has become insolvent (that is, it does not have enough money to pay its debts,) then an indemnity from the corporation will not really assist the director.

For this reason, anyone who is considering taking on the role of a director should also consider whether it is appropriate for the corporation to purchase directors' and officers' liability insurance. The *BCA* and *CBCA* both allow a corporation to buy insurance for the benefit of an individual who acts as director or officer of the corporation.[37] The benefit of purchasing this insurance, from the director's perspective, is that it provides protection to the director *even if* the company becomes insolvent. As long as the terms of the insurance contract are met, the insurance company will pay the costs of litigation, and neither the corporation nor the director will suffer financially. In practicality, many individuals would not agree to act as a director or officer of a corporation – particularly a large corporation – if the *BCA* and *CBCA* did not allow a corporation to purchase directors' and officers' liability insurance. (Note that this insurance also applies to officers of the company.) The personal risk to the individual would be too great. However, in smaller, non-offering corporations, it may be cost-prohibitive to purchase this insurance when the corporation is first formed, and the risk of this type of litigation may be low. In each case, the costs and benefits of purchasing liability insurance should be explored with a client that intends to act as a director or officer of a corporation, and if necessary, should be revisited as the corporation grows.

(c) Conflicts of Interest

Because of the special powers and duties of a director, it is critical that a director avoid any perceived or actual conflicts of interest. A director has a statutory fiduciary duty to act in the best interests of the corporation, and a duty of care to act as a reasonably prudent person would act in comparable circumstances.[38] Fulfilling these duties includes avoiding any conflicts of interest, such as those listed in section 132 of the *BCA* and section 120 of the *CBCA*.[39] (These provisions are substantially the same.) Subsections 132(1) and (2) of the *BCA* provide:

132(1) A director or officer of a corporation who,

(a) is a party to a material contract or transaction or proposed material contract or transaction with the corporation; or

---

36 *Business Corporations Act*, R.S.O. 1990, c. B.16, s. 136; *Canada Business Corporations Act*, R.S.C. 1985, c. C-44, s.124.

37 *Business Corporations Act*, R.S.O. 1990, c. B.16, s. 136(4.3); *Canada Business Corporations Act*, R.S.C. 1985, c. C-44, s. 124(6).

38 *Business Corporations Act*, R.S.O. 1990, c. B.16, s. 134; *Canada Business Corporations Act*, R.S.C. 1985, c. C-44, s. 122; see also *Pente Investment Management Ltd. v. Schneider Corp.*, 1998 CarswellOnt 4035, 42 O.R. (3d) 177 (Ont. C.A.), summarized in this chapter.

39 *Business Corporations Act*, R.S.O. 1990, c. B.16, s. 132; *Canada Business Corporations Act*, R.S.C. 1985, c. C-44, s. 120.

(b) is a director or an officer of, or has a material interest in, any person who is a party to a material contract or transaction or proposed material contract or transaction with the corporation,

shall disclose in writing to the corporation or request to have entered in the minutes of meetings of directors the nature and extent of his or her interest. R.S.O. 1990, c. B.16, s. 132 (1).

(2) The disclosure required by subsection (1) shall be made, in the case of a director,

(a) at the meeting at which a proposed contract or transaction is first considered;

(b) if the director was not then interested in a proposed contract or transaction, at the first meeting after he or she becomes so interested;

(c) if the director becomes interested after a contract is made or a transaction is entered into, at the first meeting after he or she becomes so interested; or

(d) if a person who is interested in a contract or transaction later becomes a director, at the first meeting after he or she becomes a director. R.S.O. 1990, c. B.16, s. 132 (2).[40]

> Assume that Javid, Helena and Mike are all directors of Entertainment Group Ltd. They are discussing the opening night event, and Mike would like to recommend a band that his brother plays in. He thinks they are a great band, and he wants to help his brother out, too. Does this pose a conflict of interest for Mike? What should Mike do or not do?

A director who has a conflict of interest – or even one who may be perceived to have a conflict of interest – should disclose that conflict in writing to the rest of the board of directors. In addition, that director should not attend any meetings where that contract or conflict of interest is being discussed, and the director should not vote on any resolution to approve the contract or transaction, unless the contract or transaction is:

- One that relates primarily to his/her own remuneration as a director of the corporation (or a director of an affiliated corporation)

- One that relates to an indemnity or insurance to protect the director from liability

- One that is with an affiliated company[41]

There are situations where shareholders may approve a contract or transaction, even if there was a conflict of interest with a director or officer when the contract was entered into. For example, if Mike does not disclose that his brother is in the band that he is recommending, but later Javid and Mike find out, the shareholders of the corporation – Javid, Helena and Mike – can still decide that they want to hire the band for opening night. Subsection 132(8) of the *BCA* and subsection 120(7.1) of the *CBCA* describe the

---

40 *Business Corporations Act*, R.S.O. 1990, c. B.16, s. 132.
41 *Business Corporations Act*, R.S.O. 1990, c. B.16, s. 132(4) – 132(5); *Canada Business Corporations Act*, R.S.C. 1985, c. C-44, s. 120(4)–(5).

circumstances and process by which shareholders may approve a contract or transaction in which a director or officer has a conflict of interest.[42]

There are also situations, however, where the director or officer does not disclose the conflict of interest in a contract or transaction, and the shareholders or the corporation (through its board of directors) would like to set aside the contract or transaction. In this case, the *BCA* and *CBCA* both provide a remedy to the corporation and its shareholders – they can apply to the court for an order setting aside the contract or transaction, and directing that the officer or director that had the undisclosed conflict of interest account to the corporation for any profit or gain realized. The court may also make any other order that it thinks fit in the circumstances.[43]

Assume that Javid, Helena and Mike are directors of Entertainment Group Ltd. For their opening night event, Mike would like to recommend a band that his brother plays in. Mike does not tell Javid and Helena that his brother is in the band, because he thinks it is a great band and the fact that his brother is in the band is irrelevant. Javid and Helena agree to hire the band, relying on Mike's advice. On opening night, the band performs well but plays a different kind of music than what was advertised. The clientele is disappointed, and opening night is a disaster. Javid calculates that they lost about $20,000 that night in lost revenue and expenses. Javid and Helena then discover that Mike's brother was in the band. What can they do?

Avoiding a conflict of interest is a natural consequence of assigning a fiduciary duty to directors and officers of a corporation. As a result, it makes sense that directors are not allowed to make secret profits at the expense of the corporation, and that they are not allowed to take a "corporate opportunity" that rightfully belongs to the company. Both of these situations have been explored extensively in the caselaw. The following Supreme Court of Canada case discusses the concept of "corporate opportunity".

Canadian Aero Service Ltd. v. O'Malley (1973), [1974] S.C.R. 592 (S.C.C.)

The plaintiff-appellant ("Canaero") sued two of its directors (who were also senior officers) of the corporation for breach of fiduciary duty. The individuals being sued pursued government funding for a project in Guyana, on behalf of Canaero, from 1961 to 1965. Thereafter, they resigned from their positions at Canaero, incorporated a new company, and pursued the same project. The project was awarded to their newly incorporated company. Canaero sued on the basis that the defendants wrongfully took a corporate opportunity which they had first found and negotiated on behalf of Canaero.

The S.C.C. stated that both directors and officers owe a fiduciary duty to the corporation. The caselaw clearly establishes that this fiduciary duty prevents directors and officers from taking, or diverting to another party with whom they are associated, a business opportunity that the company is actively pursuing. This is true even after

---

42   *Business Corporations Act*, R.S.O. 1990, c. B.16, s. 132(8); *Canada Business Corporations Act*, R.S.C. 1985, c. C-44, s. 120(7.1).
43   *Business Corporations Act*, R.S.O. 1990, c. B.16, s. 132(9); *Canada Business Corporations Act*, R.S.C. 1985, c. C-44, s. 120(8).

the director or officer has resigned, if the reason for the resignation was to pursue that business opportunity, or where his previous position with the company led him to that opportunity.

The court acknowledged that obtaining a profit at the corporation's expense is clearly a breach of fiduciary duty. However, it also indicated that there may be situations where a breach of fiduciary duty might occur even if the corporation was not able to take advantage of the opportunity, because directors and officers must not use their positions in a corporation in order to reap a personal profit.

Directors and officers must exhibit loyalty, good faith and avoidance of conflict of duty and self-interest, because of the degree of control which their positions give them in corporate operations. Strict application of this principle is necessary, the court stated, to protect the public interest.

Finally, the court held that:

> The general standards of loyalty, good faith and avoidance of a conflict of duty and self-interest to which the conduct of a director or senior officer must conform, must be tested in each case by many factors which it would be reckless to attempt to enumerate exhaustively. Among them are the factor of position or office held, the nature of the corporate opportunity, its ripeness, its specificness and the director's or managerial officer's relation to it, the amount of knowledge possessed, the circumstances in which it was obtained and whether it was special or, indeed, even private, the factor of time in the continuation of fiduciary duty where the alleged breach occurs after termination of the relationship with the company, and the circumstances under which the relationship was terminated, that is whether by retirement or resignation or discharge.

The appeal was allowed against the directors of the corporation, and damages of $125,000 were awarded against them.

3. Officers

(a) The Roles and Responsibilities of Officers

The officers of a corporation are the individuals who are hired to be part of the senior management team. Most non-offering corporations will have, at minimum, a President and a Secretary-Treasurer (although the role of the Secretary can be kept separate from the role of the Treasurer.) Large, public corporations may have an extensive management team. Walmart, for example, has the following "Executive Officers" listed in its 2011 Annual Report:

1. C.E.O. (Chief Executive Officer)

2. Executive Vice-President, President and CEO, Walmart International

3. Executive Vice-President, President and CEO, Walmart U.S.

4. Executive Vice-President, President and CEO of Sam's Club

5. Executive Vice-President, General Counsel and Corporate Secretary

6. Executive Vice-President, People Division

7. Executive Vice-President, Corporate Affairs

8. Executive Vice-President, Chief Information Officer

9. Executive Vice-President and Chief Financial Officer

10. Senior Vice President and Controller

11. Vice Chairman, responsible for Global eCommerce and Global Sourcing[44]

While the President and C.E.O. is considered the highest position amongst officers, the other positions listed above are in no particular order. (In Walmart's 2011 Annual Report, they are listed in alphabetical order according to the individual's last name.) Walmart also includes the Chairman of the Board of Directors as a member of the group of Executive Officers,[45] implying that the Chairman of the Board of Directors participates in meetings (and other functions) of this group. Strictly speaking, however, the role of "Chairman of the Board" is a role held by a director of the corporation.

The *BCA* discusses officers in section 133, as follows:

133. Subject to the articles, the by-laws or any unanimous shareholder agreement,

(a) the directors may designate the offices of the corporation, appoint officers, specify their duties and delegate to them powers to manage the business and affairs of the corporation, except, subject to section 184, powers to do anything referred to in subsection 127 (3);

(b) a director may be appointed to any office of the corporation; and

(c) two or more offices of the corporation may be held by the same person. R.S.O. 1990, c. B.16, s. 133.[46]

The corresponding provision is the *CBCA* is virtually identical.[47]

As these provisions indicate, directors decide what offices (positions) to have in the management team, and who to appoint to those positions. Directors also determine what the officers' responsibilities are, and how much each member of the management team will get paid.[48] In part 2 of this chapter, we indicated that directors make the strategic decisions relating to the corporation and its business. Officers – at least, in theory – are the individuals who implement the strategic decisions made by the board of directors. This is why they are in the second level of the pyramid shown at the beginning of the chapter. For example, if the board of directors of Entertainment Group Ltd. decides to look for a location for the nightclub in downtown Toronto, it will be the officers who actually visit different premises and recommend a specific location for the nightclub. Similarly, if the board decides to market the nightclub as one that plays a particular type of music, then it will be the officers who identify the bands or DJs that will actually play at the nightclub. The officers' mandate, according to the *BCA* and *CBCA*, is to "manage

---

44 *Walmart 2011 Annual Report*, 2011 Walmart Executive Officers, http://walmartstores.com/sites/annualreport/2011/officers.aspx.

45 *Ibid.*

46 *Business Corporations Act*, R.S.O. 1990, c. B. 16, s. 133.

47 *Canada Business Corporations Act*, R.S.C. 1985, c. C-44, s.121.

48 *Business Corporations Act*, R.S.O. 1990, c. B.16, s. 137; *Canada Business Corporations Act*, R.S.C. 1985, c. C-44, s.125.

the business and affairs of corporation," within certain limits.[49] On an ongoing basis, the officers will hire and supervise employees, identify and deal with suppliers, obtain marketing materials, and do all the day-to-day activities involved in managing a business.

In the case of Entertainment Group Ltd. and most non-offering corporations, the roles of officers and directors, and their decision-making powers, seem to merge because, in many cases, the directors are also officers. Subsection 133(b) of the *BCA* and subsection 121(b) of the *CBCA* permit a director to also be an officer of the corporation.[50] However, as the corporation becomes larger, it often becomes necessary to have different people in the roles of director and officer in order to manage the workload – and this is when the different roles, responsibilities and powers of directors and officers become more important. (Recall that a director who is also an officer of the corporation is often referred to as an "inside director".)

Note that section 133(c) of the *BCA* and the corresponding section 121(c) of the *CBCA* also state that one person can hold more than one position as an officer.[51] In many cases, legal professionals will incorporate a company with only one person – and that person will serve as the sole director, the President and Secretary-Treasurer. The office of the President is viewed as the leader of the management team, with overriding decision-making authority amongst the other officers. The Secretary of the corporation is the officer that ensures that all government, tax and other legal requirements of the corporation are fulfilled. It is a critical role that requires some knowledge of corporate and tax law, but individuals without that knowledge can certainly obtain guidance from legal professionals. The Treasurer of the corporation also plays a critical role in managing the financial assets of the corporation, and in ensuring that accounting records are maintained accurately. Again, the Treasurer may seek the assistance of an accounting professional, when required.

(b) Officers' Duties & Liability

As indicated in part 1(b) of this chapter, the provisions that discuss the duties and standards of care for directors, also apply to officers. Section 134 of the *BCA* states:

> 134(1) Every director and officer of a corporation in exercising his or her powers and discharging his or her duties to the corporation shall,
>
> (a) act honestly and in good faith with a view to the best interests of the corporation; and
>
> (b) exercise the care, diligence and skill that a reasonably prudent person would exercise in comparable circumstances. R.S.O. 1990, c. B.16, s. 134 (1); 2006, c. 34, Sched. B, s. 24.
>
> . . .
>
> (2) Every director and officer of a corporation shall comply with this Act, the regulations, articles, by-laws and any unanimous shareholder agreement. R.S.O. 1990, c. B.16, s. 134 (2).

---

49 *Business Corporations Act*, R.S.O. 1990, c. B.16, s. 133; *Canada Business Corporations Act*, R.S.C. 1985, c. C-44, s.121.

50 *Business Corporations Act*, R.S.O. 1990, c. B.16, s. 133(b); *Canada Business Corporations Act*, R.S.C. 1985, c. C-44, s.121(b).

51 *Business Corporations Act*, R.S.O. 1990, c. B.16, s. 133(c); *Canada Business Corporations Act*, R.S.C. 1985, c. C-44, s.121(c).

. . .

(3) Subject to subsection 108 (5), no provision in a contract, the articles, the by-laws or a resolution relieves a director or officer from the duty to act in accordance with this Act and the regulations or relieves him or her from liability for a breach thereof.[52]

The comparable provision in the *CBCA* is section 122.[53] As these provisions have been discussed in part 2 of this chapter, we will not discuss them again here. In addition, the caselaw indicates that the fiduciary duties of directors also apply to officers. Please refer to the *Canadian Aero Service Ltd. v. O'Malley*[54] case, summarized earlier in this chapter.

Note that the corporation can indemnify officers (as well as directors), and can purchase liability insurance for key officers as well. Both of these topics were discussed in part 2(b) of this chapter.

In part 2(c), we discussed the issue of conflict of interest in relation to directors. Those provisions also apply to officers, as specified in the *BCA* and the *CBCA*.[55] Subsection 132(3) of the BCA states, in relation to disclosure of a conflict of interest by an officer who is not a director:

The disclosure required by subsection (1) shall be made, in the case of an officer who is not a director,

(a) forthwith after the officer becomes aware that the contract or transaction or proposed contract or transaction is to be considered or has been considered at a meeting of directors;

(b) if the officer becomes interested after a contract is made or a transaction is entered into, forthwith after he or she becomes so interested; or

(c) if a person who is interested in a contract or transaction later becomes an officer, forthwith after he or she becomes an officer.[56]

4. Related Issues

(a) Indoor Management Rule

As we have discussed in this chapter, directors and officers have distinct roles in the corporation. In day-to-day business transactions, however, most people who do business with the corporation will not know the details of the corporate structure or of specific powers or limitations provided in the corporation's Articles of Incorporation or by-laws. Can the corporation get out of a business transaction by saying that the person who entered into it did not have the authority to do so?

---

52 *Business Corporations Act*, R.S.O. 1990, c. B.16, s. 134.
53 *Canada Business Corporations Act*, R.S.C. 1985, c. C-44, s.122.
54 *Canadian Aero Service Ltd. v. O'Malley* (1973), 1973 CarswellOnt 236, 1973 CarswellOnt 236F, [1974] S.C.R. 592 (S.C.C.).
55 *Business Corporations Act*, R.S.O. 1990, c. B. 16, s. 132(3); *Canada Business Corporations Act*, R.S.C. 1985, c. C-44, s.120(3).
56 *Business Corporations Act*, R.S.O. 1990, c. B. 16, s. 132(3)

> Assume that Javid, Helena and Mike agree that, for contracts over $5,000, all three of them must sign the contract to approve it. Javid is the President and Secretary-Treasurer of Entertainment Group Ltd., Helena is the Vice-President, Operations and Mike is the Marketing Manager. Helena orders unique furniture for the nightclub, at a cost of $25,000. She gives the supplier a business card which states that she is the Vice-President, Operations. She also tells him that she is a director of the corporation, and that she has full authority to sign the contract. After the contract is signed, Helena presents it to Javid and Mike, who are very upset. While the furniture is very unique, it is far more expensive than what they had budgeted. In the meantime, the furniture is shipped to Entertainment Group Ltd., and when Helena tells the supplier that she wants to cancel the contract, he tells her that she must honour it. Can Entertainment Group Ltd. escape the obligation to pay for the furniture by stating that Helena did not have the authority to enter into the contract?

Section 19 of the *BCA* provides:

A corporation or a guarantor of an obligation of a corporation may not assert against a person dealing with the corporation or with any person who has acquired rights from the corporation that,

    (a) the articles, by-laws or any unanimous shareholder agreement have not been complied with;

    (b) the persons named in the most recent notice filed under the *Corporations Information Act*, or named in the articles, whichever is more current, are not the directors of the corporation;

    (c) the location named in the most recent notice filed under subsection 14 (3) or named in the articles, whichever is more current, is not the registered office of the corporation;

[**Note:** On a day to be named by proclamation of the Lieutenant Governor, clause (c) is amended by striking out "subsection 14 (3)" and substituting "the *Corporations Information Act*". See: 2011, c. 1, Sched. 2, ss. 1 (4), 9 (2).]

    (d) a person held out by a corporation as a director, an officer or an agent of the corporation has not been duly appointed or does not have authority to exercise the powers and perform the duties that are customary in the business of the corporation or usual for such director, officer or agent;

    (e) a document issued by any director, officer or agent of a corporation with actual or usual authority to issue the document is not valid or not genuine; or

    (f) a sale, lease or exchange of property referred to in subsection 184 (3) was not authorized,

except where the person has or ought to have, by virtue of the person's position with or relationship to the corporation, knowledge to that effect.[57]

---

57 *Business Corporations Act*, R.S.O. 1990, c. B.16, s. 19; *Canada Business Corporations Act*, R.S.C. 1985, c. C-44, s.18.

This provision of the *BCA* (and the corresponding provision in the *CBCA*) is referred to as the "indoor management rule".[58]

In order to allow corporations to enter into transactions freely, it is essential that suppliers, customers and others be able to assume that those individuals who hold themselves out to be in a position of authority, are in fact able to enter into the transactions which they say they can enter into. If this was not the case, customers and suppliers would hesitate to enter into contracts with corporations, or would require formal verification of the corporate structure before entering into contracts. Both of these options would make the corporation a less desirable vehicle for running a business. Requiring formal verification of the corporate structure may seem like a simple thing to do, but it would add time and cost to each transaction. Imagine a large corporation the size of a college or university. Would it be practical for each supplier of paper, pens, markers, erasers, etc. to require confirmation of corporate structure before agreeing to provide those supplies to the corporation? Many corporations enter into hundreds (or even more) transactions in a day. Making it difficult for those corporations to do business would, ultimately, be detrimental to the economic growth of the province and the country.

As a result, section 19 of the *BCA* and section 18 of the *CBCA* provide protection to "persons dealing with the corporation" and "any person who has acquired rights from the corporation".[59] Those persons can assume that:

(a) the articles, by-laws or, if applicable, the unanimous shareholder agreement of a corporation have been complied with

(b) the persons named in certain government or legal records as directors of the corporation, are in fact the directors

(c) the location of the registered office is the location stated in certain government or legal records

(d) a person who appears to be and acts as a director, officer or agent of the corporation, has the powers and performs the duties that are customary in the business

(e) a document provided by a director, officer or agent in the normal course of business is valid

(f) a sale, lease or exchange of property has been duly authorized,
except where that person knows or should know that these assumptions are false.[60]

For example, if Javid, Mike and Helena (as directors) agree to place restrictions on how much liquor Helena can order at one time (such as a maximum of $5,000 per order,) they must let the supplier of that liquor know, in advance, that she has that restriction. Otherwise, as Vice-President, Operations, she appears to have authority to order liquor on behalf of the corporation without restriction, and under the indoor management rule, the supplier would be entitled to assume that she can order as much liquor as she deems appropriate.

---

58 *Business Corporations Act*, R.S.O. 1990, c. B.16, s. 19.
59 *Ibid.*
60 *Ibid.*

Ramey v. Winkleigh Co-operative Housing Corp., 2010 CarswellOnt 6357 (Ont. S.C.J.)

The plaintiff was a contractor carrying on business as Ramey's Contracting. The defendant housing corporation ("Winkleigh") was a not-for-profit corporation that provided subsidized and low-cost housing. Mary Mullins, also a defendant, was a resident and also director and treasurer of the housing corporation. She knew the plaintiff personally, as he was the grandfather of her two children. In the fall of 2005, the plaintiff was hired to be a "handyman" for Winkleigh, after being told of the opportunity by Mullins and then meeting with the chairman of Winkleigh's board of directors. Clarissa Powell, another defendant, was an employee of Winkleigh, and signed certain documentation approving the employment arrangement with the plaintiff. The plaintiff testified that Powell told him that "everything had to go through the board." Mullins was told by the chairman of Winkleigh's board that she had to resign, because she had not disclosed her personal relationship with the plaintiff. After reviewing this and other evidence, the court found that the plaintiff was aware that all contracts had to be approved by the board of directors in order to be binding. There were subsequent contracts with the plaintiff, signed by Powell and Mullins without approval by the board of directors. The plaintiff is suing for breach of contract, for amounts owing to him under those contracts.

One of the bases for the plaintiff's claim was reliance on s. 19 of the *BCA*, the indoor management rule.

> Section 19 represents a codification of the common law 'indoor management rule' which originated in the English case of *Royal British Bank v. Turquand* (1856), 119 E.R. 886 (Eng. Exch.) . . .
>
> The rule provides that 'if a corporation makes a representation to a third party by holding someone out as a director, officer, or agent, the corporation cannot deny that the person is duly appointed or that she has the authority customary or usual for such a director, officer, or agent.' See Van Duzer, J. Anthony, The Law of Partnerships and Corporations, 3d Ed. (Toronto, Irwin Law, 2009) at 217. The rule is based upon the general principle of agency law that acts of an agent bind the principal to the extent that those acts are within the actual, usual or apparent authority of the agent. The policy underlying the rule is that 'third parties should not have to worry about whether internal housekeeping is in order', (Van Duzer, supra, at 218). The purpose of the rule and s. 19 of the O.B.C.A. is to ensure that internal corporate restrictions on authority or failure of the corporation to follow its procedures do not stand in the way of its obligations to a third party.

However, the court emphasized that section 19 of the *BCA* has a very important qualifier or condition – a third party cannot benefit from the protection provided in section 19 if he knew or ought to have known that the person who he was dealing with did not have proper authority to bind the corporation.

In this case, the court held that the plaintiff did know that all contracts required prior approval of the board of directors, and so he could not rely upon section 19 of the *BCA* to receive compensation. (The court did award judgment to the plaintiff on alternate grounds.)

The indoor management rule does not always work against the corporation, as we can see from the next case summarized in this chapter.

Pacific National Leasing Corp. (Receiver of) v. Marina Travel Agency Ltd., 1999 CarswellOnt 385 (Ont. C.A.)

Network Leasing ("NL") entered into a contract to lease computer equipment with Marina Travel Agency Ltd. ("Marina"). The contract was assigned by NL to Pacific National Leasing Corp. ("Pacific"), who is suing under the contract. The contract was signed by Maurizio, on behalf of Marina. However, Maurizio was not an officer, director or shareholder of Marina, and he did not have signing authority at the bank. Maurizio was the son of Aurelio, the sole shareholder and President of Marina, and Maurizio signed this contract when Aurelio was out of the country. Aurelio did not know about the contract, and did not authorize it. Maurizio (who had worked for Marina as a travel agent for 10 or 11 years) signed his own name and his father's name on various documents related to the contract. Aurelio discovered the situation when he returned to the country and found withdrawals being made from Marina's bank account, and upon discovery of the situation, he fired Maurizio.

The court found that, based on the evidence, Maurizio did not have actual authority to enter into the contract. However, the plaintiff relied on the indoor management rule in section 19 of the *BCA* and argued that the defendant was liable under the contract.

The court stated that section 19: "only applies if the corporation has 'held out' the agent as having authority either by appointing that person to a position which would normally carry such authority or by representing that the person has been appointed to such a position or by some other specific representation . . . [S]uch latter representation may be expressed or may be implied by a course of conduct."

In this case, there was never any contact between NL and Marina; the only person they dealt with was Maurizio. Maurizio signed all of the documents in his own name, except for the Pre-Authorized Payments form and cheque (on which he forged his father's signature.) Aurelio knew nothing about the contract and never authorized it. The court held that:

> Maurizio held himself out as being authorized by Marina to enter into the contracts but . . . there was not such a representation from the corporation and, indeed, I find that the corporation . . . neither authorized [n]or held out Maurizio as having authority to enter into the contract and, indeed, that the corporation was not aware of the contract.

Moreover, the onus was on the plaintiff to show that Marina had given Maurizio authority to act on the corporation's behalf, either by expressly stating that he had that authority or through its conduct. (The plaintiff would also have to show that it relied on that representation to its detriment.) The plaintiff failed to satisfy that onus, and the court held that Marina was not liable under the contract. (Note that a second issue, which is not summarized here, also led to the same conclusion regarding liability.)

The action was dismissed at trial, and that decision was affirmed by the Court of Appeal.

(b) Insider Liability

Directors, officers, and shareholders of a corporation can have confidential information about a corporation that they can use for their own personal benefit. Just as directors and officers cannot be involved in a conflict of interest situation, directors, officers and shareholders cannot use confidential information about the corporation in a way that creates an advantage for themselves, particularly by affecting the price of shares in the corporation.

Section 138 of the *BCA* deals with "Insider Liability" *with respect to a non-offering corporation* and provides:

> (5) An insider who, in connection with a transaction in a security of the corporation or any of its affiliates, makes use of any specific confidential information for the insider's own benefit or advantage that, if generally known, might reasonably be expected to affect materially the value of the security,
>
> > (a) is liable to compensate any person for any direct loss suffered by that person as a result of the transaction, unless the information was known or in the exercise of reasonable diligence should have been known to that person; and
> >
> > (b) is accountable to the corporation for any direct benefit or advantage received or receivable by the insider as a result of the transaction.[61]

An "insider" includes:

- the corporation (in this section, a non-offering corporation)

- an affiliate, director or officer of the corporation

- a shareholder owning or controlling more than 10% of the voting shares of the corporation

- a person employed or retained by the corporation

- a person who receives confidential information from any other insider, knowing that the person who provides the information is an insider

- another corporation, in certain circumstances (such as amalgamation)[62]

For *CBCA* corporations, refer to sections 126–131 of the *CBCA*[63] for provisions on insider trading. Note that the area of "insider trading" in public corporations is also addressed by the *Securities Act*[64] in Ontario, and is beyond the scope of this textbook. (Refer to reference material on securities law for more information on this topic.) Finally, as we have discussed earlier in this chapter, the caselaw also indicates that directors and officers have a fiduciary duty to the corporation, as such, they must not misuse confidential information for their own personal benefit.[65]

---

61 *Business Corporations Act*, R.S.O. 1990, c. B.16, s. 138(5).
62 *Ibid.*, s. 138(1)–(3).
63 R.S.C. 1985, c. C-44, ss. 126–131.
64 R.S.O. 1990, c. S.5
65 See *Canadian Aero Service Ltd. v. O'Malley* (1973), 1973 CarswellOnt 236, 1973 CarswellOnt 236F, [1974] S.C.R. 592 (S.C.C.), summarized earlier in this chapter.

CHAPTER 7: THE "CORPORATE PLAYERS" – SHAREHOLDERS

Overview:

- Who are shareholders?
- Duties, liabilities and general powers
- Unanimous shareholder agreement
- Oppression remedy
- Derivative actions
- Right to Dissent
- Shareholder Agreements
- Workbook:
  - Review Exercise
- Appendix:
  - Checklist for Comprehensive Shareholder Agreement

1. Who Are Shareholders?

In Chapter 6, we identified the "corporate players" as being divided into three groups: directors, officers and shareholders. Recall that only one person is required to form a corporation, [1] but even if there is only one incorporator, that person must play each of the roles depicted in the diagram below:

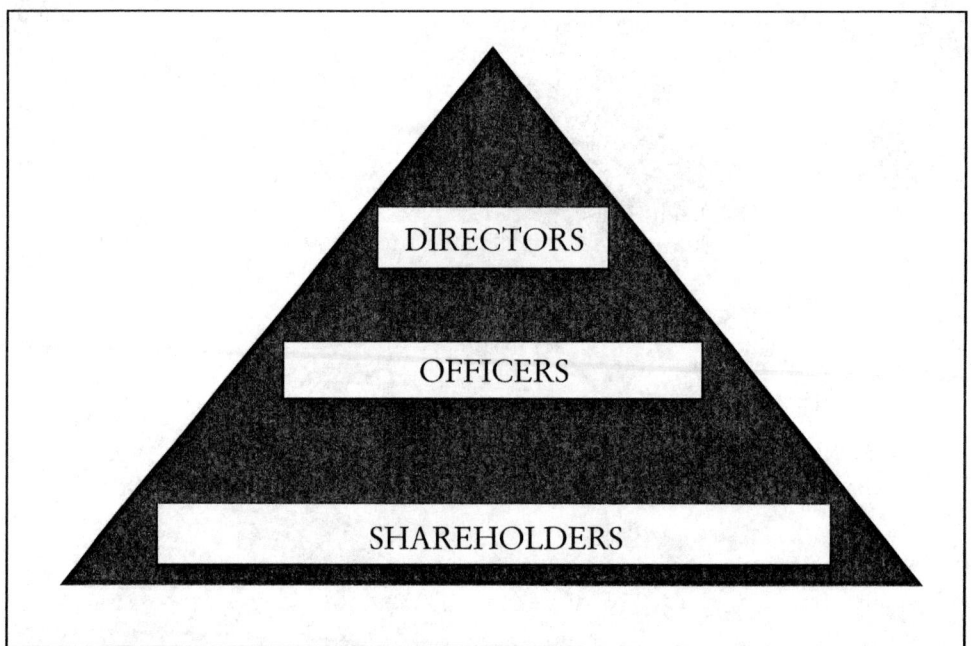

How can one incorporator be a director, officer and shareholder? He can be a director, officer and shareholder at the same time, in the same way that a person can be a husband, father and son at the same time. When the same person is performing all three roles in the corporation, the duties, liabilities and responsibilities that relate to each role become blurred in practice, because the same person is doing everything. However, as you have more people involved in the corporation, knowing "who does what" in the corporation becomes increasingly important. It also becomes very important to understand the powers and liabilities that are assigned to each role.

In Chapter 6, we discussed directors and officers. Directors are at the top of the pyramid shown above because they are typically fewer in number, but they have the most power in a corporation (at least, theoretically.) Officers are in the middle tier because they actually manage the corporation, under the direction and supervision of the directors. Typically, there are also more officers than directors (although this may not always be the case.) In this chapter, we will focus on the lowest layer in the pyramid – the shareholders.

---

1 *Business Corporations Act*, R.S.O. 1990, c. B.16, s. 4(1); *Canada Business Corporations Act*, R.S.C. 1985, c. C-44, s. 5(1).

It may surprise some readers to learn that the shareholders are the owners of the corporation. Shareholders are the individuals that invest money in the corporation. If this is the case, why are they "at the bottom of the pyramid", so to speak? While shareholders are usually the largest group amongst directors, officers and shareholders, they have the least amount of decision-making power in a corporation (unless they enter into a unanimous shareholder agreement, which will be discussed later in this chapter.) Shareholders generally do not make business decisions, and by law, their ability to affect the financial direction of the corporation is limited. Note, however, that in a non-offering corporation, it is very common for the shareholders to also be officers and/or directors. As a result of these additional roles (as officers and/or directors,) they are able to participate in decision-making. However, if these individuals are only shareholders, their role in the day-to-day activities of the corporation is minimal, except in certain circumstances which will be discussed later in this chapter.

2. Duties, Liabilities & General Powers

Unlike directors and officers, shareholders can act completely in their own self-interest. Shareholders do not owe a duty to the corporation. Caselaw has also established that majority shareholders and directors generally do not owe a fiduciary duty to minority shareholders, unless there are special circumstances, which create a special relationship of trust amongst the parties. "Courts impose fiduciary duties only in situations where someone stands in a particular position of trust by virtue of an agreement or as a result of the circumstances and relationship of the parties."[2] Rather, caselaw emphasizes that votes (attached to shares) are proprietary rights, and a shareholder can exercise those votes with his or her own selfish motives. A shareholder has no obligation to act in the best interest of the corporation, and may even enter into agreements with other shareholders to vote in a particular way. It will only be in limited circumstances that the courts will intervene to prevent a "fraud on the minority."[3]

A key benefit of being a shareholder is found in subsection 92(1) of the *BCA*:

92(1) The shareholders of a corporation are not, as shareholders, liable for any act, default, obligation or liability of the corporation except under subsection 34 (5), subsection 108 (5) and section 243. R.S.O. 1990, c. B.16, s. 92 (1).

[**Note:** On a day to be named by proclamation of the Lieutenant Governor, subsection (1) is amended by striking out "except under subsection 34 (5), subsection 108 (5) and section 243" at the end and substituting "except under subsections 34 (5), 108 (5) and 130 (5) and section 243". See: 2011, c. 1, Sched. 2, ss. 1 (6), 9 (2).[4]]

Subsection 45(1) of the *CBCA* is substantially the same.[5] Recall that the reason that many individuals choose to incorporate is the limited liability that the owners have in a corporation as shareholders. In this way, the shareholders' personal assets are protected, and only the corporation's assets can be pursued by creditors and others.

---

2 *Brant Investments Ltd. v. KeepRite Inc.*, 1991 CarswellOnt 133, 3 O.R. (3d) 289 (Ont. C.A.).

3 *Benson v. Third Canadian General Investment Trust Ltd.*, 1993 CarswellOnt 166, 14 O.R. (3d) 493 (Ont. Gen. Div. [Commercial List]).

4 *Business Corporations Act*, R.S.O. 1990, c. B.16, s. 92(1).

5 *Canada Business Corporations Act*, R.S.C. 1985, c. C-44, s. 495(1).

> Assume that Javid's uncle, Sam Khan, would like to invest in Entertainment Group Ltd., but because Sam lives in Quebec, he cannot be involved with the management of the business. As a result, Sam, Javid, Helena and Mike become the shareholders of Entertainment Group Ltd., and only Javid, Helena and Mike become directors and officers. After hearing nothing from Javid, Helena and Mike for several months, Sam starts getting concerned. Can he demand to see the corporation's financial records? What can he do to get some information about how the business is operating?

While shareholders cannot interfere with the day-to-day operations of the corporation and cannot force directors to make certain decisions, they do have certain powers which can influence business decisions. A critical power that shareholders have is the ability to elect the directors (who in turn, will appoint officers.) If a shareholder does not think that a director is doing a good job, the shareholder can vote for a different person to become director at the shareholders' annual meeting. As a result, a shareholder who controls a majority of shares in the corporation, in practice, actually controls the corporation by his or her ability to elect the board of directors that he or she desires. As stated in the dictum of Viscount Simon, L.C. in *British American Tobacco Co. v. Inland Revenue Commissioners* at p. 15: "The owners of the majority of the voting power of a company are the persons who are in effective control of its affairs and functions."[6]

The *BCA* and *CBCA* also give shareholders the right to appoint an auditor who will review the financial statements of the corporation and provide a report to the shareholders at their annual shareholders' meeting.[7] Since shareholders do not have the right to view financial statements of the corporation at any time, they are dependent upon the information provided to them by directors at shareholders' meetings. Having an auditor gives the shareholders some security in knowing that an impartial third party has reviewed the financial statements of the corporation, and has indicated that they have been prepared according to the standards of the accounting profession. However, hiring an auditor can be expensive, and may not make sense for corporations in which all of the shareholders are also directors of the corporation – or in a situation where the corporation is clearly unable to pay for the services of an auditor. For this reason, the *BCA* also provides that a non-offering corporation can be exempt from the requirements of appointing an auditor for a given year, if all of the shareholders of the corporation consent in writing. This issue must be addressed by the shareholders every year, as the exemption is only valid for that year.[8] The provisions in the *CBCA* are almost identical; however, consent to exempt the corporation from appointing an auditor must be obtained from all shareholders, *including those that are normally not entitled to vote.*[9]

Subsection 108(1) of the *BCA* and subsection 145.1 of the *CBCA* give shareholders the power to create "voting blocks" amongst themselves. In other words, shareholders

---

6 *British American Tobacco Co. v. Inland Revenue Commissioners* (1942), [1943] 1 All E.R. 13 (U.K. H.L.).

7 *Business Corporations Act*, R.S.O. 1990, c. B.16, ss. 148 – 160; *Canada Business Corporations Act*, R.S.C. 1985, c. C-44, ss. 160–172.

8 *Business Corporations Act*, R.S.O. 1990, c. B.16, s. 148.

9 *Canada Business Corporations Act*, R.S.C. 1985, c. C-44, s. 163.

can have a written agreement amongst themselves to exercise their voting rights in a particular way.[10] For example, in Entertainment Group Ltd., assume that Javid has more shares than either Helena or Mike, and therefore, he has more votes as a shareholder than either Helena or Mike. In order to ensure that both Helena and Mike remain directors and are not ousted by Javid, Helena and Mike can enter into a written agreement which indicates that they will both vote for each other to become directors of the corporation. In this way, they can ensure that they retain some control over the corporation as directors. Unless otherwise stated in the Articles of Incorporation, each share of a corporation entitles the shareholder to one vote.[11]

Finally, a corporation must hold an annual meeting of its shareholders not later than 18 months after its incorporation, and after that, not more than 15 months after the last annual meeting.[12] At this meeting, shareholders can raise any matter relevant to the affairs and business of the corporation. The following standard matters will also be addressed:

- consideration of the minutes of an earlier meeting

- consideration of the financial statements and auditor's report (if any)

- elections of directors

- appointment of the auditor (or waiver of the right to appoint an auditor)

Generally speaking, shareholders in an offering corporation must receive at least 21 days notice of the annual shareholders' meeting, whereas shareholders in a non-offering corporation must receive at least 10 days notice. In both cases, the notice of the annual shareholders' meeting must not exceed 50 days. The directors may also call a special meeting of the shareholders at any time.[13] Sections 95 to 108 of the *BCA* address procedures and rights related to shareholders meetings, including (without limitation) notice requirements, voting rights, resolution of controversies and voting agreements. Please refer to these sections of the Act for more details on these matters.

Note that subsection 96(5) defines "special business" at a shareholders' annual meeting to be anything *other than*:

- consideration of minutes of an earlier meeting

- consideration of the financial statements and auditor's report

- election of directors, or

- reappointment of the incumbent auditor[14]

---

10 *Business Corporations Act*, R.S.O. 1990, c. B.16, s. 108(1); *Canada Business Corporations Act*, R.S.C. 1985, c. C-44, s. 145.1.

11 *Business Corporations Act*, R.S.O. 1990, c. B.16, s. 102(1); *Canada Business Corporations Act*, R.S.C. 1985, c. C-44, s. 140(1).

12 *Business Corporations Act*, R.S.O. 1990, c. B.16, s. 94(1); *Canada Business Corporations Act*, R.S.C. 1985, c. C-44, s. 133(1).

13 *Business Corporations Act*, R.S.O. 1990, c. B.16, s. 96(1); *Canada Business Corporations Act*, R.S.C. 1985, c. C-44, s. 133(2).

14 *Business Corporations Act*, R.S.O. 1990, c. B.16, s. 96(5); *Canada Business Corporations Act*, R.S.C. 1985, c. C-44, s. 135(5)–(6).

If special business is to be conducted at the shareholders' annual meeting, the notice sent to shareholders to inform them of the meeting must provide details of the special business, in order to allow them to make a reasoned judgement at the meeting. If a special resolution or by-law is to be submitted at the meeting, the text of that special resolution or by-law must accompany the notice.

3. Unanimous Shareholder Agreement

One of the most powerful tools that shareholders can use is the unanimous shareholder agreement. Subsections 108(2) and 108(3) of the *BCA* provide:

> (2) A written agreement among all the shareholders of a corporation or among all the shareholders and one or more persons who are not shareholders may restrict in whole or in part the powers of the directors to manage or supervise the management of the business and affairs of the corporation.

> *Unanimous shareholder agreement*

> (3) Where a person who is the registered holder of all the issued shares of a corporation makes a written declaration that restricts in whole or in part the powers of the directors to manage or supervise the management of the business and affairs of a corporation, the declaration shall be deemed to be a unanimous shareholder agreement.[15]

The *CBCA* has similar provisions regarding a unanimous shareholder agreement.[16]

A unanimous shareholder agreement is an agreement amongst all of the shareholders of the corporation that, essentially, allows the shareholders to take over the corporation. In other words, the directors' powers to supervise or manage the supervision of the corporation are usurped, and the shareholders begin to play the role of directors. Subsection 108(5) of the *BCA* states:

> A shareholder who is a party to a unanimous shareholder agreement has all the rights, powers, duties and liabilities of a director of a corporation, whether arising under this Act or otherwise, including any defences available to the directors, to which the agreement relates to the extent that the agreement restricts the discretion or powers of the directors to manage or supervise the management of the business and affairs of the corporation and the directors are relieved of their duties and liabilities, including any liabilities under section 131, to the same extent.[17]

Subsection 146(5) of the *CBCA* is substantially the same.[18] The *BCA* and *CBCA* do not provide a detailed list of what can be in a unanimous shareholder agreement; instead, subsection 108(6) of the *BCA* simply states that the shareholder agreement may provide that:

- it can be amended in the manner described in the unanimous shareholder agreement, and

---

15 *Business Corporations Act*, R.S.O. 1990, c. B.16, s. 108(2)–(3).
16 *Canada Business Corporations Act*, R.S.C. 1985, c. C-44, s. 146(1)–(2).
17 *Business Corporations Act*, R.S.O. 1990, c. B.16, s. 108(5).
18 *Canada Business Corporations Act*, R.S.C. 1985, c. C-44, s. 146(5).

- any disputes or disagreements relating to the agreement may be referred to arbitration.[19]

(The *CBCA* does not have a similar provision.) In practice, however, the unanimous shareholder agreement can be a lengthy contract that specifies the powers that the shareholders are taking away from the directors, and how they intend to run the corporation.

Since the unanimous shareholder agreement requires all shareholders to sign the agreement, what happens if the corporation issues shares to a new shareholder that was not a party to the unanimous shareholder agreement? The *CBCA* simply states that a person who buys shares of a corporation that is subject to a unanimous shareholder agreement is automatically deemed to be a party to the unanimous shareholder agreement, and must abide by its terms; the same is true of a transferee that receives shares that are subject to a unanimous shareholder agreement.[20] The *BCA*, however, provides additional detail in subsection 108(6). It states that, if a unanimous shareholder agreement is in place when the corporation issues shares to a new shareholder, then:

(a) the new shareholder is deemed to be a party to the unanimous shareholder agreement, even if that person had no knowledge of the unanimous shareholder agreement when the shares were issued;

(b) the issue of shares does not terminate the unanimous shareholder agreement; and

(c) if the new shareholder purchased the shares without being informed of the unanimous shareholder agreement, the new shareholder may choose to return the shares (and rescind his/her contract with the corporation) within 60 days after the person receives a complete copy of the unanimous shareholder agreement.[21]

The *BCA* has similar provisions for a transfer of shares that are subject to a unanimous shareholder agreement.[22]

Note, however, that the share certificate obtained by a new shareholder must contain a reference to the unanimous shareholder agreement. (Share certificates are documents that indicate the number and type of shares of a corporation that a particular shareholder has acquired. A share certificate acts like a "receipt" for those shares, and is issued once the shares are sold or transferred by the corporation.) If the share certificates do not state that the shares are subject to a unanimous shareholder agreement, the purchaser of those shares may send a notice of objection to the corporation and may, ultimately, choose to return the shares and rescind his/her contract with the corporation, or demand compensation from a transferee of those shares.[23]

Finally, with reference to unanimous shareholder agreements, subsection 108(5.1) states that "[n]othing in this section prevents shareholders from fettering their discretion when exercising the power of directors under a unanimous shareholder agreement."[24] As

---

19 *Business Corporations Act*, R.S.O. 1990, c. B.16, s. 108(6).
20 *Ibid.*, s. 146(3).
21 *Business Corporations Act*, R.S.O. 1990, c. B.16, s. 108(7).
22 *Ibid.*, s. 108(8).
23 *Ibid.*, s. 108(10)–(11).
24 *Ibid.*, s. 108(5.1).

described in the *Duha Printers*[25] case summarized later in this chapter, the common law (prior to the introduction of the *CBCA* and other corporate statutes) did not allow shareholders to fetter – or interfere with – the powers of the directors, even if all the shareholders agreed to do so. Statutory intervention was required in order to allow a unanimous shareholder agreement to supplant the power of the directors. Subsection 146(6) of the *CBCA* is identical to subsection 108(5.1) of the *BCA*.

Duha Printers (Western) Ltd. v. R., [1998] 1 S.C.R. 795 (S.C.C.)

In this case, the Supreme Court of Canada was asked to define "control" for the purposes of s. 111(5) of the *Income Tax Act*, which required consideration of a unanimous shareholder agreement ("USA"). In this regard, the SCC held that a unanimous shareholder agreement is part of the "corporate constitution", along with the corporation's Articles of Incorporation and by-laws. It pointed out that, prior to the statutory provisions for USAs in the *CBCA* and other statutes, the shareholders could not control the day-to-day business decisions of directors and officers, and their power was essentially limited to electing and dismissing directors. The common law also prevented shareholders from agreeing, even unanimously, to interfere (or fetter) the discretion of directors.

Statutory changes to the *CBCA* and other statutes changed the common law. Several key provisions of the *CBCA* are made subject to the Articles of Incorporation, by-laws and/or a USA. It is clear that the legislators gave the USA the same importance as the Articles of Incorporation and by-laws of the corporation. The SCC stated:

> The advent of the USA, first in the *CBCA* and then in other statutes modeled after it, materially altered this situation by providing a mechanism by which the shareholders, through a unanimous agreement, could strip the directors of some or all of their managerial powers as desired by the shareholders. Rather than removing the directors from their positions, a USA simply relieves them of their powers, rights, duties, and associated responsibilities. This may be accomplished without specific formality; all that is required appears to be some unanimous written expression of shareholder will. . . .
>
> The result, however, amounts to a fundamental change in the management of the company, as s. 140(5) of the *Corporations Act* provides that the shareholders who are parties to the USA assume all the rights, powers, duties and liabilities of the directors which are removed by the agreement, and. that the directors are relieved of their duties and liabilities to the same extent. As I have already intimated, what is in effect created is an 'incorporated partnership' with statutory force.

(This case will not be summarized in its entirety; its primary focus is income tax law, which is beyond the scope of this textbook.)

---

4. Oppression Remedy

One of the most powerful remedies that have been provided to shareholders by corporate statutes such as the *CBCA* and the *BCA* is the oppression remedy. "Oppression" is a legal term that has been discussed in the caselaw, but as a starting point, it is useful

---

25 *Duha Printers (Western) Ltd. v. R.*, 1998 CarswellNat 750, 1998 CarswellNat 751, (*sub nom.* Duha Printers (Western) Ltd. v. Canada) [1998] 1 S.C.R. 795 (S.C.C.).

to consider its definition in the Oxford Dictionaries: "inflicting harsh and authoritarian treatment."[26] The oppression remedy was, therefore, designed to assist shareholders – and others – who felt that they were being treated in a manner that was unfair, prejudicial or otherwise tainted with bad faith.

In the *BCA*, the oppression remedy is found in section 248, which reads as follows:

248(1) A complainant and, in the case of an offering corporation, the Commission may apply to the court for an order under this section. . . .

(2) Where, upon an application under subsection (1), the court is satisfied that in respect of a corporation or any of its affiliates,

   (a) any act or omission of the corporation or any of its affiliates effects or threatens to effect a result;

   (b) the business or affairs of the corporation or any of its affiliates are, have been or are threatened to be carried on or conducted in a manner; or

   (c) the powers of the directors of the corporation or any of its affiliates are, have been or are threatened to be exercised in a manner,

that is oppressive or unfairly prejudicial to or that unfairly disregards the interests of any security holder, creditor, director or officer of the corporation, the court may make an order to rectify the matters complained of.[27]

In the *CBCA*, the oppression remedy is found in section 241, and it is substantially the same as section 248 under the *BCA*.[28] As these provisions indicate, the oppression remedy is not limited to shareholders only – for Ontario companies, any "complainant" or the Ontario Securities Commission can apply to the court for the remedy. The term "complainant" is defined in section 245 of the *BCA* as:

   (a) a registered holder or beneficial owner, and a former registered holder or beneficial owner, of a security of a corporation or any of its affiliates,

   (b) a director or an officer or a former director or officer of a corporation or of any of its affiliates,

   (c) any other person who, in the discretion of the court, is a proper person to make an application under this Part.[29]

The relevant provisions of the *CBCA* are substantially the same, but provide that the Director under the *CBCA* (not the Ontario Securities Commission) may apply for the oppression remedy under the federal statute.[30] Note that subsection 248(2) of the *BCA* and subsection 241(2) of the *CBCA* specifically mention the interests of a creditor, and caselaw confirms that creditors may also apply for this remedy.

---

26 *Oxford Dictionaries Online* <http://oxforddictionaries.com/definition/oppressive>.
27 *Business Corporations Act*, R.S.O. 1990, c. B.16, s. 248(1)–(2).
28 *Canada Business Corporations Act*, R.S.C. 1985, c. C-44, s. 241.
29 *Business Corporations Act*, R.S.O. 1990, c. B.16, s. 245.
30 *Canada Business Corporations Act*, R.S.C. 1985, c. C-44, ss. 2 & 238.

1413910 Ontario Inc. v. McLennan (2009), 309 D.L.R. (4th) 756 (Ont. Div. Ct.)

The appellant, McLennan, was an officer, director and sole shareholder of a corporation that was also the sole shareholder of Select Restaurant Plaza Corporation ("Select"). The appellant elected her brother, McCullough, to be the president of Select. As a result, the appellant indirectly had control over and owned the shares of Select. The respondent corporation, 1413910 Ontario Inc. operating as Bulls Eye Steakhouse & Grill ("Bulls Eye,") was a tenant in a commercial plaza owned by Select.

In 2004, Bulls Eye was awarded damages in a lawsuit against Select for wrongful termination of its lease, and subsequent appeals were quashed. Damages were assessed and awarded in 2006, in the amount of $699,465.48. After judgment was first granted in 2004, Select sold the commercial plaza (in 2005) and, within days, approximately $3.8 million was deposited into the appellant's personal bank account. Prior to the closing of the sale, Bulls Eye made a motion to the court to appoint a receiver to control the sale of the plaza, or alternatively, to order Select to pay $600,000 into court pending assessment of Bulls Eye's damages. Based on evidence provided by McCullough at the motion, the judge did not grant the motion on the basis that there was no evidence that Select would remove assets from the jurisdiction or otherwise dissipate its assets to avoid paying Bulls Eye's judgment. Once damages were assessed in 2006, Select no longer had any assets to pay those damages (because the funds had been deposited into the appellant's personal bank account); as a result, Bulls Eye made an application to the court under s. 248(2) of the OBCA (the oppression remedy.)

The court held that Bulls Eye was a "creditor" under s. 248(2) of the OBCA, because it had a legal right to damages. There was no need to restrict the definition of "creditor" to à "judgment creditor" (someone who was owed money for repayment of a debt.) Both statutory and common law recognize that a creditor can include a person who has the right to require performance of any legal obligation, including someone who has a right to damages arising out of contract or tort.

The court stated that:

> [t]he oppression remedy is designed to address, where oppression is found, the imbalance of power on the part of those in control with the vulnerability on the part of those having a genuine stake in the affairs of corporation but no control over its conduct. In my view, a person to whom the corporation owes an obligation affirmed by judgment but as yet unquantified by assessment of damages, is in no less vulnerable position vis à vis the corporation and has no less a legitimate stake or interest in the manner in which the affairs of the corporation are conducted than one to whom a liquidated sum is owed.

With respect to whether or not there was oppression in these circumstances, the judge referred to *BCE Inc., Re*, 2008 SCC 69, 2008 CarswellQue 12595, 2008 CarswellQue 12596 (S.C.C.), which will be summarized later in this chapter. The court stated that, to find oppression, Bulls Eye must have had an objective, reasonable expectation that there would be funds available to satisfy its judgment, and that the thwarting of that expectation (by diverting funds elsewhere) amounted to oppression. The court held that Bulls Eye did have a reasonable expectation of being paid the damages that were owed to it, based on evidence provided in the motion to appoint a receiver. The court dismissed the appeal, with costs to the respondent (affirming the trial judge's decision to award Bulls Eye payment of its damages plus interest.)

As the following case illustrates, even an employee has been found to be a "complainant" for the purposes of the oppression remedy.

Fortnum v. Royal City Plymouth Chrysler (1991) Ltd., 2006 CarswellOnt 8362 (Ont. S.C.J.)

This case was an application by an employee for damages resulting from a breach of an employment contract with Royal City Plymouth Chrysler (1991) Ltd. ("Royal City"). The employee was terminated in January 2002, and Royal City was sold to another company in February 2002. In May 2004, the applicant was awarded damages in the amount of $125,000, plus interest and costs. In March and April of 2002, the proceeds of the sale of Royal City were deposited into the personal bank accounts of Chris and Georgina Stogios. While some of the proceeds were then transferred into Royal City's bank account, at least $220,000 was kept in the personal bank accounts of the Stogios, and additional funds were paid by Royal City to both Chris and Georgina Stogios subsequently. The applicant claimed that the actions of Chris and Georgina Stogios stripped Royal City of its assets, making the corporation unable to pay the damages owing to him. Chris Stogios was the sole director, officer and shareholder of Royal City, and Georgina Stogios was his wife.

> I agree with the view expressed by Farley J. in *Royal Trust Corp. of Canada v. Hordo* that debt actions should not "be routinely turned into oppression actions." . . .[C]reditors should not be elevated to the status of a "complainant" entitled to an oppression remedy where the creditor's interest "in the affairs of a corporation is too remote" or where the creditor has no "particular or legitimate interest in the manner in which the affairs of the company are managed." . . .
>
> [I]n order to have the necessary status to seek an oppression remedy, a party must establish he has a reasonable expectation that a company's affairs will be conducted with a view to protecting his interests.

The court held that, in this case, the applicant was a "complainant" for the purposes of s. 248(2) of the *OBCA*. He had notified Chris Stogios of his intention to sue the company for breach of his employment contract before the sale of the company took place, and as such, he had a reasonable expectation that Royal City would account for the amounts due to him from the proceeds of that sale, and he had taken reasonable steps to protect himself in the circumstances. The diversion of assets from Royal City to the respondents was conduct that was both unfairly prejudicial and unfairly disregarded the interests of the applicant, in favour of the personal interests of the director of the company.

Under s. 248(3) of the *OBCA*, the court can make any order that it sees fit. In this case, the court ordered that the Chris Stogios was personally liable for the amounts owing to the applicant. However, personal liability did not extend to his wife, as she was unaware of the circumstances leading to the transfer of assets to her bank account, and she had nothing to do with directing or controlling Royal City. Mr. Stogios was ordered to pay to the applicant the sum of $141,250.00, plus interest at the rate of 4% per year from May 20, 2004 to the date of payment or judgment.

Both the *BCA* and the *CBCA* give the court broad powers to "rectify the matters complained of",[31] but they also list the kinds of orders that a court may make under the oppression remedy, such as:

- an order to restrain oppressive conduct

- an order appointing a receiver or a receiver-manager

- an order amending the Articles of Incorporation or by-laws of a corporation, or an order to create or amend a unanimous shareholder agreement

- an order to issue or exchange securities (shares)

- an order appointing directors

- an order, subject to the limitation provided in subsection 248(6) of the *BCA* and subsection 241(6) of the *CBCA*, directing the corporation or any other person to purchase securities or repay a security holder

- an order setting aside a contract or transaction, and providing compensation to the corporation or any other party to the contract or transaction

- an order requiring the corporation to provide financial statements or an accounting

- an order compensating an aggrieved person

- an order amending the corporation's registers or other corporate records

- an order winding up the corporation

- an order directing an investigation under Part XIII of the *BCA* or Part XIX of the *CBCA*, which both deal with Investigation

- an order requiring the trial of any issue.[32]

If an order of the court requires the Articles of Incorporation or by-laws of the corporation to be amended, the directors have a duty to make the changes and send amended articles to the Director. (Articles of Amendment will be discussed in Chapter 12.) In addition, the directors cannot make any further amendments to the articles or by-laws without court approval, unless the court orders otherwise.[33] A shareholder cannot dissent to such amendment of the Articles of Incorporation.[34]

Note that an order directing the corporation or any other person to purchase securities or repay a security holder, was made subject to the limitation provided in subsection

31 *Business Corporations Act*, R.S.O. 1990, c. B.16, s. 248(2); *Canada Business Corporations Act*, R.S.C. 1985, c. C-44, s. 241(2).

32 *Business Corporations Act*, R.S.O. 1990, c. B.16, s. 248(3) – (4); *Canada Business Corporations Act*, R.S.C. 1985, c. C-44, s. 241(3)–(4).

33 *Business Corporations Act*, R.S.O. 1990, c. B.16, s. 248(4); *Canada Business Corporations Act*, R.S.C. 1985, c. C-44, s. 241(4).

34 *Business Corporations Act*, R.S.O. 1990, c. B.16, s. 248(5); *Canada Business Corporations Act*, R.S.C. 1985, c. C-44, s. 241(5).

248(6) of the *BCA* and subsection 241(6) of the *CBCA*. Subsection 248(6) of the *BCA* states:

> 248(6) A corporation shall not make a payment to a shareholder under clause (3) (f) or (g) if there are reasonable grounds for believing that,
>
> (a) the corporation is or, after the payment, would be unable to pay its liabilities as they become due; or
>
> (b) the realizable value of the corporation's assets would thereby be less than the aggregate of its liabilities.[35]

Subsection 241(6) of the *CBCA* is virtually identical. The limitation found in these provisions of the *BCA* and *CBCA* recognizes that, in certain circumstances, ordering a corporation to make certain payments would put the company out of business – which would not be in anyone's best interest or in the best interest of the corporation. As a result, the statutes seem to be directing the courts to take a longer-term view of the situation, to ensure the viability of the corporation.

BCE Inc., Re, [2008] 3 S.C.R. 560 (S.C.C.)

In September 2007, nearly 98% of BCE's shareholders approved a deal led by the Ontario Teachers Pension Plan Board to purchase all of the shares of BCE Inc. ("BCE"). The deal included the assumption of $30 billion of debt by Bell Canada, a subsidiary of BCE. The debenture holders of Bell Canada opposed the deal because the assumption of this debt would reduce the value of their bonds. The Superior Court found the transaction to be fair and dismissed the debenture holders' claim of oppression. The Quebec Court of Appeal reversed that decision, which was then appealed to the Supreme Court of Canada. A key issue in the case was the debenture holders' right to relief under s. 241 of the *CBCA*, the oppression remedy.

Debenture holders are security holders that can bring an action under s. 241 of the *CBCA*. After analyzing two different approaches in the caselaw, the SCC held that analyzing s. 241(2) requires two steps: first, establishing that the complainant had a reasonable expectation, and second, considering whether the defendant's conduct amounts to "oppression", "unfair prejudice" or "unfair disregard" as stated in s. 241(2). In addition, the court noted that the oppression remedy is an equitable remedy, which means that the courts can enforce "not just what is legal but what is fair", and what is fair must be judged according to the facts of each specific case. "Conduct that is oppressive in one situation may not be in another." . . .

With respect to the first step of the analysis – that is, did the complainant have a reasonable expectation – the court indicated that the concept of reasonable expectations is objective, and must be viewed in the context of the specific case. The court noted that the interests and expectations of different stakeholders may conflict. Ultimately, stakeholders are entitled to reasonably expect fair treatment, and they are reasonably entitled to expect that directors act in the best interests of the corporation (not in the best interests of the stakeholders.) Factors to consider whether the complainant had a reasonable expectation include: general commercial practice, the nature of the corporation, the relationship between the parties, past practice, steps the claim-

---

35 *Business Corporations Act,* R.S.O. 1990, c. B.16, s. 248(6).

ant could have taken to protect itself, representations and agreements, and the fair resolution of conflicting interests between corporate stakeholders.

With respect to the second step in the analysis – whether the conduct complained of was "oppression", "unfair prejudice" or "unfair disregard" of relevant interests – the court stated that oppression is a wrong of the most serious sort. "Unfair prejudice" is less offensive than oppression, may include squeezing out a minority shareholder, failing to disclose related party transactions, changing corporate structure to drastically alter debt ratios, adopting a "poison pill" to prevent a takeover bid, paying dividends without a formal declaration, preferring some shareholders with management fees and paying directors' fees higher than the industry norm. "Unfair disregard" is the least serious of the three categories, and could include favouring a director by failing to properly prosecute claims, improperly reducing a shareholder's dividend, or failing to deliver property belonging to the claimant. As in any action in equity, wrongful conduct, causation and compensable injury must be established in a claim for oppression.

. . .

In this case, the debenture holders argued that they had a reasonable expectation that the investment grade status of the debentures would be maintained as a result of the transaction. The court held that this was not a reasonable expectation, and pointed out that directors may be put in situations where they have to approve transactions that, while in the best interest of the corporation, benefit some stakeholders at the expense of others. The evidence showed that the directors did consider the interests of the debenture holders, but there was no way that they could restructure the transaction to provide a satisfactory price to shareholders and preserve the high market value of the debentures. All of the takeover bids were leveraged, involving a significant increase in Bell Canada's debt; as such, there was no evidence that the directors could do anything to protect the value of the debentures. Ultimately, the directors acted in the best interests of the corporation.

The SCC found, therefore, that the debenture holders failed to establish a claim under s. 241 of the *CBCA*.

5. Derivative Actions

The *BCA* and *CBCA* also give shareholders options other than (or in addition to) pursuing the oppression remedy, depending upon the circumstances. Section 246 of the *BCA* and section 239 of the *CBCA* give a "complainant" the option of applying to the court for permission to bring an action on behalf of the corporation, or to intervene in an existing action on behalf of the corporation. This is referred to as a "derivative action". Subsection 246(1) of the *BCA* states:

> Subject to subsection (2), a complainant may apply to the court for leave to bring an action in the name and on behalf of a corporation or any of its subsidiaries, or intervene in an action to which any such body corporate is a party, for the purpose of prosecuting, defending or discontinuing the action on behalf of the body corporate.[36]

A "complainant", as we have discussed previously, is defined in section 245 of the *BCA* as including:

---

36 *Business Corporations Act*, R.S.O. 1990, c. B.16, s. 246(1).

(a) a registered holder or beneficial owner, and a former registered holder or beneficial owner, of a security of a corporation or any of its affiliates,

(b) a director or an officer or a former director or officer of a corporation or of any of its affiliates,

(c) any other person who, in the discretion of the court, is a proper person to make an application under this Part.[37]

Why would a shareholder, for example, apply to the court to bring an action on behalf of the corporation? Typically, the shareholder will want to bring such an action if the directors of the corporation are not willing to do so themselves (perhaps because the directors are at fault.) Recall that a corporation is a person under the law.[38] As a legal person, the corporation should commence any lawsuits against individuals (to recover funds, for example) itself. However, in reality, the corporation is only a legal structure, and the controlling minds of the corporation are its directors. If the directors themselves are at fault, or if, for other reasons, they do not wish to commence a lawsuit that is for the benefit of the corporation, then the corporation will not sue and its other stakeholders will suffer. The *BCA* and *CBCA* address this problem by granting "complainants" the option to apply to a court for leave to commence a derivative action.

Note that commencing a derivative action is not an automatic right – the complainant must apply to the court for leave (or permission) to start a lawsuit on behalf of the corporation. In granting that permission, the courts will consider many factors, outlined in *Jennings v. Bernstein* [39] case summarized later in this chapter. In addition, the *BCA* and the *CBCA* outline certain procedural requirements. First, an application for a derivative action under subsection 246(1) of the *BCA* or subsection 239(2) of the *CBCA* cannot be made unless the complainant first provides the directors of the corporation with fourteen days' notice of its intention to apply to the court. However, the *BCA* does provide exceptions where this notice to the directors is not required,[40] and also provides that the court can make an interim order for relief when the court finds it appropriate to do so.[41]

Before granting leave to commence an action or to intervene in an action on behalf of a corporation (pursuant to subsection 246(1) of the *BCA* or subsection 239(2) of the *CBCA*), the court must be satisfied that:

- the directors of the corporation will not bring, diligently prosecute, defend or discontinue the action, as the case may be

- the complainant is acting in good faith

- it appears to be in the interests of the corporation to bring, prosecute, defend or discontinue the action, as the case may be.[42]

---

37 *Ibid.*, s. 245.

38 *Ibid.*, s. 1(1).

39 2000 CarswellOnt 4039, 11 B.L.R. (3d) 259 (Ont. S.C.J.), additional reasons 2001 CarswellOnt 654 (Ont. S.C.J.)

40 *Business Corporations Act*, R.S.O. 1990, c. B.16, ss. 246(2.1)–(3).

41 *Ibid.*, s. 246(4).

42 *Business Corporations Act*, R.S.O. 1990, c. B.16, s. 246(2); *Canada Business Corporations Act*, R.S.C. 1985, c. C-44, s. 239(2).

Finally, the court is given broad powers under subsection 247 of the *BCA* and section 240 of the *CBCA* to make any order it thinks fit, in connection with an application for a derivative action. For example, the court may:

- authorize the complainant or any other person to control the conduct of the action (lawsuit)

- give directions on how to conduct the action

- direct that any amounts found to be payable by the defendants in the action be paid to security holders of the corporation, instead of to the corporation itself

- require the corporation to pay reasonable legal fees and costs incurred by the complainant in connection with the action.

The court may also make any other order that is appropriate in the circumstances.[43]

Jennings v. Bernstein (2000), 11 B.L.R. (3d) 259 (Ont. S.C.J.), additional reasons 2001 CarswellOnt 654 (Ont. S.C.J.)

Jennings applied, pursuant to s. 246 of the *BCA*, to commence a derivative action on behalf of 1172774 Ontario Ltd. ("117") against Stanley K. Bernstein ("Bernstein"), Dr. Stanley K. Bernstein's Health and Diet Clinics (*"Clinics"*), 1228011 Ontario Ltd. (*"122"*) and Post Road Health and Diet Ltd. ("Post Road"). In September 1996, Jennings entered into a contract with Bernstein to open five "Dr. Bernstein's Health and Diet Clinics" in Hamilton, Burlington and Oakville, utilizing the services of a management corporation called Post Road. Bernstein is the sole director, officer and shareholder of Post Road. In October 1996, Bernstein entered into a licensing agreement with 117; half of the shares of 117 were owned by Bernstein, and the other half were owned by 1201100 Ontario Inc. (a holding company owned by Jennings.) The licensing agreement allowed 117 to use trade names, trademarks and products associated with the business for five years. Jennings provided the capital and other support to start a clinic in Burlington, but according to Bernstein, failed to provide capital or negotiate a line of credit to open other clinics. There is some disagreement about who terminated the licensing agreement, but it was terminated on January 10, 1997. From that date onwards, Clinics operated the Burlington clinic (with Bernstein as the sole director, officer and shareholder,) and subsequently, 122 opened and operated a clinic in Hamilton (with Bernstein as the sole director, officer and shareholder.) Jennings claimed that Bernstein, through Clinics, operated the clinics originally contracted for 117, to the exclusion of 117 and without an accounting of revenues to 117.

The court summarized the issues in the case as follows:

1. Can leave to commence a derivative action be by way of Notice of Motion?

2. Does the leave application in question satisfy the statutory pre-requisites of s.246?

With respect to the first issue, the court examined the *BCA* and the Rules of Civil Procedure and found that an application for *leave to commence* a derivative action

---

43 *Business Corporations Act*, R.S.O. 1990, c. B.16, s. 247; *Canada Business Corporations Act*, R.S.C. 1985, c. C-44, s. 240.

should be done by way of a motion. (Italics added.) The derivative action itself would be commenced by a Statement of Claim.

With respect to the second issue, the court stated:

To obtain leave to commence a derivative action assuming as there is here no issue as to notice, the plaintiff must satisfy the court that:

    (a) he or she is a complainant within the definition contained in section 245;

    (b) the directors of the corporation will not bring, diligently prosecute or defend or discontinue the action;

    (c) the complainant is acting in good faith;

    (d) the action '*appears*' to be in the interest of the corporation.

In this case, Jennings was clearly a complainant as an officer and director of 117. Both Jennings and Bernstein were directors of 117, were both embroiled in other legal proceedings against each other (using the oppression remedy.) They were clearly not co-operating, and Bernstein was unlikely to act against his own self-interest. Therefore, the directors of 117 could not be expected to bring the proposed action themselves. With respect to good faith, the court stated that, while the concept of good faith is based on honesty, it is not devoid of self-interest and there is a possibility of personal gain.

. . . The practical objective for a complainant acting in good faith within the context of section 246 is "*a person who could reasonably be entrusted with the responsibility of advancing the interests of the corporation by seeking to remedy a wrong allegedly done to the corporation.*" (Hollingworth J. in commenting upon an analogous situation in *Canadian Opera Co. v. 670800 Ontario Inc.* (1989), 69 O.R. (2d) 532 (Ont. H.C.) at p.536.) . . . Good faith has to have an objectively reasonable component especially in light of the practical objective . . . A derivative action which is motivated less by potential return to the corporation and more by the prospect of a potential tactical advantage against the respondent, is anathema to the requirement of good faith. *Vedova v. Garden House Inn Ltd.* (1985), 29 B.L.R. 236 (Ont. H.C.) Anderson J.

In this case, the proposed action on behalf of 117 seeks an accounting and damages, and was conducted in good faith (even though Jennings and Bernstein had already commenced oppression actions against each other.) With respect to the final requirement that the derivative action be in the best interests of the corporation, the court held that the action must not be meritless, vexatious or frivolous, and must "appear to be" in the best interests of the corporation. Therefore, it was not necessary for the court to find that the action was, in fact, in the best interest of the corporation, but rather, that there was an arguable case that it was in the best interest of the corporation. The court did find that the proposed action appeared to be in the best interest of 117.

Leave was granted for Jennings to commence a derivative action on behalf of 117, with legal fees and costs to be paid by 117.

6. Right to Dissent

In addition to the more powerful remedies of oppression and derivative action, a shareholder also has the right of dissent. Subsection 185 of the *BCA* provides that a shareholder can disagree with a corporate resolution to:

- amend the Articles of Incorporation to change restrictions on shares, the nature of the business, and powers of the corporation

- amalgamate with another corporation

- be continued under the laws of another jurisdiction

- sell, lease or exchange substantially all of the corporation's property, other than in the ordinary course of business[44]

(Amalgamation and continuance will be discussed in Chapter 12.)

What makes the right to dissent powerful is that dissenting shareholders have the right to be paid the "fair value" of their shares in the circumstances described in subsection 185(1), which are listed above. These rights are in addition to any other rights that the shareholder may have.[45] For example, if the directors of Entertainment Group Ltd. pass a resolution to change share restrictions in a way that Sam Khan (a shareholder) finds unacceptable, Sam has a right to demand that the corporation pay him the fair value of his shares, so that he can leave the corporation. However, Sam must claim compensation for *all* of his shares (in the particular class of shares that are affected,) as the *BCA* does not allow a "partial dissent".[46]

Note that, while "fair value" of the shares is often equated with "fair market value" of the shares, it can be difficult to determine the market value of a corporation's shares where those shares are not freely traded. The case *Brant Investments Ltd. v. KeepRite Inc.*[47] discusses the concept of "fair value" and is summarized at the end of this chapter. The case illustrates that "fair value" of a corporation's shares may not always be the same as the "market value" of those shares.

In order to exercise the right of dissent, a shareholder like Sam Khan must first send the corporation a written objection to the resolution that is to be proposed at a shareholders meeting.[48] After the shareholders as a group have adopted the resolution (by majority vote), the corporation must send each shareholder who has filed an objection a notice that indicates that the resolution was adopted.[49] For example, if Javid, Helena and Mike are shareholders, directors and officers of Entertainment Group Ltd., and Sam Khan is the only additional shareholder, Javid, Helena and Mike can easily pass a shareholders' resolution that Sam disagrees with. However, Sam can file an objection under section 185, and after Javid, Helena and Mike approve the resolution, the corporation must send Sam a notice to indicate that the resolution has been adopted. The notice must contain

---

44 *Business Corporations Act*, R.S.O. 1990, c. B.16, ss. 185(1)–(3).
45 *Ibid.*, s. 185(4).
46 *Ibid.*, s. 185(5).
47 1991 CarswellOnt 133, 3 O.R. (3d) 289 (Ont. C.A.).
48 *Ibid.*, ss. 185(6)–(7).
49 *Ibid.*, ss. 185(8).

the rights of the dissenting shareholder, and the process for enforcing those rights.[50] Within twenty days of receiving this notice, the dissenting shareholder (in our example, Sam) must send the corporation a written notice including his or her name and address, the number and class of shares involved, and a demand for payment of fair value of those shares.[51] In addition, the dissenting shareholder (Sam) must then send the relevant share certificates back to the corporation, within thirty days of the shareholder's notice demanding payment of fair value for those shares.[52] The procedural requirements for exercise a right to dissent are fairly strict, as a shareholder who does not follow the proper process may lose the right to dissent under section 185 of the *BCA*.[53]

Once the process outlined above has been followed, the dissenting shareholder normally loses any rights as a shareholder, except the right to be paid fair value for the shares. The dissenting shareholder can retain rights as a shareholder, however, where:

- the shareholder withdraws notice before the corporation's offer to pay

- the corporation fails to make an offer to pay and the dissenting shareholder withdraws his or her notice, or

- the directors revoke the resolution that caused the shareholder to dissent in the first place[54]

Note that the corporation only has up to seven days from the date on which the corporation approved the resolution or the shareholder gave notice to demand payment (whichever is later) to provide dissenting shareholders with an offer to pay for the dissenting shareholder's shares. In other words, if the directors of Entertainment Group Ltd. approve a resolution and Sam Khan gives notice of a demand for payment the next day, the corporation must make an offer to pay Sam Khan fair market value for his shares within seven days of his notice of a demand for payment. This is, in practical terms, a short timeframe, as determining the fair value of the shares of a corporation – particularly a non-offering (private) corporation – is not a simple exercise. It can also be a costly exercise, as it may require hiring a professional to provide a business valuation. It also may pose liquidity problems for Entertainment Group Ltd., as the corporation will have to come up with the cash to pay for those shares relatively quickly, and most non-offering corporations have the bulk of their assets tied up in illiquid (that is, non-cash) assets. As a result, the directors may then consider revoking the resolution that the shareholder disagreed with, in order to avoid financial problems or additional legal expenses.

Once the corporation makes an offer to the dissenting shareholder to pay a certain amount for his or her shares, the dissenting shareholder has up to thirty days to accept the offer, after which the corporation has a further ten days to pay the full amount.[55] Where the dissenting shareholder does not accept the corporation's offer (usually because the shareholder feels that the amount offered is less than the fair market value of the

---

50 *Ibid.*, ss. 185(9).
51 *Ibid.*, ss. 185(10).
52 *Ibid.*, ss. 185(11).
53 *Ibid.*, ss. 185(12).
54 *Ibid.*, ss. 185(14).
55 *Ibid.*, ss. 185(17).

shares,) either the corporation or the dissenting shareholder can apply to the court to determine the fair value of the shares of the dissenting shareholder.[56]

The *BCA* recognizes, however, that a corporation may be unable to pay the fair value of a dissenting shareholder's shares. Subsection 185(30) states that:

A corporation shall not make a payment to a dissenting shareholder under this section if there are reasonable grounds for believing that,

(a) the corporation is or, after the payment, would be unable to pay its liabilities as they become due; or

(b) the realizable value of the corporation's assets would thereby be less than the aggregate of its liabilities.[57]

Within ten days of receiving a court order to pay a certain amount for the dissenting shareholder's shares, the corporation must notify the dissenting shareholder that it is "unable lawfully to pay."[58] The dissenting shareholder must then choose between two options:

- to withdraw the notice of dissent and resume full rights as a shareholder in the corporation, or

- to remain a claimant against the corporation, to be paid as soon as the corporation is lawfully able to do so, or if the corporation is liquidated, to receive payment after creditors but before other shareholders.[59]

Finally, the *BCA* gives the corporation a final trump card – it can apply to the court for an order that the right of shareholders to dissent and demand payment of the fair value of their shares pursuant to subsection 185(4), should not apply in a given circumstance. If the court agrees, the rights under subsection 185(4) will not apply, and the court may make any order that thinks fit in those circumstances (which may contain a requirement by the corporation to comply with terms and conditions that the court specifies.)[60]

The right to dissent is found in section 190 of the *CBCA* for federal corporations. The provisions in the *CBCA* are substantially the same as those in section 185 of the *BCA*, but the *CBCA* specifically mentions that a shareholder can exercise the right to dissent where there is a corporate resolution to take the company private (if it is currently an offering corporation) or a squeeze-out transaction.[61]

---

56 *Ibid.*, ss. 185(18)–(27).
57 *Ibid.*, ss. 185(30).
58 *Ibid.*, ss. 185(28).
59 *Ibid.*, ss. 185(29).
60 *Ibid.*, ss. 185(31).
61 *Canada Business Corporations Act*, R.S.C. 1985, c. C-44, s.190(1).

Brant Investments Ltd. v. KeepRite Inc. (1991), 3 O.R. (3d) 289 (Ont. C.A.)

There were two proceedings in this case: an oppression action by minority share-holders, and an action by KeepRite Inc. ("KeepRite") for the court to fix the fair market value of shares of dissenting shareholders (the "valuation action".) KeepRite (a public company) was a wholly owned subsidiary of Inter-City Manufacturing Ltd. ("ICM"). ICG Manufacturing Ltd. ("ICG") was a wholly owned subsidiary of ICM. KeepRite and ICG negotiated a transaction in which KeepRite would purchase equip-ment from ICG for approximately $20 million, and would finance that purchase by offering shareholders the right to purchase additional shares. KeepRite's shareholders approved the transaction with a two-thirds majority, and dissenting shareholders reg-istered their objection.

Plaintiffs in the oppression action were owners of 28% of the shares of KeepRite. With respect to the claim under the oppression remedy in the *CBCA*, the court held that directors and majority shareholders do not owe a fiduciary duty to minority share-holders. Acting in the best interest of the corporation may, sometimes, require directors or officers to act against the interest of a particular stakeholder in the corporation. The court also stated that there is no need to find malice in order to establish "oppression", and that the courts should not generally substitute its own business judgment for that of the directors, managers or an independent committee that was designed to study the transaction (as in this case.) Ultimately, the court found that there was no oppres-sion either in the transaction or in the process used to consider the transaction in this case. The oppression action was dismissed with costs. . . .

With respect to the valuation action, KeepRite offered the dissenting shareholders $9 per share, which they refused. The trial judge fixed the fair market value of the shares at $13 per share, which the dissenting shareholders appealed to the Court of Appeal. The Court of Appeal stated:

"[m]arket value" has frequently been defined as the best price that can be obtained in an open market by a willing seller from a willing purchaser. It is true that such a value is notional and hypothetical. It is also true that in the context of a case such as this, there is seldom any real market for the shares against which one can test "market value" as determined from the various elements of "evidence, assumptions, calculations and judgment" referred to by An-derson J. . . . I agree that, in this case, "fair value" and "market value" can be equated; however, for reasons stated earlier, I consider that there may be situations where an amount not normally included in "market value" might be included in "fair value" under s. [190(3)] of the *CBCA* . . .

There are four widely accepted approaches to valuation of corporate shares: (a) the market value approach, or the quoted market price on the stock exchange; (b) the asset value approach, or the value of the assets of the corporation, either on a going concern or a liqui-dation basis; (c) the earnings approach, or the capitalized value of a projected stream of maintainable earnings; or (d) some combination of the preceding three approaches

. . . All experts agreed that an earnings approach to valuation was appropriate in this case, because KeepRite was not unduly capital-intensive, and was fundamentally viable as a going concern at the valuation date. . . .

The Court of Appeal held that the trial judge had properly considered the expert and other evidence provided in this case. In arriving at the figure of $13 per share, the trial judge was slightly more generous than necessary, and as such, there was no reason to increase the share price further. The valuation appeal was dismissed with costs.

7. Shareholder Agreements

We have already discussed unanimous shareholder agreements and voting agreements earlier in this chapter. There may, however, be other circumstances in which shareholders enter into an agreement with one another.

It is always advisable for shareholders who are starting a business in the form of a corporation, to negotiate a shareholders agreement prior to incorporation. This is a comprehensive agreement (as opposed to an agreement of limited scope) that covers many of the issues that will have to be addressed during or after incorporation. Dealing with these issues when all parties are getting along can prevent complications and costly disagreements later. For example, shareholders may wish to specify that all shareholders will be first directors of the corporation, or that particular shares will carry more than one vote. Contribution of capital, financing, share transfers, directors, officers and other employees, dividends and buy/sell arrangements are all important considerations to include in a comprehensive shareholder agreement.

If the corporation is already in existence, the Articles of Incorporation and by-laws should be attached to the shareholder agreement as schedules. If the corporation has not yet been incorporated, the articles and by-laws will be drafted after the shareholders' agreement has been signed. Please refer to the Appendix to this chapter for a summary of some of the key clauses in a comprehensive shareholder agreement.

APPENDIX: Checklist for Comprehensive Shareholder Agreement

CLAUSE	DETAILS
Preamble	• include date, parties, authorized capital of the corporation, number of issued shares, and a full description of consideration (and receipt thereof) for each of the parties entering into the agreement
Definitions	• define key terms
First Right of Refusal	• gives existing shareholders the right to buy shares from another existing shareholder, before that shareholder can sell, assign, transfer, convey or otherwise dispose of the shares to someone else • include convenants by each shareholder not to pledge, charge or otherwise encumber shares without the consent of all shareholders • can allow for permitted sales and transfers in certain circumstances
Pre-emptive Rights	• gives existing shareholders the right to purchase newly issued shares from the corporation first, before those shares can be offered to another party
Compulsory Buy/Sell Arrangements	• deals with the situation when existing shareholders die, are permanently disabled or retire • include insurance clause (insurance on life of each shareholder)
Special Voting Arrangements	• may include nominees on Board of Directors
Share Restrictions	• restrictions on transfer, mortgage, pledge or other disposition of shares (should also be indicated on share certificates)
Board of Directors	• number and composition of the board • may include the right of certain parties to elect members to the board
Financing	• addresses borrowing by the corporation, and loans made by shareholders to the corporation
Employment Contracts	• details regarding employment contracts where some or all of the shareholders will also be employees of the corporation
Corporate Bank Account	• addresses authorized signing officers, and possibly limitations on the ability of officers/employees to borrow, sign cheques or withdraw sums from the account
Waiving Appointment of Auditor	• common in a non-offering corporation • provides for a waiver of the requirement to have an auditor

Shareholder Defaults	• consequences if a shareholder defaults on financial or other obligations
Miscellaneous	• arbitration clause • notice provisions • nominees • amendments to the agreement • share certificates • further assurances • errors • remedies for non-compliance • acknowledgement by and consent of the corporation to the agreement • governing law • time of essence

CHAPTER 8: HOW DOES A CORPORATION RAISE MONEY?

Overview:

- Raising Money
- Loans
- Equity Financing
- Shares
    - What are shares?
        - Common & preferred shares
        - Dividends
        - Additional rights
        - Lien on shares
        - Subscription for shares
- Bonds & other securities
- Workbook:
    - Review exercise
    - Case studies

1. Raising Money

Nirvana Nightclub has been operating for 3 months, and already, it becomes clear that the business will need more money to survive. Javid decides to speak to his uncle, Sam, who has experience in the nightclub business. How can the company get access to additional capital?

There are essentially two ways to raise money for a corporation: equity and debt. Equity is defined in a variety of ways, depending on whether you take an accounting or finance approach, but in basic terms, it refers to an ownership interest in a corporation. Therefore, shareholders, who are the owners of a corporation, have an equity – or ownership – interest in the corporation. By contrast, creditors (lenders) are not owners of a corporation. When a corporation raises money through debt financing, that means that the corporation is getting a loan from one or more creditors. Those creditors could be formal institutions like banks, or they could be individuals. A creditor does not own part of the corporation, but is entitled to receive the amount of the loan, plus interest, on a specified basis. Upon dissolution of the company, creditors must be paid before shareholders receive any money.

For example, if Mike was purchasing a car for his own personal use and he did not have enough money to buy it himself, what could he do to finance his purchase? One option would be to borrow money from a family member, for example. Let's assume that Mike borrowed $10,000 from his mother to buy a car. Mike would be the only owner of the car, and his mother would be a creditor. She would have the legal right to repayment of her loan, plus interest (on the terms negotiated between Mike and his mother.) However, Mike's mother is not the owner of the car, and she does not have the rights of an owner – such as the right to sell the car, use it as collateral for another loan, give it away, or destroy it (within the limits of the law.) This first option – that is, getting a loan to buy the car – involves incurring debt. On the other hand, Mike could talk to his mother about buying the car together. He would have to convince her that it is to her benefit to purchase a car with him. For example, Mike may agree to drive his mother to work every day and to pay all gasoline expenses, in return for being a joint owner of the automobile. If Mike's mother agrees, she will provide the amount of money Mike requires, and both she and Mike will become owners of the vehicle. Their rights will be based on the terms that they have negotiated between themselves, and on any applicable laws. This second option involves equity, or ownership.

Similarly, Entertainment Group Ltd. has to weigh the advantages and disadvantages of obtaining additional funds through debt (a loan) or through equity financing (adding new shareholders.) There are also many options available today that combine elements of both equity and debt financing; however, a detailed analysis of the variety of financing options available to corporations goes beyond the scope of this introductory textbook, and for many small businesses, beyond the scope of what they will consider as financing options.

2. Loans

For most small businesses, debt financing will be the first option that the business will consider for raising additional capital. Some of the factors that Entertainment Group Ltd. would have to consider before it obtains a loan include:

- how much money it will need in the short term, and in the longer term

- who would be willing to lend the corporation the money

- what rate of interest would be charged

- can the corporation realistically make the loan payments

One of the challenges that a new corporation like Entertainment Group Ltd. can expect to face is that creditors will be hesitant to lend money to a corporation with no credit history or business experience. Creditors are in the business of lending money, with a view to making a profit from repayment of the loan plus interest. In determining the rate of interest that they will charge, they must assess the creditworthiness of the borrower, and the level of risk in giving the loan. A company like Entertainment Group Ltd. has no credit history, and no history of business success, so it will be difficult for it to obtain debt financing at the market rate. However, there are creditors that do lend money to higher risk individuals or corporations; these creditors will charge a higher rate of interest to compensate for the higher risk that they are assuming in granting the loan. (The risk to the creditor is, of course, the risk of not being repaid in accordance with the terms of the loan agreement.)

> Sam, Javid's uncle, suggests that Javid speak to an individual who he knows has lent money to other businesses. However, Sam warns Javid that this person charges a very high rate of interest. Javid is uncomfortable dealing with this person, and says that he would rather deal with a bank. Is there any way that Javid can convince a major bank to lend Entertainment Group Ltd. the money it needs?

When negotiating a loan agreement, banks and other financial institutions will generally require a personal guarantee from shareholders of a corporation that does not have a strong credit history or an established business. From the bank's perspective, this personal guarantee is only effective if the guarantor or guarantors – or possibly, someone else involved in the business – has a good credit history and significant personal assets. This gives the bank some assurance that, if a corporation like Entertainment Group Ltd. defaults on its loan, there is a guarantor that has sufficient assets to satisfy the requirements of the loan. From the shareholders' perspective (assuming that the guarantors are the shareholders,) this arrangement is far from ideal, but it may be the only way to get debt financing. Recall that the primary reason for incorporating the business was to protect shareholders from personal liability. By acting as guarantors for the loan to the corporation, the shareholders have agreed to assume personal liability for the amount of the loan. While the liability is limited to the amount of the loan, it still involves putting the shareholders' personal assets at risk.

In addition to a personal guarantee, a bank or other financial institution will likely take a security interest – often referred to as a lien – on tangible and intangible assets of the business. For Entertainment Group Ltd., these assets could include inventory, furniture, equipment, vehicles and other personal property. By taking a security interest in these assets, the bank now has a claim on those assets if the loan is not repaid in accordance with its terms. (The process of registering a security interest will be discussed in Chapter 13.)

In summary, some of the key advantages of debt financing for new corporations include:

- no effect on the ownership structure of the company

- no dilution of the profits payable to shareholders

Some of the key disadvantages of debt financing for new corporations include:

- the business must be able to make loan payments as they come due, with serious consequences if the business is unable to do so

- shareholders (and/or others) will likely have to provide personal guarantees

- creditors will likely place a security interest on the assets of the corporation

- a new corporation will likely have to pay a higher interest rate than a more established one

> The directors of Entertainment Group Ltd. have been talking about approaching the bank for a loan for $50,000 to help the company through its initial start-up period. Javid has already invested as much money as he is willing to invest, and neither Mike nor Helena has any funds to invest. Javid tells the other directors that Sam is hesitant to invest any more money in the company, but he may be willing to lend the corporation money. Can a shareholder lend money to a corporation (thereby becoming a creditor, as well as a shareholder)? Even if Sam or others are willing to lend money to the corporation, Javid is concerned about being able to make monthly loan payments. What other options can the directors consider?

3. Equity Financing

The shareholders of Entertainment Group Ltd. may decide that the disadvantages of obtaining a loan to help them through their initial start-up period may be greater than the advantages. Javid is most concerned about a loan default, since he and Sam are the only shareholders with significant assets and they would be asked to provide personal guarantees. If the corporation is unable to make loan payments, creditors could seize the company's assets and also pursue Javid and Sam's personal assets to satisfy the debt. For Javid, the risk appears to be too high.

If debt financing is not a viable option for a corporation – usually because creditors are not willing to lend the company money, or the company is unlikely to be able to make monthly loan payments in the initial period of the loan – equity financing becomes another option to consider. This means that the corporation will add one or more shareholders to the corporation, with each of those shareholders investing money in the corporation in return for their shares. For example, Sam may ultimately decide that he is willing to invest more money in the corporation, with the result that he will now own more shares in the corporation than he previously did. Alternatively, an entirely new shareholder – such as Helena's brother, for example – may decide to invest money in the corporation, in return for shares.

Some of the key advantages to equity financing include:

- there is no obligation for the corporation to make regular payments (as in a loan) or to repay the investment

- there is no need for shareholders to provide personal guarantees

- the corporation is not required to provide security interests on its assets

- the risk is borne by the shareholder, who invests money in the corporation because the shareholder believes that the business will grow and the value of his/her shares will increase over time

Some of the key disadvantages of equity financing include:

- loss of control, as there is now an additional shareholder to contend with

- initial dilution of profits, since the corporations profits must now be split between more individuals

- new shareholders may demand additional rights, giving them greater power than the initial shareholders may be willing to give

While there appear to be fewer disadvantages to equity financing, the addition of a particularly difficult shareholder can significantly change the dynamics of a corporation. If the shareholder is aware that the corporation is in dire need of additional capital, the new shareholder may demand additional rights – such as greater voting rights – which sway the balance of power amongst shareholders. The initial shareholders may not know the new shareholder as well as they know one another, and may be concerned about losing some control when the "stranger" gains voting rights in the corporation. (In part 4 of this Chapter, we will address different types of shares, including those that do not have voting rights.) Moreover, as the number of shares sold in the corporation increases, the value of each share decreases – that is, until the business becomes more profitable. For example, if you buy a cake for a birthday party with eight people and then twelve people show up, each person gets a smaller piece of cake than was originally intended. In a business, however, the goal is that the money that the new shareholder provides will help the business to grow, so that all the shareholders can ultimately get more money from the business. So in our simple example, if the four extra guests who show up at the birthday party also bring a cake for eight people, all twelve guests end up with more cake.

4. Shares

(a) What are Shares?

As discussed in Chapter 7, each shareholder owns shares in a corporation. What are shares? Shares are evidence of an ownership interest in the corporation. They indicate that a person owns a proportionate interest in the net worth of the corporation. Assume, for example, that a corporation has two shareholders and each of them contributes $50,000 to start a business. The Articles of Incorporation indicate that the corporation may issue an unlimited number of common shares. In other words, the "authorized share capital" of the corporation is an unlimited number of common shares. The corporation decides to issue 50 common shares to Shareholder A and 50 common shares to Shareholder B. Therefore, the "issued" or "allotted" share capital of the corporation is 100 common shares. (Unissued share capital is the difference between the maximum number of shares that a corporation can issue, and the number of shares it has actually issued.) In our example, there are 100 shares outstanding and the business is currently worth $100,000; therefore, each share is worth $1,000.

> Net worth of business = $50,000 (from Shareholder A) + $50,000 (from Shareholder B) = $100,000
> Issued share capital = 100
> Each share is worth: $100,000 / 100 = $1,000
> Shareholder A owns 50 / 100 shares = 50% of the issued shares
> Shareholder B owns 50 / 100 shares = 50% of the issued shares

In the same example, assume that the business grows over time, and the business is now worth $200,000. (Businesses are valued by financial analysis that takes into account many factors, including, amongst other things, the assets, liabilities, profits, cash flow, and reputation of the business.) The fifty shares owned by Shareholder A are now worth a total of $100,000, which means that Shareholder A's profit is equal to his initial investment.

> Net worth of business = $200,000
> Issued share capital = 100
> Each share is worth: $200,000 / 100 = $2,000
> Shareholder A owns 50 / 100 shares = 50% of the issued shares
> Shareholder A's investment is worth: 50 x $2,000 = $100,000 (OR $200,000 x 50% = $100,000)
> Shareholder B owns 50 / 100 shares = 50% of the issued shares
> Shareholder B's investment is worth: 50 x $2,000 = $100,000 (OR $200,000 x 50% = $100,000)

Shares are not defined in the *Business Corporation Act* or in the *Canada Business Corporations Act*, but are described in the *BCA* in the following way: "The shares of a corporation are personal property."[1]

The term "personal property" is also not defined in the *BCA*, but is defined in the *Personal Property Security Act*:

"personal property" means chattel paper, documents of title, goods, instruments, intangibles, money and investment property, and includes fixtures but does not include building materials that have been affixed to real property;[2]

Personal property can be contrasted with real property, which relates to land and fixtures attached to land. Therefore, a house is considered real property, but the furniture in it is considered personal property. Similarly, shares are a form of personal property that can be bought, sold or pledged as collateral for a loan.

---

1 *Business Corporations Act*, R.S.O. 1990, c. B.16, s.41.
2 *Personal Property Security Act*, R.S.O. 1990, c. P.10, s. 1(1).

Ownership of shares is usually evidenced by a share certificate, but according to section 54 of the *BCA*, shares can also be "uncertificated" if the directors of the corporation pass a resolution stating that some or all of the shares of a corporation will not have share certificates.[3] By contrast, the *CBCA* specifies that a security holder is entitled to request a security certificate (at his/her option) or a non-transferable written acknowledgement of his/her right to obtain a security certificate; the corporation can charge a fee to comply with this request.[4] In most cases, private corporations will issue share certificates as part of the organizational process after incorporation. (More details on this process will be provided in Chapters 9 and 10.) Share certificates are documents that indicate the number and type of shares that a particular shareholder has acquired. A share certificate acts like a "receipt" for those shares, and is issued once the shares are sold or transferred by the corporation; it is a way of proving that the shareholder owns a certain number of shares in a corporation. Share certificates must be signed by at least one of the following persons:

- a director or officer of the corporation

- a registrar or transfer agent of the corporation

- a trustee

An original signature is not necessary; the signature can be printed or otherwise mechanically reproduced on the share certificate.[5]

Each share certificate must contain the following information:

- name of the corporation

- the words "Incorporated under the law of the Province of Ontario", "Subject to the *Ontario Business Corporations Act*" or a similar statement

- the name of the shareholder

- the number and class of shares (and any series, if applicable)

If the Articles of Incorporation allow a corporation to issue more than one class or series of shares (more on this later,) then the rights, privileges and restrictions relating to each class of shares must be indicated on the share certificate.[6] (The *CBCA* has similar provisions regarding the content of share certificates.[7]) In the past, shares also indicated a "par value" or "nominal value" on the share certificate. The *BCA* and *CBCA* now state that shares must be in registered form, *without* nominal or par value.[8] Since the value of shares typically fluctuates over time, the concept of a fixed value assigned to shares is no longer considered appropriate. Finally, for non-offering or private companies, the restriction on transfer of shares must be clearly stated on the share certificate, along with

---

3 *Business Corporations Act*, R.S.O. 1990, c. B.16, s. 54.

4 *Canada Business Corporations Act*, R.S.C. 1985, c. C-44, ss. 49(1) – (2)

5 *Business Corporations Act*, R.S.O. 1990, c. B. 16, s. 55; *Canada Business Corporations Act*, R.S.C. 1985, c. C-44, ss. 49(4) & (6).

6 *Ibid.*, s. 56.

7 *Canada Business Corporations Act*, R.S.C. 1985, c. C-44, s. 49(7).

8 *Business Corporations Act*, R.S.O. 1990, c. B. 16, ss. 22 & 56(6); *Canada Business Corporations Act*, R.S.C. 1985, c. C-44, s. 24(1).

a statement indicating that the corporation will provide a copy of the full text of the restriction to the shareholder upon demand and without charge.[9] Offering or public corporations cannot impose restrictions on share transfer unless those restrictions are authorized in the Articles of Incorporation.[10] Federal corporations have similar requirements regarding restrictions on share certificates in subsections 49(8), 49(10) and 49(12).[11]

Sometimes, more than one person will collectively own shares of a corporation. In this case, if one of the joint holders dies, the other becomes the sole owner of the shares of the corporation, as long as the living holder can provide satisfactory proof of the death of the other holder.[12] For example, if Javid and Sam are the joint holders of shares in ABC Corporation, and then Sam dies, Javid automatically becomes the sole owner of those shares after he provides a copy of Sam's death certificate to ABC Corporation.

Finally, a corporation is entitled to assume that the person whose name is registered as a shareholder is the person who has the exclusive right to vote, receive notices, receive dividends or other payments in relation to the shares, and otherwise exercise the rights of a shareholder. However, there may be situations where a shareholder cannot be present to exercise his/her rights. For example, a shareholder may be out of the country for a period of time, and will want his interests in the corporation protected while he is away. In this case, the shareholder could appoint a proxyholder – that is, a representative who can vote on his/her behalf. Similarly, an executor of an estate can exercise rights in relation to a deceased shareholder's shares, as can a liquidator or trustee in bankruptcy for a shareholder who goes bankrupt.[13]

Part VIII of the *BCA* and sections 27 to 29.3 of the General Regulation[14] address the topic of proxies. Section 109 of the *BCA* defines the term "proxy" as "a completed and signed form of proxy by means of which a shareholder has appointed a proxyholder to attend and act on a shareholder's behalf at a meeting of shareholders."[15] In general business terminology, the term "proxy" is used to describe both the person who acts as a shareholder's representative (called a "proxyholder" in the *BCA*,) and the document that a shareholder signs to give that person the authority to exercise rights on his/her behalf. According to the *BCA*, a proxyholder does not have to be a shareholder in the corporation,[16] and in an offering corporation, a proxy that appoints a proxyholder to vote at a shareholder's meeting(s) expires one year after the date on the proxy.[17] Note, however, that a shareholder can revoke or cancel a proxy by complying with the requirements specified in the *BCA*.[18] Often, public companies will send proxy notices to shareholders, giving them the opportunity to appoint management (officers) as their proxies to vote on

---

9 *Business Corporations Act*, R.S.O. 1990, c. B.16, ss. 56(8)–(9).

10 *Ibid.*, s. 42(1).

11 *Canada Business Corporations Act*, R.S.C. 1985, c. C-44, ss. 49(8), (10) & (12).

12 *Business Corporations Act*, R.S.O. 1990, c. B.16, s. 67(6); *Canada Business Corporations Act*, R.S.C. 1985, c. C-44, s. 51(6).

13 *Business Corporations Act*, R.S.O. 1990, c. B.16, ss. 67(1)(4); *Canada Business Corporations Act*, R.S.C. 1985, c. C-44, ss. 51(1)(3).

14 *Business Corporations Act, General*, R.R.O. 1990, Reg. 62, ss. 27–29.3.

15 *Business Corporations Act*, R.S.O. 1990, c. B.16, s. 109.

16 *Ibid.*, s. 110(1).

17 *Ibid.*, s. 110(2.1).

18 Ibid., ss. 110(4)(4.1).

a particular matter. Part VIII provides details on proxies, with additional requirements imposed on offering (public) corporations, and specifies that the form of every proxy must comply with the regulations.[19] Note that Part XIII of the *CBCA* addresses the issue of proxies, and is very similar to the provisions of the *BCA*. There are differences, however; for example, the *CBCA* provides that a proxy is only valid at the meeting in respect of which it was given[20] (not for one year, as with the *BCA*.)

(b) Types of Shares

As we have discussed, shares carry different bundles of rights, such as the right to vote and the right to a share of the net worth of a corporation upon dissolution, after creditors are paid. There are circumstances where a corporation may not want to give all shareholders the same rights, or where, for tax or other reasons, it is necessary to create different types of shares. The *BCA* refers to the different types of shares as different "classes" of shares. Generally speaking, each share within a class is the same as every other share of that class.[21] However, a corporation may decide to further subdivide a class of shares into different "series" of shares with further distinctions.[22] A corporation may also have two or more classes or two or more series of shares that have the same rights, privileges, restrictions and conditions.[23] A corporation is required to keep track of the different classes and series of shares by having a separate stated capital account for each class and series of shares that it issues.[24]

The *BCA* states:

22(3) Where a corporation has only one class of shares, the rights of the holders thereof are equal in all respects and include the rights,

    (a) to vote at all meetings of shareholders; and

    (b) to receive the remaining property of the corporation upon dissolution. . . .

(4) The articles may provide for more than one class of shares and where they so provide,

    (a) the rights, privileges, restrictions and conditions attaching to the shares of each class shall be set out therein; and

    (b) each of the rights set out in subsection (3) shall be attached to at least one class of shares, but both such rights are not required to be attached to any one class.[25]

Form 1 under the *BCA* (Articles of Incorporation) reflects this language in articles six and seven. Article six requires the drafter to state the classes and maximum number of shares that the corporation is allowed to issue. Article 7 requires the drafter to indicate the rights, privileges, restrictions and conditions (if any) attaching to each class of shares, and directors' authority with respect to any class of shares issued in series. (Note, however, that it is not necessary to state in the Articles of Incorporation that the shareholders

---

19 *Ibid.*, ss. 110(3),111 &112; *General*, R.R.O. 1990, Reg. 62, ss. 27–29.3.
20 *Canada Business Corporations Act*, R.S.C. 1985, c. C-44, ss. 147–154.
21 *Business Corporations Act*, R.S.O. 1990, c. B.16, s. 22(6).
22 *Ibid.*, s. 25.
23 *Ibid.*, s. 22(7).
24 *Ibid.*, s. 24; *Canada Business Corporations Act*, R.S.C. 1985, c. C-44, s. 26.
25 *Ibid.*, ss. 22(3)–(4).

of a particular class of shares have one vote for each share, or that they are entitled to receive the residual property of the corporation upon dissolution.[26]) Subsections 24(3) and 24(4) of the *CBCA* are substantially the same as subsections 22(3) and 22(4) of the *BCA*.[27]

Both the *BCA* and *CBCA* explicitly state that the issuance of shares is the prerogative of directors. In other words, directors of a corporation decide what type of shares to issue, how many and to whom, subject to the Articles of Incorporation, by-laws, unanimous shareholder agreement or section 26 of the *BCA* or section 28 of the *CBCA*, as the case may be.[28] (Section 26 of the *BCA* and section 28 of the *CBCA* deal with pre-emptive rights, which will be addressed later in this Chapter under part 4(b)(iii) "Additional Rights".) Shares can only be issued, however, once the shares have been fully paid for in money, property or past service that is worth at least the same amount that the corporation would have received if the shares had been issued for money. In the case of shares issued for property or past service, the directors will determine the value of that property or past service and the corresponding value of the shares.[29]

(i) Common & Preferred Shares

Where a corporation chooses to have only one class of shares – as many new, Ontario corporations will – then those shares are referred to as common shares. Common shares are voting shares that carry a right to receive the residual property of a corporation upon dissolution (after all creditors and preferred shareholders have been paid.)

Preferred or preference shares are typically non-voting shares that have a right to receive a dividend, and a priority interest in the residual value of a corporation, ahead of common shareholders. In other words, when a corporation dissolves and all the creditors have been paid, preferred shareholders will receive their portion of the value of the corporation before common shareholders receive anything. However, preferred shareholders give up the right to vote, which means that they do not have much, if any, influence on how a corporation operates. Today, corporate lawyers or law clerks often refer to these two types of shares as "Class A" shares (which are then further described as common shares) and "Class B" shares (described as preferred or preference shares) in Articles of Incorporation.

Corporations may have only one type of shares – common shares – or many different classes and series of shares, if they so desire. The goal, for a legal professional, is to determine what share structure meets the needs of a corporation. Many legal professionals provide for both common and preferred shares in the Articles of Incorporation, with the view that it allows the corporation some flexibility and avoids the necessity of changing the share structure of a corporation (by filing Articles of Amendment) at a later date. However, a complicated share structure is not likely to be beneficial for most new corporations starting to do business in Ontario. Even if the corporation decides that it requires

---

26 *Ibid.*, s. 22(5).

27 *Canada Business Corporations Act*, R.S.C. 1985, c. C-44, ss. 24(3)–(4).

28 *Business Corporations Act*, R.S.O. 1990, c. B.16, s. 2; *Canada Business Corporations Act*, R.S.C. 1985, c. C-44, s. 25(1).

29 *Business Corporations Act*, R.S.O. 1990, c. B.16, s. 23(3) – (6); *Canada Business Corporations Act*, R.S.C. 1985, c. C-44, ss. 25(3)–(5).

a different share structure – perhaps for tax reasons – the likelihood is that the share structure would have to be designed with advice from an accountant, to meet the needs of the business at that point in time. Trying to anticipate what a business may need in the future is difficult, and as such, Articles of Amendment may still be necessary if a detailed share structure is included in the Articles of Incorporation. For this reason, it is quite acceptable to provide for only common shares, or possibly, for both Class A and Class B shares that are described in a flexible manner.

For example, some Articles of Incorporation will include a statement that Class B (preferred) shares are entitled to a dividend of $10.00 per share on January 1 of every year. This provision may become problematic if the corporation is not in a financial position to give a dividend of $10.00 per share on January 1 of a particular year, and Articles of Amendment may be required in order to change the date or amount of the dividend at that time. Instead, if the articles state that Class B shares are entitled to payment of a dividend annually, in an amount to be determined by the directors, the corporation has more flexibility and Articles of Amendment may not be necessary. In any case, a legal professional must be aware of the goals of the corporation, and the likelihood that it will require different types of shares, before drafting Articles of Incorporation. Within the context of these goals, a simpler approach is often better than an unduly complicated one.

Finally, corporations today issue shares that have characteristics of both common and preferred shares. For example, a corporation may have Class A, B, C, and D shares described as follows:

Class A – voting, common shares
Class B – non-voting, common shares
Class C – voting, preferred shares with an annual dividend
Class D – non-voting, preferred shares with an annual dividend

In other words, shares can be structured in a variety of ways that incorporate features of both common and preferred shares. In the sections below, we will explore additional features of shares that can be incorporated into the share structure of a corporation.

(ii) Dividends

A dividend is a payment made to the shareholders of a company from the profits of the corporation. Shareholders are typically most concerned about making a profit from their investment, and as such, the provision of dividends is an important consideration when a shareholder decides what type of shares to purchase. Shareholders who hold preferred shares will be entitled to receive a dividend before shareholders who own common shares. (However, preferred shareholders give up other rights in return for this privilege.)

Subsection 38(1) of the *BCA* provides that:

> Subject to its articles and any unanimous shareholder agreement, the directors may declare and a corporation may pay a dividend by issuing fully paid shares of the corporation or options or rights to acquire fully paid shares of the corporation and, subject to subsection (3), a corporation may pay a dividend in money or property.[30]

---

30 *Business Corporations Act*, R.S.O. 1990, c. B.16, s. 38(1).

Sections 42 and 43 of the *CBCA* address dividends.[31] In both the *BCA* and *CBCA*, it is clear that a dividend can be declared in money, property, or by issuing additional shares in the corporation (within the limits provided in the *BCA* or *CBCA*.) The corporation can also issue options or rights to acquire fully paid shares of the corporation. The most common way of issuing dividends is to do so in money, and usually in terms of a certain amount of money per share (such as $10.00 per share.)

However, there are circumstances when a corporation cannot issue a dividend. The *BCA* provides that a corporation cannot issue a dividend if there are reasonable grounds to believe that:

- after paying the dividend, the corporation would be unable to pay its liabilities as they become due, or

- after paying the dividend, the realizable value of the corporation's assets would be less than the total of the corporation's liabilities plus its stated capital of all classes of shares.[32]

This provision in the *BCA* (and an almost identical provision in the *CBCA*[33]) is designed to protect creditors and others who have a claim on the corporation's assets. It prevents the corporation from being able to give all its money away to the shareholders in order to avoid paying debts or fulfilling other financial obligations to others. For example, consider a corporation in which all the shareholders are officers and directors. The business is suffering and it is clear that it is unlikely to succeed in the long run. The corporation owes money to several creditors, so if the business is dissolved, there is unlikely to be any money left for the shareholders after creditors are paid. Without the restriction described above, the directors could issue a dividend to the shareholders amounting to all the profits of the corporation, leaving nothing behind to pay creditors. The creditors could only sue the corporation (not the shareholders personally,) and there would be nothing left in the corporation to pay judgment. In order to avoid this situation, the *BCA* specifically restricts provision of dividends in the circumstances described above (see subsection 38(3) of the *BCA*.)

Like shares themselves, the right to receive a dividend can also be structured in a variety of different ways in different classes of shares. A corporation may simply state that Class B (preferred) shares have a right to receive a dividend before Class A (common) shares. Alternatively, the corporation can provide that Class B shares will receive a dividend of a certain, fixed amount within a specified period of time. For example, a corporation could indicate that Class B shares will receive a dividend of $10 per share on December 31 of every year. (This can be restricting to the corporation, for the reasons explained previously in this chapter.)

The right to receive a dividend can also be described as cumulative, non-cumulative or partially cumulative. These terms are defined below.

- Cumulative dividends – Assume that Class B shares in a corporation have the right to receive a dividend annually. The right to receive this dividend does not expire at the end of the year. So, if the corporation does not actually declare a

31 *Canada Business Corporations Act*, R.S.C. 1985, c. C-44, ss. 42 & 43.

32 *Business Corporations Act*, R.S.O. 1990, c. B.16, s. 38(3).

33 *Canada Business Corporations Act*, R.S.C. 1985, c. C-44, s. 42.

dividend in one year, then next year, it must declare a dividend for Class B shareholders for the current and previous years, before it can declare a dividend for any other class of shares.

> Assume that Entertainment Group Ltd. has two classes of shares: Class A common shares and Class B preferred shares. The Class B shares have the right to receive cumulative, annual dividends. In Year 1, Entertainment Group Ltd. is unable to declare a dividend on Class B shares. In Year 2, Entertainment Group Ltd. must pay the Class B dividends for both Year 1 and Year 2, before it can declare any dividends for the Class A shares.

- Non-cumulative dividends – This type of dividend is payable on preferred shares before any dividend can be declared on common shares. However, if the corporation does not issue a dividend in a given year, the right for a dividend for that year disappears.

> Assume that Entertainment Group Ltd. has two classes of shares: Class A common shares and Class B preferred shares. The Class B shares have the right to receive ***non-cumulative***, annual dividends. In Year 1, Entertainment Group Ltd. is unable to declare a dividend on Class B shares. In Year 2, Entertainment Group Ltd. must pay the Class B dividends for Year 2 before it can declare a dividend for the Class A shares. Class B shareholders are not entitled to claim the unpaid dividend for Year 1.

- Partially-Cumulative dividends – This type of dividend provides that preferred shareholders will receive a cumulative dividend, and after that dividend is paid, they also receive the same dividend that common shareholders receive. The right to receive the preferred dividend is cumulative, but the right to share in the dividends received by common shareholders is not cumulative.

> Assume that Entertainment Group Ltd. has two classes of shares: Class A common shares and Class B preferred shares. The Class B shares have the right to receive *partially cumulative*, annual dividends. In Year 1, Entertainment Group Ltd. is unable to declare a dividend on Class B shares. In Year 2, Entertainment Group Ltd. must pay the Class B dividends for both Year 1 and Year 2, before it can declare any dividends for the Class A shares. Assume that the corporation does this, and then declares a dividend for Class A shares. At this point, Class B shareholders are also entitled to receive a further dividend that is equal to the amount received by Class A shareholders.

(iii) Additional Rights

A share may have additional rights attached to it. For example, a particular class of shares may have the exclusive right to elect a director or directors. If this is the only distinction between shares, then a corporation could have Class A common shares that can vote on all matters other than the right to elect a director, and Class B common shares that can vote on all matters including the exclusive right to vote for directors. For example, in Entertainment Group Ltd., Javid may demand the exclusive right to vote for directors since he is the only shareholder who is investing money in the corporation, and he wants to ensure that he always remains a director of the corporation. Similarly, preferred shares (which typically do not carry the right to vote) may be given the right to vote on certain matters affecting the corporation. Finally, shares can also have conditions or restrictions placed upon them, such as the right to vote only in certain circumstances. In every case, the way the shares are structured should reflect the goals of the corporation. For example, in most corporations, shareholders will not accept shares that have restrictions placed upon them, if they have invested an equal amount in the corporation. With Entertainment Group Ltd., however, Mike and Helena may accept shares with restrictions (even though they would prefer to have shares that are the same as those held by Javid and Sam,) since they do not have any capital to invest in the company when it is being incorporated. (Mike and Helena are basically receiving shares in Entertainment Group Ltd. in return for their skills, experience and personal contributions to the business.)

A more common right that can be attached to a particular class or series of shares is the right to convert shares from one class (or series) into shares of other class (or series). Convertible shares are shares that can be converted into another class of share, or another type of security altogether (such as a bond, which is discussed in part 5 of this Chapter.) For example, Class B preferred shares can have the right to convert to Class A common shares, usually at a stated price and within a fixed period of time. It is also possible to convert one share of one class into a different number of shares of a different class. For example, it would be possible to convert one Class B share into two Class A shares (or even one Class B share into $\frac{1}{2}$ of a Class A share) within a specified time at a stated price.

> Assume that Entertainment Group Ltd. has two classes of shares: Class A common shares and Class B preferred shares. The Class B shares are convertible – they can be converted into Class A shares within the first 2 years after incorporation, upon payment of $200 per share. Assume that Sam owns 50 Class B, convertible shares, and within the first two years of incorporation, he decides to exercise this right. He will have to pay $10,000 ($200 x 50 shares) to Entertainment Group Ltd. in order to convert his Class B shares into Class A shares. (Why would he be willing to do this?) Sam will also have to return his Class B share certificate(s) to the corporation, in exchange for a new Class A share certificate.

Subsection 27(1) of the *BCA* and subsection 29(1) of the *CBCA* give a corporation the right to issue convertible shares, as long as the corporation specifies the conditions for converting the shares on the share certificate, or in other certificates or documents. The conversion privileges can be transferable or non-transferable, and the corporation must maintain sufficient reserve of authorized shares to allow the exercises of such conversion privileges.[34] Subsection 35(8) of the *BCA* also addresses convertible shares in the following way:

---

34 *Business Corporations Act*, R.S.O. 1990, c. B.16, s. 27; *Canada Business Corporations Act*, R.S.C. 1985, c. C-44, s. 29.

Where shares of a class or series are changed under section 168, 186 or 248, or converted pursuant to their terms, into the same or another number of shares of another class or series, such shares become the same in all respects as the shares of the class or series respectively into which they are changed or converted, and if the articles limit the number of shares of either of such classes or series, the number of authorized shares of such class or series is changed and the articles amended accordingly.[35]

The *CBCA* has similar provisions in section 39.[36]

Shares can also be characterized as redeemable shares. Let's start with the premise that a corporation can buy its own shares, just like any other "person". Subsections 30(1) and 30(2) of the *BCA* state:

30(1) Subject to subsection (2) and to its articles, a corporation may purchase or otherwise acquire any of its issued shares or warrants.

(2) A corporation shall not make any payment to purchase or otherwise acquire shares issued by it if there are reasonable grounds for believing that,

(a) the corporation is or, after the payment, would be unable to pay its liabilities as they become due; or

(b) after the payment, the realizable value of the corporation's assets would be less than the aggregate of,

(i) its liabilities, and

(ii) its stated capital of all classes.[37]

A corporation may decide to purchase a shareholder's shares (thereby removing the shareholder from the corporation, as an owner) in order to settle a debt or a claim against the corporation, in order to eliminate fractional shares, or to fulfill an agreement that the corporation has made to purchase those shares.[38] For example, assume that the directors of Entertainment Group Ltd. decide that they do not want Sam involved in the corporation any longer. The corporation can pay Sam the value of his shares, thereby "purchasing" the shares from him. Now, Sam is no longer a shareholder in the corporation. Note that this does not affect his status as an officer or director of the corporation, if he plays one of those roles.

With this context in mind, a corporation can issue shares that are "redeemable." This means that the corporation can "buy back" the shares of a shareholder, thereby ridding itself of the obligation to pay dividends and any other privileges those shareholders may have. The share can be structured as redeemable at the option of the shareholder (meaning that the shareholder decides whether or not to make the corporation buy back its shares) or at the option of the corporation (meaning that the corporation decides whether or not to buy back the shares.) Usually, redemption is at the option of the corporation, so that the corporation can be sure that there are sufficient funds to redeem the shares.

---

35 *Business Corporations Act*, R.S.O. 1990, c. B.16, s. 35(8).

36 *Canada Business Corporations Act*, R.S.C. 1985, c. C-44, s. 39(9)–10).

37 *Business Corporations Act*, R.S.O. 1990, c. B.16, ss. 30(1)–(2); see also *Canada Business Corporations Act*, R.S.C. 1985, c. C-44, s. 34(1).

38 *Business Corporations Act*, R.S.O. 1990, c. B.16, s. 31; see also *Canada Business Corporations Act*, R.S.C. 1985, c. C-44, s. 35(1).

Section 32 of the *BCA* and section 36 of the *CBCA* address redemption of shares, and state that a corporation may purchase redeemable shares according to the redemption price (or formula) stated in the Articles of Incorporation. However, a corporation cannot redeem shares if there are reasonable grounds for believing that, after redemption:

- the corporation would be unable to pay its liabilities as they become due; or

- the realizable value of the corporation's assets would be less than the total of its liabilities plus the amount required for redemption (including any amounts that have to be paid to other shareholders before redemption, if applicable)[39]

Finally, shares of a corporation may carry pre-emptive rights. This means that, before those shares can be sold to anyone else, they must first be offered for sale to existing shareholders of the corporation. Section 26 of the *BCA* states:

> If it is so provided in the articles or a unanimous shareholder agreement, no shares of a class or series shall be issued unless the shares have first been offered to the shareholders of the corporation holding shares of that class or series of another class or series on such terms as are provided in the articles or unanimous shareholder agreement.[40]

The comparable provision in the *CBCA* is similar.[41] Pre-emptive rights allow the shareholders of a corporation to maintain control over the corporation, by preventing dilution of the value of their shares and loss of voting control.

Assume that Entertainment Group Ltd. has four shareholders, and authorized share capital of an unlimited number of common shares (designated as Class A shares):

Javid   -   100 common shares

Sam   -   50 common shares

Mike   -   50 common shares

Helena   -   50 common shares

Assuming that each share carries one vote, Javid and Sam can (together) have a majority vote on any issue requiring a majority decision (because collectively, they have 150 shares and Mike and Helena only have a total of 100 shares.) Assume that Entertainment Group Ltd. needs more money, so it decides to issue an additional 100 common shares (in return for $50,000, for example.) Assume that Helena's brother-in-law, Juan, is interested in purchasing the 100 common shares. **If the common shares carry pre-emptive rights,** the additional 100 common shares must first be offered to Javid, Sam, Helena and Mike, before they can be sold to Juan. Javid and/or Sam will likely try to purchase the 100 common shares, if they can afford to do so, in order to maintain voting control of the corporation. However, if they cannot afford to buy the shares, note how the voting power in the corporation changes:

Javid   -   100 common shares

Sam   -   50 common shares

---

39 *Business Corporations Act*, R.S.O. 1990, c. B.16, s. 32; *Canada Business Corporations Act*, R.S.C. 1985, c. C-44, s. 36.

40 *Business Corporations Act*, R.S.O. 1990, c. B.16, s. 26.

41 *Canada Business Corporations Act*, R.S.C. 1985, c. C-44, s. 28.

> Mike - 50 common shares
>
> Helena - 50 common shares
>
> Juan - 100 common shares
>
> Now, if Mike, Helena and Juan vote on an issue as a "voting block", they can override the views of Javid and Sam. Javid and Sam have lost their control over decisions made by shareholders.

(iv) Lien on Shares

If a shareholder owes a debt to a corporation, the corporation can have a lien on the shares registered in the name of that shareholder. For example, if Sam purchases shares of Entertainment Group Ltd., but only pays half up front with the balance payable in three months, then for those three months, Sam owes a debt to Entertainment Group Ltd. For those three months, Entertainment Group Ltd. has a lien on the shares – so if Sam decides to sell the shares to someone else in that period of time, he must first pay Entertainment Group Ltd. the balance owing from his purchase of the shares (or he can arrange for the new purchaser to assume this debt.) In order for the corporation to have a lien on shares, the articles or by-laws of the corporation (or in the case of a non-offering corporation, a unanimous shareholder agreement) must provide that the corporation has a lien on shares registered in the name of a shareholder that owes a debt to the corporation.[42] Note that the *BCA* states that this provision does not apply to publicly traded shares.[43]

(v) Subscription for Shares

Shares can generally be acquired in one of two ways: either by purchasing them from an existing shareholder, or by purchasing them from the corporation. If a shareholder wishes to purchase shares from a corporation (perhaps in response to the corporation's solicitations,) the shareholder "applies" for those shares by submitting a share subscription to the corporation. In contract law terminology, the corporation's solicitation for subscriptions is an "invitation to treat" and the shareholder's submission of a subscription for shares is an "offer". The corporation has no obligation to accept the shareholder's offer, but if it does, then there is a binding contract, and the corporation will issue shares to the new shareholder. All the requirements of a valid contract apply to this contractual relationship. For example, the shareholder can withdraw its subscription (that is, its offer to purchase shares in the corporation) at any time before that offer is accepted.

5. Bonds & Other Securities

The *BCA* recognizes that a corporation may issue securities other than shares. The term "security" is defined in the *BCA* as "a share of any class or series of shares or a

---

42 *Business Corporations Act*, R.S.O. 1990, c. B.16, s. 40(1) & (3); *Canada Business Corporations Act*, R.S.C. 1985, c. C-44, ss. 45(2)–(3).
43 *Business Corporations Act*, R.S.O. 1990, c. B.16, s. 40(2).

debt obligation of a body corporate."[44] Similarly, a "security certificate" is defined as "a certificate evidencing a security."[45] A bond is a type of debt obligation which can be issued by a corporation and is evidenced by a bond certificate. When a person – called a "bondholder" – buys a bond, that person is essentially lending money to the corporation at a fixed rate of interest. Bondholders typically purchase bonds instead of shares because they feel that there is less risk in investing in a bond. With bonds, the purchaser is guaranteed to receive the principal and interest within a specified period of time, whereas with shares, the purchaser is hoping that the shares will increase in value as the business grows. Shares hold the potential to make more money, but bonds have less risk – assuming that the corporation is able to pay its debts as they become due. Some of the factors that purchasers of bonds must consider are:

- whether the corporation is likely to be able to repay the debt, plus interest, in the specified period of time

- whether the corporation's assets are liquid, or tied up in assets

- what the corporation intends to use the money for, and whether that is likely to lead to business expansion and growth in profits

- what external factors – like the state of the economy – are likely to affect the corporation's ability to increase its profits over time.

Many individuals are familiar with Canada Savings Bonds, and while government bonds are different from corporate bonds, they serve as a useful example to learn about bonds. Information about Canada Savings Bonds is available from the official website, <www.csb.gc.ca>. On October 3, 2011, the government of Canada published interest rates for the November 1, 2011 bond issues. For example, the Canada Premium Bond Series 78 bond carries an interest rate of 1% and will mature in one year. Someone who purchases this bond will receive their principal plus 1% on November 1, 2012 (one year later.)[46] Clearly, this is a very low rate of interest, but it is also a very safe investment. As the amount of time to maturity and the risk level of a bond increases, the interest rate also increases. In Canada, corporate bonds are considered to be riskier than Canada Savings Bonds, because it is much more likely that a corporation will be unable to pay its debts than it is for the Canadian government to be unable to pay its debts. For this reason, corporations must offer a higher rate of interest – and therefore, a higher return on investment – for individuals that purchase corporate bonds than the government of Canada needs to offer.

Before we discuss an example, it is necessary to review some basic terms related to bonds. The "face value" of the bond is the principal amount that the bondholder invests. If a bond has a face value of $1,000, the bondholder must pay $1,000 to purchase that bond. The "coupon rate" or interest rate is the amount of money that the corporation must pay to the bondholder, as compensation for the loan. The interest rate is usually expressed as a rate "per annum", but that interest can be paid at different points in time,

---

44 *Ibid.*, s. 1(1); see also *Canada Business Corporations Act*, R.S.C. 1985, c. C-44, s. 2(1) for a very similar definition.
45 *Business Corporations Act*, R.S.O. 1990, c. B.16, s. 1(1).
46 "Rates," online: Canada Savings Bonds <http://www.csb.gc.ca/about/rates/>.

such as annually, semi-annually, or monthly. The "maturity date" is the date that the corporation must pay the bondholder the face value of the bond, plus any interest payable at that time.

Entertainment Group Ltd. needs to raise more money to grow its business. The directors do not want to issue additional shares, because they are uncomfortable about adding new shareholders to the company. (Note that the directors are also shareholders in the corporation.) Javid and Sam are concerned about the impact of adding new shareholders on their ability to control the outcome of voting at shareholder meetings, and a possible dilution in the value of their shares. As a result, the corporation decides to issue bonds. Juan, Helena's brother-in-law, purchases a corporate bond with a face value of $10,000, at a 10% annual interest rate, payable semi-annually and maturing in 2 years. (The example has been kept simple to make the calculations easier to understand, but typically, a corporation will issue many bonds in smaller denominations, such as $1,000.)

This means that, over two years, Entertainment Group Ltd. will have paid $2,000 in interest, and since interest is payable semi-annually, the corporation must pay $500 every 6 months for the next two years. The corporation must also pay the face value of the bond - $10,000 – at the end of two years. The bondholder's investment can be depicted in the following timeline:

Buy Bond	$500	$500	$500	$10,500
↓	↓	↓	↓	↓
0 months	6 months	12 months	18 months	24 months

The advantage to Entertainment Group Ltd. is that Juan (the bondholder) has no effect on shareholder control and no impact on the value of shares, because he is not a shareholder. But what will happen if Entertainment Group Ltd. uses the $10,000 provided by Juan, and it is still not able to grow its business? What will the corporation have to do in two years, when the bond matures?

Section 43 of the *BCA* is the section that allows a corporation to issue bonds. It simply states that "[n]othing in this Act prohibits the issue of a debt obligation in bearer form."[47] Note that section 27, which was discussed earlier in this chapter in relation to shares, also applies to bonds. Section 27 of the *BCA* states:

27(1) A corporation may issue warrants as evidence of conversion privileges or options or rights to acquire securities of the corporation, and shall set out the conditions thereof,

(a) in certificates evidencing the securities to which the conversion privileges, options or rights are attached; or

(b) in separate certificates or other documents.

---

47 *Ibid.*, s. 43.

. . .

(2)Conversion privileges and options or rights to purchase securities of a corporation may be made transferable or non-transferable, and options or rights to purchase may be made separable or inseparable from any securities to which they are attached.

. . .

(3)Where a corporation has granted privileges to convert any securities, other than shares issued by the corporation, into shares of the corporation or has issued or granted options or rights to acquire shares of the corporation and where the articles limit the number of authorized shares, the corporation shall reserve and continue to reserve sufficient authorized shares to meet the exercise of such conversion privileges, options and rights.

Section 27 of the *BCA* provides the basis for a corporation to issue securities that can be converted into another type of security, upon satisfaction of specified conditions. For example, a convertible bond is a bond that can be converted into shares if certain conditions are met.

> The directors of Entertainment Group Ltd. need to raise money but do not want to issue shares in the corporation at this point in time. Since the corporation is new, they do not want to add additional shareholders, and thereby lose some control over the corporation, at a point when they feel that they must grow the business in a certain way. However, they are also concerned about issuing bonds because they are worried about being able to pay back the face value of the bonds, plus interest, when the bonds mature. To address these issues, the directors decide to issue convertible bonds – that is (in this case,) bonds that will be converted into preferred shares if the corporation cannot repay the face value of the bonds (plus interest) on the maturity date.

Subsections 39(11), (12) and 48(2) of the *CBCA* discuss debt obligations, which include bonds.[48]

---

48 *Canada Business Corporations Act*, R.S.C. 1985, c. C-44, ss. 39(11), (12) & 48(2).

CHAPTER 9: PREPARING A MINUTE BOOK – PART 1

Overview:

- Statutory requirements
- Minute book
  - Articles of Incorporation & related documents
  - By-laws
  - Minutes & Resolutions
    - Directors' Organizational Resolutions
    - Shareholders' Organizational Resolutions
- Workbook:
  - By-Law No. 1
  - Directors' and Shareholders' Organizational Resolutions
- Appendices:
  - By-law No. 1
  - By-law No. 2
  - Directors' Organizational Resolutions
  - Special resolution regarding number of directors
  - Shareholders' Organizational Resolutions (voting shareholders)
  - Shareholders' Organizational Resolutions (all voting & non-voting share-holders)

1. Statutory Requirements

As we discussed in Chapter 5, filing Articles of Incorporation is the first step in the incorporation process. The next step is creating a minute book for the corporation. The term "minute book" is not used in the *BCA* or the *CBCA*, but is the term used legal professionals use to describe a binder, which contains the key records for a corporation. Subsection 140(1) of the *BCA* requires that a corporation prepares and maintains the following records at its registered office, or at such other place in Ontario designated by the directors:

- the articles and by-laws of the corporation (including any amendments), and a copy of any unanimous shareholder agreement known to the directors

- minutes of shareholder meetings and resolutions

- minutes of directors' meetings and resolutions

- a directors' register, listing all the directors of the corporation and the dates that they became (and if applicable, ceased to be) directors

- a securities register that complies with section 141, and

- adequate accounting records.[1]

In addition, section 24 of the *BCA* and section 26 of the *CBCA* require that the corporation maintain a separate stated capital account for each class and series of shares issued by the corporation.[2]

Any records required to be kept by the corporation can be kept in a bound or loose-leaf book – such as a minute book – or in electronic format.[3] The securities register must include the names of the persons who are or have been registered shareholders of the corporation for the last six years, and the number and class of shares held by each shareholder. Similarly, the securities register must list the registered holders of debt obligations (such as bondholders) for the last six years, and the holders of certain types of warrants. The corporation must also maintain a register of transfers which shows the transfer of securities either from the corporation, or amongst shareholders.[4] Similar requirements can be found in sections 20 to 22 of the *CBCA*.[5]

In practice, most minute books will contain the following tabs or sections, reflecting the requirements discussed above:

1. Articles of Incorporation

2. By-laws

3. Minutes & Resolutions

4. Directors' Register

---

1 *Business Corporations Act*, R.S.O. 1990, c. B.16, s. 140.
2 *Ibid.*, s. 24; *Canada Business Corporations Act*, R.S.C. 1985, c. C-44, s. 26.
3 *Business Corporations Act*, R.S.O. 1990, c. B.16, s. 139.
4 *Ibid.*, s. 141.
5 *Canada Business Corporations Act*, R.S.C. 1985, c. C-44, ss. 20–22.

5. Officers' Register

6. Shareholders' Register

7. Share Transfer Register

8. Shareholders' Ledger (as many as required)

9. Shareholders' Agreements

10. Register of Debt Obligations

11. Forms Filed

12. Miscellaneous

13. Share Certificates

Each of these documents, other than the Articles of Incorporation (which were discussed in Chapter 5), will be reviewed in Chapters 9 and 10.

Note that directors may examine records mentioned in sections 140 and 141 of the *BCA* during normal business hours, and except where specified in the Act, the records must usually be kept at the registered office of the corporation.[6] In the past, lawyers kept clients' minute books at their offices (for ease of reference, and to ensure that they were updated as required.) However, as a lawyer's practice grows, this may not be a practical option if there are storage constraints. Registered shareholders, beneficial owners of shares and even creditors of a corporation may examine records referred to in section 140(1) of the *BCA* during normal business hours, and if the corporation is an offering corporation, they may take copies of those records free of charge. If the corporation is a non-offering corporation, they may take copies upon payment of a reasonable fee.[7] Subsections 20(4) and 21(1)–(3) of the *CBCA* have similar provisions.[8]

2. The Minute Book

This part of the chapter will provide details on what you need to include in each tab (or section) of the corporate minute book for an Ontario corporation. A minute book for a federal corporation can be created with the same format, but the forms will differ. For example, Articles of Amendment for an Ontario corporation are designated as Form 3 under the *BCA*, whereas Articles of Amendment for a federal corporation are Form 4 under the *CBCA* and are separate from the Change of Registered Office Address, which is Form 3 under the *CBCA*. As mentioned previously in this book, current copies of forms for Ontario corporations can be found on the Ontario Central Forms Repository website, and forms for federal corporations can be found on the Corporations Canada website. (Please refer to Chapters 2 and 5 for details on these websites.)

---

6 *Business Corporations Act*, R.S.O. 1990, c. B.16, s. 141.
7 Ibid., s. 145(1).
8 *Canada Business Corporations Act*, R.S.C. 1985, c. C-44, ss. 20(4) & 21(1)–(3).

(a) Articles of Incorporation& Related Documents

The first tab of a minute book is for Articles of Incorporation, as this is the "birth certificate" for a corporation. Please refer to Chapter 5 for a discussion on how to prepare Articles of Incorporation. Note that this section of the minute book should also contain any Articles of Amendment (Form 3 under the *BCA*) and the Consent to Act as First Director (Form 2 under the *BCA,*) if applicable.

Assume that Javid, Helena, Mike and Sam decide to change the name of their corporation from Entertainment Group Ltd. to Nirvana Nightclub Ltd. In order to do this, you would have to file duplicate copies of Articles of Amendment (Form 3 under the *BCA,*) with the Ministry of Government Services, Personal Property and Security Branch. The filing fee is currently $150. Detailed instructions are provided online with the form; as always, legal professionals should pay careful attention to these instructions to avoid unnecessary delays. Note that, since this is a change in the name of a corporation, a NUANS search report with the new corporate name must be attached to the Articles of Amendment. (Articles of Amendment are discussed in greater detail in Chapter 12, which includes a sample form for Entertainment Group Ltd.)

(b) By-laws

The word "by-law" comes from Scandinavian origin and meant a "village law". Over time, it has come to mean "subordinate laws". From a corporate perspective, by-laws are the rules and regulations which govern how a corporation operates. They are usually prepared immediately after the Articles of Incorporation are certified. In fact, section 117 of the *BCA* and section 104 of the *CBCA* specify what directors must do at their first meeting, after incorporation. Specifically, the directors must:

- make by-laws

- adopt forms of security certificates (such as share certificates) and corporate records

- authorize the issue of securities (such as the issuance of shares to shareholders)

- appoint officers

- appoint one or more auditors to hold office until the first annual meeting of shareholders, or a special meeting of the shareholders

- make banking arrangements, and

- transact any other business.[9]

First on this list is the responsibility to make by-laws.

Section 116 of the *BCA* and section 103 of the *CBCA* address by-laws of a corporation. These sections specify that it is the directors' prerogative to make, amend or repeal by-laws of a corporation, unless the Articles of Incorporation, by-laws or a unanimous shareholder agreement states otherwise. However, after the directors have created, amended or repealed the by-laws, the shareholders of the corporation have the oppor-

---

9 *Business Corporations Act*, R.S.O. 1990, c. B.16, s. 117; *Canada Business Corporations Act*, R.S.C. 1985, c. C-44, s. 104.

tunity to confirm, reject or amend the by-law at the next shareholders' meeting. The process is as follows:

- By-laws are made, amended or repealed

- Directors pass an ordinary resolution (requiring 50% of the directors eligible to vote) to approve the by-laws. The by-laws are effective as of the date of this directors' resolution.

- The by-laws must be presented to shareholders for approval at the next shareholders' meeting. If, at that meeting,

    - the shareholders approve the by-laws, the by-laws continue in effect

    - the shareholders reject the by-laws or suggest a change to the by-laws, the by-laws cease to be effective on the date of the shareholders' rejection. While all previous business conducted according to those by-laws is still effective, no further business can be conducted until new by-laws are confirmed by the shareholders.[10]

In Ontario, the common practice is for legal professionals to draft one set of by-laws, often referred to as the "General By-law", or simply, "By-law No. 1". In the past, it was also common to draft a "Borrowing By-law" or "By-law No. 2." By-law No. 2 stated that the corporation had the authority to borrow money and issue debt obligations (such as bonds.) Today, many legal professionals do not prepare By-law No. 2, because the *BCA* (and the *CBCA*) already confer upon the corporation the power to do both of these things, and more. In fact, as a "legal person", the corporation can do anything, in a business context, that an individual can. Section 184 of the *BCA* makes this clear by stating:

> Unless the articles or by-laws of or a unanimous shareholder agreement otherwise provide, the articles of a corporation shall be deemed to state that the directors of a corporation may, without authorization of the shareholders,
>
> (a) borrow money upon the credit of the corporation;
>
> (b) issue, reissue, sell or pledge debt obligations of the corporation;
>
> (c) give a guarantee on behalf of the corporation to secure performance of an obligation of any person; and
>
> (d) mortgage, hypothecate, pledge or otherwise create a security interest in all or any property of the corporation, owned or subsequently acquired, to secure any obligation of the corporation.[11]

While drafting By-law No. 2 is, therefore, unnecessary, there may be situations where a legal professional is asked to provide a copy of By-law No. 2. Banks or other financial institutions may ask clients to complete their own form of By-law No. 2 (on the bank's

---

10 *Business Corporations Act*, R.S.O. 1990, c. B.16, s. 116; *Canada Business Corporations Act*, R.S.C. 1985, c. C-44, s. 103.

11 *Business Corporations Act*, R.S.O. 1990, c. B.16, s. 184; *Canada Business Corporations Act*, R.S.C. 1985, c. C-44, s. 189.

standard form) or they may ask the client to provide a copy of By-law No. 2. If this occurs, the lawyer or law clerk can draft By-law No. 2 for the client.

It is possible to buy precedent forms for By-law No. 1 and By-law No. 2 from companies that provide legal precedents. In this case, it is important to select the correct version of the by-laws; typically, there is one version of By-law No. 1 for companies with a single director and single shareholder, and another version for companies with multiple directors (and there may be other versions as well.) Alternatively, many law firms will have their own precedents, or will use the precedents provided by corporate law software packages such as Fast Company.[12] (This software will be discussed in Chapter 14.)

Appendix A and B to this chapter include samples of By-law No. 1 and By-law No. 2 for Entertainment Group Ltd. They have been produced using Fast Company.[13] In By-law No. 1, note that the following provisions have been tailored for Entertainment Group Ltd.; these provisions would have to be tailored for any corporation:

- section 2.3 – Fiscal Year

- section 2.4 – Execution of Documents

- section 3.3 – Number of Directors

- section 4.7 – Quorum for Directors' Meetings

- section 4.9 – Casting Vote in a Directors Meeting

- section 7.8 – Quorum for Shareholders' Meetings

- section 7.16 – Votes to Govern in a Shareholders Meeting

The edited portion of these sections is marked with an asterisk (*) and can, therefore, be easily searched and identified on the computer. A law clerk or lawyer should also consider whether other areas of By-law No. 1 need to be tailored to suit a particular client's objectives. It is important to view a precedent as a helpful starting point, but not a simple "fill-in-the-blanks" form that can be printed off the computer without careful consideration. Some additional areas to consider include:

- section 5.4 – List of Officers

- section 8.7 – Lien for Indebtedness (which must appear in By-law No. 1 *or* in the Articles of Incorporation. If this provision is in the Articles of Incorporation, it should be deleted from By-law No. 1.)

The fiscal year of the corporation – referred to in the *BCA* as the "financial year" – may not be known at the time that the minute book is being prepared. If this is the case, simply delete section 2.3 of the sample By-law No. 1 provided in Appendix A to this chapter, and ensure that a directors' resolution is drafted to address this issue in due course. Since resolutions can be changed much more easily than a by-law, a lawyer may decide to omit section 2.3 of By-law No. 1 *even if* the fiscal year is known at the time the by-law is being drafted. By including the fiscal year in the organizational resolutions

---

12 A product of Do Process Software Ltd.
13 *Ibid.*

of the directors, a change can be easily made later, if the fiscal year of the corporation is amended.

Section 2.2 of the sample By-law No. 1 provided in this chapter deals with the corporate seal. It has been left in this sample because, while it allows the corporation to have a corporate seal, it does not require it. Section 13 of the *BCA* states that a corporation "may, but need not, have a corporate seal."[14] A corporate seal can usually be ordered from suppliers of minute books, and they come in many formats. Historically, corporate seals were required by corporations to show to third parties that a contract signed on behalf of a corporation had, in fact, been approved by the corporation. As commerce grew, it became impractical to require every contract entered into by a corporation to be stamped with the corporate seal, and as such, the *BCA* specifically addressed the matter by making corporate seals optional. Having said that, some clients do want to have a corporate seal and are willing to pay to have one. This is a matter to be discussed with every client, as it is certainly not necessary to incur the expense of purchasing a corporate seal.

Finally, many of the topics addressed in By-law No. 1 are also referred to in the *BCA* and the *CBCA*. With respect to directors, for example, section 126 of the *BCA* addresses a number of matters related to directors' meetings, including where the meeting can be held, quorum (that is, the number of directors that are required to hold a meeting,) notice requirements, the ability to waive notice, and meetings by telephone. Section 126 of the *BCA* provides – as do other provisions in the *BCA* and *CBCA* – that the procedures outlined in that section are subject to what is stated in a corporation's Articles of Incorporation or by-laws. In other words, the statutes provide a basic "operations manual" for corporations to follow, but each corporation can tailor its processes to suit its own purposes (within the limits established by those statutes.)[15] The provisions that address directors and officers are found in Part IX of the *BCA*.

Similarly, Part VII of the *BCA* addresses shareholders. Section 97 of the *BCA* discusses voting at a shareholders' meeting, and states that the chairman of a shareholders' meeting shall not have a casting vote, unless the by-laws or Articles or a unanimous shareholder agreement states otherwise.[16] Section 98 discusses notice requirements for shareholder meetings and the ability to waive notice.[17] Section 101 of the *BCA* addresses quorum at shareholders' meetings, and again, states that the holders of the majority of shares at a shareholders meeting constitutes quorum, unless the by-laws of a corporation state otherwise.[18] The goal of the governing statutes appears to be to provide guidance on these issues, but to allow a corporation to create its own procedures for day-to-day operation of the corporation, within stated limits.

---

14 *Business Corporations Act*, R.S.O. 1990, c. B.16, s. 13.
15 *Business Corporations Act*, R.S.O. 1990, c. B.16, s. 126.
16 *Ibid.*, s. 97.
17 *Ibid.*, s. 98.
18 Ibid., s. 101.

(c) Minutes and Resolutions

The next part of a minute book is called "Minutes and Resolutions." In this chapter, we will address the first entry in this portion of the minute book – the organizational resolutions of directors and the organizational resolutions of shareholders.

As a starting point, it is important to remember that a corporation can only act if its directors – and sometimes, its shareholders – approve that action. After all, a corporation is a legal fiction – it exists in the law, but is not a human being that can act on its own. Approval of corporate actions occurs at directors' and shareholders' meetings. However, directors and shareholders may not want to meet to discuss something that they have already agreed upon – and if the shareholders of a corporation are all directors (or if there is only one shareholder who acts as the sole director and assumes the role of President and Secretary-Treasurer) – then it may be redundant to have a meeting for the sake of formality. The corporate statutes recognize this, and as a result, many corporate matters can be dealt with by resolution, rather than by holding a meeting. A resolution is a written record of decisions made either by directors (in which case it is called a "directors' resolution") or shareholders (in which case it is called a "shareholders' resolution.") By contrast, "minutes" refer to notes taken (in a particular format) at either a directors' meeting or a shareholders' meeting, including a record of decisions taken at that meeting. Therefore, there would either be resolutions recording particular decisions (if there was no formal meeting held to approve certain decisions), *or* minutes (if an actual meeting was held to discuss them.)

(i) Directors' Organizational Resolutions

Both the *BCA* and the *CBCA* require the corporation to hold a meeting of the first directors. Section 117 of the *BCA*, which we have referred to in part 2(b) ("By-laws") above, states:

> 117(1) After incorporation, a meeting of the directors of the corporation shall be held at which the directors may,
>
> > (a) make by-laws;
> >
> > (b) adopt forms of security certificates and corporate records;
> >
> > (c) authorize the issue of securities;
> >
> > (d) appoint officers;
> >
> > (e) appoint one or more auditors to hold office until the first annual or special meeting of the shareholders;
> >
> > (f) make banking arrangements; and
> >
> > (g) transact any other business.
>
> (2) Any matter referred to in subsection (1) may be dealt with by the directors by a resolution in writing in accordance with subsection 129(1).[19]

---

19 *Business Corporations Act*, R.S.O. 1990, c. B.16, s. 117; see also *Canada Business Corporations Act*, R.S.C. 1985, c. C-44, s. 104.

However, in most cases, first directors may not want to meet in person to address these matters. It is often easier to address these organizational matters by preparing resolutions. The *BCA* recognizes this in subsection 129(1) and provides:

> A resolution in writing, signed by all of the directors entitled to vote on that resolution at a meeting of directors or a committee of directors, is as valid as if it had been passed at a meeting of directors or a committee of directors.[20]

The normal practice, therefore, is for the legal professional to prepare directors' resolutions that address the matters referred to in section 117 of the *BCA*. Those resolutions – called "organizational resolutions" – must be signed by all of the directors who would be entitled to attend the first meeting of directors. (Generally, this means that all of the first directors must sign the organizational resolutions.)

In addition to the matters discussed in s. 117 of the *BCA* (noted previously), organizational resolutions of the directors typically also address:

- adoption of a corporate seal, if applicable

- location of the registered office of the corporation

- the financial/fiscal year end of the corporation, if it has been established and was not included in the by-laws

- adoption of any pre-incorporation contracts (such as a lease for the corporation's premises), if applicable

Finally, if the Articles of Incorporation provide for a range of directors, subsection 125(3) of the *BCA* requires that the directors pass a special resolution indicating the number of directors that the corporation will elect at the present time.[21] For example, if the Articles of Incorporation state that the corporation may have between 1 to 10 directors, and the corporation intends to start its business with 3 directors, then a special resolution of the directors must be passed to indicate that the corporation will have 3 directors at this point in time. A special resolution is defined in s.1(1) of the *BCA* as:

> A resolution that is,
>
> (a) submitted to a special meeting of the shareholders of a corporation duly called for the purpose of considering the resolution passed, with or without amendment, at the meeting by at least two-thirds of the votes cast, or
>
> (b) consented to in writing by each shareholder of the corporation entitled to vote at such a meeting or the shareholder's attorney authorized in writing.[22]

This is in contrast to an "ordinary resolution", which is also defined in subsection 1(1) as "a resolution submitted to a meeting of the shareholders of a corporation and

---

20 *Business Corporations Act*, R.S.O. 1990, c. B.16, s. 129; see also *Canada Business Corporations Act*, R.S.C. 1985, c. C-44, s. 117

21 *Business Corporations Act*, R.S.O. 1990, c. B.16, s. 125(3).

22 *Business Corporations Act*, R.S.O. 1990, c. B.16, s. 1(1); see also *Canada Business Corporations Act*, R.S.C. 1985, c. C-44, s. 2(1).

passed, with or without amendment, at the meeting by at least a majority of the votes cast."[23]

While both the *BCA* and the *CBCA* define "ordinary resolution" and "special resolution" in terms of shareholders, the same principles are generally applied to directors' resolutions. With respect to the special resolution indicating the number of directors (referred to previously,) the resolution should be signed by all of the directors entitled to vote at a special meeting of directors (which will likely be all of the first directors, since this resolution is being passed immediately after the organizational resolutions of the directors.)

Appendix C to this Chapter includes sample organizational resolutions of the directors of Entertainment Group Ltd. Each "paragraph" that begins with "Resolved that . . ." is referred to as a resolution of the directors, but they can all be grouped together in one document, as shown in Appendix C. Note that the resolutions end with a confirmation clause, which indicates that the resolutions have been passed in accordance with the governing statute (either the *BCA* or *CBCA*,) as well as the date and signature lines for all of the directors of the corporation.

(ii) Shareholders' Organizational Resolutions

While shareholders have limited power in the corporation (as compared to directors,) they do have certain important rights and responsibilities relating to the organization of the corporation. The second document included in the "Minutes and Resolutions" section of the minute book will be the shareholders' organizational resolutions. (The first document was the directors' organizational resolutions.) Shareholders' organizational resolutions typically include:

- Electing the directors of the corporation

- Waiving the right to have an auditor

- Appointing the accountant for the corporation

(Please refer to Chapter 7 for a discussion on why shareholders may opt to waive the right to have an auditor. Note that Part XII of the *BCA* and sections 161 to 172 of the *CBCA* deal with auditors and financial statements of a corporation.)

Appendices D and E to this Chapter provide sample shareholders' resolutions regarding the election of directors (including a special resolution regarding the number of directors.) Appendices F and G provide examples of the organizational resolutions of the shareholders of Entertainment Group Ltd.

---

23 *Ibid.*

APPENDIX A:

By-Law No. 1

A by-law relating generally to the conduct of the business and affairs of

ENTERTAINMENT GROUP LTD.

CONTENTS

BE IT ENACTED as a by-law of Entertainment Group Ltd. as follows:

1. Interpretation

1.1 <u>Definitions</u> - In this by-law and all other by-laws and resolutions of the Corporation, unless the context otherwise requires:

"Act" means the *Business Corporations Act (Ontario)*, including the Regulations made pursuant thereto, and any statute or regulations substituted therefor, as amended from time to time;

"appoint" includes "elect", and *vice versa*

"articles" means the Articles of Incorporation and/or other constating documents of the Corporation as amended or restated from time to time;

"board" means the board of directors of the Corporation and *"director"* means a member of the board;

"by-laws" means this by-law and all other by-laws, including special by-laws, of the Corporation as amended from time to time and which are, from time to time, in force and effect;

"Corporation" means this Corporation, being the corporation to which the Articles pertain, and named "Entertainment Group Ltd.";

"meeting of shareholders" includes an annual meeting of shareholders and a special meeting of shareholders; *"special meeting of shareholders"* means a special meeting of all sharehold-

ers entitled to vote at an annual meeting of shareholders and a meeting of any class or classes of shareholders entitled to vote on the question at issue;

"recorded address" means, in the case of a shareholder, his address as recorded in the shareholders' register; and in the case of joint shareholders, the address appearing in the shareholders' register in respect of such joint holding or the first address so appearing if there is more than one; in the case of a director, officer, auditor or member of a committee of the board, his latest address as shown in the records of the Corporation or in the most recent notice filed under the *Corporations Information Act*, whichever is the more current. The secretary may change or cause to be changed the recorded address of any person in accordance with any information believed by him to be reliable.

1.2 Rules - In the interpretation of this by-law, unless the context otherwise requires, the following rules shall apply:

a) Except where specifically defined herein, words, terms and expressions appearing in this by-law, including the terms "resident Canadian" and "unanimous shareholder agreement" shall have the meaning ascribed to them under the Act;

b) Words importing the singular include the plural and *vice versa*;

c) Words importing gender include the masculine, feminine and neuter genders;

d) Words importing a person include an individual, sole proprietorship, partnership, unincorporated association, unincorporated syndicate, unincorporated organization, trust, body corporate, and a natural person in his capacity as trustee, executor, administrator, or other legal representative.

2. General Business Matters

2.1 Registered Office - The shareholders may, by special resolution, from time to time change the municipality or geographic township within Ontario in which the registered office of the Corporation shall be located, but unless and until such special resolution has been passed, the registered office shall be where initially specified in the articles. The directors shall from time to time fix the location of the registered office within such municipality or geographic township.

2.2 Corporate Seal - The Corporation may, but need not, have a corporate seal; if adopted, such seal shall be in the form approved from time to time by the board.

2.3 Fiscal Year - Unless and until another date has been effectively determined, the fiscal year or financial year of the Corporation shall end on December 30th* in each year.

2.4 Execution of Documents - Deeds, transfers, assignments, contracts, obligations and other instruments in writing requiring execution by the Corporation may be signed by any two of the President, Vice-President, Secretary or Treasurer*.

Notwithstanding the foregoing, the board may from time to time direct the manner in which and the person or persons by whom a particular document or class of documents shall be executed. Any person authorized to sign any document may affix the corporate seal thereto.

2.5 Banking - All matters pertaining to the banking of the Corporation shall be transacted with such banks, trust companies or other financial organizations as the board may designate or authorize from time to time. All such banking business shall be transacted on behalf of the Corporation pursuant to such agreements, instructions and delegations of powers as may, from time to time, be prescribed by the board.

3. Directors

3.1 Powers - Subject to the express provisions of a unanimous shareholder agreement, the directors shall manage or supervise the management of the business and affairs of the Corporation.

3.2 Transaction of Business - Business may be transacted by resolutions passed at meetings of directors or committees of directors at which a quorum is present or by resolution in writing, signed by all the directors entitled to vote on that resolution at a meeting of directors or a committee of directors. A copy of every such resolution in writing shall be kept with the minutes of the proceedings of the directors or committee of directors.

3.3 Number - Until changed in accordance with the Act, the board shall consist of that number of directors, being a minimum of one (1) and a maximum of ten (10)*, as determined from time to time by special resolution or, if the special resolution empowers the directors to determine the number, by resolution of the board.

3.4 Resident Canadians - If the board consists of only one director, that director shall be a resident Canadian. If the board consists of two directors, at least one of the two directors shall be a resident Canadian. Except as aforesaid, not less than 25% of the directors of the Corporation shall be resident Canadians.

3.5 Qualifications - Each director shall be an individual who is not less than 18 years of age. No person who is of unsound mind and has been so found by a court in Canada or elsewhere or who has the status of a bankrupt shall be a director. If a director acquires the status of a bankrupt or becomes of unsound mind and is so found, he shall thereupon cease to be a director. A director need not be a shareholder.

3.6 Election and Term - The election of directors shall take place at the first meeting of shareholders and at each annual meeting of shareholders and all the directors then in office shall retire, but, if qualified, shall be eligible for re-election. The number of directors to be elected at any such meeting shall be the number of directors then in office unless the directors or shareholders shall have otherwise determined in accordance with the Act. Where the shareholders adopt an amendment to the articles to increase the number or minimum number of directors, the shareholders may, at the meeting at which they adopt the amendment, elect the additional number of directors authorized by the amendment. The election shall be by resolution. If an election of directors is not held at the proper time, the incumbent directors shall continue in office until their successors are elected.

3.7 Resignation - A director who is not named in the articles may resign from office upon giving a written resignation to the Corporation and such resignation becomes effective when received by the Corporation or at the time specified in the resignation, whichever is later. A director named in the articles shall not be permitted to resign his office unless at the time the resignation is to become effective a successor is elected or appointed.

3.8 Removal - Subject to the provisions of the Act, the shareholders may, by ordinary resolution passed at an annual or special meeting of shareholders, remove any director from office before the expiration of his term and may elect a qualified individual to fill the resulting vacancy for the remainder of the term of the director so removed, failing which such vacancy may be filled by the board. Notice of intention to pass such resolution shall be given in the notice calling the meeting.

3.9 <u>Vacation of office</u> - A director ceases to hold office when he dies, resigns, is removed from office by the shareholders, or becomes disqualified to serve as director.

3.10 <u>Vacancies</u> - Subject to the provisions of the Act, a vacancy on the board may be filled for the remainder of its term by a qualified individual by resolution of a quorum of the board. If there is not a quorum of directors or if a vacancy results from the failure to elect the number of directors required to be elected at any meeting of shareholders, the directors then in office shall forthwith call a special meeting of shareholders to fill the vacancy and, if they fail to call a meeting or if there are no directors then in office, the meeting may be called by any shareholder.

4. <u>Meetings of Directors</u>

4.1 <u>Place of Meetings</u> - Meetings of the board may be held at the registered office of the Corporation or at any other place within or outside of Ontario, and it is not necessary that, in any financial year of the Corporation, a majority of such meetings be held in Canada.

4.2 <u>Participation by Telephone</u> - With the unanimous consent of all of the directors present at or participating in the meeting, a director may participate in a meeting of the board or in a meeting of a committee of directors by means of such telephone, electronic or other communication facilities as permit all persons participating in the meeting to communicate with each other simultaneously and instantaneously, and a director participating in such a meeting by such means is deemed for the purposes of the Act and this by-law to be present at that meeting. A consent pursuant to this provision may be given before or after the meeting to which it relates and may be a "blanket" consent, relating to all meetings of the board and/or committees of the board and need not be in writing.

4.3 <u>Calling of Meetings</u> - In addition to any other provisions in the articles or by-laws of a Corporation for calling meetings of directors, a quorum of the directors may, at any time, call a meeting of any business, the general nature of which is specified in the notice calling the meeting. Where the Corporation has only one director, that director may constitute a meeting.

4.4 <u>Notice of Meeting</u> - Notice of the time and place for the holding of a meeting of the board shall be given to every director of the Corporation not less than two clear days (excluding Sundays and holidays as defined by the *Interpretation Act*) before the date of the meeting. Notwithstanding the foregoing, notice of a meeting shall not be necessary if all of the directors are present, and none objects to the holding of the meeting, or if those absent have waived notice of or have otherwise signified their consent to the holding of such meeting. Notice of an adjourned meeting is not required if the time and place of the adjourned meeting is announced at the original meeting.

4.5 <u>First Meeting of New Board</u> - Provided that a quorum of directors is present, a newly elected board may, without notice, hold its first meeting immediately following the meeting of shareholders at which such board is elected.

4.6 <u>Regular Meetings</u> - The board may appoint a day or days in any month or months for regular meetings of the board at a place and hour to be named. A copy of any resolution of the board fixing the place and time of such regular meetings of the board shall be sent to each director forthwith after being passed, but no other notice shall be required for any such regular meeting except where the Act requires the purpose thereof or the business to be transacted thereat to be specified.

4.7 <u>Quorum</u> - A majority of the directors elected to office* constitutes a quorum at any meeting of the board.

4.8 <u>Chairman</u> - The Chairman of any meeting of the board shall be the first mentioned of such of the following officers as have been appointed and who is a director and is present at the meeting:

Chairman of the Board
President,
A Vice-President, or
Managing Director

If no such officer is present, the directors present shall choose one of their number to be Chairman of such meeting.

4.9 <u>Votes to Govern</u> - At all meetings of the board, every question shall be decided by a majority of the votes cast on the question; and in the case of an equality of votes, the Chairman of the meeting shall *be entitled to a second or casting vote.

4.10 <u>Disclosure- Conflict of Interest</u> - A director or officer of the Corporation who is a party to, or who is a director or an officer of, or has a material interest in any person who is a party to, a material contract or transaction or proposed material contract or transaction with the Corporation, shall disclose in writing to the Corporation or request to have entered in the minutes of meetings of directors the nature and extent of his interest. Disclosure, as aforesaid, shall be made at the time and in the manner required by the Act, and a director so having an interest in a contract or transaction shall, unless expressly permitted by the Act, not vote on any resolution to approve the contract or transaction.

4.11 <u>Delegation by Directors (Committees)</u> - The board may appoint from their number a managing director, or a committee of directors, and delegate to such managing director or committee any of the powers of the board except those which relate to matters over which a managing director or committee shall, pursuant to the Act, not have authority. Unless otherwise determined by the board, a committee shall have the power to fix its quorum at not less than a majority of its members, to elect its chairman and to regulate its procedure.

4.8 <u>Remuneration and Expenses</u> - Subject to the articles and any unanimous shareholder agreement, the board may fix the remuneration of the directors, which remuneration shall be in addition to any remuneration which may be payable to a director who serves the Corporation in any other capacity. The directors shall also be entitled to be reimbursed for travelling and other expenses properly incurred by them in attending meetings of the board, committees or shareholders and for such other out-of-pocket expenses incurred in respect of the performance of their duties as the board may from time to time determine.

5. <u>Officers</u>

5.1 <u>Appointment</u> - The board may from time to time designate the offices of the Corporation, appoint officers (and assistants to officers), specify their duties and, subject to the Act or the provisions of any unanimous shareholder agreement, delegate to such officers powers to manage the business and affairs of the Corporation. A director may be appointed to any office of the Corporation. Except for the chairman of the board and the managing director, an officer may but need not be a director. Two or more offices may be held by the same person.

5.2 <u>Term of Office (Removal)</u> - In the absence of a written agreement to the contrary, the board may remove, whether for cause or without cause, any officer of the Corporation. Unless so removed, an officer shall hold office until his successor is appointed or until his resignation, whichever shall first occur.

5.3 <u>Terms of Employment, Duties and Remuneration</u> - The terms of employment and remuneration of all officers elected or appointed by the board shall be determined from time to time and may be varied from time to time by the board. The fact that any officer or employee is a director or shareholder of the Corporation shall not disqualify him from receiving such remuneration as may be determined. All officers, in the absence of agreement to the contrary, shall be subject to removal by resolution of the Board of Directors at any time, with or without cause.

5.4 <u>Description of Offices</u> - Unless otherwise specified by the board (which may, subject to the Act, modify, restrict or supplement such duties and powers), the offices of the Corporation, if designated and if officers are appointed thereto, shall have the following duties and powers associated therewith:

a) **Chairman of the Board** - The chairman of the board, if one is to be appointed, shall be a director. The board may assign to him any of the powers and duties which, pursuant to the by-laws, are capable of being assigned to the managing director or to the president. During the absence or disability of the Chairman of the Board, the President shall assume all his powers and duties.

b) **Managing Director** - The managing director, if one is to be appointed, shall exercise such powers and have such authority as may be delegated to him by the Board in accordance with the provisions of Section 127 of the Act.

c) **President** - The President shall be the chief executive officer of the Corporation unless otherwise determined by resolution of the Board of Directors and shall have responsibility for the general management and direction of the business and affairs of the Corporation, subject to the authority of the Board of Directors. Where no Chairman of the Board is elected or during the absence or inability to act of Chairman of the Board, the President, when present, shall preside at all meetings of shareholders, and if he is a director, at all meetings of the Board of Directors or meetings of a committee of directors;

d) **Vice-President** - During the absence or inability of the President, his duties may be performed and his powers may be exercised by the Vice-President, or if there are more than one, by the Vice-President in order of seniority (as determined by the Board of Directors) save that no Vice-President shall preside at a meeting of the Board of Directors or at a meeting of shareholders who is not qualified to attend the meeting as a director or shareholder, as the case may be. A Vice-President shall also perform such duties and exercise such powers as the President may from time to time delegate to him or as the Board of Directors may prescribe;

e) **General Manager** - The General Manager, if one be appointed, shall have the responsibility for the general management, and direction, subject to the authority of the Board of Directors and the supervision of the President, of the Corporation's business and affairs and the power to appoint and remove any and all officers, employees and agents of the Corporation not appointed directly by the Board of Directors and to settle the terms of their employment and remuneration.

f) **Secretary** - The secretary, when in attendance, shall be the secretary of all meetings of the board, shareholders and committees of the board and, whether or not he attends, the secretary shall enter or cause to be entered in the Corporation's minute book, minutes of all proceedings at such meetings; he shall give, or cause to be given, as and when instructed, notices to shareholders, directors, auditors and members of committees; he shall be the custodian of the corporate seal as well as all books, papers, records, documents and other instruments belonging to the Corporation. He shall perform such other duties as may from time to time be prescribed by the Board of Directors;

g) **Treasurer** - The treasurer shall be responsible for the maintenance of proper accounting records in compliance with the Act as well as the deposit of money, the safekeeping of securities and the disbursement of funds of the Corporation; whenever required, he shall render to the board an account of his transactions as treasurer and of the financial position of the Corporation.

The duties of all other officers of the Corporation shall be such as the terms of their engagement call for or the board requires of them. Any of the powers and duties of an officer to whom an assistant has been appointed may be exercised and performed by such assistant, unless the board otherwise directs.

5.5 <u>Vacancies</u> - If the office of the Chairman of the Board, Managing Director, President, Vice-President, Secretary, Assistant Secretary, Treasurer, Assistant Secretary, or any one of such offices, or any other office shall be or become vacant by reason of death, resignation, disqualification or otherwise, the Board of Directors by resolution shall in the case of the President or Secretary, and may in the case of any other office, appoint a person to fill such vacancy.

5.6 <u>Agents and Attorneys</u> - The board shall have power from time to time to appoint agents or attorneys for the Corporation in or out of Ontario with such powers of management, administration or otherwise (including the power to sub-delegate) as the board considers fit.

5.7 <u>Disclosure- Conflict of Interest</u> - An officer shall have the same duty to disclose his interest in a material contract or transaction or proposed material contract or transaction with the Corporation, as is, pursuant to the provisions of the Act and the by-laws, imposed upon directors.

6. <u>Protection of Directors, Officers and Others</u>

6.1 <u>Standard of Care</u> - Every director and officer of the Corporation in exercising his powers and discharging his duties shall act honestly and in good faith with a view to the best interests of the Corporation and shall exercise the care, diligence and skill that a reasonably prudent person would exercise in comparable circumstances. Every director and officer of the Corporation shall comply with the Act, the regulations, articles, by-laws and any unanimous shareholder agreement.

6.2 <u>Limitation of Liability</u> - Provided that the standard of care required of him has been satisfied, no director or officer shall be liable for the acts, receipts, neglects or defaults of any other director or officer or employee, or for joining in any receipt or other act for conformity, or for any loss, damage or expense happening to the Corporation through the insufficiency or deficiency of title to any property acquired for or on behalf of the Corporation, or for the insufficiency or deficiency of any security in or upon which any of the monies of the Corporation shall be invested, or for any loss or damage arising from the bankruptcy, insolvency or tortious acts of any person with whom any of the monies, securities or effects of the Corporation shall be deposited, or for any loss occasioned by any error of judgment or oversight on his part, or for any other loss, damage or misfortune which shall happen in the execution of the duties of his office or in relation thereto, unless the same are occasioned by his own willful neglect or default.

6.3 Indemnity of Directors and Officers - Subject to the Act, the Corporation shall indemnify a director or officer of the Corporation, a former director of officer of the Corporation or a person who acts or acted at the Corporation's request as a director or officer of a body corporate of which the Corporation is or was a shareholder or creditor, and his heirs and legal representatives, against all costs, charges and expenses, including an amount paid to settle an action or satisfy a judgment, reasonably incurred by him in respect of any civil, criminal administrative, investigative or other action or proceeding to which he is made a party by reason of being or having been a director or officer of such corporation or body corporate if,

a) he acted honestly and in good faith with a view to the best interests of the Corporation; and

b) in the case of a criminal or administrative action or proceeding that is enforced by a monetary penalty, he had reasonable grounds for believing that his conduct was lawful.

The Corporation shall indemnify such person in all such other matters, actions, proceedings and circumstances as may be permitted by the Act or the law.

6.4 Insurance - Subject to the Act, the Corporation may purchase and maintain such insurance for the benefit of any person entitled to be indemnified by the Corporation pursuant to the immediately preceding section as the board may from time to time determine.

6.5 Financial Assistance - The Corporation or any corporation with which it is affiliated, shall not, directly or indirectly, give financial assistance by means of a loan, guarantee or otherwise, to any shareholder, director, officer or employee of the Corporation or affiliated corporation or to an associate of any such person for any purpose; or to any person for the purpose of or in connection with a purchase of a share or security convertible into or exchangeable for a share, issued or to be issued by the Corporation or affiliated corporation, where there are reasonable grounds for believing that:

(a) the Corporation is, or after giving the financial assistance, would be unable to pay its liabilities as they become due; or

(b) the realizable value of the Corporation's assets, excluding the amount of any financial assistance in the form of a loan and in the form of any secured guarantee, after giving the financial assistance, would be less than the aggregate of the Corporation's liabilities and stated capital of all classes.

The Corporation may give financial assistance by means of a loan, guarantee or otherwise, to any person in the ordinary course of business if the lending of money is part of the ordinary business of the Corporation; to any person on account of expenditures incurred or to be incurred on behalf of the Corporation; to its holding body corporate if the Corporation is a wholly owned subsidiary of the holding body corporate; to a subsidiary body corporate of the Corporation; or to employees of the Corporation or any of its affiliates, to enable or assist them to purchase or erect living accommodation for their own occupation, or in accordance with a plan for the purchase of shares of the Corporation or any of its affiliates.

7. Meetings of Shareholders

7.1 Annual Meetings - The board shall call, at such date and time as it determines, the first annual meeting of shareholders not later than eighteen months after the Corporation comes into existence and thereafter not later than fifteen months after holding the last preceding annual meeting, so as to consider the financial statements and reports required by the Act to be presented thereat, to elect directors, appoint auditors and to transact such other business as may properly be brought before the meeting.

7.2 Special Meetings - The board, the chairman of the board, the managing director or the president may at any time call a special meeting of shareholders for the transaction of any business which may properly be brought before such meeting of shareholders.

7.3 Place of Meetings - Meetings of shareholders shall be held at such place in or outside Ontario as the board determines or, in the absence of such a determination, at the place where the registered office of the Corporation is located.

7.4 Special Business - All business transacted at a special meeting or an annual meeting of shareholders, except consideration of the minutes of an earlier meeting, the financial statements and auditor's report, election of directors and reappointment of the incumbent auditor constitutes special business.

7.5 Notice of Meetings - Notice of the time and place of a meeting of shareholders shall be sent not less than 10 days, or if the Corporation is an offering corporation, not less than twenty-one (21) days, but in either case not more than 50 days before the date of the meeting:

a)   to each shareholder entitled to vote at the meeting (according to the records of the Corporation at the close of business on the day preceding the giving of the notice);

b)   to each director; and

c)   to the auditor of the Corporation.

A meeting of shareholders may be held at any time without notice if all the shareholders entitled to vote thereat are present or represented by proxy and do not object to the holding of the meeting or those not so present by proxy have waived notice, if all the directors are present or have waived notice of or otherwise consent to the meeting and if the auditor, if any, is present or has waived notice of or otherwise consents to the meeting.

Notice of a meeting of shareholders at which special business is to be transacted shall state:

a)   the nature of that business in sufficient detail to permit the shareholder to form a reasoned judgment thereon; and

b)   the text of any special resolution or by-law to be submitted to the meeting.

In the event of the adjournment of a meeting, notice, if any is required, shall be given in accordance with the provisions of the Act.

7.6 <u>Waiving Notice</u> - A shareholder and any other person entitled to attend a meeting of shareholders may in any manner and at any time waive notice of a meeting of shareholders, and attendance of any such person at a meeting of shareholders is a waiver of notice of the meeting, except where such person attends a meeting for the express purpose of objecting to the transaction of any business on the grounds that the meeting is not lawfully called.

7.7 <u>Persons Entitled to be Present</u> - The only persons entitled to be present at a meeting of shareholders shall be those entitled to vote thereat, the directors and the auditor of the Corporation, if any and such other persons who are entitled or required under any provision of the Act, articles or by-laws of the Corporation to be present at the meeting. Any other person may be admitted only on the invitation of the chairman of the meeting or with the consent of the meeting.

7.8 <u>Quorum</u> - The holders of a majority of shares entitled to vote at a meeting of shareholders*, whether present in person or represented by proxy, constitute a quorum for the transaction of business at any meeting of shareholders. If a quorum is present at the opening of a meeting of shareholders, the shareholders present may proceed with the business of the meeting even if a quorum is not present throughout the meeting. If the Corporation has only one shareholder, or only one holder of any class or series of shares, the shareholder present in person or by proxy constitutes a meeting.

7.9 <u>Right to Vote</u> - Unless the articles otherwise provide, each share of the Corporation entitles the holder thereof to one vote at a meeting of shareholders. At each meeting of shareholders every shareholder shall be entitled to vote who is entered on the books of the Corporation as a holder of one or more shares carrying the right to vote at such meeting in accordance with a shareholder list which, in the case of a record date, shall be a list of those registered at the close of business on that record date, and where there is no record date, at the close of business on the day immediately preceding the day on which notice is given or, where no notice is given, those registered on the day on which the meeting is held. When a share or shares have been mortgaged or hypothecated, the person who mortgaged or hypothecated such share or shares (or his proxy) may nevertheless represent the shares at meetings and vote in respect thereof unless in the instrument creating the mortgage or hypothec, he has expressly empowered the holder of such mortgage or hypothec to vote thereon, in which case such holder (or his proxy) may attend meetings to vote in respect of such shares upon filing with the Secretary of the meeting sufficient proof of the terms of such instrument.

7.10 <u>Representatives</u> - An executor, administrator, committee of a mentally incompetent person, guardian or trustee and where a Corporation is such executor, administrator, committee, guardian or trustee, any person duly a proxy appointed for such corporation, upon filing with the secretary of the meeting sufficient proof of his appointment, shall represent the shares in his or its hands at all meetings of the shareholders of the Corporation and may vote accordingly as a shareholder in the same manner and to the same extent as the shareholder of record. Where two or more persons hold the same share or shares jointly, any one of such persons present at a meeting of shareholders has the right, in the absence of the other or others, to vote in respect of such share or shares but if more than one of such persons are present or represented by proxy and vote, they shall vote together as one on the share or shares jointly held by them.

7.11 Scrutineers - At each meeting of shareholders one or more scrutineers may be appointed by a resolution of the meeting or by the Chairman with the consent of the meeting to serve at the meeting. Such scrutineers need not be shareholders of the Corporation.

7.12 Proxies - Every shareholder entitled to vote at a meeting of shareholders may by means of a proxy appoint a proxyholder or one or more alternate proxyholders who need not be shareholders, as the shareholder's nominee to attend and act at the meeting in the manner, to the extent and with the authority conferred by the proxy. A proxy shall be in writing, shall be executed by the shareholder or by his attorney authorized in writing or, if the shareholder is a body corporate, by an officer or attorney thereof duly authorized, and shall cease to be valid after the expiration of one year from the date thereof. The instrument appointing a proxy shall comply with the provisions of the Act and regulations thereto and shall be in such form as the Board of Directors may from time to time prescribe or in such other form as the Chairman of the meeting may accept as sufficient and shall be deposited with the Secretary of the meeting before any vote is cast under its authority, or at such earlier time and in such manner as the Board of Directors may prescribe in accordance with the Act.

7.13 Time for Deposit of Proxies - The Corporation shall recognize a proxy only if it has been deposited with the Corporation and it shall be so deposited before any vote is taken under its authority, or at such earlier time as the board, in compliance with the Act, prescribes and which has been specified in the notice calling the meeting.

7.14 Corporate Shareholders and Associations - As an alternative to depositing a proxy, a body corporate or an association may deposit a certified copy of a resolution of its directors or governing body authorizing an individual to represent it at meetings of shareholders of the Corporation.

7.15 Joint Shareholders - Where two or more persons hold shares jointly, one of those holders present at a meeting of shareholders may in the absence of the others vote the shares, but if two or more of those persons are present, in person or by proxy, they shall vote as one on the shares jointly held by them.

7.16 Votes to Govern - Subject to the Act, the articles, the by-laws and any unanimous shareholder agreement, all questions proposed for the consideration of the shareholders shall be determined by a majority of the votes cast thereon and, in case of an equality of votes, the chairman of the meeting shall *have a second or casting vote.

7.17 Show of Hands - Except where a ballot is demanded as hereafter set out, voting on any question proposed for consideration at a meeting of shareholders shall be by show of hands, and a declaration by the chairman as to whether or not the question or motion has been carried and an entry to that effect in the minutes of the meeting shall, in the absence of evidence to the contrary, be evidence of the fact without proof of the number or proportion of the votes recorded in favour of or against the motion.

7.18 Ballots - For any question proposed for consideration at a meeting of shareholders, either before or after a vote by show of hands has been taken, the chairman, or any shareholder or proxyholder may demand a ballot, in which case the ballot shall be taken in such manner as the chairman directs and the decision of the shareholders on the question shall be determined by the result of such ballot.

7.19 Resolution in Lieu of Meeting - Except where, pursuant to the Act, a written statement is submitted to the Corporation by a director or representations in writing are submitted to the Corporation by an auditor:

a) a resolution in writing signed by all the shareholders entitled to vote on that resolution at a meeting of shareholders is as valid as if it had been passed at a meeting of the shareholders; and

b) a resolution in writing dealing with all matters required by the Act to be dealt with at a meeting of shareholders, and signed by all the shareholders entitled to vote at that meeting, satisfies all the requirements of the Act relating to that meeting of shareholders.

7.20 One Shareholder - Where the Corporation has only one shareholder, all business which the Corporation may transact at an annual or special meeting of shareholders shall be transacted in the manner provided for in paragraph 7.18 hereof.

7.21 Adjournment - The Chairman of the meeting of shareholders may, with the consent of the meeting and subject to such conditions as the meeting may decide, or where otherwise permitted under the provisions of the Act, adjourn the meeting from time to time and from place to place.

8. Shares

8.1 Allotment - Subject to the Act, the articles and any unanimous shareholder agreement, the board may from time to time issue, allot or grant options to purchase the whole or any part of the authorized and unissued shares of the Corporation, at such times and to such persons and for such consideration as the board shall determine, provided that no share shall be issued until it is fully paid as provided by the Act.

8.2 Share Certificates - Share certificates and the form of stock transfer power shall be in such form as the board shall from time to time approve and shall be signed by the Chairman of the Board or the President or a Vice-President and the Secretary or Assistant Secretary holding office at the time of signing. Every shareholder of the Corporation is entitled upon request to a share certificate or to a non-transferable written acknowledgment of his right to obtain a share certificate in respect of the shares held by him.

Unless otherwise provided in the Articles, the Board may provide by resolution that all or any classes and series of shares or other securities shall be uncertified securities, provided that such resolution shall not apply to securities represented by a certificate until such certificate is surrendered to the Corporation.

The signature of the Chairman of the Board, the Vice-Chairman of the Board, the President or a Vice-President may be printed, engraved, lithographed or otherwise mechanically reproduced upon certificates for shares of the Corporation. Certificates so signed shall be deemed to have been manually signed by the Chairman of the Board, the Vice-Chairman of the Board, the President or the Vice-President whose signature is so printed, engraved, lithographed or otherwise mechanically reproduced thereon and shall be as valid to all intents and purposes as if they had been signed manually. Where the Corporation has appointed a trustee, registrar, transfer agent, branch transfer agent or other authenticating agent, for the shares of the Corporation the signature of the Secretary or Assistant Secretary may also be printed, engraved, lithographed or otherwise mechanically reproduced on certificates representing the shares (or the shares of the class or classes in respect of which any such appointment has been made) of the Corporation and when countersigned by or on behalf of a trustee, registrar, transfer agent, branch transfer agent or other authenticating agent such certificates so signed shall be as valid to all intents and purposes as if they had been signed manually. A share certificate containing the signature of a person which is printed, engraved, lithographed or otherwise mechanically reproduced thereon may be issued notwithstanding that the person has ceased to be an officer of the Corporation and shall be as valid as if he were an officer at the date of its issue.

8.3 Joint Shareholders - If two or more persons are registered as joint holders of any share, it shall be sufficient for the Corporation to issue one certificate in respect thereof and it shall also be sufficient for the Corporation to accept, from any one of such persons, receipts for the certificate or for any dividend, bonus, return of capital or other money payable or warrant issuable in respect of such share.

8.4 Deceased Shareholders - In the event of the death of a shareholder, the Corporation shall not be required to make an entry in its records in respect of such death and nor shall it be required to make any dividend or other payment in respect of such shares until such documents have been produced to the Corporation as are required by the Act and the law and as are reasonably required by the Corporation and its transfer agents.

8.5 Replacement of Share Certificates - Subject to the Act, the board may prescribe, either generally or for a particular instance, the conditions upon which a new share certificate may be issued to replace a share certificate which has been or is claimed to have been defaced, lost, stolen or destroyed.

8.6 Payment of Commission - The board may, from time to time, authorize the Corporation to pay a reasonable commission to any person in consideration of his purchasing or agreeing to purchase shares of the Corporation from the Corporation or from any other person, or for procuring or agreeing to procure purchasers for any such shares.

8.7 Lien for Indebtedness - Subject to the Act, the Corporation has a lien on shares registered in the name of a shareholder or his legal representative for a debt of that shareholder to the Corporation which lien may be enforced, subject to the articles and to any unanimous shareholder agreement, by the sale of such shares or by any other proceeding or remedy available by law to the Corporation and, until such indebtedness has been satisfied, the Corporation may refuse to register a transfer of any such shares.

8.8 Central Securities Register - A securities register and the register of transfers of the Corporation shall be kept at the registered office of the Corporation or such other office or place in Ontario as may from time to time be designated by resolution of the Board of Directors and a branch securities register or registers of transfers may be kept at such office or offices of the Corporation or other place or places, either in or outside Ontario, as may from time to time be designated by resolution of the Board of Directors.

8.9 Transfer of Securities - No transfer of shares shall be recorded or registered unless or until the certificate representing the shares to be transferred has been surrendered and cancelled.

9. Dividends

9.1 Declaration - Subject to the Act, the articles and any unanimous shareholder agreement, the board may declare and the Corporation may pay dividends to the shareholders according to their respective rights and interests in the Corporation. Any such dividend may be paid by issuing fully paid shares of the Corporation or options or rights to acquire fully paid shares of the Corporation or, subject to the Act, the Corporation may pay a dividend in money or property.

9.2 <u>Payment</u> - A dividend payable in money shall be paid by cheque to the order of each registered holder of shares of the class or series in respect of which it has been declared and, unless the shareholder otherwise directs, mailed by prepaid ordinary mail to such registered holder at his last address appearing on the records of the Corporation. In the case of joint shareholders, unless they otherwise direct, the cheque shall be made payable to the order of all of such joint holders and mailed by prepaid ordinary mail to them at the address appearing on the records of the Corporation for them or, if addresses appear for more than one such joint holder, it shall be mailed to the first address so appearing. The mailing of such cheque as aforesaid, unless it is not honoured on presentation, shall satisfy and discharge the liability for the dividend to the extent of the aggregate of the sum represented by such cheque plus the amount of any tax which the Corporation is required to and does withhold. The board may prescribe, either generally or for a particular instance, the terms as to indemnity, reimbursement of expenses and evidence of non-receipt, upon which a replacement cheque may be issued to a person to whom a dividend cheque was sent and who claims that such cheque was not received or has been defaced, lost, stolen or destroyed.

10. Notices

10.1 <u>Method of Giving Notices</u> - Any notice, communication or other document required to be given by the Corporation to a shareholder, director, officer, member of a committee of the board or auditor of the Corporation pursuant to the Act, the regulations, the articles or by-laws or otherwise shall be sufficiently given to such person if:

a) delivered personally to him, in which case it shall be deemed to have been given when so delivered;

b) delivered to his recorded address, in which case it shall be deemed to have been given when so delivered;

c) mailed to him at his recorded address by prepaid ordinary mail, in which case it shall be deemed to have been given on the fifth day after it is deposited in a post office or public letter box; or

d) sent to him at his recorded address by any means of prepaid transmitted or recorded communication, in which case it shall be deemed to have been given when dispatched or delivered to the appropriate communication company or agency or its representative for dispatch.

If a notice or document is sent to a shareholder by prepaid mail in accordance with this paragraph and the notice or document is returned on three consecutive occasions because the shareholder cannot be found, it shall not be necessary to send any further notices or documents to the shareholder until he informs the Corporation in writing of his new address.

10.2 <u>Notice to Joint Shareholders</u> - Notice required to be given to a shareholder where two or more persons are registered as joint holders of any share shall be sufficiently given to all of them if given to any one of them.

10.3 <u>Notices Given to Predecessors</u> - Every person who by transfer, death of a shareholder, operation of law or otherwise becomes entitled to shares, is bound by every notice in respect of such shares which was duly given to the registered holder of such shares from whom his title is derived prior to entry of his name and address in the records of the Corporation and prior to his providing to the Corporation the proof of authority or evidence of his entitlement as prescribed by the Act.

10.4 <u>Computation of Time</u> - In computing the date when notice must be given under any provision requiring a specified number of days' notice of any meeting or other event, the date of giving the notice and the date of the meeting or other event shall be excluded.

10.5 <u>Omissions and Errors</u> - The accidental omission to give any notice to any shareholder, director, officer, member of a committee of the board or auditor, or the non-receipt of any notice by any such person or any error in any notice not affecting its substance shall not invalidate any action taken at any meeting to which the notice pertained or otherwise founded on such notice.

10.6 <u>Waiver of Notice</u> - Any shareholder, proxyholder, director, officer, member of a committee of the board or auditor may waive or abridge the time for any notice required to be given him, and such waiver or abridgement, whether given before or after the meeting or other event of which notice is required to be given shall cure any default in the giving or in the time of such notice, as the case may be. Any such waiver or abridgement shall be in writing except a waiver of notice of a meeting of shareholders or of the board or of a committee of the board, which may be given in any manner.

11. Effective Date

11.1 <u>Effective Date</u> - Subject to its being confirmed by the shareholders, this by-law shall come into force when enacted by the board, subject to the provisions of the Act.

ENACTED by the board this _____ day of _____, 20_____.

_____
President

_____
Secretary   c/s

The foregoing by-law is hereby enacted by the directors of the Corporation as evidenced by the respective signatures hereto of all of the directors of the Corporation in accordance with the provisions of section 129(1) of the *Business Corporations Act* (Ontario).

DATED the _____ day of _____, 20_____.

_____   _____
JAVID KHAN   HELENA KRISTINA MADEJ

_____
MICHAEL ANDREW SMITH

In lieu of confirmation at a general meeting of the shareholders, the foregoing by-law is hereby confirmed by all of the shareholders of the Corporation entitled to vote at a meeting of shareholders in accordance with the provisions of section 104(1) of the *Business Corporations Act* (Ontario), this day of , 20.

DATED the _____ day of _____, 20_____.

_____   _____
JAVID KHAN   SAM KHAN

_____   _____
HELENA KRISTINA MADEJ   MICHAEL ANDREW SMITH

APPENDIX B:

By-Law No. 2

A by-law respecting the borrowing of money,

the issuing of securities and the securing of liabilities by

ENTERTAINMENT GROUP LTD.

(herein called the "Corporation")

BE IT ENACTED as a by-law of the Corporation as follows:

1. <u>Borrowing Powers</u> - Without limiting the borrowing powers of the Corporation as set forth in the Act, the board may, subject to the articles and any unanimous shareholder agreement, from time to time, on behalf of the Corporation, without the authorization of the shareholders:

   a) borrow money on the credit of the Corporation;

   b) issue, re-issue, sell or pledge debt obligations of the Corporation, whether secured or unsecured;

   c) subject to the Act, give a guarantee on behalf of the Corporation to secure performance of an obligation of any person; and

   d) mortgage, hypothecate, pledge or otherwise create a security interest in all or any property of the Corporation, owned or subsequently acquired, to secure any obligation of the Corporation.

2. <u>Delegation of Powers</u> - Subject to the Act, the articles, the by-laws and any unanimous shareholder agreement, the board may, from time to time, delegate any or all of the powers hereinbefore specified, to a director, a committee of directors or one or more officers of the Corporation.

ENACTED by the board this _____ day of _____, 20_____.

_____
President

_____
Secretary   c/s

The foregoing by-law is hereby enacted by the directors of the Corporation as evidenced by the respective signatures hereto of all of the directors of the Corporation in accordance with the provisions of section 129(1) of the *Business Corporations Act* (Ontario).

DATED the _____ day of _____, 20_____.

_____   _____
JAVID KHAN   HELENA KRISTINA MADEJ

_____
MICHAEL ANDREW SMITH

In lieu of confirmation at a general meeting of the shareholders, the foregoing by-law is hereby confirmed by all of the shareholders of the Corporation entitled to vote at a meeting of shareholders in accordance with the provisions of section 104(1) of the *Business Corporations Act* (Ontario), this _____ day of _____, 20_____.

DATED the _____ day of _____, 20_____.

_____   _____
JAVID KHAN   SAM KHAN

_____   _____
HELENA KRISTINA MADEJ   MICHAEL ANDREW SMITH

APPENDIX C:

Resolutions of the Directors

of

Entertainment Group Ltd.

1. Articles of Incorporation

BE IT RESOLVED THAT:

the directors acknowledge that the Corporation has been incorporated by Articles of Incorporation issued under the *Business Corporations Act* (Ontario), bearing date the 21st day of October, 2011 and they hereby direct that a copy of such Articles of Incorporation be inserted and retained in the minute book of the Corporation.

2. By-Law No. 1

BE IT RESOLVED THAT:

the directors of the Corporation do hereby approve and adopt By-Law No. 1, being a by-law relating generally to the conduct of the business and affairs of the Corporation, and the President and the Secretary be and they are hereby authorized and directed to sign and to affix the seal of the Corporation thereto.

3. Approval of Share Certificates

BE IT RESOLVED THAT:

the forms of share certificates annexed to these resolutions, and initialed for identification by the president, be and the same are hereby approved and adopted as the forms of share certificates of the Corporation to be issued in respect of the:
unlimited number of Common shares;
unlimited number of non-voting Class "A" shares;
unlimited number of voting, redeemable, retractable Class "B" shares with non-cumulative dividends;
unlimited number of voting, participating, redeemable, retractable Class "C" shares with cumulative dividends;
unlimited number of non-voting Class "D" shares with non-cumulative dividends.
as indicated on the said certificates.

4. Corporate Seal

BE IT RESOLVED THAT:

the form of corporate seal, an impression of which is affixed beside this resolution be and the same is hereby adopted as the corporate seal of the Corporation.

5. Location of Registered Office

BE IT RESOLVED THAT:

the location of the registered office of the Corporation be and the same is hereby fixed at:

555 Hotspot Blvd.
Toronto, Ontario
L4S 5T6
in the City of Toronto
in the Province of Ontario

6. Banking and Signing Officers

BE IT RESOLVED THAT:

an account be opened with:

TD BANK 2222
600 Hotspot Blvd.
Toronto, Ontario
L4S 5T6

and that the resolution respecting banking with TD Bank 2222 providing for signature by any two of the President, Secretary or Treasurer on behalf of the Corporation, a copy of which is annexed to these resolutions, be and the same is hereby passed and adopted.

7. Corporate Solicitors

BE IT RESOLVED THAT:

SMART & SMARTER LLP, Barristers and Solicitors, be and they are hereby retained as the Corporation's solicitors and be and they are hereby authorized to accept and carry out such instructions as the directors, officers, and authorized agents of the Corporation may give them from time to time.

8. Appointment of Officers

BE IT RESOLVED THAT:

The following persons be and they are hereby elected or appointed officers of the Corporation to hold office during the pleasure of the board:

JAVID KHAN	President
HELENA KRISTINA MADEJ	Secretary-Treasurer
MICHAEL ANDREW SMITH	1st Vice President

9. Allotment and Issue of Common Shares for Cash

BE IT RESOLVED THAT:

a) the subscriptions from Javid Khan, Sam Khan, Helena Kristina Madej and Michael Andrew Smith for three hundred (300) Common shares in the capital of the Corporation be and the same are hereby accepted;

b) the board of directors of the Corporation, acting in good faith and in the best interests of the Corporation, hereby fixes the sum of $30,000.00 as the aggregate consideration for the allotment and issue of the said three hundred (300) Common shares;

c) three hundred Common shares in the capital of the Corporation be and they are hereby allotted and issued, subject to payment therefor, to the following persons in the numbers and at the subscription prices set opposite their respective names:

SUBSCRIPTION	NO. OF SHARES	PRICE PER SHARE
JAVID KHAN	100	$100.00
SAM KHAN	100	$100.00
HELENA KRISTINA MADEJ	50	$100.00
MICHAEL ANDREW SMITH	50	$100.00

d) upon receipt by the Corporation of the sum of $30,000.00 in respect of the consideration for the allotment and issue of the said three hundred (300) Common shares, the said Common shares be allotted and issued to Javid Khan, Sam Khan, Helena Kristina Madej and Michael Andrew Smith as fully paid and non-assessable, and certificates therefor be issued to them or as they may in writing direct.

10. Allotment and Issue of Class "B" Shares For Cash

BE IT RESOLVED THAT:

a) the subscription from Javid Khan for one hundred (100) Class "B" shares in the capital of the Corporation be and the same is hereby accepted;

b) the board of directors of the Corporation, acting in good faith and in the best interests of the Corporation, hereby fixes the sum of $15,000.00 as the aggregate consideration for the allotment and issue of the said one hundred (100) Class "B" shares;

c) one hundred Class "B" shares in the capital of the Corporation be and they are hereby allotted and issued, subject to payment therefor, to Javid Khan at the subscription price set opposite his name:

SUBSCRIPTION	NO. OF SHARES	PRICE PER SHARE
JAVID KHAN	100	$150.00

d) upon receipt by the Corporation of the sum of $150.00 in respect of the consideration for the allotment and issue of the said one hundred (100) Class "B" shares, the said Class "B" shares be allotted and issued to Javid Khan as fully paid and non-assessable, and a certificate therefor be issued to him or as he may in writing direct.

11. Fiscal Year End

BE IT RESOLVED THAT:

the fiscal year end of the Corporation shall terminate on December 30th in each year.

12. Location of Minute Book

BE IT RESOLVED THAT:

a) the office of:

NIRVANA NIGHTCLUB
555 Hotspot Blvd.
Toronto, Ontario
L4S 5T6

is hereby designated as a location at which the minute book, including the registers and corporate records of the Corporation, may be prepared, maintained and kept; and

b) the certificate of incorporation be placed and retained in the minute book.

EACH AND EVERY OF THE FOREGOING RESOLUTIONS is hereby consented to by all of the directors of the Corporation, as evidenced by their respective signatures hereto in accordance with the provisions of subsection 129(1) of the *Business Corporations Act* (Ontario), this _____ day of _____, 20_____.

_____

JAVID KHAN

_____

HELENA KRISTINA MADEJ

_____

MICHAEL ANDREW SMITH

APPENDIX D:

Resolution of the Shareholders

of

Entertainment Group Ltd.

13. ELECTION OF DIRECTORS

WHEREAS the number of directors comprising the board of directors of the Corporation has been fixed at three (3).

NOW THEREFORE BE IT RESOLVED THAT:

The following persons be and they are hereby elected directors of the Corporation to hold office until the completion of the first annual meeting of the shareholders of the Corporation or until their respective successors are duly elected, subject to the provisions of the by-laws of the Corporation and the provisions of the *Business Corporations Act* (Ontario):

JAVID KHAN
HELENA KRISTINA MADEJ
MICHAEL ANDREW SMITH

THE FOREGOING RESOLUTION is hereby consented to by all of the shareholders of the Corporation entitled to vote thereon at a meeting of shareholders, as evidenced by their respective signatures hereto in accordance with the provisions of section 104(1) of the *Business Corporations Act* (Ontario), this _____ day of _____, 20____.

_____

JAVID KHAN

_____

SAM KHAN

_____

HELENA KRISTINA MADEJ

_____

MICHAEL ANDREW SMITH

APPENDIX E:

Special Resolution

of

Entertainment Group LTD.

14. Number and Election of Directors

    WHEREAS the Articles of the Corporation provide that the number of directors for the Corporation is a range with a minimum of one (1) and a maximum of ten (10);

    NOW THEREFORE BE IT RESOLVED AS A SPECIAL RESOLUTION OF THE CORPORATION THAT:

    i)   the number of directors comprising the board of directors of the Corporation shall be fixed at three (3), being a number within the prescribed range;

    ii)   the following persons be and they are hereby elected directors of the Corporation to hold office until the first annual meeting or annual resolutions of the share-holders of the Corporation or until their respective successors are duly elected, subject to the provisions of the by-laws of the Corporation and the provisions of the *Business Corporations Act* (Ontario):

JAVID KHAN
HELENA KRISTINA MADEJ
MICHAEL ANDREW SMITH

    iii)   the directors of the Corporation are hereby empowered to determine the number of directors of the Corporation hereafter from time to time by resolution of the board.

    THE FOREGOING SPECIAL RESOLUTION is hereby consented to by all of the directors of the Corporation, as evidenced by their respective signatures hereto in accordance with the provisions of subsection 129(1) of the *Business Corporations Act* (Ontario), this _____ day of _____, 20_____.

_____   _____

JAVID KHAN   HELENA KRISTINA MADEJ

_____

MICHAEL ANDREW SMITH

    THE FOREGOING SPECIAL RESOLUTION is hereby consented to and passed by all of the shareholders of the Corporation entitled to vote thereon at a meeting of shareholders, as evidenced by their respective signatures hereto in accordance with the provisions of subsection 104(1) of the *Business Corporations Act* (Ontario), this _____ day of _____, 20_____.

JAVID KHAN

SAM KHAN

HELENA KRISTINA MADEJ

MICHAEL ANDREW SMITH

APPENDIX F:

Resolutions of the Shareholders

of

Entertainment Group LTD.

15. <u>BY-LAW NO. 1</u>

BE IT RESOLVED THAT:

By-Law No. 1, being a by-law relating generally to the conduct of the business and affairs of the Corporation, in the form enacted by the board of directors be and the same is hereby confirmed.

16. <u>BY-LAW NO. 2</u>

BE IT RESOLVED THAT:

By-Law No. 2, being a by-law respecting the borrowing of money and the issuing of securities by the Corporation, in the form enacted by the board of directors be and the same is hereby confirmed.

17. <u>APPOINTMENT OF ACCOUNTANT</u>

BE IT RESOLVED THAT:

Pecuniary Associates be and he is hereby appointed the accountant of the Corporation to hold office until the completion of the first annual meeting of the shareholders of the Corporation, or until a successor is appointed, at such remuneration as may be fixed by the board of directors and the board of directors is hereby authorized to fix such remuneration.

18. <u>INDEMNIFICATION OF DIRECTORS AND OFFICERS</u>

BE IT RESOLVED THAT:

the Corporation indemnify and save harmless each director and officer of the Corporation and his or her heirs, executors, administrators and estates and other legal personal representatives from and against any and all liabilities, costs, charges and expenses to the extent specified in section 136 of the *Business Corporations Act* (Ontario), subject to the by-laws of the Corporation.

EACH AND EVERY OF THE FOREGOING RESOLUTIONS is hereby consented to by all of the shareholders of the Corporation entitled to vote thereon at a meeting of shareholders, as evidenced by their respective signatures hereto in accordance with the provisions of section 104(1) of the *Business Corporations Act* (Ontario), this _____ day of _____, 20_____.

JAVID KHAN

SAM KHAN

HELENA KRISTINA MADEJ

MICHAEL ANDREW SMITH

APPENDIX G:

Resolution of the Shareholders

of

Entertainment Group LTD.

1. Exemption From Audit Provisions

BE IT RESOLVED THAT:

pursuant to section 148 of the *Business Corporations Act* (Ontario), all of the shareholders of the Corporation hereby consent to the exemption of the Corporation from the requirements of Part XII of the *Business Corporations Act* (Ontario) regarding the appointment and duties of an auditor in respect of the first fiscal year of the Corporation, and in respect of each fiscal year thereafter until this consent is revoked.

THE FOREGOING RESOLUTION is hereby consented to by all of the shareholders of the Corporation, as evidenced by their respective signatures hereto in accordance with the provisions of section 104(1) of the *Business Corporations Act* (Ontario), this _____ day of _____, 20_____.

_____

JAVID KHAN

_____

SAM KHAN

_____

HELENA KRISTINA MADEJ

_____

MICHAEL ANDREW SMITH[24]

---

24 All documents in the Appendices to this Chapter have been produced using Fast Company, a product of Do Process software (discussed in Chapter 14).

CHAPTER 10: PREPARING A MINUTE BOOK – PART 2

Overview:

- Statutory Requirements
- Registers
- Ledgers
- Shares
- Change of Directors
- Workbook:
  - Registers
  - Ledgers
- Appendices:
  - Directors' Register
  - Officers' Register
  - Shareholders' Register
  - Share Transfer Register
  - Shareholder's Ledgers
  - Share Subscription
  - Share Certificates
  - Director's Resignation Letter
  - Director's Consent Letter

1. Statutory Requirements

An overview of the statutory requirements related to minute books was provided at the beginning of Chapter 9. Note that subsection 140(1) of the *BCA* requires that a corporation prepares and maintains the following records at its registered office, or at such other place in Ontario designated by the directors:

- the articles and by-laws of the corporation (including any amendments), and a copy of any unanimous shareholder agreement known to the directors

- minutes of shareholder meetings and resolutions

- minutes of directors' meetings and resolutions

- a directors' register, listing all the directors of the corporation and the dates that they became (and if applicable, ceased to be) directors

- a securities register that complies with section 141, and

- adequate accounting records.[1]

The securities register must include certain information (refer to Chapter 9 for details) and, a corporation must also maintain a register which shows transfers of securities from the corporation or amongst shareholders. Finally, a corporation must maintain a separate stated capital account for each class and series of shares that it issues.[2]

In this chapter, we will focus on preparation of registers & ledgers, share subscriptions and share certificates. We will also discuss other documents, such as a resignation letter from a director and a consent to act as a director, which may be required from time to time. Finally, we will provide a brief discussion of the role of an "office incorporator" – a practice that is no longer common amongst corporate law practitioners, but is important to understand.

2. Registers

Most minute books will include the following registers:

1. Directors' Register

2. Officers' Register

3. Shareholders' Register

4. Share Transfer Register

The directors' register is, simply, a list of all of the directors of the corporation, from the date of incorporation onwards. It notes the date that an individual became a director, and if that person resigns, the date of resignation. If a corporation has committees on its board of directors, then the position of each director will also be noted; however, in most private corporations, the document will simply designate the position of a director as "Chairman" or "Director". (Note that many female directors who chair a board prefer to

---

1 *Business Corporations Act*, R.S.O. 1990, c. B.16, s. 140.
2 Ibid., ss. 24, 26, 141; *Canada Business Corporations Act*, R.S.C. 1985, c. C-44, ss. 20–22 & 26.

be called Chairman or Chairperson; the term "Chairwoman" is not used often today.) Please refer to Appendix A to this Chapter for a sample directors' register for Entertainment Group Ltd.

Similarly, an officers' register will list all of the officers of a corporation from the date of incorporation onwards. Most private corporations will have designated at least the following positions:

1. President

2. Secretary

3. Treasurer

Alternatively, the second and third roles listed above can be combined into one position – that is, the role of "Secretary-Treasurer." Note that the term "Secretary" in a corporation denotes the individual that is typically responsible for corporate compliance, including compliance with the requirements of the *BCA* or *CBCA*, as the case may be. It is the Secretary that will ensure that the minute book is kept up to date (if the corporation's law firm is not assuming this responsibility) and that all corporate filings are current and other requirements are being met. The "Treasurer" manages all the financial matters related to the corporation, and the "President" has the overall responsibility for managing the business. Please refer to Appendix B to this Chapter for the officers' register for Entertainment Group Ltd.

A shareholders' register lists all of the shareholders of a corporation from the date of incorporation. It also indicates when each shareholder purchased shares, the class of shares purchased and the number of shares purchased. If a shareholder sells his/her shares, that is also reflected in the shareholders' register. Therefore, the shareholders' register should always represent an accurate reflection of the issued or allotted share capital of a corporation – that is, the number of shares that have been issued by the corporation at a specific date.

Assume that Javid and Sam each received 100 common (Class A) shares upon incorporation, and Mike and Helena each received 50 common (Class A) shares. In addition, Javid received 100 preferred (Class B) shares. One month later (November 21, 2011,) Javid agrees to sell 50 preferred (Class B) shares to Sam. The shareholders' register for Entertainment Group Ltd. (provided in Appendix C to this Chapter) reflects these shareholdings.

Finally, the share transfer register shows transactions relating the shares of the corporation. The first transactions will occur when the corporation issues shares to the first shareholders of the corporation. Please refer to the sample share transfer register for Entertainment Group Ltd., provided in Appendix D to this chapter. Note that, when a corporation issues shares to a shareholder, the share transfer register should indicate that the shares were issued from "Treasury". The "transfer number" is simply a number allocated to each transaction, starting from "1" and increasing from there as required. (So if there are five transactions to record on the share transfer register, they will be numbered from "1" to "5" in the column called "transfer number".) The column for "certificate number" will indicate the number on the share certificate that is prepared and given to each shareholder. When Javid sells 50 preferred (Class B) shares to Sam, he has to return his share certificate for 100 preferred (Class B) shares to the corporation, and he will receive a new share certificate for 50 preferred (Class B) shares. Sam will also receive a share certificate for 50 preferred (Class B) shares. Note that the share certificate numbers listed on the share transfer register must correspond to the actual numbers on the share certificates themselves. (We will discuss the preparation of share certificates in part 4 of this Chapter.)

It is very important that all registers are updated as required by the Secretary of the corporation, or by a legal practitioner hired by the corporation. The directors' and officers' registers may be important in, for example, determining whether a director that has resigned still has liability for something that occurred while he was a director of the corporation. While the dates of his resignation as a director can be obtained from other documents, updated registers are an easy way to determine this information. Similarly, an updated shareholders' register provides the corporation with quick and easy access to the information needed to give shareholders notice of an upcoming meeting, or to determine the issued share capital of a corporation at a given point in time. The share transfer register can clarify how a shareholder's shareholdings have changed over time, if there is some confusion about how many shares a shareholder should have. However, registers become much less useful if they are only completed when the minute book is created, and never revisited again. It can be a useful practice for a legal professional to offer to review and update a corporation's minute book annually, during the process of generating annual minutes (which will be discussed in Chapter 11.)

3. Ledgers

A shareholder's ledger is a statement of account for a particular shareholder, with respect to a specific class of shares. In other words, it is a document (usually in a chart format, similar to a register) that shows how many shares of a particular class a shareholder owns. It will also show any transactions that have occurred with respect to those shares, for one shareholder only. In other words, in Javid's ledger for preferred (Class B) shares, we will be able to see that he has sold 50 shares, but we cannot determine to whom those shares were sold. In some cases, a shareholder's ledger may also include contact information for the shareholder, and other relevant information.

When a minute book is prepared, there should be a separate ledger for each shareholder, and each class of shares. The shareholder ledgers that would be prepared for a minute book for Entertainment Group Ltd., for example, would be:

1. ledger for Javid Khan's common (Class A) shares.

2. ledger for Javid Khan's preferred (Class B) shares.

3. ledger for Sam Khan's common (Class A) shares.

4. ledger for Sam Khan's preferred (Class B) shares.

5. ledger for Helena Madej's common (Class A) shares.

6. ledger for Michael Smith's common (Class A) shares.

For illustration purposes, please refer to the sample ledgers for Javid Khan's shares, provided in Appendix E to this Chapter. Note that the references to "transfer number" and "certificate number" must match the information entered into the share transfer register. For example, in the share transfer register, transfer number "1" was the issuance of common shares to Javid Khan. In Javid's shareholder's ledger for common shares, therefore, the column called "transfer number" will be filled in with "1". This is one example of how the documents in a minute book must all relate to – and be consistent with – one another. Similarly, in the share transfer register, we indicated that Javid Khan's share certificate for common shares was share certificate number "1". This information must be consistent with what is entered into Javid's shareholder's ledger for common shares, as well as on the share certificate itself. Finally, the latest entry in a shareholder's ledger always indicates the current number of shares that are owned by that shareholder (in the column called "Balance Held".)

4. Shares

There are two groups of documents that you will need to prepare when shares are being issued by a corporation to a shareholder:

(a) share subscriptions

(b) share certificates

A share subscription is, essentially, an "application form" in which a shareholder indicates that he or she would like to purchase a certain number of shares of the corporation for a specified amount. In the terminology of contract law, it is an offer made by the prospective shareholder to the corporation. A sample share subscription form is provided in Appendix F to this chapter.

Unlike the *CBCA*, the *BCA* provides that a security (which includes a share) of a corporation may or may not be represented by a security certificate. In other words, it is possible for the board of directors of an Ontario corporation to decide that they will not have share certificates.[3] By contrast, the *CBCA* states that every security holder is entitled to receive a security certificate, if he/she wishes to do so.[4] In general, however, most legal practitioners will prepare share certificates when the corporate minute book is being prepared.

Both the *BCA* and *CBCA* specify the information that must be included on a share certificate.[5] The *BCA* specifies that a share certicate must include:

* the name of the corporation

* the words "Incorporated under the law of the Province of Ontario", "Subject to the *Ontario Business Corporations Act*" or a similar statement

* the name of the person to whom the certificate is issued, and

* the number and class of shares being issued, and the designation of any class or series that the certificate represents

---

3 *Business Corporations Act*, R.S.O. 1990, c. B.16, s. 140, s. 54.
4 *Canada Business Corporations Act*, R.S.C. 1985, c. C-44, s. 49.
5 *Business Corporations Act*, R.S.O. 1990, c. B.16, s. 140, ss. 55–56; *Canada Business Corporations Act*, R.S.C. 1985, c. C-44, s. 49.

- if the corporation is authorized to issue more than one class of shares (or more than one series), then the rights, privileges and restrictions that attach to those shares *or* a statement that indicates that there are rights, privileges, restrictions or conditions attached to those shares, and the corporation will provide those to the shareholder upon request

- certain other restrictions related to paragraphs 42(2)(c) or (d) must also be noted.[6]

In practice, legal practitioners will either generate share certificates through a corporate software designed to do so, or will order share certificates from companies that provide pre-printed forms. Appendix G to this Chapter provides sample share certificates held by Javid Khan in Entertainment Group Ltd. These share certificates were generated through Fast Company software, which will be discussed in Chapter 14.

5. Change in Directors

While it is not common today, there used to be a common practice in which law clerks or lawyers would act as an "office incorporator" for the purposes of incorporating a new company. In other words, the law clerk would act as the first director and shareholder of the corporation, and after the organizational resolutions were signed for the minute book, the law clerk would resign as a director and transfer his/her share in the corporation back to treasury. The new or "real" directors and shareholders would then be put in place. The practice was developed for the convenience of clients who either did not want to, or could not participate in the initial procedures related to starting a corporation (such as signing the Articles of Incorporation and other documents related to the minute book.) For example, if a client was out of the country at the time that a business was being incorporated, the office incorporator could act as first director and first shareholder of the corporation, and thereby allow the process to continue while the client was away.

The practice of having "office incorporators" is no longer common today, because online filing of documents such as Articles of Incorporation no longer requires the client's signature. Therefore, the incorporation process can continue without the client being present. All the documents can be prepared first, and then the client can simply come into the office once to sign all the required documents. In addition, law firms are no longer prepared to assume the risk of any liability that might be incurred during the time that an employee of the law firm acted as office incorporator. While the risk of liability is usually low, there is no need to incur the liability if the same objective – convenience for the client – can be obtained through online filing of documents.

Having said that, there will be situations where an individual may choose to resign as director of a corporation. To document this change, one would need to prepare:

- a directors' resolution indicating that a director was resigning

- a shareholders' resolution electing a new director to take his/her place

- a resignation letter from the resigning director

- a consent letter from the new director

---

6 *Business Corporations Act*, R.S.O. 1990, c. B.16, s. 140, s. 56.

A sample directors' resolution is provided in Appendix H; since we have discussed resolutions in Chapter 9, however, we will focus on the resignation letter and consent letter in this chapter.

A resignation letter can simply be a letter from the resigning director to the corporation, indicating that the individual is resigning as a director of the corporation as of a specific date. A sample is provided in Appendix I to this Chapter. Note that the letter can be very simple (as in the sample provided,) and it can be tailored as required. The important point is to provide a written record of a director's resignation, in order to protect the resigning director from incurring liability after resignation, and to give notice to the corporation that the shareholders must replace the director (if a certain number of directors are required, or if the number falls below the required range.)

Once a new director is elected, the new director must indicate his/her consent to become a director of the corporation (and to thereby assume the duties, responsibilities and liabilities of a director) by providing a consent letter to the corporation. It can be very similar to the resignation letter described above. A sample is provided in Appendix J to this chapter.

APPENDIX A:

Directors' Register

NAME	DATE ELECTED	DATE RETIRED	OFFICE HELD
JAVID KHAN 313 River Road Drive, Toronto, ON M4W 5S7	OCTOBER 21, 2011		CHAIRMAN
HELENA KRISTINA MADEJ 6768 Murray Ross Drive, Unit 2105, Toronto, ON M3S 2F5	OCTOBER 21, 2011		DIRECTOR
MICHAEL ANDREW SMITH 948 Bergamont Drive, Brampton, ON L6X 8S4	OCTOBER 21, 2011		DIRECTOR

APPENDIX B:

Officers' Register

NAME OF OFFICER	OFFICE HELD	DATE BECAME AN OFFICER	DATE CEASED TO BE AN OFFICER
JAVID KHAN 313 River Road Drive, Toronto, ON M4W 5S7	PRESIDENT	OCTOBER 21, 2011	
HELENA KRISTINA MADEJ 6768 Murray Ross Drive, Unit 2105, Toronto, ON M3S 2F5	SECRETARY-TREASURER	OCTOBER 21, 2011	
MICHAEL ANDREW SMITH 948 Bergamont Drive, Brampton, ON L6X 8S4	VP, MARKETING	OCTOBER 21, 2011	

Shareholders' Register

DATE	NAME	SHARES HELD – CLASS A	SHARES HELD – CLASS B
~~OCTOBER 21, 2011~~	~~JAVID KHAN 313 River Road Drive, Toronto, ON M4W 5S7~~	~~100~~	~~100~~
~~OCTOBER 21, 2011~~	~~SAM KHAN 5225 Corby Crescent, Markham ON L3R 9A9~~	~~100~~	
OCTOBER 21, 2011	HELENA KRISTINA MADEJ 6768 Murray Ross Drive, Unit 2105, Toronto, ON M3S 2F5	50	
OCTOBER 21, 2011	MICHAEL ANDREW SMITH 948 Bergamont Drive, Brampton, ON L6X 8S4	50	
NOVEMBER 21, 2011	SAM KHAN 5225 Corby Crescent, Markham ON L3R 9A9	100	50
NOVEMBER 21, 2011	JAVID KHAN 313 River Road Drive, Toronto, ON M4W 5S7	100	50

APPENDIX D:

Share Transfer Register

Transfer No.	Date	Class Of Shares	Cert. Surrendered No.	Cert. Surrendered *Shares*	Transferor	Transferee	New Cert. Issued-No.	New Cert. Issued-Shares
1	OCT. 21, 2011	A			TREASURY	J. KHAN	A-1	100
2	OCT. 21, 2011	A			TREASURY	S. KHAN	A-2	50
3	OCT. 21, 2011	A			TREASURY	H.K. MADEJ	A-3	50
4	OCT. 12, 2011	A			TREASURY	M.A. SMITH	A-4	50
5	OCT. 21, 2011	B			TREASURY	J. KHAN	B-1	100
6	NOV. 21, 2011	B	B-1	50	J.KHAN	S. KHAN	B-2	50
7	NOV. 21, 2011	B	B-1	50	J. KHAN	J. KHAN	B-3	50

APPENDIX E:

Shareholders' Ledger

NAME: JAVID KHAN

ADDRESS: 313 RIVER ROAD DRIVE, TORONTO, ON M3S 2E5

PHONE NO.:   **OFFICE:** (416) 123-3333 **RESIDENCE:** (416) 123-4567

CLASS OF SHARES: A – COMMON

DATE	CERT. NO.	TRANS. NO.	TO OR FROM WHOM	SHARES TRANSFERRED	SHARES ACQUIRED	BALANCE HELD
OCT. 21, 2011	A-1	1	FROM TREASURY		100	100

Shareholders' Ledger

NAME: JAVID KHAN

ADDRESS: 313 RIVER ROAD DRIVE, TORONTO, ON M3S 2E5

PHONE NO.: **OFFICE:** (416) 123-3333 **RESIDENCE:** (416) 123-4567

CLASS OF SHARES: B – PREFERRED

DATE	CERT. NO.	TRANS. NO.	TO OR FROM WHOM	SHARES TRANSFERRED	SHARES ACQUIRED	BALANCE HELD
OCT. 21, 2011	B-1	5	FROM TREASURY		100	100
NOV. 21, 2011	B-1	6	TO SAM KHAN	50		50
NOV. 21, 2011	B-3	7	REPLACEMENT CERTIFICATE (TO REPLACE B-1)			50

APPENDIX F: SHARE SUBSCRIPTION FORM

TO: **ENTERTAINMENT GROUP LTD.**

AND TO: **THE BOARD OF DIRECTORS THEREOF**

The undersigned hereby subscribes for 100 COMMON shares in the capital of ENTERTAINMENT GROUP LTD. without par value at the issue price of $100 per share, and encloses a cheque for $10,000.00 in payment therefor.

Kindly allot and issue the said shares to JAVID KHAN.

DATED the 21st day of October, 2011

_____

JAVID KHAN

APPENDIX G: SAMPLE SHARE CERTIFICATES – COMMON & PREFERRED

Common Shares

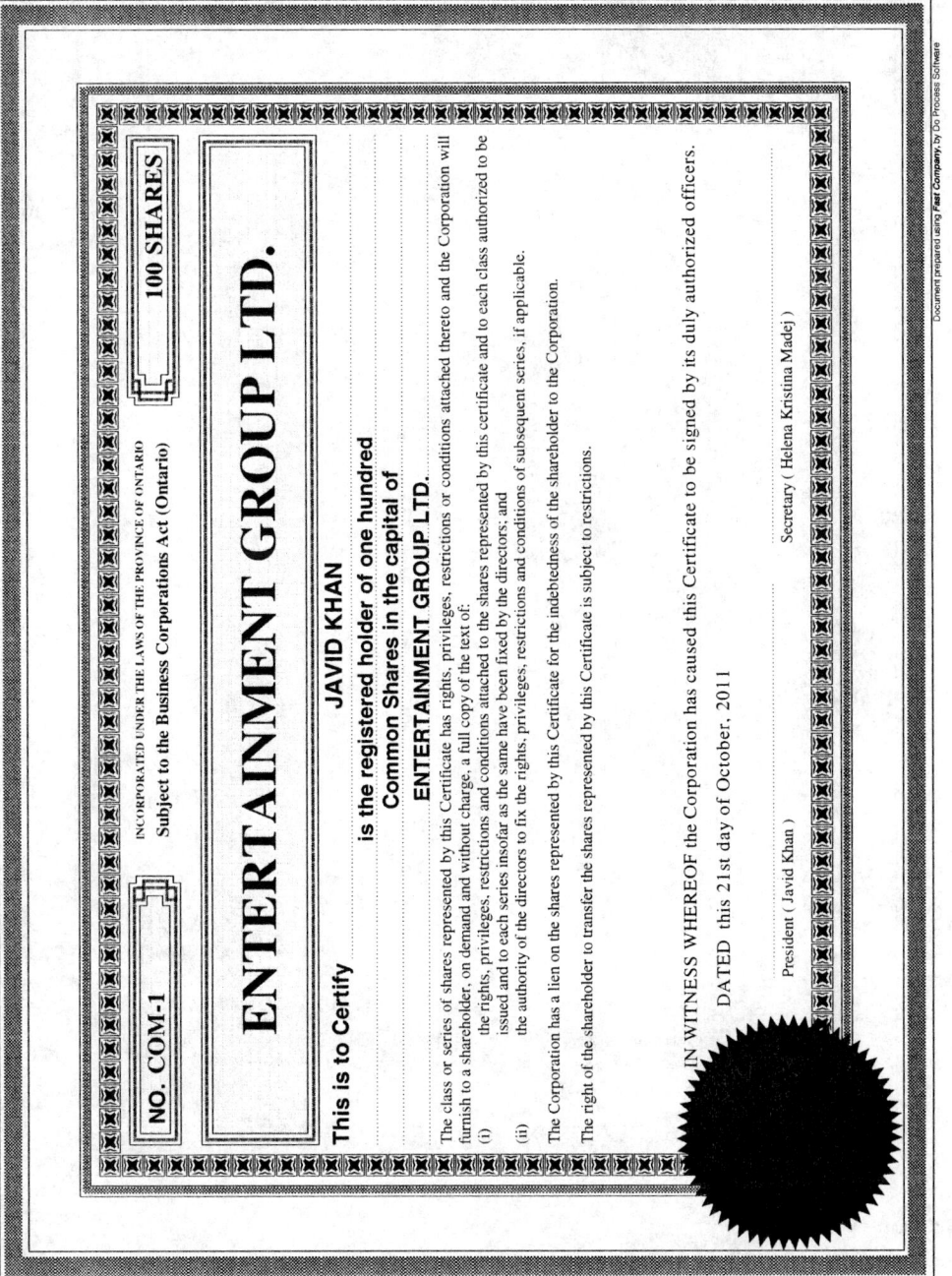

Preferred

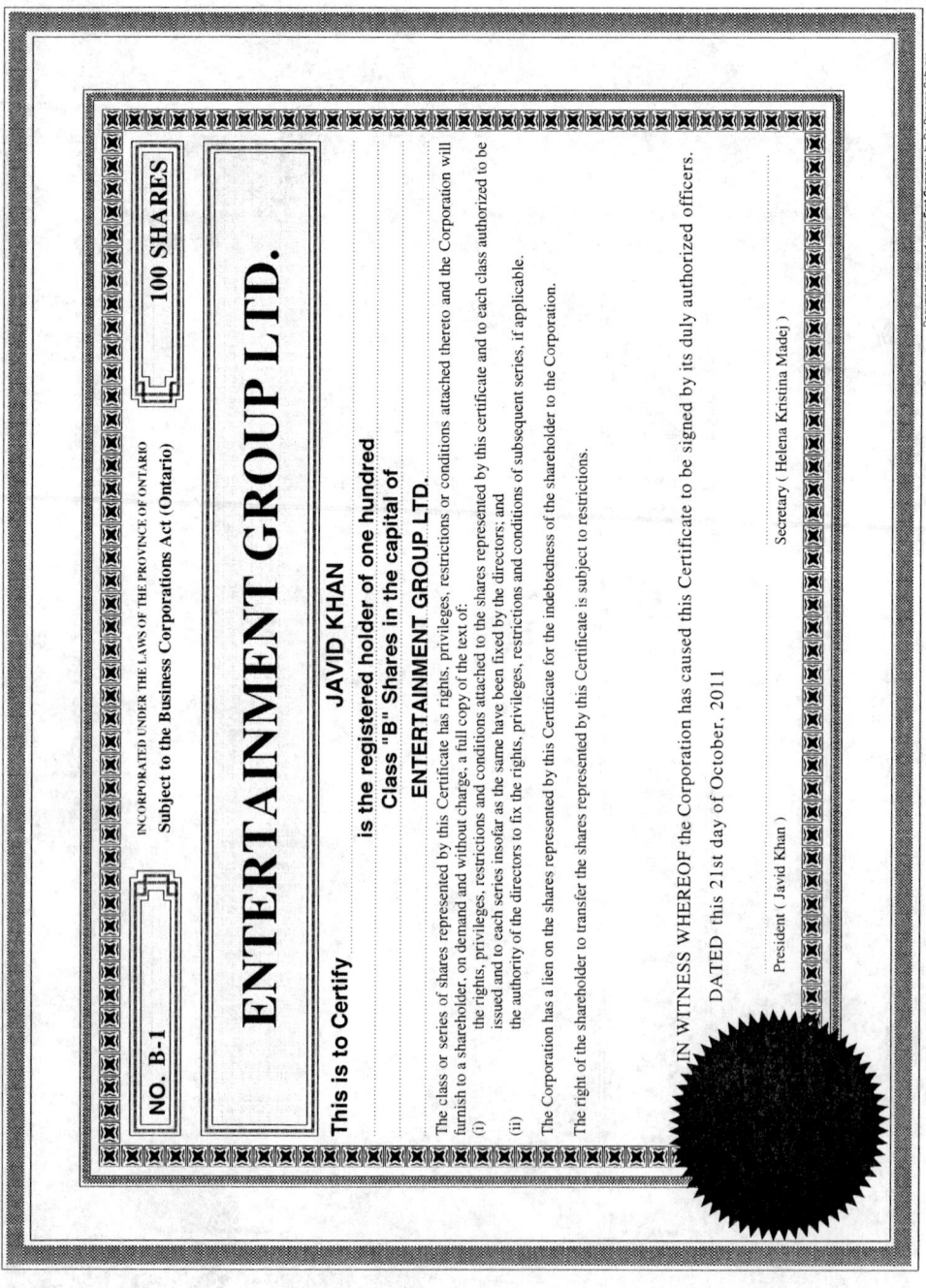

NO. B-1

INCORPORATED UNDER THE LAWS OF THE PROVINCE OF ONTARIO
Subject to the Business Corporations Act (Ontario)

100 SHARES

ENTERTAINMENT GROUP LTD.

This is to Certify

JAVID KHAN

is the registered holder of one hundred
Class "B" Shares in the capital of
ENTERTAINMENT GROUP LTD.

The class or series of shares represented by this Certificate has rights, privileges, restrictions or conditions attached thereto and the Corporation will
furnish to a shareholder, on demand and without charge, a full copy of the text of:

(i) the rights, privileges, restrictions and conditions attached to the shares represented by this certificate and to each class authorized to be
issued and to each series insofar as the same have been fixed by the directors; and

(ii) the authority of the directors to fix the rights, privileges, restrictions and conditions of subsequent series, if applicable.

The Corporation has a lien on the shares represented by this Certificate for the indebtedness of the shareholder to the Corporation.

The right of the shareholder to transfer the shares represented by this Certificate is subject to restrictions.

IN WITNESS WHEREOF the Corporation has caused this Certificate to be signed by its duly authorized officers.

DATED this 21st day of October, 2011

President (Javid Khan)   Secretary (Helena Kristina Madej)

Document prepared using *Fast Company* by Do Process Software

APPENDIX H: DIRECTORS' RESOLUTIONS REGARDING RESIGNATION OF DIRECTOR

Resolution of the Shareholders

of

Entertainment Group LTD.

1. Resignation of Director

WHEREAS the number of directors comprising the board of directors of the Corporation has been fixed at three (3), and

WHEREAS Helena Kristina Madej has resigned as a director of the Corporation as of _____, 20___

NOW THEREFOREBE IT RESOLVED THAT:

The following person be and is hereby elected director of the Corporation to hold office until the next annual meeting of the shareholders of the Corporation or until his respective successor is duly elected, subject to the provisions of the by-laws of the Corporation and the provisions of the *Business Corporations Act* (Ontario):

JOSEF MADEJ

THE FOREGOING RESOLUTION is hereby consented to by all of the shareholders of the Corporation entitled to vote thereon at a meeting of shareholders, as evidenced by their respective signatures hereto in accordance with the provisions of section 104(1) of the *Business Corporations Act* (Ontario), this _____ day of _____, 20_____.

_____
JAVID KHAN

_____
SAM KHAN

_____
HELENA KRISTINA MADEJ

_____
MICHAEL ANDREW SMITH

APPENDIX I: DIRECTOR'S LETTER OF RESIGNATION

April 19, 2012

Entertainment Group Ltd.
555 Hotspot Blvd.
Toronto, Ontario
L4S 5T6

ATTENTION: Board of Directors of Entertainment Group Ltd. c/o Javid Khan, Chairman

Dear Mr. Khan:

Re: Resignation of Director

Please be advised that I hereby resign as director of Entertainment Group Ltd., effective today.

Yours very truly,

Helena Kristina Madej

APPENDIX J: DIRECTOR'S LETTER OF CONSENT

June 2, 2012

Entertainment Group Ltd.
555 Hotspot Blvd.
Toronto, Ontario
L4S 5T6

ATTENTION: Board of Directors of Entertainment Group Ltd. c/o Javid Khan, Chairman

Dear Mr. Khan:

Re: Consent to Become Director

Please be advised that I hereby agree to become a director of Entertainment Group Ltd., effective today.

Yours very truly,

Jonathan Samuel Myers

CHAPTER 11: AFTER THE MINUTE BOOK

Overview:

- Reports
    - Reporting letter to the client
    - Reporting letter to the auditor accountant
- Corporate Bank Account
- *Corporations Information Act*
- Corporate Tax
    - Filing the Annual Return under the *Corporations Information Act*
- Annual Meetings
- Auditors and Financial Statements
- Workbook:
    - Form 1, *Corporations Information Act*
- Appendices:
    - Reporting Letter to Client
    - Schedule 546 (Annual Return under the *CIA*)
    - Minutes of a Meeting of the Board of Directors
    - Minutes of a Meeting of the Shareholders
    - Consent of Shareholders to Exemption from Audit

The last two chapters have focused on how to prepare a minute book for a newly incorporated company. Once the minute book is completed, there are a number of other tasks for the legal professional to address, including:

1. preparing a reporting letter and statement of account for the client

2. preparing a reporting letter for the auditor/accountant

3. advising the client to open a corporate bank account

4. filing the Initial Return under the *Corporations Information Act (CIA)*[1]

These steps will be explained in this chapter. Related matters, such as the Annual Return under the *CIA* and tax considerations, will also be discussed briefly; note, however, that a thorough examination of tax implications is beyond the scope of this textbook. Annual meetings and financial statements will also be addressed in this chapter.

1. Reports

(a) Reporting Letter to the Client

While it is not technically part of a minute book, a lawyer will normally present a reporting letter to the client at the same time that the lawyer gives the client the corporate minute book. The reporting letter is a summary of key corporate information included in a minute book. Some lawyers provide a very detailed reporting letter, while others opt for a more succinct version. The following are some of the topics that may be included in a reporting letter:

- Date of incorporation

- Corporate name

- Authorized share capital

- Share transfer restrictions and other special provisions

- Restrictions on business, if applicable

- Registered office of the corporation

- Accountant

- Fiscal year end

- Corporate banking information

- Authority to execute documents

- Directors

- Officers

- Issued Share Capital (and, if applicable, any transfer of shares that has occurred)

---

1 R.S.O. 1990, c. C.39.

- Quorum requirements

- Initial Return/Notice of Change under the *CIA*

- Tax matters (or possibly, a paragraph instructing the client to contact the corporation's accountant regarding tax matters)

- Business Style

- Enclosures with the reporting letter (such as the statement of account)

- A reminder of documents that will need to be prepared in the future, and a request for the client to provide instructions regarding preparation of these documents

A sample reporting letter that would accompany the minute book for Entertainment Group Ltd. is provided in Appendix A to this chapter. It should be printed on firm letterhead (that is, formal stationary with the firm's name and address printed at the top.) The statement of account will accompany the reporting letter to the client, and should separate legal fees and disbursements. Disbursements are out of pocket expenses that the lawyer has incurred on behalf of the client. Disbursements typically include the incorporation fee charged by the government, additional fees charged by online service providers (if applicable), fees for obtaining a NUANS search, the cost of obtaining a minute book, seal, share certificates and other corporate supplies, cost of photocopying, faxing or long distance charges, and any other out of pocket expenses that are permitted to be charged pursuant to the Rules of Professional Conduct and other standards established by the Law Society of Upper Canada. Legal fees are the amount of money charged for the lawyer's services (which incorporates the time spent by law clerks and other legal professionals who have also been involved in the file.)

(b) Reporting Letter to the Accountant

In order to set up the necessary accounting records for a corporation, the corporation's accountant will require information about incorporation and other information from the minute book. The lawyer must obtain specific instructions from the client (preferably confirmed in writing) indicating whether:

1. the client prefers to deal directly with the accountant in this regard, *or*

2. the client would like the lawyer to provide information to the accountant.

If the client chooses the first option, then it is the client's responsibility to provide the required information to the accountant. The lawyer should simply confirm the client's instructions about this in writing. If the client chooses the second option, the lawyer can simply provide the accountant with a copy of the reporting letter to the client; the lawyer should also attach a cover letter to the accountant (copied to the client,) indicating that the accountant can contact the lawyer if any additional information is required.

2. Corporate Bank Account

It is the client's responsibility to set up a corporate bank account at the bank that has been named in the directors' organizational resolutions. The client may, however, ask for some guidance from the legal professional that incorporated the company. While all banks will have their own pre-printed forms to complete, clients can be told that they will likely be asked to provide a copy of the Articles of Incorporation for the company, and possibly a copy of the by-laws and directors' organizational resolutions. Assuming that the client will be given the minute book before the corporate account is opened, it may be easiest for the client to take the entire minute book and the corporate seal (if applicable) with them when they open the account. The individuals with signing authority on the account will likely have to provide personal identification, such as government issued identification and/or photo identification. Those individuals should be present at the time the account is opened, as they will be asked to sign certain forms.

Clients can be asked to complete a variety of forms to open a corporate bank account, such as:

- a form that identifies who is authorized to sign cheques on the corporate bank account, where bank statements will be sent, and other pertinent information

- a certificate of incumbency, which is a list of all of the directors and officers of the corporation

- a document that requires an impression of the corporate seal, if the corporation has one

- a document that outlines service charges and other fees charged by the bank

- a specimen signature card, which will be signed by each person that has the authority to access the account

While By-law No. 2 – the borrowing by-law – is not required under the *BCA*, some banks may continue with the practice of having clients complete a pre-printed version of By-law No. 2. (There was a time when By-law No. 2 was required, so some banks may still continue with this practice.) Assuming that the by-law states that the corporation has the authority to borrow money and conduct other financial transactions in the normal course of business, the client can complete this form as required by the bank.

3. *Corporations Information Act*

The *Corporations Information Act*[2] ("*CIA*") provides a way for the government to maintain and update its records about corporate information. It also enables the public to find information about a corporation, perhaps in the context of a lawsuit, or other legal or financial matters. The way in which the *CIA* accomplishes these goals is to require every corporation (as defined in the Act) to file an Initial Return within sixty days of incorporation, and an Annual Return every year.[3] A corporation is defined in the *CIA* as "any corporation with or without share capital wherever or however incorporated and includes an extra-provincial corporation."[4] Extra-provincial corporations (discussed in Chapter 4) must file an Initial Return within sixty days of starting business in Ontario.[5]

---

2 R.S.O. 1990, c. C.39.

3 *Ibid.*, ss. 2–3.

4 *Ibid.*, s. 1.

5 *Ibid.*, s. 3(2).

The Initial Return is referred to as Form 1 under the *CIA*. This form can be obtained from the Ontario Central Forms Repository website, introduced in Chapter 2. The form can be completed online, and then printed for filing purposes. Form 1 contains general information about the corporation, including its name, corporation number, registered address, mailing address, details about directors and officers, and other relevant information. The same form is also used to report a change in this information, and is then referred to as a Notice of Change. Section 4 of the *CIA* requires corporations to file a Notice of Change for every change of information filed in the Initial Return or an Annual Return, within 15 days after the change takes place.[6] However, a Notice of Change is *not* required if:

- a director retires and is then re-elected for the next term of office, or

- the only change is that the corporation has changed its name.[7]

It is important to advise clients of the requirements related to filing a Notice of Change, possibly in a reporting letter to the client after Form 1 is filed. Many clients will not realize that there are significant consequences to forgetting to file a Notice of Change, or for doing something else that does not comply with the *CIA*. Failure to comply with the requirements of the *CIA*, or filing false or misleading information, can lead to a fine of up to $25,000 for a corporation, or to imprisonment of an individual for a term of up to one year, or both. There are also provisions in the *CIA* which indicate that a director or officer may be personally fined up to $2,000 for allowing or participating in an offence under the *CIA*.[8] In addition, section 18 of the *CIA* provides that:

18(1) A corporation that is in default of a requirement under this Act to file a return or notice or that has unpaid fees or penalties is not capable of maintaining a proceeding in a court in Ontario in respect of the business carried on by the corporation, except with leave of the court.

(2) The court shall grant leave if the court is satisfied that,

(a) the failure to file the return or notice or pay the fees or penalties was inadvertent;

(b) there is no evidence that the public has been deceived or misled; and

(c) at the time of the application to court, the corporation has filed all returns and notices required by this Act and has no unpaid fees or penalties.[9]

The Act defines "court" as "the Superior Court of Justice presided over by a judge designated by the Chief Justice of Ontario to hear applications under this Act."[10] Late filing of a document under the *CIA* will also result in a late filing fee.[11]

Finally, members of the public – including legal professionals – can find information about a corporation by examining documents filed under the *CIA*. Section 10 of the *CIA* gives members of the public the right to examine these records, upon payment of the

---

6 *Ibid.*, s. 4.

7 Ibid., ss. 4(3)-(4).

8 Ibid., ss. 13–14.

9 *Ibid.*, s. 18.

10 *Ibid.*, s. 1.

11 *Ibid.*, s. 17.

required fee, and the right to obtain certified copies of the contents of such documents.[12] Section 19 also refers to the types of certificates that may be issued by the Minister, including:

- whether or not a document referred to in the *CIA* has been filed

- the time when facts upon which legal proceedings are based first came to the knowledge of the Minister

- that a person named in the certificate is or was a director, officer, manager or attorney for service of the corporation during a specified period of time

- that the information set out in the certificate has been filed pursuant to the *CIA*

- other information relating to the corporation based on the records of the Ministry.[13]

Please refer to the copy of Form 1 provided in the Workbook. Note that Box "1" at the top right hand corner indicates whether the form is being used as an Initial Return, or a Notice of Change. In addition to the Initial Return, the *CIA* requires corporations to file an Annual Return. The Annual Return is related to the topic of corporate tax, and as such, it will be discussed in the next part of this chapter.

4. Corporate Tax

(a) Introduction

In Canada, all corporations (and individuals) must pay federal tax and provincial tax. In Ontario, the basic corporate tax rate for corporations is as follows:

- 11.5% effective July 1, 2011

- 11% effective July 1, 2012

- 10% effective July 1, 2013[14]

A corporation that is a Canadian Controlled Private Corporation ("CCPC") throughout the taxation year can also claim the Ontario small business deduction, which amounts to 7.5% effective July 1, 2010. This reduces the Ontario tax rate payable by a CCPC; on July 1, 2011, for example, the Ontario tax rate payable by a CCPC would be only 4% (that is, 11.5% minus 7.5%).[15]

A CCPC is a private, Canadian corporation that is not controlled, directly or indirectly, by public corporations, non-residents of Canada, or a combination of the two. Operating as a CCPC allows a corporation to take advantage of a number of tax benefits that are designed to assist small businesses, including:

---

12 *Ibid.*, s. 10.

13 *Ibid.*, s. 19.

14 Canada Revenue Agency, Corporations, "Corporation Tax Rates", online: Canada Revenue Agency <http://www.cra-arc.gc.ca/tx/bsnss/tpcs/crprtns/prv/on/menu-eng.html>.

15 Canada Revenue Agency, Corporations, "Corporation Tax Rates", online: Canada Revenue Agency <http://www.cra-arc.gc.ca/tx/bsnss/tpcs/crprtns/prv/on/smllbsnssddctn-eng.html.>.

- the ability to reduce income tax by claiming the small business deduction (discussed above)

- additional time to pay certain taxes

- enhanced investment tax credits for certain expenditures on scientific research and experimental development

- shareholder entitlement to the capital gains exemption, when qualified shares of the corporation are sold, and

- deferral of an employee's taxable benefit, if the employee exercises stock options provided by a CCPC[16]

In addition to Ontario corporate tax, every corporation must also pay federal income tax. The basic federal tax rate is 38%; however, that tax rate is reduced by the federal tax abatement of 28%. For a CCPC, the net federal tax rate is 11%. For other corporations, the net federal tax rate is:

- 16.5% effective January 1, 2011

- 15% effective January 1, 2012[17]

> Javid has heard that corporations in Canada pay a lot of tax. He contacts his accountant to find out how much Entertainment Group Ltd. will have to pay for taxes as of July 1, 2012. Assuming that Entertainment Group Ltd. is a CCPC, what is its net corporate tax rate as of July 1, 2012? (Consider both federal and provincial tax.)

(b) Filing the Annual Return under the *CIA*

As of January 1, 2009, the Canada Revenue Agency (CRA) has taken over administration of Ontario corporate taxes and the Annual Return that must be filed pursuant to the *CIA*. This has streamlined the regulatory process, and made it easier for corporations to comply with government requirements. From a practical perspective, it also means that the Annual Return is generally prepared by the accountant for the corporation, not by the lawyer.

A corporation's tax return is referred to as its "T2 return". All resident corporations, except registered charities, must file a T2 return for every tax year, even if there is no income tax payable in that year. This includes non-profit organizations, tax-exempt corporations and inactive corporations. A non-resident corporation also has to file a T2 return if, at any time during the tax year, any one of the following situations occurred:

- the corporation carried on business in Canada

- the corporation had a taxable capital gain

---

16 Canada Revenue Agency, *Income Tax Interpretation Bulletin No. IT-458R2 (May 31, 2000)*, online: Canada Revenue Agency <http://www.cra-arc.gc.ca/E/pub/tp/it458r2/it458r2-e.html.>.

17 Canada Revenue Agency, Corporations, "Corporation Tax Rates", online: Canada Revenue Agency <http://www.cra-arc.gc.ca/tx/bsnss/tpcs/crprtns/rts-eng.html.>.

- the corporations disposed of taxable Canadian property, except if the disposition took place after 2008 and certain conditions were met.[18]

Schedule 546 to the T2 return is the *"Corporations Information Act* Annual Return for Ontario Corporations" for 2009 and later tax returns. This schedule must be completed by any corporation that is incorporated, continued or amalgamated in Ontario and subject to the *BCA*, except for registered charities. (Continuation and amalgamation will be discussed in Chapter 12.) Schedule 546 – that is, the Annual Return under the *CIA* – must be completed within six months after the end of the corporation's taxation year. The Ministry of Government Services (MGS) will consider the Annual Return to have been filed on the date that it is filed with the T2 return with the Canada Revenue Agency (CRA). As stated on Schedule 546, it is the corporation's responsibility to ensure that the information shown on the MGS public record is current and accurate. A corporation can obtain a Corporation Profile Report through the ServiceOntario website to verify the information included in the MGS public record. Please see Appendix B to this Chapter for a blank copy of Schedule 546. Note that Parts 1 to 4 will be completed annually by the corporation's accountant, and parts 5 to 7 are only completed to report a change to the information recorded on the MGS public record.

5. Annual Meetings

There are two types of meetings contemplated by the corporate statutes: directors' meetings and shareholders' meetings. In practice, many of the legal requirements for directors can be satisfied by passing resolutions, instead of holding a formal meeting and documenting the decisions made at that meeting in "minutes" (to be discussed later in this chapter.) Directors are required to have a "first directors meeting" pursuant to s. 117(1) of the *BCA*;[19] however, s. 117(2) of the *BCA* also provides that any matter to be discussed in the first directors meeting may also be dealt with by a resolution in writing.[20] Subsection 129(1) of the *BCA* further provides that a resolution in writing must be signed by all of the directors entitled to vote on that resolution at a meeting of the directors.[21] For most non-offering corporations, therefore, legal requirements pertaining to directors' decisions will usually be satisfied by passing directors' resolutions signed by all the directors of the corporation.

Shareholders' meetings are discussed in Part VII of the *BCA* and Part XII of the *CBCA*. While we will only discuss the rules relating to Ontario corporations in this part of the chapter, please refer to Part XII of the *CBCA* for comparable provisions relating to federal corporations. The *BCA* provides that directors must call an annual meeting of the shareholders of the corporation not later than eighteen months after the corporation

---

18 Canada Revenue Agency, Corporations, "Who has to File a Corporation Income Tax (T2) Return", online: Canada Revenue Agency <http://www.cra-arc.gc.ca/tx/bsnss/tpcs/crprtns/rtrn/fl-eng.html.>.

19 *Business Corporations Act*, R.S.O. 1990, c. B.16, s. 117(1); see also *Canada Business Corporations Act*, R.S.C. 1985, c. C-44, s. 104(1).

20 *Business Corporations Act*, R.S.O. 1990, c. B.16, s. 117(2); see also *Canada Business Corporations Act*, R.S.C. 1985, c. C-44, s. 117(1).

21 *Business Corporations Act*, R.S.O. 1990, c. B.16, s. 129(1); see also *Canada Business Corporations Act*, R.S.C. 1985, c. C-44, s. 117(1).

comes into existence, and thereafter, not later than fifteen months after holding the last annual shareholders' meeting. The directors may also call a special meeting of the shareholders at any time.[22] For a legal practitioner, it is important to know the technicalities around calling and administering meetings, and to advise clients of their responsibilities an annual basis.

For small, non-offering corporations where the shareholders are also directors, the process can be relatively simple. Recall that section 104 of the *BCA* allows the corporation to pass annual shareholders resolutions, instead of holding an annual shareholder meeting. Specifically, section 104 of the *BCA* provides:

> 104. (1) Except where a written statement is submitted by a director under subsection 123(2) or where representations in writing are submitted by an auditor under subsection 149(6),
>
> > (a) a resolution in writing signed by all of the shareholders or their attorney authorized in writing entitled to vote on that resolution at a meeting of shareholders is as valid as if it had been passed at a meeting of the shareholders; and
> >
> > (b) a resolution in writing dealing with all matters required by this Act to be dealt with at a meeting of shareholders, and signed by all the shareholders or their attorney authorized in writing entitled to vote at that meeting, satisfies all the requirements of this Act relating to that meeting of shareholders.
>
> (2) A copy of every resolution referred to in subsection (1) shall be kept with the minutes of the meetings of shareholders.[23]

One way of addressing the requirement to have annual shareholders' meetings, therefore, is simply to pass shareholders' resolutions, signed by all of the shareholders entitled to vote at the shareholders meeting, on an annual basis. The content of these resolutions can be fairly straightforward, including:

- consideration of the minutes of an earlier meeting

- approval of financial statements and, if applicable, the auditor's report

- election of directors for the next term

- reappointment of the incumbent auditor, if applicable, or consent to exemption of the requirement to have an auditor for that year

(Note that section 148 of the *BCA* allows a non-offering corporation to be exempt from the requirements of Part XII of the *BCA* – called "Auditors and Financial Statements – regarding the appointment and duties of an auditor, if the corporation is not an offering corporation *and* all of the shareholders of the corporation consent in writing to that exemption in respect of that year.)[24]

Where there are many shareholders in a corporation, it may be advisable to call an annual shareholders' meeting. The meeting can be held through electronic means if necessary.[25] In the case of a corporation where shareholders are changing frequently – such as an offering corporation – it may be necessary to fix a "record date", that is, the date

---

22 *Business Corporations Act*, R.S.O. 1990, c. B.16, s. 94.

23 *Ibid.*, s. 104.

24 *Ibid.*, s. 148.

25 *Ibid.*, s. 94(2).

upon which shareholders of a corporation will be identified for the purpose of providing notice for a shareholders meeting, or for other purposes specified in the *BCA*.[26] For most non-offering corporations, however, this is not an issue, as shareholders do not change frequently. Notice of the time and place of a shareholders' meeting must be sent at least 21 days before the meeting for an offering corporation, and at least ten days before the meeting for a non-offering corporation (but in either case, not more than 50 days in advance.) Such notice must be provided to:

- each shareholder entitled to vote at the meeting

- each director, and

- the auditor of the corporation, if there is one.[27]

Note, however, that anyone entitled to receive notice of a shareholders meeting may waive that notice, except in certain limited circumstances.[28]

If the shareholders' meeting will involve discussion of "special business", notice of the meeting must include certain features. Anything *other than* the following is considered "special business" in the context of a shareholders meeting:

- consideration of minutes of an earlier meeting

- review of financial statements and auditor's report

- election of directors

- reappointment of the incumbent auditor[29]

Subsection 96(6) of the *BCA* provides that:

Notice of a meeting of shareholders at which special business is to be transacted shall state or be accompanied by a statement of,

(a) the nature of that business in sufficient detail to permit the shareholder to form a reasoned judgment thereon; and

(b) the text of any special resolution or by-law to be submitted to the meeting.[30]

Note that subsection 1(1) of the *BCA* defines "special resolution" as:

a resolution that is,

(a) submitted to a special meeting of shareholders of a corporation duly called for the purpose of considering the resolution and passed, with or without amendment, at the meeting by at least two-thirds of the votes cast, or

(b) consented to in writing by each shareholder of the corporation entitled to vote at such a meeting or the shareholder's attorney authorized in writing.[31]

---

26 *Ibid.*, s. 95.
27 *Ibid.*, s. 96(1)
28 *Ibid.*, s. 98.
29 *Ibid.*, s. 96(5).
30 *Ibid.*, s. 96(6).
31 *Ibid.*, s. 1(1).

Note that a special resolution can be either a resolution signed by shareholders having at least 2/3 majority of the votes at an actual meeting, <u>or</u> a resolution consented to and signed by all of the shareholders of the corporation in writing. This means that, *if the shareholders do not wish to hold an actual meeting,* a special resolution requires all of the shareholders to agree to and sign the resolution.

The *BCA* also contemplates the situation where a shareholder may wish to submit a proposal for consideration at a shareholders' meeting.[32] Similarly, the holders of at least five percent of the issued voting shares of a corporation may requisition the directors of a corporation to call a shareholders' meeting (for the purposes stated in the requisition.)[33] These and other details related to calling shareholders meetings can be found in Part VII of the *BCA*, and should be reviewed by a legal practitioner prior to arranging a shareholders' meeting.

From a practical perspective, most legal practitioners will simply prepare standard minutes for annual shareholders' meetings. While these matters can be dealt with by a shareholders' resolution signed by all the shareholders in the corporation, it is common practice in many law firms to prepare "minutes" for annual shareholders meetings. Minutes are a formal record of the decisions made and consented to at a meeting of directors or shareholders of a corporation. They typically have a certain format, and should be included in the minute book of the corporation on an annual basis if they are prepared for the purpose of the annual shareholders meeting. (A legal practitioner should contact corporate clients every year to remind them of this requirement, and to confirm instructions to prepare the minutes.) Corporate software or precedents can make the preparation of such minutes much easier for a legal practitioner. For example, the sample minutes for Entertainment Group Ltd. (provided in the Appendices to this Chapter) have been prepared using Fast Company, a product of Do Process Software; Fast Company will be discussed in greater detail in Chapter 14. Appendix C provides sample minutes of a meeting of directors, and Appendix D provides sample minutes from an annual shareholders' meeting. Finally, Appendix E to this Chapter includes the consent of shareholders to be exempt from the audit requirements of the *BCA*.

6. Auditors and Financial Statements

An auditor is an accounting professional that reviews the financial statements of a corporation, and expresses an opinion on whether those financial statements have been prepared in accordance with the standards of the accounting profession. The *BCA* addresses auditors and financial statements in Part XII (called "Auditors and Financial Statements"); similarly, the *CBCA* addresses these issues in Part XIV (called "Financial Disclosure".)

As mentioned in Part 5 of this Chapter ("Annual Meetings") the shareholders of a non-offering corporations may choose not to have an auditor. While having an auditor review the financial statements of a corporation does give shareholders some assurance that those financial statements can be relied upon, that sense of comfort comes at a cost. Hiring an auditor to review financial statements may be cost prohibitive for a small, private company, and may not even seem necessary in a situation where all of the share-

---

32   *Ibid.,* s. 99.
33   *Ibid.,* s. 105.

holders are also directors of the company. For this reason, section 148 of the *BCA* allows a corporation to decide *not* to have an auditor. Specifically, section 148 states:

> 148. In respect of a financial year of a corporation, the corporation is exempt from the requirements of this Part regarding the appointment and duties of an auditor if,
>
>> (a) The corporation is not an offering corporation; and
>>
>> (b) all of the shareholders consent in writing to the exemption in respect of that year.[34]

Note that this issue must be addressed by shareholders at *every* annual meeting, since the exemption is only for one financial year. Since most non-offering corporations will choose to exempt themselves from the requirement to have an auditor, we will not cover the qualifications, duties and role of the auditor in further detail. Please refer to the relevant parts of the *BCA* or *CBCA* (noted at the beginning of part 6 of this Chapter,) for further information in this regard.

Finally, Part XII of the *BCA* also addresses the financial statements of a corporation. For example, it provides that financial statements of a corporation must be presented at an annual meeting of shareholders,[35] and must be prepared in accordance with generally accepted accounting principles.[36] Financial statements must be approved by the board of directors of the corporation, and where there is an auditor's report, it should be attached to the financial statements.[37]

---

34 *Ibid.*, s. 148; see also *Canada Business Corporations Act*, R.S.C. 1985, c. C-44, s. 163.
35 *Business Corporations Act*, R.S.O. 1990, c. B.16, s. 154; *Canada Business Corporations Act*, R.S.C. 1985, c. C-44, s. 155.
36 *Business Corporations Act*, R.S.O. 1990, c. B.16, s. 155.
37 *Business Corporations Act*, R.S.O. 1990, c. B.16, s. 159; *Canada Business Corporations Act*, R.S.C. 1985, c. C-44, s. 158.

APPENDIX A: REPORTING LETTER TO THE CLIENT

November 30, 2011

555 Hotspot Blvd.
Toronto, Ontario
L4S 5T6

ATTENTION: Javid Khan

Dear Mr. Khan:

Re: Entertainment Group Ltd.
Incorporation and Organization
Our File No. 1

We are pleased to submit our report at this time concerning the completion of services performed on behalf of your Corporation, as detailed below.

Certificate of Incorporation

The corporation was incorporated under the name:

ENTERTAINMENT GROUP LTD.

on October 21, 2011 by the issuance of a Certificate of Incorporation pursuant to the *Business Corporations Act* (Ontario). The Ontario Corporation Number for Entertainment Group Ltd. is 1234567.

We are enclosing herewith a photocopy of the Certificate of Incorporation for your records.

Approval of Corporate Name

Prior to filing the Articles of Incorporation, we obtained and reviewed with you a NUANS corporate name search for the proposed name of the Corporation, being the statutory prescribed computerized name search report which is used to search for conflicting names of federal and provincial companies; a copy of this search is enclosed for your records and the original has been filed with the Ministry of Consumer and Business Services.

The name search system is neither exhaustive nor conclusive and, the corporate name may be challenged at a future date if its use is contrary to the rules prescribed by the *Business Corporations Act* (Ontario), for example, by reason of a conflict between the name and another corporate name, business style and/or trade mark having priority, whether or not disclosed in the name search report.

Under the Act, the Corporation may use either the full or the abbreviated form of the last word of its corporate name which denotes the Corporation's limited liability.

Authorized Capital

The authorized capital of the corporation consists of the following classes of shares:
An unlimited number of Common shares;
An unlimited number of non-voting Class "A" shares;
An unlimited number of voting, redeemable, retractable Class "B" shares with non-cumulative dividends;
An unlimited number of voting, participating, redeemable, retractable Class "C" shares with cumulative dividends;
An unlimited number of non-voting Class "D" shares with non-cumulative dividends.

The particular rights, privileges, restrictions and conditions associated with each class of shares are set out on page 3 of the Articles of Incorporation.

Share Transfer Restrictions and Special Provisions

For particulars of restrictions on the transfer of shares of the Corporation, refer to page 4 of the Articles of Incorporation.

For the text of other special provisions, including restrictions on the total number of shareholders as well as on invitations to the public to subscribe for shares of the Corporation, refer to page 5 of the Articles of Incorporation.

Registered Office

The registered office address of the Corporation is in the City of Toronto in the Province of Ontario and is fixed at:

555 Hotspot Blvd.
Toronto, Ontario
L4S 5T6

The municipality or geographic township within Ontario in which the registered office is situate may be changed from time to time by special resolution, a certified copy of which must be filed with the Ministry of Consumer and Business Services; the street address within such municipality or geographic township may be changed by an ordinary resolution of the directors.

Accountant

A resolution has been prepared and entered into the minute book for the Corporation pursuant to which Pecuniary Associates has been appointed to serve as the accountant of the Corporation.

Fiscal Year End

In accordance with information provided to our office, the minute book reflects that the fiscal period of the Corporation shall end on December 30th of each year.

Corporate Bank

A directors' resolution has been prepared adopting:

TD BANK 2222
600 Hotspot Blvd.
Toronto, Ontario
L4S 5T6

as the banker of the corporation.

If you have not already provided the same to our office, we require, for insertion into the minute book, a copy of the banking resolution which should have been provided to you when the corporate account was opened providing for signature by any two of the President, Secretary or Treasurer on behalf of the Corporation.

Execution of Documents

Pursuant to By-Law No. 1, deeds, contracts and other documents or instruments in writing required to be signed on behalf of the Corporation shall be signed by any two of the President, Vice-President, Secretary or Treasurer and the seal of the Corporation shall be affixed to such documents as require same. However, the board of directors may from time to time authorize other persons to execute any particular document or class of documents.

Directors

Pursuant to the charter of the Corporation, the number of directors comprising the board is a range with a minimum of one (1) and a maximum of ten (10). By special resolution, the number of directors, for the time being, has been fixed at three (3).

A quorum of directors, that is, the number of directors required to be present at a meeting in order to transact business of the company, is a majority of the directors elected to office. In the event of a tied vote on any issue, the Chairman of the meeting has a casting vote.

Currently, the directors of the Corporation are:
JAVID KHAN
HELENA KRISTINA MADEJ
MICHAEL ANDREW SMITH

Officers

Effective October 21, 2011, the directors elected Javid Khan as President, Helena Kristina Madej as Secretary-Treasurer and Michael Andrew Smith as 1st Vice President of the Corporation.

Issued Common Shares

Pursuant to their subscriptions therefor, 300 Common shares of the capital stock of the Corporation were issued to the following persons in the numbers and at the price per share shown below, on October 21, 2011:

SUBSCRIPTION	NO. OF SHARES	CERT. NO.	$ PER SHARE
JAVID KHAN	100	COM-1	$100.00
SAM KHAN	100	COM-2	$100.00
HELENA KRISTINA MADEJ	50	COM-3	$100.00
MICHAEL ANDREW SMITH	50	COM-4	$100.00

If it has not already been done, the shareholders should deposit into the bank account of the Corporation the sum of $30,000.00 representing the purchase price of the said 300 Common shares issued by the Corporation.

Issued Class "B" Shares

Pursuant to his subscription therefor, 100 Class "B" shares of the capital stock of the Corporation were issued to Javid Khan at the price per share shown below:

SUBSCRIPTION	NO. OF SHARES	CERT. NO.	$ PER SHARE
JAVID KHAN	100	B-1	$150.00

If it has not already been done, the shareholder should deposit into the bank account of the Corporation the sum of $15,000.00 representing the purchase price of the said 100 Class "B" shares issued by the Corporation.

Meetings of Shareholders

A quorum of shareholders, that is, the number of shareholders required to be present at a meeting in order to transact the business of the shareholders, is the holders of a majority of shares entitled to vote at a meeting of shareholders. In the event of a tied vote on any issue, the Chairman of the meeting has a casting vote.

Transfer of Class "B" Shares

Effective November 21, 2011, the following transfer of fifty (50) Class "B" shares in the capital of the Corporation was approved, and the shares were transferred accordingly:

TRANSFER FROM	TRANSFER TO	NO. & CLASS
JAVID KHAN	SAM KHAN	50 Class "B"

Initial Return/Notices of Change

In accordance with the provisions of the *Corporations Information Act*, we have filed with the Ministry of Consumer and Business Services an "Initial Return/Notice of Change" form which sets out the names and addresses of the current directors and officers of the Corporation as well as the location of the head office of the Corporation. A copy is enclosed herewith for your records.

In the event of a change of directors or officers or any of their respective addresses or in the event of a relocation of the head office or place of business, the Corporation is required to file a Notice of Change with the Ministry of Consumer and Business Services within 15 days of such change, and failure to do so could result in the laying of charges against the Corporation and its directors and officers pursuant to sections 13 and 14 of the *Corporations Information Act*.

Therefore, please notify our office promptly if a change in corporate status occurs in order that we may attend to preparation and filing of the appropriate Notice of Change.

Corporate Tax

The Corporation is required to comply with the provisions of the *Corporations Tax Act*. Please contact Pecuniary Associates for filing and other requirements.

BUSINESS OR STYLE NAME

Pursuant to the *Business Names Act (Ontario)*, the Corporation may not carry on business or identify itself to the public in Ontario by a name or style other than its corporate name unless such business name or style is first registered with the Ministry of Consumer and Business Services. This registration operates as notice to the public of the entity so carrying on business but does not confer upon the Corporation any right to such name or style that the Corporation does not otherwise have.

If the Corporation carries on business or identifies itself to the public in Ontario by such a registered name, it is required to set out such registered name as well as its full corporate name in all contracts, invoices, negotiable instruments and orders involving goods or services issued or made by the Corporation.

Please contact our office if you wish our assistance or further information in this regard.

Enclosures

We are enclosing herewith the following:
Copy of NUANS corporate name search.

Copy of Articles of Incorporation.
Copy of Initial Return.
Our statement of account.

If you have any questions or comments with respect to the incorporation and orga-nization of the company or our reporting letter, please do not hesitate to contact me.

Please note that annual resolutions of the directors and shareholders must be prepared for the year ending December 30, 2011. Kindly contact our office to provide your in-structions in this regard.

As always, please also keep our office informed of any change in the corporation, including a change in the location of the head office and/or any change of directors or officers or their respective addresses.

Enclosed is our account for services rendered, which we trust you will find satisfactory.

Yours very truly,

Farah Jamal Karmali

FJK

APPENDIX B: ANNUAL RETURN UNDER THE CIA (SCHEDULE 546)

Canada Revenue Agency / Agence du revenu du Canada	**SCHEDULE 546** Code 0902

CORPORATIONS INFORMATION ACT ANNUAL RETURN FOR ONTARIO CORPORATIONS
(2009 and later tax years)

Corporation's name	Business Number	Tax year-end Year · Month · Day

- This schedule should be completed by a corporation that is incorporated, continued, or amalgamated in Ontario and subject to the Ontario *Business Corporations Act* (BCA) or Ontario *Corporations Act* (CA), except for registered charities under the federal *Income Tax Act*. This completed schedule serves as a *Corporations Information Act* Annual Return under the Ontario *Corporations Information Act*.

- Complete parts 1 to 4. Complete parts 5 to 7 only to report change(s) in the information recorded on the Ontario Ministry of Government Services (MGS) public record.

- This schedule must set out the required information for the corporation as of the date of delivery of this schedule.

- A completed Ontario *Corporations Information Act* Annual Return must be delivered within six months after the end of the corporation's tax year-end. The MGS considers this return to be delivered on the date that it is filed with the Canada Revenue Agency (CRA) together with the corporation's income tax return.

- It is the corporation's responsibility to ensure that the information shown on the MGS public record is accurate and up-to-date. To review the information shown for the corporation on the public record maintained by the MGS, obtain a Corporation Profile Report. Visit **www.ServiceOntario.ca** for more information.

- This schedule contains non-tax information collected under the authority of the Ontario *Corporations Information Act*. This information will be sent to the MGS for the purposes of recording the information on the public record maintained by the MGS.

Part 1 – Identification

100 Corporation's name (exactly as shown on the MGS public record)

Jurisdiction incorporated, continued, or amalgamated, whichever is the most recent **Ontario**	**110** Date of incorporation or amalgamation, whichever is the most recent Year · Month · Day	**120** Ontario Corporation No. 0 0

Part 2 – Head or registered office address (P.O. box not acceptable as stand-alone address)

200 Care of (if applicable)

210 Street number **220** Street name/Rural route/Lot and Concession number **230** Suite number

240 Additional address information if applicable (line 220 must be completed first)

250 Municipality (e.g., city, town) **260** Province **270** Country **280** Postal code

---

Part 3 – Change identifier

Have there been any changes in any of the information most recently filed for the public record maintained by the MGS for the corporation with respect to names, addresses for service, and the date elected/appointed and, if applicable, the date the election/appointment ceased of the directors and five most senior officers, or with respect to the corporation's mailing address or language of preference? To review the information shown for the corporation on the public record maintained by the MGS, obtain a Corporation Profile Report. For more information, visit **www.ServiceOntario.ca**.

300 ☐ If there have been no changes, enter **1** in this box and then go to "Part 4 – Certification."
If there are changes, enter **2** in this box and complete the applicable parts on the next page, and then go to "Part 4 – Certification."

Part 4 – Certification

I certify that all information given in this *Corporations Information Act* Annual Return is true, correct, and complete.

450 _____ **451** _____ **454** _____
Last name ·· First name ·· Middle name(s)

460 ☐ Please enter one of the following numbers in this box for the above-named person: **1** for director, **2** for officer, or **3** for other individual having knowledge of the affairs of the corporation. If you are a director and officer, enter **1** or **2**.

Note: Sections 13 and 14 of the Ontario *Corporations Information Act* provide penalties for making false or misleading statements or omissions.

Complete the applicable parts to report changes in the information recorded on the MGS public record.

Part 5 – Mailing address

500 ☐ Please enter one of the following numbers in this box: **1** – Show no mailing address on the MGS public record.
2 – The corporation's mailing address is the same as the head or registered office address in Part 2 of this schedule.
3 – The corporation's complete mailing address is as follows:

510 Care of (if applicable)

520 Street number	**530** Street name/Rural route/Lot and Concession number	**540** Suite number

550 Additional address information if applicable (line 530 must be completed first)

560 Municipality (e.g., city, town)	**570** Province/state	**580** Country	**590** Postal/zip code

Part 6 – Language of preference

600 ☐ Indicate your language of preference by entering **1** for English or **2** for French. This is the language of preference recorded on the MGS public record for communications with the corporation. It may be different from line 990 on the T2 return.

Part 7 – Director/Officer information

CRA internal form identifier 547, Code 0902

- **Director:** If the individual named in this part is a director (or must be reported ceased as a director), complete lines 700 to 797.
- **Officer:** If the individual named in this part is one of the corporation's five most senior officers (or must be reported ceased in an officer position), complete lines 700 to 790 and the applicable lines from 801 to 912.
- **Director and officer:** If the individual named in this part is a director and one of the corporation's five most senior officers (or must be reported ceased in these position(s)), complete lines 700 to 797 and the applicable lines from 801 to 912.
- The corporation is required to show information on the MGS public record for all its directors and a maximum of five of its most senior officers. If the MGS public record shows more than five officer positions, report cease dates for all except the corporation's five most senior officer positions.
- To report changes to the name of a director/officer, or changes to both the address and the date elected/appointed of a director/officer, enter the director/officer information exactly as shown incorrectly on the public record, with a cease date, and then photocopy and complete only Part 7 with the correct director/officer information.

Please photocopy this page and complete Part 7 only for each additional individual for whom director/officer information changes are being reported.

Full name and address for service (P.O. box not acceptable as stand-alone address). The name entered in lines 700 to 710 must be exactly as shown on the MGS public record.

700 Last name	**705** First name	**710** Middle name(s)

720 Street number	**730** Street name/Rural route/Lot and Concession number	**740** Suite number

750 Additional address information if applicable (line 730 must be completed first)

760 Municipality (e.g., city, town)	**770** Province/state	**780** Country	**790** Postal/zip code

Director

Is this director a resident Canadian?... **795** 1 Yes ☐ 2 No ☐
(applies to directors of corporations with share capital only)

	Date elected/appointed				Date ceased, if applicable		
	Year	Month	Day		Year	Month	Day
796				**797**			

Officer information

	Date appointed				Date ceased, if applicable		
	Year	Month	Day		Year	Month	Day
President	**801**				**802**		
Secretary	**806**				**807**		
Treasurer	**811**				**812**		
General Manager	**816**				**817**		
Chair	**821**				**822**		
Chairperson	**826**				**827**		
Chairman	**831**				**832**		
Chairwoman	**836**				**837**		
Vice-Chair	**841**				**842**		
Vice-President	**846**				**847**		
Assistant Secretary	**851**				**852**		
Assistant Treasurer	**856**				**857**		
Chief Manager	**861**				**862**		
Executive Director	**866**				**867**		
Managing Director	**871**				**872**		
Chief Executive Officer	**876**				**877**		
Chief Financial Officer	**881**				**882**		
Chief Information Officer	**886**				**887**		
Chief Operating Officer	**891**				**892**		
Chief Administrative Officer	**896**				**897**		
Comptroller	**901**				**902**		
Authorized Signing Officer	**906**				**907**		
Other (untitled)	**911**				**912**		

Once you have completed this page, complete the certification in Part 4 of this schedule.

APPENDIX C:

Minutes of a Meeting of the Board of Directors of

Entertainment Group LTD.

held at the Registered Office of the Corporation

on the _____ day of _____, 20_____

at the hour of 10:00 o'clock in the afternoon.

Present:

A quorum of directors was present, namely:

JAVID KHAN
HELENA KRISTINA MADEJ
MICHAEL ANDREW SMITH

The President, Javid Khan, acted as Chairman and Helena Kristina Madej acted as Secretary of the meeting.

A quorum of the directors being present, and all the directors of the Corporation having waived notice of the meeting, the Chairman declared the meeting to be duly constituted.

1. Approval of Financial Statements

On motion duly made, seconded and unanimously carried, the following resolution was passed:

Be It Resolved That:

the unaudited financial statements of the Corporation for the fiscal period ended December 30, 2010, which have been prepared by the accountant of the Corporation, consisting of a Statement of Profit and Loss for the period ended December 30, 2010 and a Balance Sheet as of the end of such period, together with a draft of the accountant's comments thereon be and the same are hereby approved, and the directors are hereby authorized to sign the Balance Sheet to evidence such approval, and be it further resolved that the said financial statements be submitted to the shareholders of the Corporation.

2. Shareholders Meeting

On motion duly made, seconded and unanimously carried, the following resolution was passed:

Be It Resolved That:

the annual meeting of the shareholders be held for the purposes of receiving and considering the financial statements of the Corporation for the fiscal period ended December 30, 2010, electing directors, appointing the accountant and transacting such other business as may properly come before the meeting.

There being no further business, the meeting was terminated.

_____   _____

Chairman   Secretary

APPENDIX D:

Minutes of a Meeting of the Shareholders of

Entertainment Group LTD.

held at the Registered Office of the Corporation

on the _____ day of _____, 20_____

at the hour of 10:30 o'clock in the forenoon.

Present:

The following shareholders were present at the meeting:

JAVID KHAN
SAM KHAN
HELENA KRISTINA MADEJ
MICHAEL ANDREW SMITH

The President, Javid Khan, acted as Chairman and Helena Kristina Madej acted as Secretary of the meeting.

A quorum of shareholders being present either personally or by proxy, and all of the shareholders of the Corporation having waived notice of the meeting, the Chairman declared the meeting to be duly constituted.

3. Approval of Financial Statements

The Chairman presented to the meeting the unaudited financial statements of the Corporation for the fiscal period ended December 30, 2010, together with the accountant's comments thereon.

On motion duly made, seconded and unanimously carried, the following resolution was passed:

Be It Resolved That:

the unaudited financial statements of the Corporation for the fiscal period ended December 30, 2010 be and the same are hereby accepted by the shareholders of the Corporation.

4. Confirmation of Proceedings

On motion duly made, seconded and unanimously carried, the following resolution was passed:

Be It Resolved That:

all acts, by-laws, resolutions, contracts, proceedings, elections, appointments and payments enacted, passed, made, done or taken by the directors and officers of the Corporation since the date of the last annual meeting of shareholders of the Corporation be and the same are hereby approved, ratified and confirmed.

5. Election of Directors

The Chairman then stated that it was in order to proceed with the election of directors and called for nominations. The following persons were nominated:

JAVID KHAN
HELENA KRISTINA MADEJ
MICHAEL ANDREW SMITH

There being no further nominations, the Chairman declared nominations closed.

On motion duly made, seconded and unanimously carried, the following resolution was passed:

Be It Resolved That:

The following persons be and they are hereby elected directors of the Corporation to hold office until the completion of the first annual meeting of the shareholders of the Corporation or until their respective successors are duly elected, subject to the provisions of the by-laws of the Corporation and the provisions of the *Business Corporations Act* (Ontario):

JAVID KHAN
HELENA KRISTINA MADEJ
MICHAEL ANDREW SMITH

6. Appointment of Accountant

Be It Resolved That:

Pecuniary Associates be and he is hereby appointed the accountant of the Corporation to hold office until the completion of the first annual meeting of the shareholders of the Corporation, or until a successor is appointed, at such remuneration as may be fixed by the board of directors and the board of directors is hereby authorized to fix such remuneration.

There being no further business, the meeting was terminated.

_____   _____
Chairman   Secretary

Appendix E:

Consent of Shareholders to Exemption From Audit
Entertainment Group LTD.

The undersigned, being all of the shareholders of ENTERTAINMENT GROUP LTD. (the "Corporation"), hereby declare that the Corporation is not offering its securities to the public.

Pursuant to section 148 of the *Business Corporations Act* (Ontario), we hereby consent to the exemption of the Corporation from the audit provisions set out in Part XII of the said Act in respect of the first fiscal year of the Corporation, and in respect of each fiscal year thereafter until this consent is revoked.

DATED the _____ day of _____, 20_____.

_____   _____
JAVID KHAN   SAM KHAN

_____   _____
HELENA KRISTINA MADEJ   MICHAEL ANDREW SMITH

CHAPTER 12: CHANGES IN CORPORATE STRUCTURE

Overview:

- Amendments
- Amalgamation
- Continuance
- Arrangement and reorganization
- Sale of the business
- Dissolution & winding up
    - Voluntary winding up
    - Winding up by court order
    - Voluntary dissolution
    - Cancellation by Director of *BCA*
- Workbook:
    - Review Exercise
    - Articles of Amendment
- Appendices:
    - Articles of Amendment
    - Articles of Amalgamation
    - Statement of Directors
    - Articles of Dissolution (Form 10, *BCA*)

1. Introduction

Many changes can occur over the life of a corporation. The corporation may change its name, number of directors, share structure or other characteristics. The directors of a corporation may decide that the corporation can be more successful if it joins forces with another corporation. Alternatively, the corporation may decide to change jurisdictions. Finally, the directors of a corporation may even decide that it is time to sell or end the life of the corporation. Each of these changes in corporate structure will be discussed in this chapter.

2. Amendments

> Helena would like to purchase shares in Entertainment Group Ltd. for her 5 year old daughter, but of course, these shares must be non-voting shares. She proposes that the corporation add a new class of shares, namely non-voting preferred shares. Unfortunately, the Articles of Incorporation do not include a class of non-voting preferred shares. How can this change be accomplished?

Sometimes, the directors of a corporation may decide to change basic characteristics of the company that are addressed in the Articles of Incorporation. For example, a corporation may:

- change its name
- add, change or remove a restriction on the business that the corporation may carry on or the powers the corporation may exercise
- add, change or remove the maximum number of shares that the corporation is authorized to issue (that is, the "authorized share capital" of the corporation)
- create a new class of shares
- change the features of any existing class of shares
- convert one class of shares into another class of shares
- divide a class of shares into different series of shares, with different rights, privileges, restrictions and conditions
- change the number of directors
- add, change or remove restrictions on the issue, transfer or ownership of shares of any class or series

These and other amendments are addressed in section 168 of the *BCA*, which gives a corporation the right to amend its Articles of Incorporation to add, change or remove any provision that is permitted by the Act, including but not limited to the changes listed above.[1] These changes must be authorized by a special resolution of the shareholders of the corporation.[2] (Recall that a "special resolution" is a resolution that is,

(a) submitted to a special meeting of the shareholders of a corporation duly called for the purpose of considering the resolution and passed, with or without amendment, at the meeting by at least two-thirds of the votes cast, or

(b) consented to in writing by each shareholder of the corporation entitled to vote at such a meeting or the shareholder's attorney authorized in writing.[3]

By contrast, an "ordinary resolution" is a resolution that is passed, with or without amendment, by a majority – that is, at least fifty percent – of the shareholders who vote at a meeting.[4])

For Ontario corporations, there are a limited number of changes that can be made with a directors' resolution only, including changing a numbered company name into a name that is not a number name.[5] Note that the directors, or any shareholder who is entitled to vote at an annual shareholders' meeting, may make a proposal to amend the Articles of Incorporation.[6] Where the change affects the share structure of the corporation, a legal professional should review section 170 to determine how shareholders are allowed to vote on that change.[7]

Once an amendment to the Articles of Incorporation has been approved in the manner specified in Part XIV of the *BCA* ("Fundamental Changes") the legal professional acting on behalf of the corporation should prepare Articles of Amendment. Articles of Amendment can be obtained from the Ontario Central Forms Repository, introduced in Chapter 2. Articles of Amendment for an Ontario corporation are referred to as Form 3 under the *BCA*.

Appendix A to this Chapter includes sample Articles of Amendment for Entertainment Group Ltd., which has decided to change its name to Nirvana Nightclub Ltd. As usual, it is very important to read the instructions to the form to prevent any unnecessary delay. For example, the instructions indicate that the form must be submitted in duplicate, either by mail or in person, and it must be completed in block capital letters. In addition, a name change requires the legal professional to obtain and submit a NUANS search report for the proposed name; that report cannot be dated more than 90 days before the date of submission of the Articles of Amendment. Pay special attention to the instructions for Article 5, which indicate exactly how that portion of the document must be completed.

---

1 *Business Corporations Act*, R.S.O. 1990, c. B.16, s. 168; see also *Canada Business Corporations Act*, R.S.C. 1985, c. C-44, s. 173.

2 *Business Corporations Act*, R.S.O. 1990, c. B.16, s. 168(5); see also *Canada Business Corporations Act*, R.S.C. 1985, c. C-44, s. 173(1).

3 *Business Corporations Act*, R.S.O. 1990, c. B.16, s. 1(1); see also *Canada Business Corporations Act*, R.S.C. 1985, c. C-44, s. 173(1).*Ibid.*, s. 2(1).

4 *Business Corporations Act*, R.S.O. 1990, c. B.16, s. 1(1); see also *Canada Business Corporations Act*, R.S.C. 1985, c. C-44, s. 173(1).*Ibid.*, s. 2(1).

5 *Business Corporations Act*, R.S.O. 1990, c. B.16, s. 168(2)–(5).

6 *Business Corporations Act*, R.S.O. 1990, c. B.16, s. 169(1); see also *Canada Business Corporations Act*, R.S.C. 1985, c. C-44, s. 175.

7 *Business Corporations Act*, R.S.O. 1990, c. B.16, s. 170; see also *Canada Business Corporations Act*, R.S.C. 1985, c. C-44, s. 176.

(It must be an extract from the resolution to amend the Articles of Incorporation.) Details such as the cost of filing the form and the locations at which it can be filed are available in the instructions to Form 3 (which are attached to the form), or on the ServiceOntario website at www.ServiceOntario.ca.

Note that a corporation may not change its name if the corporation is unable to pay its liabilities as they become due, or if the realizable value of the corporation's assets is less than the total amount of its liabilities.[8]

Once Articles of Amendment are filed, they will be endorsed with a Certificate of Amendment.[9] If there have been several amendments to the Articles of Incorporation, the directors may decided to submit Restated Articles of Incorporation, which are referred to as Form 5 under the *BCA* and are available from the Ontario Central Forms Repository. Form 5 is essentially the same as the Articles of Incorporation (Form 1) and is used to consolidate all the amendments and the original Articles of Incorporation into one, updated form. Please refer to Form 5 online at the Ontario Central Forms Repository. Note that the Restated Articles of Incorporation will also have a Restated Certificate of Incorporation.[10]

3. Amalgamation

Nirvana Nightclub has not been as successful as Javid, Helena and Mike had hoped. They know that they have a great location and a unique concept for the business, but their lack of business experience seems to be working against them. They are surprised, but excited, when the directors of Red Flag Entertainment Inc. approach them to discuss how they can work together. Red Flag Entertainment Inc. has been in the nightclub business for 20 years, and has successful nightclubs in Ontario and Quebec. The directors of Red Flag Entertainment Inc. like the business model and location for Nirvana Nightclub, but feel that they have the marketing knowledge and overall experience to make it a successful business. After several discussions, the parties agree that the two corporations will amalgamate, and that the newly amalgamated company will keep the name "Red Flag Entertainment Inc."

Amalgamation is like the "marriage" of two companies – individual corporations decide to merge and, thereafter, operate as one corporation. Section 174 of the *BCA* provides that "two or more corporations, including holding or subsidiary corporations, may amalgamate and continue as one corporation."[11] The relevant provisions in the *BCA* are sections 174 to 179; similar provisions are also found in sections 181 to 186.1 in the *CBCA*.

Corporations may choose to amalgamate for a variety of reasons. Sometimes, amalgamation is part of the process of buying a business, or it may take place as part of a

---

8 *Business Corporations Act*, R.S.O. 1990, c. B.16, s. 171(3).

9 *Business Corporations Act*, R.S.O. 1990, c. B.16, s. 172; see also *Canada Business Corporations Act*, R.S.C. 1985, c. C-44, s. 178.

10 *Business Corporations Act*, R.S.O. 1990, c. B.16, s. 173; see also *Canada Business Corporations Act*, R.S.C. 1985, c. C-44, s. 180.

11 *Business Corporations Act*, R.S.O. 1990, c. B.16, s. 174; see also *Canada Business Corporations Act*, R.S.C. 1985, c. C-44, s. 181.

reorganization for corporate or tax reasons. For example, a parent company may decide that there is no benefit to be derived from maintaining an inactive, wholly owned subsidiary (and there will still be some legal, accounting or other costs related to maintaining it.) To save on the cost and extra paperwork related to the inactive corporation, the parent company may choose to amalgamate with its wholly owned subsidiary. (The concept of parent company and wholly owned subsidiary is explained in further detail below.) Alternatively, an accountant may recommend that corporations amalgamate for tax reasons. In any case, it is important to consult with a tax professional to ensure that amalgamation does not result in adverse tax implications to the corporations or their shareholders. A legal professional should also review key contracts, leases, licenses, mortgages, security documents and key agreements with suppliers, customers and employees to ensure that any notice provisions are complied with, and to determine if consent is required before amalgamation can take place.[12]

A basic rule in understanding amalgamations is that only corporations from the same jurisdiction may amalgamate. In other words, an Ontario company can only amalgamate with another Ontario company. Similarly, a federal company can only amalgamate with a federal company. There may be situations, however, where two corporations from different jurisdictions – such as a federal company and an Ontario company – wish to amalgamate. In this case, one of the corporations will have to change its jurisdiction, in a process referred to as "continuance".[13] Continuance will be discussed later in part 4 of this chapter.

Amalgamations are generally referred to as "short form amalgamations" and "long form amalgamations", although the *BCA* does not use this terminology. In the *CBCA*, short form amalgamations are referred to as:

- vertical short-form amalgamations, and

- horizontal short-form amalgamations

It is important to distinguish between short form and long form amalgamations, because this distinction determines the legal process to be followed. While we will focus on the rules provided in the *BCA*, the provisions in the *CBCA* are very similar and will be referred to in the footnotes to this chapter.

As a starting point, it is useful to define some important terms. First, a "parent" or "holding" company is a company that owns shares in another company – usually, a sufficient number of shares to influence voting and control of the other company (which is called the "subsidiary").

---

12 "How to Amalgamate Corporations", online: Law Society of Upper Canada <http://rc.lscuc.on.ca/jsp/ht/amalgamatecorportions.jsp>.

13 *Ibid.*, see also the definitions of corporation in subsection 1(1) of the *BCA* and subsection 1(2) of the *CBCA*.

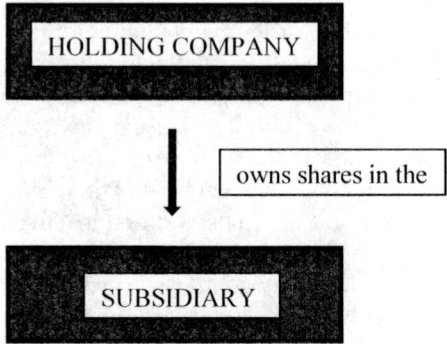

A "wholly owned subsidiary" is a company whose shares are owned entirely - that is, 100 percent – by its parent or holding company.

Wholly Owned Subsidiary:

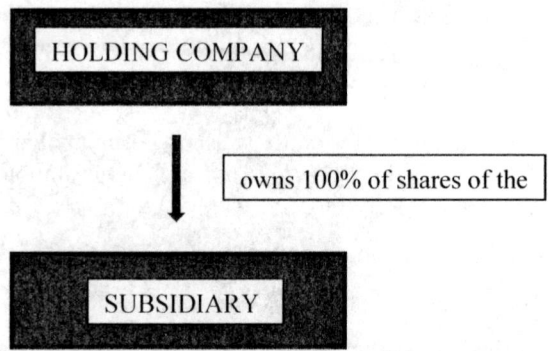

A short form amalgamation is:

* an amalgamation between the parent or holding company, and one or more wholly owned subsidiaries (called a "vertical short form amalgamation" in the CBCA) *or*

* an amalgamation between two or more wholly owned subsidiaries of the same parent company (called a horizontal short form amalgamation in the CBCA.)[14]

---

14 *Business Corporations Act*, R.S.O. 1990, c. B.16, s. 177; see also *Canada Business Corporations Act*, R.S.C. 1985, c. C-44, s. 184.

Vertical Short Form Amalgamation:

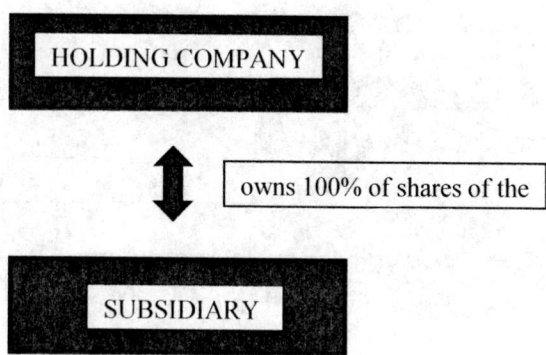

results in:

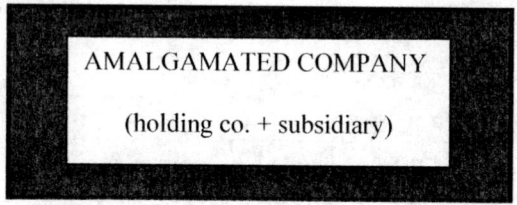

Horizontal Short Form Amalgamation:

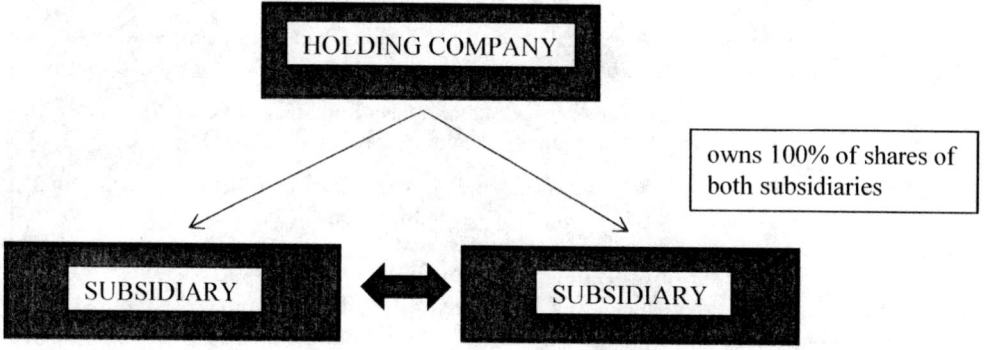

results in:

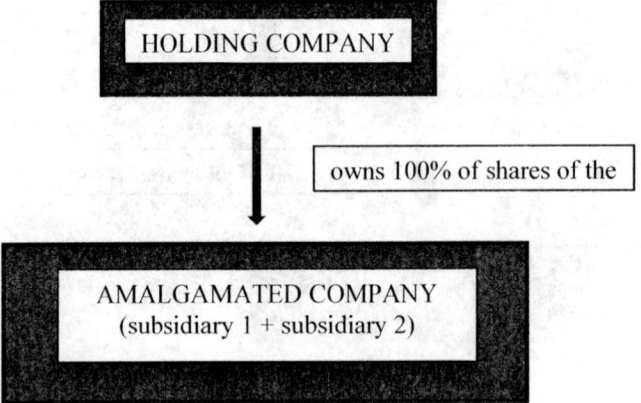

The process for completing a short form amalgamation of Ontario companies is described in the table below.

SHORT FORM AMALGAMATION - ONTARIO
• Directors of each of the amalgamating companies must pass a resolution approving the transaction.[15] Refer to s. 177(1) for specific statements that must be included in the resolution. The resolution must state that (i) the shares of each amalgamating subsidiary corporation shall be cancelled without any repayment of capital in respect thereof, (i.1) the by-laws of the amalgamated corporation shall be the same as the by-laws of the amalgamating holding corporation, (ii) except as may be prescribed, the articles of amalgamation shall be the same as the articles of the amalgamating holding corporation, and (iii) no securities shall be issued and no assets shall be distributed by the amalgamated corporation in conjunction with the amalgamation.[16]
• With a vertical short form amalgamation, the shares of each of the amalgamating companies must be cancelled without any repayment of capital. For a horizontal amalgamation, the shares of all but one of the amalgamating subsidiaries must be cancelled without repayment of capital.[17]

---

15 *Business Corporations Act*, R.S.O. 1990, c. B.16, s. 177(1); see also *Canada Business Corporations Act*, R.S.C. 1985, c. C-44, s. 184(1).

16 *Ibid.*

17 "How to Amalgamate Corporations", online: Law Society of Upper Canada <http://rc.lscuc.on.ca/jsp/ht/amalgamatecorportions.jsp>.

- With a vertical short form amalgamation, the by-laws of the amalgamated corporation must be the same as the by-laws of the holding (parent) company. For a horizontal amalgamation, the by-laws of the amalgamated corporation must be the same as the by-laws of the subsidiary whose shares are not cancelled.[18]

- With a vertical short form amalgamation, the Articles of Incorporation must be the same as the Articles of Incorporation of the holding (parent) company. For a horizontal amalgamation, the Articles of Incorporation must be the same as the Articles of Incorporation of the subsidiary whose shares are not cancelled. The only change permitted to the articles on a vertical short form amalgamation is that a different name and registered office address may be used. For a horizontal short form amalgamation, however, the articles may provide for:

    (a) a different name

    (b) a different minimum and maximum number of directors

    (c) a different address for the registered office, and

    (d) change, removal or addition of restrictions on the business of the amalgamated company[19]

- With a vertical short form amalgamation, no shares can be issued or assets distributed by the amalgamated corporation. For a horizontal amalgamation, the stated capital of the subsidiary whose shares are cancelled must be added to the stated capital of the other subsidiary corporation (to form the stated capital of the amalgamated corporation.)[20]

- Articles of Amalgamation must be filed in duplicate, with a statement of a director or officer of each amalgamating corporation. Generally, the statement is intended to confirm that the corporation is solvent, and that creditors will not be prejudiced by the amalgamation. Refer to subsection 178(2) for the specific provisions that must be included in this statement. It may be necessary to provide notice to creditors, in accordance with subsection 178(2) of the *BCA*.[21]

- A Certificate of Amalgamation will be issued.[22]

---

18 *Ibid.*
19 *Ibid.*
20 *Ibid.*
21 *Business Corporations Act*, R.S.O. 1990, c. B.16, s. 178; see also *Canada Business Corporations Act*, R.S.C. 1985, c. C-44, s. 185.
22 *Business Corporations Act*, R.S.O. 1990, c. B.16, ss. 178(4) & 179; see also *Canada Business Corporations Act*, R.S.C. 1985, c. C-44, ss. 185(4) & 186.

- After amalgamation, it is common practice to hold a meeting for the amalgamated corporation's directors and shareholders, to complete organizational matters such as the adoption of by-laws, appointment of officers and adoption of share certificates. A new minute book should be created for the amalgamated corporation, similar to a minute book for a new incorporation. The directors of the newly amalgamated company should consult with accounting or tax professionals to ensure that tax obligations (such as obtaining new tax filing numbers) are complied with. Finally, the newly amalgamated company must file Form 1 (Initial Return) under the *Corporations Information Act*[23] within 60 days of the date of the amalgamation.[24]

The process for a long form amalgamation – which is any amalgamation that is not a short form horizontal amalgamation or a short form vertical amalgamation – is somewhat more involved because it requires the negotiation of an amalgamation agreement between the companies proposing to amalgamate, and shareholder approval from all of the amalgamating companies. The table below summarizes the steps to follow. (Some of the steps will be the same as those in the table for short form amalgamations.)

LONG FORM AMALGAMATION - ONTARIO
• The corporations that propose to amalgamate must enter into an amalgamation agreement that addresses certain matters. (Refer to section 175 of the *BCA* for a complete list of matters which must be addressed by the amalgamation agreement.)[25]
• The shareholders of each amalgamating corporation must approve the amalgamation by special resolution. Notice of the meeting where shareholders will vote on the amalgamation must include a copy or summary of the amalgamation agreement. Refer to subsection 176(3) for provisions that address voting by the shareholders.[26]
• Dissenting shareholders – that is, shareholders who do not agree with the proposal to amalgamate – are entitled to be paid fair value for their shares.[27]

23 R.S.O. 1990, c. C-39.
24 "How to Amalgamate Corporations", online: Law Society of Upper Canada <http://rc.lscuc.on.ca/jsp/ht/amalgamatecorportions.jsp>.
25 *Business Corporations Act*, R.S.O. 1990, c. B.16, s. 175; see also *Canada Business Corporations Act*, R.S.C. 1985, c. C-44, s. 182.
26 "How to Amalgamate Corporations", online: Law Society of Upper Canada <http://rc.lscuc.on.ca/jsp/ht/amalgamatecorportions.jsp>.
27 *Business Corporations Act*, R.S.O. 1990, c. B.16, s. 185; see also *Canada Business Corporations Act*, R.S.C. 1985, c. C-44, s. 190.

- Articles of Amalgamation must be filed in duplicate, with a statement of a director or officer of each amalgamating corporation. Generally, the statement is intended to confirm that the corporation is solvent, and that creditors will not be prejudiced by the amalgamation. Refer to subsection 178(2) for the specific provisions that must be included in this statement. It may be necessary to provide notice to creditors, in accordance with subsection 178(2) of the *BCA*.[28]

- A Certificate of Amalgamation will be issued.[29]

- After amalgamation, it is common practice to hold a meeting for the amalgamated corporation's directors and shareholders, to complete organizational matters such as the adoption of by-laws, appointment of officers and adoption of share certificates. A new minute book should be created for the amalgamated corporation, similar to a minute book for a new incorporation. The directors of the newly amalgamated company should consult with accounting or tax professionals to ensure that tax obligations (such as obtaining new tax filing numbers) are complied with. Finally, the newly amalgamated company must file Form 1 (Initial Return) under the *Corporations Information Act*[30] within 60 days of the date of the amalgamation.[31]

Articles of Amalgamation are referred to as Form 4 under the *BCA*. The instructions indicate that the following must be attached to Form 4 (in addition to the required fee):

- a NUANS search report that is not more than 90 days old, if the name of the newly amalgamated corporation is a new name; note that a NUANS search report is <u>not</u> required if the newly amalgamated company is going to keep the name of one of the amalgamating companies. (However, the amalgamated company cannot retain the *number name* of one of the amalgamating corporations.)

- if it is a short form amalgamation, a copy of the directors' resolutions approving the amalgamation for each of the amalgamating companies (in duplicate)

- if it is a long form amalgamation, a copy of the amalgamation agreement (in duplicate)

- a cover letter, with the information specified in the instructions.

Articles of Amalgamation may be filed in person or by mail, at the address provided in the instructions to Form 4. Note that, upon receipt of the Certificate of Amalgamation, the Articles of Amalgamation are deemed to be the Articles of Incorporation of the newly amalgamated company.[32]

---

28 *Business Corporations Act*, R.S.O. 1990, c. B.16, s. 178; see also *Canada Business Corporations Act*, R.S.C. 1985, c. C-44, s. 185.

29 *Business Corporations Act*, R.S.O. 1990, c. B.16, ss. 178(4) & 179; see also *Canada Business Corporations Act*, R.S.C. 1985, c. C-44, ss. 185(4) & 186.

30 R.S.O. 1990, c. C-39.

31 "How to Amalgamate Corporations", online: Law Society of Upper Canada <http://rc.lscuc.on.ca/jsp/ht/amalgamatecorportions.jsp>.

32 *Business Corporations Act*, R.S.O. 1990, c. B.16, s. 179; see also *Canada Business Corporations Act*, R.S.C. 1985, c. C-44, s. 186.

Please refer to the sample Articles of Amalgamation provided in Appendix B to this Chapter. These Articles of Amalgamation are based on the amalgamation of Entertainment Group Ltd. and Red Flag Entertainment Inc., which was referred to at the beginning of part 3 in this Chapter. A sample statement of the directors of Entertainment Group Ltd. is also provided in Appendix C, for your reference.

Witco Chemical Co. v. Oakville (Town) (1974), [1975] 1 S.C.R. 273, 43 D.L.R. (3d) 413, 1 N.R. 453 (S.C.C.)

A firm of lawyers represented the plaintiff, Whitco Chemical Co. ("Whitco"). One associate in the firm arranged for the amalgamation of Whitco and Argus Chemical Canada Limited ("Argus"). A day after the Certificate of Amalgamation was issued, another associate in the same law firm arranged for a lawsuit to be commenced by Whitco against the Town of Oakville. The name of the plaintiff was "Whitco", not Argus (the name of the amalgamated company.) Once the mistake was recognized, the lawyer applied to the court to amend the Statement of Claim; however, at this point, the limitation period for the claim had expired. The defendant argued that the claim should be dismissed because it had been started by a non-existent company.

The Supreme Court of Canada held that:

> there was not an extinguishment of the corporate identity of the Witco Chemical Company, Canada, Limited, sufficient to justify the Court in holding that the writ had been issued in the name of a non-existent plaintiff." The amendment to the statement of claim sought by the plaintiff was allowed.

Note that, today, section 179 of the *BCA* clarifies this issue and states that:

Upon the articles of amalgamation becoming effective,

(a) the amalgamating corporations are amalgamated and continue as one corporation under the terms and conditions prescribed in the amalgamation agreement;

(a.1) the amalgamating corporations cease to exist as entities separate from the amalgamated corporation;

(b) the amalgamated corporation possesses all the property, rights, privileges and franchises and is subject to all liabilities, including civil, criminal and quasi-criminal, and all contracts, disabilities and debts of each of the amalgamating corporations;

(c) a conviction against, or ruling, order or judgment in favour or against an amalgamating corporation may be enforced by or against the amalgamated corporation;

(d) the articles of amalgamation are deemed to be the Articles of Incorporation of the amalgamated corporation and, except for the purposes of subsection 117(1), the certificate of amalgamation is deemed to be the certificate of incorporation of the amalgamated corporation; and

(e) the amalgamated corporation shall be deemed to be the party plaintiff or the party defendant, as the case may be, in any civil action commenced by or against an amalgamating corporation before the amalgamation has become effective.

4. Continuance

> ABC Company is an Ontario corporation that proposes to amalgamate with XYZ Company, which is an Alberta corporation. Can the two companies amalgamate?

Recall that a basic rule for amalgamation of corporations under the *BCA* and the *CBCA* is that only corporations from the same jurisdiction may amalgamate. So for ABC Company to amalgamate with XYZ Company, one of them will have to change its jurisdiction. Since this textbook focuses on corporate law in Ontario, we will assume that XYZ Company agrees to change its jurisdiction to Ontario. Our analogy for amalgamation at the beginning of this Chapter was that amalgamation is like a "marriage" of corporations. Two individual corporations agree to come together to operate as one entity. In order to make that possible, both corporations must be in the same jurisdiction. In that context, "changing jurisdictions" –called "continuance" – is like an individual moving to Ontario to marry someone in Ontario.

A corporation that would like to be continued in Ontario – that is, to change its jurisdiction to Ontario and have Ontario laws govern it – may file Articles of Continuance. These Articles of Continuance will make any changes required to make the corporation comply with the laws of Ontario, providing that shareholder approval has been obtained. Upon receipt of the Articles of Continuance and any other required documents, a Certificate of Continuance shall be issued. At this point, the Articles of Continuance are deemed to be the Articles of Incorporation of the continued corporation, and the corporation becomes an Ontario corporation subject to the *BCA*. A copy of the Certificate of Continuance will be sent to the previous jurisdiction of that corporation.[33]

Section 181 of the *BCA* authorizes an Ontario corporation to apply to another jurisdiction to be continued into that jurisdiction. (For example, an Ontario corporation may decide to become a federal corporation, and section 181 of the *BCA* allows it to do so.) Shareholders must approve the continuance by special resolution, and dissenting shareholders are entitled to be paid the fair value of their shares in accordance with section 185 of the *BCA*. Once an Ontario corporation has received documentation from another jurisdiction that confirms that it has been continued into that jurisdiction, the corporation must file a copy of that document within sixty days after it has been issued. The *BCA* no longer applies to the corporation, once it has been continued into another jurisdiction. Finally, an Ontario corporation cannot apply to be continued under a different jurisdiction unless the laws of the new jurisdiction provide that:

- the property of the corporation remains its property

- the corporation continues to be liable for its obligations

- any existing cause of action, claim or liability is unaffected

- a civil, criminal or administrative proceeding pending by or against the corporation may continue to be prosecuted, and

---

33   *Business Corporations Act*, R.S.O. 1990, c. B.16, s. 180; see also *Canada Business Corporations Act*, R.S.C. 1985, c. C-44, s. 187.

- a conviction against the corporation may be enforced by or against the corporation.[34]

5. Arrangement & Reorganization

The *BCA* also addresses the concept of an "arrangement" whereby a corporation proposes a reorganization of the corporation or other scheme to the shareholders. If the scheme is proposed as an arrangement under the Act, sections 182 to 183 will apply. (Note that the arrangement may involve, amongst other things, an amendment to the Articles of Incorporation or even an amalgamation, but if it is structured as an arrangement, the process to follow is outlined in sections 182 to 183 of the *BCA*.) In an arrangement, the corporation is required to prepare a statement providing details on the proposal to the shareholders, who must approve the arrangement by special resolution. The corporation may also apply to the court for directions in connection with an arrangement. Once a court order has been made, Articles of Arrangement (Form 8, *BCA*) must be filed, and a Certificate of Arrangement will be issued.[35]

Finally, Part XIV of the *BCA* and Part XV of the *CBCA*– both called "Fundamental Changes" – also address a reorganization of a corporation. A "reorganization" is defined as

a court order made under section 248, an order made under the *Bankruptcy and Insolvency Act (Canada)* or an order made under the *Companies Creditors Arrangement Act (Canada)* approving a proposal.[36]

Section 248 of the *BCA* refers to the oppression remedy, discussed in Chapter 7. When a corporation is subject to a reorganization, the court may order a change in the Articles of Incorporation and the issuance of debt obligations. The court may also appoint directors to replace any or all of the directors currently in place. After a reorganization has been accomplished, Articles of Reorganization (Form 9, *BCA*) must be filed, and a Certificate of Reorganization will be issued. Note that a shareholder is not entitled to dissent under section 185 of the *BCA* if an amendment to the Articles results from this process.[37]

---

34 *Business Corporations Act*, R.S.O. 1990, c. B.16, s. 181; see also *Canada Business Corporations Act*, R.S.C. 1985, c. C-44, s. 188.

35 *Business Corporations Act*, R.S.O. 1990, c. B.16, ss. 182 – 183; see also *Canada Business Corporations Act*, R.S.C. 1985, c. C-44, s. 192.

36 *Business Corporations Act*, R.S.O. 1990, c. B.16, s. 186(1); see also *Canada Business Corporations Act*, R.S.C. 1985, c. C-44, s. 191(1) for a similar definition.

37 *Business Corporations Act*, R.S.O. 1990, c. B.16, s. 186; see also *Canada Business Corporations Act*, R.S.C. 1985, c. C-44, s. 191.

6. Sale of the Business

> Javid calls a meeting for the directors of Entertainment Group Ltd. He has exciting news – while the directors of Red Flag Entertainment Inc. are no longer interested in an amalgamation, they have indicated to Javid that they might be interested in buying Nirvana Nightclub. Javid feels that this would be an excellent option for the shareholders of Entertainment Group Ltd., as they do not want to be involved in the business any longer. Javid contacts the company's lawyer to discuss how to structure the deal.

Whenever a business is being sold, or a substantial number of assets belonging to that business are being sold, a lawyer must consider the provisions of the *Bulk Sales Act*. The sale of a business is usually structured in one of two ways:

- an asset purchase transaction, *or*

- a share purchase transaction

An asset purchase agreement is an agreement in which the vendor agrees to sell the assets of the business to the purchaser. This allows the purchaser to control which assets it wants to buy, and which liabilities (if any) it is willing to assume. By contrast, a share purchase agreement is a contract in which the vendor agrees to sell all of the shares of a corporation to the purchaser; by purchasing all of the shares of Entertainment Group Ltd., for example, Red Flag Entertainment Inc. will automatically acquire all of the assets and liabilities of Entertainment Group Ltd. Usually, vendors prefer share purchase agreements, and purchasers prefer asset purchase agreements. The way that the deal is structured will, therefore, be influenced by the negotiating power of both parties. In other words, if the vendor is desperate to sell its business, it will likely accept the terms – and the type of agreement – that the purchaser offers. If the vendor is not anxious to sell the business and the purchaser is eager to buy, the purchaser may make concessions in order to get the deal.

Asset Purchase Agreement

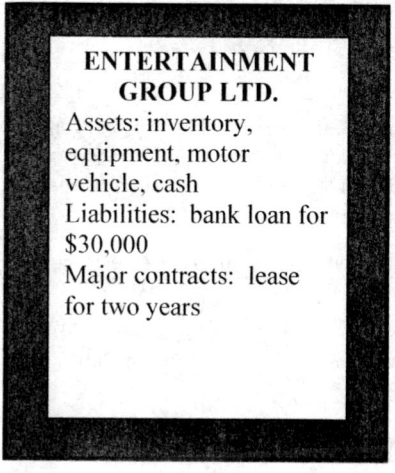

ENTERTAINMENT GROUP LTD.
Assets: inventory, equipment, motor vehicle, cash
Liabilities: bank loan for $30,000
Major contracts: lease for two years

RED FLAG ENTERTAINMENT INC.

**Agrees to buy only: inventory, equipment
Agrees to take over the lease**

Share Purchase Agreement

RED FLAG ENTERTAINMENT INC.

Buys 100% of the shares of

ENTERTAINMENT GROUP LTD.
Assets: inventory, equipment, motor vehicle, cash
Liabilities: bank loan for $30,000
Major contracts: lease for two years

While the details of asset purchase and share purchase transactions are beyond the scope of this textbook, we will discuss the implications of the *Bulk Sales Act*[38] briefly. The *Bulk Sales Act* applies to:

> every sale in bulk except a sale in bulk by an executor, an administrator, a guardian of property under the *Substitute Decisions Act, 1992*, a creditor realizing upon security, a receiver, an assignee or trustee for the benefit of creditors, a trustee under the *Bankruptcy Act* (Canada), a liquidator or official receiver, or a public official acting under judicial process.[39]

A "sale in bulk" means "a sale of stock in bulk out of the usual course of business or trade of the seller."[40]

The statute is essentially designed to protect creditors from losing their collateral in a bulk sale to another party. In order to comply with the Act, the buyer must demand –

---

38 R.S.O. 1990, c. B.14.
39 *Bulk Sales Act*, R.S.O. 1990, c. B.14, s. 2.
40 *Ibid.*, s. 1.

and the seller must provide – a list of all secured and unsecured creditors of the seller, in Form 1 to the *Bulk Sales Act*.[41] The buyer can only proceed with the transaction if it does one or more of the following:

- confirms that the total claims of all secured creditors do not exceed $2,500 and the total claims of all unsecured creditors do not exceed $2,500

- receives an affidavit from the seller indicating that the claims of all secured and unsecured creditors have been paid in full

- makes arrangements to ensure that the claims of all secured and unsecured creditors are paid in full upon completion of the sale

- receives waivers (in Form 2 to the *Bulk Sales Act*) from secured and unsecured creditors, waiving the provisions of the *Bulk Sales Act*

- receives consent forms (in Form 3 to the *Bulk Sales Act*) from unsecured creditors allowing the sale to proceed

Note that the seller may also apply to the court to exempt the sale from the provisions of the *Bulk Sales Act*.[42] (Please refer to the Act for the specific requirements related to these provisions, as this discussion only provides a general overview.)

Failure to comply with the *Bulk Sales Act* can have severe consequences. Section 16 of the Act provides:

16(1) A sale in bulk is voidable unless the buyer has complied with this Act.

(2) If a sale in bulk has been set aside or declared void and the buyer has received or taken possession of the stock in bulk, the buyer is personally liable to account to the creditors of the seller for the value thereof, including all money, security and property realized or taken by the buyer from, out of, or on account of, the sale or other disposition by the buyer of the stock in bulk.[43]

An action to set aside a sale in bulk can be brought by a creditor of the seller, or if the seller is bankrupt, by the trustee of the seller's estate. The only exception relates to real property. If real property has been sold, transferred, charged or mortgated to a purchaser in good faith for valuable consideration, without actual notice of non-compliance with the *Bulk Sales Act*, then that transaction cannot be set aside.[44]

7. Dissolution and Winding Up

> Unfortunately, Red Flag Entertainment Inc. has decided that it does not want to amalgamate with Entertainment Group Ltd., and it no longer wants to buy the business either. Javid, Helena and Mike feel that they have no option but to close down the company and get out of the nightclub business. Like many first time entrepreneurs, they have discovered that running a successful business is much harder than they thought it would be. They contact their lawyer to discuss their options.

---

41 *Ibid.*, s. 4.
42 *Ibid.*, s. 3.
43 *Ibid.*, s. 16.
44 *Ibid.*, s. 17.

Part XVI of the *BCA* is called "Liquidation and Dissolution", as is Part XVIII of the *CBCA*. This section will focus on the *BCA*; please refer to Part XVIII of the *CBCA* for relevant information about federal corporations.

There are several ways to close down a corporation under the *BCA*, including:

- voluntary winding up (sections 193 to 205)

- winding up by court order (sections 207 to 218)

- voluntary dissolution (sections 237 to 239)

- cancellation of Certificate of Incorporation by Director (sections 240 and 241)[45]

A corporation has an indefinite life – so unless it is closed down in one of these ways, it continues to exist indefinitely and must continue to comply with all legal requirements (which may involve ongoing costs.)

(a) Voluntary Winding Up

Voluntary winding up occurs when the shareholders of a corporation pass a special resolution agreeing to voluntarily wind up the corporation. The shareholders must appoint one or more individuals to act as the liquidator for the purpose of winding up the corporation's business and affairs, and distributing its property. A liquidator may be a director, officer or employee of the corporation. Once the shareholders have passed a special resolution to wind up the corporation, notice of the resolution must be filed with the Director of the *BCA* within ten days after the resolution is passed; notice must also be published in *The Ontario Gazette* within twenty days after the resolution has been passed.

Technically, the process of voluntarily winding up a corporation begins at the time that the special resolution is passed by the shareholders, or at a later time that is specified in that resolution.[46] Once the process has begun, there are several consequences. First, the corporation must cease to operate its business, except as is required to wind up the corporation. Second, the corporation cannot be sued, and certain remedies such as distress (seizing property of the corporation) cannot be exercised against the corporation without permission from the court.[47] Third, the liquidator has the power to negotiate with creditors and settle all debts and liabilities, with the approval of the shareholders.[48] Of course, the liquidator must present an account of how all matters have been dealt with at a shareholders meeting. Note that, at any time after the affairs of a corporation have been fully wound up, the liquidator (or any other person with an interest in the corporation) can apply to the court for an order dissolving the corporation. A certified copy of the order must be filed with the Director of the *BCA*, after which a notice of the order must be published in *The Ontario Gazette*.[49]

---

45 *Business Corporations Act*, R.S.O. 1990, c. B.16, ss. 191–244.
46 *Ibid.*, ss. 193–196.
47 *Ibid.*, ss. 197–199.
48 *Ibid.*, ss. 202–203.
49 Ibid., s. 205.

(b) Winding Up by Court Order

There may be times when a shareholder, creditor or even a liquidator may feel that the court must get involved in the winding up process. This can occur when a party feels that the process is not proceeding fairly or appropriately, or when the parties are in serious disagreement with one another and cannot manage the process without intervention.

Section 207 of the *BCA* explains the circumstances in which the court will wind up a corporation, including:

- where any security holder, creditor, director or officer of the corporation can prove that they have been treated oppressively, in a manner that is unfairly prejudicial or in a way that unfairly disregards their interests

- where a unanimous shareholders agreement gives a complaining shareholder the right to demand dissolution of the corporation upon the occurrence of a particular event (and that event has occurred)

- where proceedings have begun to wind up the corporation voluntarily, but it is in the interests of contributories[50] and creditors to continue the process under court supervision

- where the corporation cannot continue its business, even though it is solvent, because of its liabilities

- where it is just and equitable for any other reason, *other than* bankruptcy or insolvency of the corporation, to wind up the corporation, or

- where the shareholders authorize, by special resolution, an application to the court to wind up the corporation.[51]

A shareholder, liquidator or creditor having a claim of $2,500 or more can apply to the court for a winding-up order.[52] The court has wide powers in this situation, including making the order applied for, dismissing it, adjourning the hearing conditionally or unconditionally, or making any order that it considers just.[53] The court may also appoint a liquidator for the purpose of winding up the corporation's business and distributing its property.[54] Note that, after the process of winding up by court order has begun, no action or other proceeding can be commenced by or against the corporation without permission of the court, and actions such as distress (seizing the goods of the corporation) cannot be exercised against the corporation without the permission of the court and on such conditions as the court imposes.[55] Finally, the court can, at any time after the business and affairs of the corporation have been fully wound up, make an order to dissolve the corporation as of a specific date; the liquidator or any other interested person may apply

---

50 "Contributory" is defined in section 191 of the *BCA* as "a person who is liable to contribute to the property of a corporation in the event of the corporation being wound up under this Act.

51 *Business Corporations Act*, R.S.O. 1990, c. B.16, s. 207.

52 *Ibid.*, s. 208.

53 *Ibid.*, s. 209.

54 *Ibid.*, s. 210.

55 Ibid., s. 216; note that subsection 216(b) refers to attachment, sequestration, distress and execution against the estate or effects of the corporation.

to the court to request this order for dissolution. Once the court order has been made, it must be filed with the Director of the *BCA* within ten days, and thereafter, notice of the order must also be published in *The Ontario Gazette*.[56]

> Javid, Helena, Mike and Sam are in a meeting with their lawyer. They are discussing the possibility of winding up the corporation. Javid wants to know if the shareholders can keep all the assets that the corporation currently has, and if so, which shareholders will get paid. He is also worried that there might not be much money to share amongst the shareholders – if this is the case, will all the shareholders share whatever amount of money remains, or will some of them get nothing?

For both a voluntary wind up of a corporation and winding up by court order, the following considerations apply:

- the liquidator must use the property of the corporation to satisfy all debts, obligations and liabilities; anything that is left over after that must be distributed to shareholders, according to the shares that they hold in the corporation

- unpaid employee wages (up to three months' wages and vacation pay for up to twelve months) take priority over the claims of other creditors when the liquidator is distributing property; for any excess amount owing (greater than three months wages and twelve months vacation pay), the employees will join with other creditors and will be entitled to be paid before shareholders.

- all powers of directors cease when the liquidator is appointed, unless the liquidator allows the directors to continue to have certain powers[57]

- the costs related to the winding up process (including the liquidator's pay) are paid first out of the property of the corporation, in priority to all other claims[58]

- the powers of the liquidator are very broad, including but not limited to bringing or defending legal proceedings on behalf of the corporation, carrying on the business insofar as that is necessary for the winding up process, selling the corporation's property, and doing anything else that is necessary to wind up the corporation.[59]

- at any time during the winding up process, a shareholder, creditor or contributory may apply to the court for an order to stop the process (or put it on hold) with any conditions that the court thinks fit.[60]

Many clients are most concerned – with good reason – with how much money they can extract from the corporation as shareholders, once the corporation is wound up. Based on the considerations explained above, the corporation's property will be used to pay, in the following order:

---

56 *Ibid.*, s. 218.
57 *Ibid.*, s. 221.
58 *Ibid.*, s. 222.
59 Ibid., s. 223; see also *Canada Business Corporations Act*, R.S.C. 1985, c. C-44, s. 222.
60 *Business Corporations Act*, R.S.O. 1990, c. B.16, s. 233.

1. the liquidator, and other costs related to winding up the corporation

2. employees (for amounts up to three months wages and twelve months vacation pay)

3. ordinary creditors and others with outstanding liabilities (including unpaid employee wages and vacation pay in excess of the amount in item 2 above)

4. shareholders with preferred shares

5. shareholders with common shares

(c) Voluntary Dissolution

The key difference between winding up a corporation and dissolving a corporation, is that winding up involves a liquidator; by contrast, dissolving a corporation is a process managed primarily by the directors of the corporation, after receiving authorization from the shareholders. Because it does not require a third party to intervene and manage the process, dissolution can be a quicker, and possibly a less expensive, process.

Section 237 of the *BCA* provides that:

A corporation may be dissolved upon the authorization of,

(a) a special resolution passed at a meeting of the shareholders of the corporation duly called for the purpose or, in the case of a corporation that is not an offering corporation, by such other proportion of the votes cast as the articles provide, but such other proportion shall not be less than 50 per cent of all of the votes of the shareholders entitled to vote at the meeting;

(b) the consent in writing of all of the shareholders entitled to vote at such meeting; or

(c) all its incorporators or their personal representatives if the corporation has not commenced business and has not issued any shares.[61]

In order to dissolve the corporation pursuant to subsection 237 of the *BCA*, Articles of Dissolution must be filed with the Ministry of Government Services. However, there are two versions of the Articles of Dissolution to consider:

- Form 10 under the *BCA* – "Articles of Dissolution" – applies to voluntary dissolution of a corporation, where that dissolution has been approved by the shareholders [refer to subsections 237(a) and (b) of the *BCA*]

- Form 11 under the *BCA* – also called "Articles of Dissolution" – applies to voluntary dissolution of a corporation, where the corporation:

  - has not started a business

  - has not issued any shares

  - has authorization to dissolve from its incorporators or their personal representatives [refer to subsection 237(c) of the *BCA*][62]

---

61 *Ibid.*, s. 237.
62 *Ibid.*, s. 238(1) – 238(2).

Please see Appendix D to this Chapter for a sample Form 10 for Entertainment Group Ltd. As always, it is important to review the instructions to the forms before filing them. In this case, note that consent to dissolve must be obtained from the Minister of Revenue, and must be attached to the Articles of Dissolution. The instructions to Form 10 provide an address where you can send a request for this consent. The Articles of Dissolution must be filed within 60 days after the Minister provides consent to dissolve the corporation. Note also that the form asks for confirmation that:

- the dissolution has been authorized under subsection 237(a) or (b) of the *BCA*

- the corporation has no debts or liabilities, or has dealt with creditors and other parties with respect to debts and liabilities

- the corporation has no property to distribute to its shareholders, or has already distributed such property

- there are no proceedings pending in any court against the corporation

- the corporation has received consent to dissolve from the Minister of Revenue, and has also filed all notices and returns required under the *Corporations Information Act*[63]

Clearly, all of these matters must be dealt with before the Articles of Dissolution may be filed with the Ministry of Government Services. Once Articles of Dissolution have been filed, a Certificate of Dissolution will be issued.[64]

(d) Cancellation by Director of *BCA*

When a corporation does not comply with the requirements of the *BCA*, it may be dissolved by the Director of the *BCA*. Subsection 240(1) of the *BCA* provides that:

Where sufficient cause is shown to the Director, despite the imposition of any other penalty in respect thereof and in addition to any rights the Director may have under this or any other Act, the Director may, after having given the corporation an opportunity to be heard, by order, upon such terms and conditions as the Director thinks fit, cancel a certificate of incorporation or any other certificate issued or endorsed under this Act or a predecessor of this Act, and,

(a) in the case of the cancellation of a certificate of incorporation, the corporation is dissolved on the date fixed in the order; and

(b) in the case of the cancellation of any other certificate, the matter that became effective upon the issuance of the certificate ceases to be in effect from the date fixed in the order.[65]

The term "sufficient cause" is defined in subsection 240(2) and includes:

- failure to comply with subsection 115(2) – the required number of directors for offering and non-offering corporations – or subsection 118(3) – the Canadian residency requirements for directors

---

63 R.S.O. 1990, c. C.39.
64 *Business Corporations Act*, R.S.O. 1990, c. B.16, s. 239.
65 *Ibid.*, s. 240(1).

- a conviction of the corporation for a criminal offence, an offence under any other federal statute or an offence under the *Provincial Offences Act*, or

- conduct that is described in subsection 248(2). (Recall that subsection 248(2) is referred to as the oppression remedy, which deals with conduct that is oppressive or unfairly prejudicial to, or that unfairly disregards the interests of, any security holder, creditor, director or officer of the corporation. The oppression remedy was discussed in Chapter 7.)[66]

In addition, if the corporation has not complied with relevant tax legislation referred to in subsection 241(1) or with the requirements of the *Corporations Information Act*, the Director of the *BCA* may give notice by registered mail to the corporation, or by publication once in *The Ontario Gazette*, that an order to dissolve the corporation will be issued if the corporation does not remedy its default within 90 days after notice is given. Note that once a certificate of incorporation has been cancelled and the corporation dissolved, there are provisions of the *BCA* that provide for revival of the corporation.[67]

In order to protect third parties, however, section 242 of the *BCA* states that, even after a corporation has been dissolved, civil, criminal or administrative actions or proceedings brought by or against the corporation may be continued or commenced, as if the corporation had not been dissolved. Similarly, property of the corporation that would have been available to satisfy any judgment against the corporation remains available for that purpose. Title to land belonging to the corporation immediately before the dissolution also remains available to be sold in power of sale proceedings. Moreover, shareholders to whom corporate property has been distributed may still be liable to any person claiming under section 242 of the *BCA*.[68] These provisions ensure that parties do not dissolve a corporation simply to avoid the consequences of litigation or similar situations.

Finally, any property of the corporation that has not been disposed of at the date of its dissolution becomes the property of the government (the "Crown").[69] For this reason, it is important for legal professionals to ensure that all property of the corporation has been properly distributed, before the legal process of dissolving the corporation begins.

---

66 *Ibid.*, s. 240(2) & 248(2).
67 *Ibid.*, s. 241.
68 *Ibid.*, ss. 242–243.
69 Ibid., s. 244; see also *Canada Business Corporations Act*, R.S.C. 1985, c. C-44, s. 228.

Appendix A: Articles of Amendment

 **Ontario**

Ministry of
Government Services

Companies and Personal
Property Security Branch

393 University Avenue, Suite 200
Toronto ON M5G 2M2

Articles of Amendment
Form 3
Business Corporations Act

INSTRUCTIONS FOR COMPLETING

Articles in duplicate may be mailed to the Toronto address listed above. For over-the-counter service they may also be filed in person at the Toronto office or at some Land Registry/ServiceOntario offices in Ontario. For a list of locations see the "Offices That Endorse articles Submitted Under the *Business Corporations Act*" information sheet or visit the ServiceOntario web site at: www.ServiceOntario.ca.

FEE

$150.00   **BY MAIL** - cheque or money order payable to the Minister of Finance.

          IN PERSON (at the Toronto office) - cash, cheque or money order payable to the Minister of Finance, Visa, MasterCard, American Express or debit card. (If you are filing the documents at a Land Registry/ServiceOntario office, call first to confirm whether credit or debit cards are acceptable).

There will be a service charge payable for any cheque returned as non-negotiable by a bank or financial institution.

SUPPORTING DOCUMENTS

NAME SEARCH (if you are changing the corporation name)

If you are changing the name of the corporation, you must obtain an original Ontario-biased NUANS name search report. NUANS stands for (Newly Upgraded Automated Name Search). It is a six-page computer-printed search report consisting of corporate names, business names and trademarks that have already been incorporated/registered and are similar to the proposed corporate name. This search report must be submitted together with the duplicate Articles of Amendment and cannot be dated more than 90 days prior to the submission of the articles. For example, articles submitted on November 28th could be accompanied by a NUANS name search report dated as early as August 30th, but not dated earlier.

The NUANS name search report must be obtained from a private name search company. These companies are listed in the Yellow Pages under the heading "Searchers of Records". The Ministry does not provide this search. It is the applicant's responsibility to check the search report for similar/identical names and to obtain any consent that may be required.

The Ministry will not grant a name that is identical to the current name or former name of another corporation operating in Ontario whether active or not, unless it has been more than ten years since the other corporation dissolved or changed its name. The only exception to this rule is when the corporation meets the requirements of Subsection 6(2) of the Regulations, under the *Business Corporations Act*. In this case, Companies and Personal Property Security Branch policy requires that a legal opinion accompany the articles being filed. The legal opinion must be on legal letterhead and must be signed by an individual lawyer (not a law clerk). It must also clearly indicate that the corporations involved comply with Regulation 6(2) by referring to each clause specifically.

BILINGUAL NAMES

If you are changing the name to a name with an English and French version of the name (where the versions can be used separately), a name search is required for each version of the name (English and French). There should be a forward slash (/) separating the two versions of the name.

NUMBER NAMES

You do not require a name search for a number name. In Article two on the form, leave nine empty boxes, then type or print in block capital letters the word "ONTARIO" followed by one of the legal elements...LIMITED, LIMITÉE, INCORPORATED, INCORPOREE, CORPORATION or the corresponding abbreviation LTD., LTEE., INC., or CORP. The Director of Companies and Personal Property Security Branch will assign a number to the corporation.

APPEARANCE OF DOCUMENTS

The Articles of Amendment must be completed in duplicate on a Form 3 as approved by the Minister. All documents must be legible and compatible with the microfilming process, with the information typed or hand printed in block capital letters, on one side of good quality, white bond paper 8 1/2" X 11".

The Article headings are numbered 1 to 7 and should remain in that order. Do not leave out any of the headings. When additional pages are required, due to lack of space, they should be the same size as all the other pages and should be inserted after the applicable heading with the same number as the heading page with the addition of alphabet characters to indicate sequence. For example, pages inserted after page 1 would be numbered 1A, 1B, etc.

ARTICLE 1   Set out the current name of the corporation in block capital letters starting from the first box of the first line on the left with one letter per box and one empty box for a space. Punctuation marks are entered in separate boxes. Complete one line before starting in the first box of the next line. The name entered must be exactly the same as it appeared on the original Articles of Incorporation or Articles of Amalgamation. If there has been a name change, the name entered must be exactly the same as it appears on the most recent Articles of Amendment.

E	A	S	T		S	I	D	E		I	N	V	E	S	T	M	E	N	T		A	N	D		M	A	N	A	G
E	M	E	N	T		L	T	D	.																				

ARTICLE 2   If this is a name change; set out the new name in block capital letters starting from the first box of the first line on the left with one letter per box and one empty box for a space. Punctuation marks are entered in separate boxes. Complete one line before starting in the first box of the next line. The name entered must be exactly the same as that on the name search.

ARTICLE 3   Set out the date of incorporation or amalgamation.

ARTICLE 4   Complete only if there is a change in the "number" or "minimum and maximum" number of directors. Complete the "number" field if the corporation has a fixed number of directors **OR** the "minimum and maximum" field if the corporation has a minimum and maximum number of directors **(do not complete both)**.

ARTICLE 5   Set out an extract from the resolution to amend the articles listing the changes i.e., Resolved that:
(a) The name of the corporation is changed to ABC Holdings Inc.
(b) The authorized capital of the corporation is amended by...

If you require more space for Article 5 than is provided, please continue on page 1A, 1B etc. Page 2 should follow in sequence.

ARTICLE 6   The amendment must be authorized as required by sections 168 and 170 (as applicable) of the *Business Corporations Act*. This statement must be included in the Articles, and is already pre-printed on the form.

ARTICLE 7   Set out the date on which the resolution authorizing the amendment was approved by the shareholders/directors of the corporation.

EXECUTION   The current name of the corporation from Article 1 should be printed above the signature. Both copies of the Articles must have original signature(s) of an officer or director of the corporation. Beside the signature set out the office of the person who is signing (e.g. President, Director, Secretary). If the corporation has a seal it should be affixed to the Articles next to the signature.

Articles (in duplicate), original Ontario-biased NUANS name search report (if applicable), covering letter and filing fee should be mailed or delivered to:

Ministry of Government Services
Companies and Personal Property Security Branch
393 University Avenue, Suite 200
Toronto ON M5G 2M2
375 University Avenue, 2nd Floor (In Person)

07119 (2011/05)

For Ministry Use Only
A l'usage exclusif du ministère

Ontario Corporation Number
Numéro de la société en Ontario

1234567

ARTICLES OF AMENDMENT
STATUTS DE MODIFICATION

Form 3
Business
Corporations
Act

Formule 3
Loi sur les
sociétés par
actions

1. The name of the corporation is: (Set out in BLOCK CAPITAL LETTERS)
    Dénomination sociale actuelle de la société (écrire en LETTRES MAJUSCULES SEULEMENT) :

E	N	T	E	R	T	A	I	N	M	E	N	T		G	R	O	U	P		L	T	D	.					

2. The name of the corporation is changed to (if applicable): (Set out in BLOCK CAPITAL LETTERS)
    Nouvelle dénomination sociale de la société (s'il y a lieu) (écrire en LETTRES MAJUSCULES SEULEMENT) :

N	I	R	V	A	N	A		N	I	G	H	T	C	L	U	B		L	T	D	.							

3. Date of incorporation/amalgamation:
    Date de la constitution ou de la fusion :
    2011/10/21
    (Year, Month, Day)
    (année, mois, jour)

4. Complete only if there is a change in the number of directors or the minimum / maximum number of directors.
    Il faut remplir cette partie seulement si le nombre d'administrateurs ou si le nombre minimal ou maximal
    d'administrateurs a changé.

    Number of directors is/are: minimum and maximum number of directors is/are:
    Nombre d'administrateurs :   nombres minimum et maximum d'administrateurs :

    Number   minimum   and   maximum
    Nombre   minimum   et   maximum

                              or
                              ou

5. The articles of the corporation are amended as follows:
    Les statuts de la société sont modifiés de la façon suivante :

    RESOLVED THAT the name of the corporation is changed to Nirvana Nightclub Ltd.

6. The amendment has been duly authorized as required by sections 168 and 170 (as applicable) of the *Business Corporations Act*.
    La modification a été dûment autorisée conformément aux articles 168 et 170 (selon le cas) de la *Loi sur les sociétés par actions*.

7. The resolution authorizing the amendment was approved by the shareholders/directors (as applicable) of the corporation on
    Les actionnaires ou les administrateurs (selon le cas) de la société ont approuvé la résolution autorisant la modification le

2012/01/15
_____
(Year, Month, Day)
(année, mois, jour)

These articles are signed in duplicate.
Les presents statuts sont signés en double exemplaire.

ENTERTAINMENT GROUP LTD.
_____
(Print name of corporation from Article 1 on page 1)
(Veuillez écrire le nom de la société de l'article un à la page une)

By/
Par :

                                        PRESIDENT
_____   _____
(Signature)   (Description of Office)
(Signature)   (Fonction)

APPENDIX B: ARTICLES OF AMALGAMATION

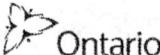 Ontario

Ministry of Government Services	Companies and Personal Property Security Branch	Articles of Amalgamation

393 University Ave, Suite 200
Toronto ON M5G 2M2

Articles of Amalgamation
Form 4
Business Corporations Act

INSTRUCTIONS FOR COMPLETING

This form together with required supporting documents and fee, must be filed with the Ministry of Government Services to amalgamate two or more Ontario business corporations under the *Business Corporations Act.*

Articles in duplicate may be mailed to the Toronto address listed below. For over-the-counter service articles may be filed in person at the Toronto office or at some Land Registry/ServiceOntario offices in Ontario. For a list of locations see the "Offices That Endorse articles Submitted Under the *Business Corporations Act*" information sheet or visit the ServiceOntario web site at: www.ServiceOntario.ca.

FEE

$330.00 (10 or fewer amalgamating corporations)

$500.00 (11 or more amalgamating corporations)

BY MAIL – Cheque or money order payable to the Minister of Finance

IN PERSON – (at the Toronto office) – cash, cheque or money order payable to Minister of Finance, Visa, MasterCard, American Express or debit card. (If you are filing the documents at a Land Registry or ServiceOntario Office, call first to confirm whether credit or debit cards are acceptable).

There will be a service charge payable for any cheque returned as non-negotiable by a bank or financial institution.

EFFECTIVE DATE

Articles are effective on the date set out in the certificate endorsed on the articles by the Branch. The certificate is dated the day the Director receives the duplicate originals of the articles together with all other required documents executed in accordance with the Act and the required fee, if they are acceptable as per the Branch's endorsement as of right policy. An effective date of up to 30 days later than the earliest date the articles can be endorsed may be requested **in writing, in the covering letter, using bold or highlighted letters,** upon submission of the articles to the branch. If you are presenting your documents in person you must also verbally bring this request to the attention of the counter clerk.

SUPPORTING DOCUMENTS

NAME SEARCH

The name of a corporation formed by the amalgamation of two or more corporations may be identical to the name of one of its amalgamating corporations, if it is **not a number name.** In this case a name search is not required.

If you are amalgamating under a new name you must obtain an original Ontario-biased NUANS name search report. NUANS is a computerized search system that compares a proposed corporate name or trade-mark with databases of existing corporate bodies and trade-marks. This comparison determines the similarity that exists between the proposed name or mark and existing names in the database, and produces a listing of names that are found to be most similar. This search must be submitted together with the duplicate Articles of Amalgamation within 90 days from production by the NUANS system. For example, articles submitted on November 28th could be accompanied by a NUANS name search report dated as early as August 30th, but not dated earlier. The Companies and Personal Property Security Branch does not provide this search.

Suppliers are listed in the Yellow Pages under the heading "Searchers of Records" or visit Industry Canada's NUANS site at, **www.nuans.com** for a list of registered search houses that can assist you with obtaining a NUANS search report and filing your corporate documents with the Ministry of Government Services. Please note the NUANS search must be **Ontario biased.**

352

NAME SEARCH
CONTINUED

It is the applicant's responsibility to check the search for similar/identical names and to obtain any consent that may be required. The Ministry will not grant a name that is identical to the current name or former name of another corporation operating in Ontario whether active or not, unless it has been more than ten years since the other corporation dissolved or changed its name. The only exception to this rule is when the corporation meets the requirements of Subsection 6(2) of Regulation 62, under the *Business Corporations Act*. In this case a legal opinion must accompany the articles being filed. The legal opinion must be on legal letterhead and signed by an individual lawyer (not a law clerk or law firm). It must also clearly indicate that the corporations involved comply with Subsection 6(2) by referring to each clause specifically.

BILINGUAL NAMES

When amalgamating a corporation with an English and French form of the name a name search is required for each form of the name (English and French) unless the English and French forms of the name are identical and the legal element in the French form is the French version of the legal element in the English form (for example, INCORPOREE and INCORPORATED). There should be a forward slash (/) separating the two forms of the name.

NUMBER NAMES

You do not require a name search for a number name. In Article one on the form, leave nine empty boxes, then type or print in block capital letters the word "ONTARIO" followed by one of the legal elements...LIMITED, LIMITÉE, INCORPORATED, INCORPOREE, CORPORATION or the corresponding abbreviation LTD., LTEE.,INC., or CORP. The Director of the Companies and Personal Property Security Branch will assign a number to the corporation.

The amalgamated corporation cannot retain the number name of an amalgamating company. When two or more corporations amalgamate a new corporation is formed. The Director assigns a new corporation number and in the case of a number name, this new number becomes the number part of the name.

SCHEDULES

SCHEDULE A A statement of a director or an officer of each of the amalgamating corporations completed as required under subsection 178(2) of the *Business Corporations Act* must be attached to both copies of the articles.

SCHEDULE B (i) A copy of the amalgamation agreement adopted by the shareholders pursuant to subsection 176(4) of the *Business Corporations Act*

Or

(ii) The director's resolutions of each amalgamating corporation as required under Section 177 of the *Business Corporations Act*

must be attached to both copies of the articles.

Schedules A and B must contain a signature of the appropriate shareholder(s), officer(s) or director(s) of the corporation as required under the Act. Photocopied amalgamation schedules that do not contain the required signature(s) will not be accepted.

COVERING LETTER

Enclose a covering letter setting out the name of a contact person, a return address and a telephone number. This will facilitate the processing of the articles should a question arise as to the content of the Articles of Amalgamation.

APPEARANCE OF DOCUMENTS

The Articles of Amalgamation must be completed in duplicate on Form 4 as approved by the Minister. All documents must be legible and compatible with the microfilming process, with the information typed or hand printed in block capital letters, on one side of good quality white bond paper 8 ½" X 11".

The article headings are numbered 1 to 12 and should remain in that order. Do not leave out any of the headings. If a section does not apply, type "nil" or "not applicable". When additional pages are required, due to lack of space, they should be the same size as all the other pages and should be inserted after the applicable heading with the same number as the heading page, but with the addition of alphabet characters to indicate sequence. For example, pages inserted after page 4 would be numbered 4A, 4B, etc.

07121 (201105)

ARTICLE 1   Set out the name of the amalgamated corporation in block capital letters starting from the first box of the first line on the left with one letter per box and one empty box for a space. Punctuation marks are entered in separate boxes. Complete one box before starting in the first box of the next line. The name entered must be exactly the same as that on the name search report or the same as one of the amalgamating corporations (if not a number name). Where a "number name" is to be used, leave the first nine boxes blank and complete as follows: "_____Ontario Inc." (see "number names")

E	A	S	T		S	I	D	E		I	N	V	E	S	T	M	E	N	T		A	N	D		M	A	N	A	G
E	M	E	N	T		L	T	D	.																				

ARTICLE 2   The address of multi-office building, include room or suite number) of the registered office of the corporation must be set out in full, including the street name, street number and suite or R.R. #, the municipality, province, country and the postal code. A post office box alone is not an acceptable address. If there is no street and number, set out the lot and concession or lot and plan numbers. The registered office must be in Ontario.

ARTICLE 3   Set out the number of directors. This can be either a fixed number of directors (i.e. 1) or a minimum and maximum number (i.e. minimum 1, maximum 10). Do not complete both.

ARTICLE 4   The name(s) (including first name, middle names and surname) and the address for service for each of the first directors must be set out. The address should include the street name, street number, suite (or R.R. #) municipality, province, country and postal code. Directors must be individuals, not corporations. State if the director(s) is/are Resident Canadian(s). At least 25 per cent of the directors must be resident Canadians (if 25% of the directors is not a whole number, round up to the nearest whole number). Where a corporation has less than four directors, at least one must be a resident Canadian

ARTICLE 5   Check the appropriate box (A) or (B):

Check box (A) Amalgamation Agreement - if the amalgamation agreement has been adopted by the shareholders of each of the amalgamating corporations under Subsection 176(4) of the Business Corporations Act. In this case Schedule "B" referred to in Article 12 on the form must be a copy of the amalgamation agreement containing the signatures of a director or authorized signing officer of each amalgamating corporation.

OR

Check box (B) Amalgamation of a holding corporation and one or more of its subsidiaries or amalgamation of subsidiaries - if the amalgamation has been approved by the directors of each of the amalgamating corporations by a resolution as required by Section 177 of the Business Corporations Act. In this case schedule "B" referred to in Article 12 must be a copy of the director's resolutions (containing the required signatures) for each amalgamating corporation. If all the directors approved the resolution without a meeting being held, each director is required to sign the resolution. If the resolution was approved at a directors' meeting, its approval must be certified in writing with a signature by the Secretary (or other authorized officer) of the corporation. If (B) is checked, on the line provided, set out the name of the amalgamating corporation containing the same provisions in substance as the Articles of Amalgamation now being submitted.

Under the corresponding headings, set out the corporation name, Ontario corporation number and the date of adoption/approval of the amalgamation agreement or directors resolutions for each of the amalgamating corporations.

ARTICLE 6   Set out restrictions, if any, on the business the corporation may carry on or on the powers that the corporation may exercise. If none, state so.

ARTICLE 7   Set out the classes and any maximum number of shares that the corporation is authorized to issue. This item must be completed (e.g., unlimited common shares).

354

ARTICLE 8	Set out the rights, privileges, restrictions, and conditions etc. (if any) attached to each class of shares, and directors' authority with respect to any class of shares which may be issued in series.
ARTICLE 9	Set out restrictions on issue, transfer or ownership of shares (if any).
ARTICLE 10	Set out other provisions (if any).
ARTICLE 11	*The statements required by Subsection 178(2) of the Business Corporations Act are attached as Schedule "A".* The statements (original or photocopy) must set out specific information as required under the Act and must contain the signature of a director or officer as evidence that the person signing has approved all of the contents of the statement This Item must be included in the articles and the required Schedule must be attached.
ARTICLE 12	*A copy of the amalgamation agreement or directors' resolutions (as the case may be) is/are attached as Schedule "B".* This Item must be included in the articles and the required schedule must be attached.
EXECUTION	Both copies of the articles must have an **original** signature of an officer or director of each of the amalgamating corporations. Set out the name of the officer/director who is signing, the name of the corporation and the office held by the individual in the corporation (e.g., president, director, secretary).

Articles with schedules "A" and "B" (in duplicate), original Ontario-biased NUANS name search report (if applicable), covering letter and filing fee should be mailed or delivered to:

Ministry of Government Services
Companies and Personal Property Security Branch
393 University Avenue, Suite 200
Toronto ON M5G 2M2

375 University Avenue, 2nd Floor (In Person)

07121 (201105)

Ontario Corporation Number
Numéro de la société en Ontario

ARTICLES OF AMALGAMATION
STATUTS DE FUSION

Form 4
*Business
Corporations
Act*

Formule 4
*Loi sur les
sociétés par
actions*

1. The name of the amalgamated corporation is: (Set out in BLOCK CAPITAL LETTERS)
    Dénomination sociale de la société issue de la fusion: (Écrire en LETTRES MAJUSCULES SEULEMENT) :

| R | E | D | | F | L | A | G | | E | N | T | E | R | T | A | I | N | M | E | N | T | | I | N | C | . | |

2. The address of the registered office is:
    Adresse du siège social :

    10 Toronto Street

    Street & Number or R.R. Number & if Multi-Office Building give Room No. /
    Rue et numéro ou numéro de la R.R. et, s'il s'agit d'un édifice à bureaux, numéro du bureau

    Toronto   **ONTARIO**   M 5 X 3 S 8

    Name of Municipality or Post Office /   Postal Code/Code postal
    Nom de la municipalité ou du bureau de poste

3. Number of directors is: Fixed number   OR minimum and maximum
    Nombre d'administrateurs :   Nombre fixe   OU minimum et maximum   1   10

4. The director(s) is/are: / Administrateur(s) :

First name, middle names and surname Prénom, autres prénoms et nom de famille	Address for service, giving Street & No. or R.R. No., Municipality, Province, Country and Postal Code Domicile élu, y compris la rue et le numéro ou le numéro de la R.R., le nom de la municipalité, la province, le pays et le code postal	Resident Canadian State 'Yes' or 'No' Résident canadien Oui/Non
Javid Khan	313 River Road Drive Toronto, Ontario M4W 5S7	Yes
Alexander T. Smith	99 Corby Court Markham, Ontario L3R 9D9	Yes

5. Method of amalgamation, check A or B
   Méthode choisie pour la fusion – Cocher A ou B :

A - **Amalgamation Agreement / Convention de fusion :**

☒

The amalgamation agreement has been duly adopted by the shareholders of each of the amalgamating corporations as required by subsection 176 (4) of the *Business Corporations Act* on the date set out below.

or
ou

Les actionnaires de chaque société qui fusionne ont dûment adopté la convention de fusion conformément au paragraphe 176(4) de la *Loi sur les sociétés par actions* à la date mentionnée ci-dessous.

B - **Amalgamation of a holding corporation and one or more of its subsidiaries or amalgamation of subsidiaries / Fusion d'une société mère avec une ou plusieurs de ses filiales ou fusion de filiales :**

☐

The amalgamation has been approved by the directors of each amalgamating corporation by a resolution as required by section 177 of the *Business Corporations Act* on the date set out below.

Les administrateurs de chaque société qui fusionne ont approuvé la fusion par voie de résolution conformément à l'article 177 de la *Loi sur les sociétés par actions* à la date mentionnée ci-dessous.

The articles of amalgamation in substance contain the provisions of the articles of incorporation of
Les statuts de fusion reprennent essentiellement les dispositions des statuts constitutifs de

and are more particularly set out in these articles.
et sont énoncés textuellement aux présents statuts.

Names of amalgamating corporations Dénomination sociale des sociétés qui fusionnent	Ontario Corporation Number Numéro de la société en Ontario	Date of Adoption/Approval Date d'adoption ou d'approbation		
		Year année	Month mois	Day jour
ENTERTAINMENT GROUP LTD.	1234567	2012/05/31		
RED FLAG ENTERTAINMENT INC.	7654321	2012/05/31		

6. Restrictions, if any, on business the corporation may carry on or on powers the corporation may exercise.
   Limites, s'il y a lieu, imposées aux activités commerciales ou aux pouvoirs de la société.

None

7. The classes and any maximum number of shares that the corporation is authorized to issue:
   Catégories et nombre maximal, s'il y a lieu, d'actions que la société est autorisée à émettre :

1. An unlimited number of Common shares, to be known as "Class A" shares

2. An unlimited number of non-voting "Class B" shares

358

8. Rights, privileges, restrictions and conditions (if any) attaching to each class of shares and directors authority with respect to any class of shares which may be issued in series:

Droits, privilèges, restrictions et conditions, s'il y a lieu, rattachés à chaque catégorie d'actions et pouvoirs des administrateurs relatifs à chaque catégorie d'actions qui peut être émise en série :

Class "B" Shares:

The rights of the holders of "Class B" Shares shall be identical to all the rights of the holders of Common Shares, save and except that the holders of the Class "B" Shares shall not have the right to vote. The rights of the holders of Class "B" shares shall in every respect rank pari passu with the holders of the Common Shares.

9. The issue, transfer or ownership of shares is/is not restricted and the restrictions (if any) are as follows.
   L'émission, le transfert ou la propriété d'actions est/n'est pas restreint. Les restrictions, s'il y a lieu, sont les suivantes :

The transfer of shares of the Corporation shall be restricted in that no shareholder shall be entitled to transfer any share or shares without either:

(a) The approval of the directors of the Corporation expressed by a resolution passed at a meeting of the board of directors or by an instrument or instruments in writing signed by a majority of the directors; or

(b) The approval of the holders of at least a majority of the shares of the Corporation entitling the holders thereof to vote in all circumstances (other than a separate class vote of the holders of another class of shares of the Corporation) for the time being outstanding expressed by a resolution passed at a meeting of the holders of such shares or by an instrument or instruments in writing signed by the holders of a majority of such shares.

10. Other provisions, (if any):
    Autres dispositions, s'il y a lieu :

(a) The Corporation shall be a private issuer within the meaning of section 2.4 of National Instrument 45-106 under the Securities Act (Ontario).

(b) The Corporation shall not at any time have outstanding securities of the Corporation that are beneficially owned, directly or indirectly, by more than 50 persons or companies that have purchased as principals, not including employees and former employees of the Corporation or its affiliates (provided that each person is counted as one beneficial owner unless the person is created or used solely to purchase or hold securities of the Corporation in which case each beneficial owner or each beneficiary of the person, as the case may be, must be counted as a separate beneficial owner)and is:

i. a director, officer, employee, founder or control person of the Corporation,

ii. a spouse, parent, grandparent, brother, sister or child of a director, executive officer, founder or control person
of the Corporation,

iii. a parent, grandparent, brother, sister or child of the spouse of a director, executive officer, founder or control person of the Corporation,

iv. a close personal friend of a director, executive officer, founder or control

11. The statements required by subsection 178(2) of the *Business Corporations Act* are attached as Schedule "A".
    Les déclarations exigées aux termes du paragraphe 178(2) de la *Loi sur les sociétés par actions* constituent l'annexe A.

12. A copy of the amalgamation agreement or directors' resolutions (as the case may be) is/are attached as Schedule "B".
    Une copie de la convention de fusion ou les résolutions des administrateurs (selon le cas) constitue(nt) l'annexe B.

360

These articles are signed in duplicate.
Les présents statuts sont signés en double exemplaire.

Name and original signature of a director or authorized signing officer of each of the amalgamating corporations. Include the name of each corporation, the signatories name and description of office (e.g. president, secretary). Only a director or authorized signing officer can sign on behalf of the corporation. / Nom et signature originale d'un administrateur ou d'un signataire autorisé de chaque société qui fusionne. Indiquer la dénomination sociale de chaque société, le nom du signataire et sa fonction (p. ex. : président, secrétaire). Seul un administrateur ou un dirigeant habilité peut signer au nom de la société.

ENTERTAINMENT GROUP LTD.
_____
Names of Corporations / Dénomination sociale des sociétés
By / Par

JAVID KHAN   PRESIDENT
_____   _____   _____
Signature / Signature   Print name of signatory /   Description of Office / Fonction
                             Nom du signataire en lettres moulées

RED FLAG ENTERTAINMENT INC.
_____
Names of Corporations / Dénomination sociale des sociétés
By / Par

ALEXANDER T. SMITH   PRESIDENT
_____   _____   _____
Signature / Signature   Print name of signatory /   Description of Office / Fonction
                             Nom du signataire en lettres moulées

_____
Names of Corporations / Dénomination sociale des sociétés
By / Par

_____   _____   _____
Signature / Signature   Print name of signatory /   Description of Office / Fonction
                             Nom du signataire en lettres moulées

_____
Names of Corporations / Dénomination sociale des sociétés
By / Par

_____   _____   _____
Signature / Signature   Print name of signatory /   Description of Office / Fonction
                             Nom du signataire en lettres moulées

_____
Names of Corporations / Dénomination sociale des sociétés
By / Par

_____   _____   _____
Signature / Signature   Print name of signatory /   Description of Office / Fonction
                             Nom du signataire en lettres moulées

APPENDIX C: STATEMENT OF DIRECTOR

I, Javid Khan, state that:

1. I am a director of Entertainment Group Ltd., one of the amalgamating corporations (hereinafter referred to as the "Corporation");

2. Pursuant to subsection 178(2) of the *Business Corporations Act*, R.S.O. 1990, c. B.16, I confirm that:

(a) there are reasonable grounds for believing that,

    (i) the Corporation is and the amalgamated corporation will be able to pay its liabilities as they become due, and

    (ii) the realizable value of the amalgamated corporation's assets will not be less than the aggregate of its liabilities and stated capital of all classes;

(b) there are reasonable grounds for believing that,

    (i) no creditor will be prejudiced by the amalgamation, or

    (ii) adequate notice has been given to all known creditors of the amalgamating corporations;

(c) the grounds upon which the objections of all creditors who have notified the Corporation that they object to the amalgamation, setting forth with reasonable particularity the grounds for such objections, are either frivolous or vexatious; and

(d) the Corporation has given notice to each person who has, in the manner referred to in clause (c), notified the Corporation of an objection to the amalgamation, that,

    (i) the grounds upon which the person's objection is based are considered to be frivolous or vexatious, and

    (ii) a creditor of a corporation who objects to an amalgamation has the status of a complainant under section 248 of the *Business Corporations Act*, R.S.O. 1990, c. B.16.

DATED THIS 31st day of May, 2012

_____

JAVID KHAN

APPENDIX D: ARTICLES OF DISSOLUTION (FORM 10, *BCA*)

 **Ontario**

Ministry of
Government Services

Central Production and
Verification Services Branch
393 University Ave, Suite 200
Toronto ON M5G 2M2

Articles of Dissolution
Form 10
Business Corporations Act

INSTRUCTIONS FOR COMPLETING

This form is to be used for voluntary dissolution of a business corporation where the dissolution has been authorized by the shareholders of the corporation.

Articles in duplicate may be mailed to the Toronto address listed below. For over-the-counter service articles may be filed in person at the Toronto office or at some Land Registry/ServiceOntario offices in Ontario. For a list of locations see the "Offices That Endorse Articles Submitted Under the *Business Corporations Act*" information sheet or visit the ServiceOntario website at www.ServiceOntario.ca.

FEE

$25.00   **BY MAIL** - cheque or money order payable to the Minister of Finance.
IN PERSON (at the Toronto office) - cash, cheque or money order payable to the Minister of Finance, Visa, MasterCard, American Express or debit card. If you are filing the documents at one of the Land Registry/ServiceOntario offices, call first to confirm whether credit or debit cards are acceptable.

There will be a service charge payable for any cheque returned as non-negotiable by a bank or financial institution.

SUPPORTING DOCUMENTS
CONSENT FROM THE MINISTER OF REVENUE

Articles must be accompanied by written consent to the dissolution from the Minister of Revenue, and must be submitted within 60 days after the Minister of Revenue provides consent. To obtain this consent, contact the Ministry of Revenue at the following address:

Ministry of Revenue
Client Accounts and Services Branch
33 King Street West
PO Box 622
Oshawa ON L1H 8H5
Fax: 905 433-5418

Telephone Enquiries can be made to the Canada Revenue Agency at:
Service in English: 1 800 959-5525
Service in French: 1 800 959-7775
TTY : 1 800 665-0354

APPEARANCE OF DOCUMENTS

The Articles of Dissolution must be completed in duplicate on a Form 10 as approved by the Minister. All documents must be legible and compatible with the microfilming process, with the information typed or hand printed in block capital letters, on one side of good quality, white bond paper 8 ½" X 11".

ARTICLES

ARTICLE 1   Set out the **current** name of the corporation in block capital letters starting from the first box on the left-hand side of the first line, with one letter per box and one empty box for a space. Punctuation marks are entered in separate boxes. Complete one line before starting in the first box of the next line. The name entered must be exactly the same as it appeared on the original Articles of Incorporation, Articles of Amalgamation or the most recent Articles of Amendment, if there has been a name change.

E	A	S	T		S	I	D	E		I	N	V	E	S	T	M	E	N	T		A	N	D		M	A	N	A	G
E	M	E	N	T		L	T	D	.																				

ARTICLE 2   Set out the date of incorporation or amalgamation.

ARTICLE 3   The dissolution must be authorized as required by section 237 (a) or (b) **(as applicable)** of the *Business Corporations Act.* **This statement must be included in the Articles.**

ARTICLE 4   Mark (X) in the box beside the one statement that applies.

ARTICLE 5   Mark (X) in the box beside the one statement that applies.

ARTICLE 6   There are no proceedings pending in any court against the corporation. **This statement must be included in the Articles.**

ARTICLE 7   The corporation has obtained consent from the Minister of Revenue to the dissolution and has filed all notices and returns required under the *Corporations Information Act.* **This statement must be included in the Articles. The requirement to file all notices and returns includes payment of any outstanding fees. A letter of consent issued by the Ministry of Revenue must accompany the application.**

EXECUTION   **The current name of the corporation should be printed above the signature in BLOCK CAPITAL LETTERS.** Both copies of the Articles must have an original signature of an officer or director of the corporation. **Beside the signature set out the office of the person who is signing i.e. President, Director, Secretary....** If the corporation has a corporate seal it should be affixed to the articles next to the signature. An executor, accountant or lawyer cannot sign Articles of Dissolution only an officer or director.

Articles (in duplicate), consent letter from the Ministry of Revenue and filing fee should be mailed or delivered to:

Ministry of Government Services
Central Production and Verification Services Branch
393 University Avenue, Suite 200
Toronto ON M5G 2M2

375 University Avenue, 2nd Floor (In Person)

07122 (2011/04)

For Ministry Use Only
À l'usage exclusif du ministère

Ontario Corporation Number
Numéro de la société en Ontario

1234567

ARTICLES OF DISSOLUTION
STATUTS DE DISSOLUTION

Form 10
Business Corporations Act

Formule 10
Loi sur les sociétés par actions

1. The name of the corporation is: (Set out in BLOCK CAPITAL LETTERS)
   Dénomination sociale de la société : (Écrire en LETTRES MAJUSCULES SEULEMENT)

E	N	T	E	R	T	A	I	N	M	E	N	T		G	R	O	U	P		L	T	D	.					

2. Date of incorporation/amalgamation:
   Date de la constitution ou de la fusion :
   2011 October 21
   (Year, Month,Day)
   (année, mois, jour)

3. The dissolution has been duly authorized under clause 237 (a) or (b) (as applicable) of the *Business Corporations Act*.
   La dissolution de la société a été dûment approuvée aux termes de l'alinéa 237 a) ou b) (le cas échéant) de la *Loi sur les sociétés par actions*.

4. The corporation has, (Mark (X) in the box beside the one statement that applies.)
   La société, selon le cas : (cocher la case appropriée)

   [x] (A) no debts, obligations or liabilities;
       (A) n'a ni dettes, ni obligations, ni passif;

   [ ] (B) duly provided for its debts, obligations or liabilities in accordance with subsection 238 (3) of the *Business Corporations Act*;
       (B) a pourvu à ses dettes, à ses obligations ou à son passif conformément au paragraphe 238(3) de la *Loi sur les sociétés par actions*;

   [ ] (C) obtained consent to its dissolution from its creditors or other persons having interests in its debts, obligations or liabilities.
       (C) a obtenu de ses créanciers ou des autres intéressés à ses dettes, à ses obligations ou à son passif, le consentement à sa dissolution.

5. After satisfying the interests of creditors in all its debts, obligations and liabilities, if any, the corporation has,
   (Mark (X) in the box beside the one statement that applies.)
   Après avoir désintéressé tous ses créanciers, s'il y a lieu, la société, selon le cas :
   (cocher la case appropriée)

   [x] (A) no property to distribute among its shareholders; **or**
       (A) n'a plus de biens à répartir entre ses actionnaires; **ou**

   [ ] (B) distributed its remaining property rateably among its shareholders according to their rights and interests in the corporation or in accordance with subsection 238 (4) of the *Business Corporations* Act where applicable.
       (B) a réparti les biens qui lui restaient entre ses actionnaires au prorata de leurs droits dans la société ou conformément au paragraphe 238 (4) de la *Loi sur les sociétés par actions*, s'il y a lieu.

6. There are no proceedings pending in any court against the corporation.
   Aucune instance n'est en cours contre la société.

7. The corporation has obtained consent from the Minister of Revenue to the dissolution and has filed all notices and returns required under the *Corporations Information Act*.
   Le ministre du Revenu a approuvé la dissolution de la société. La société a déposé tous les avis et rapports requis par la *Loi sur les renseignements exigés des personnes morales*.

These articles are signed in duplicate.
Les présents statuts sont signés en double exemplaire.

ENTERTAINMENT GROUP LTD.
_____
(Name of Corporation)
(Dénomination sociale de la société)

By
Par :
_____ PRESIDENT
(Signature)   **(Description of Office)**
(SIgnature)   **(Fonction)**

CHAPTER 13: CORPORATE SEARCHES

Overview:

- Oncorp and Cyberbahn & Marque D'Or
- Corporations Canada
- *Personal Property Security Act*
- Workbook:
    - *PPSA* Registration Questionnaire

1. Introduction

> Javid, Helena, Mike and Sam are very excited – it looks like there might be a buyer for their business. They know that they can probably get more value for their business in a sale, instead of dissolving the corporation and liquidating its assets. The potential purchasers have a numbered company called 1234567 Ontario Limited. This numbered company would be the purchaser of the business. Javid, Helena, Mike and Sam go to their lawyer to discuss their options.

Whenever a client is engaging in a transaction with a corporation – be it a purchase and sale of a business, a loan transaction, a lease or any other transaction – one of the tasks of a lawyer will be to ensure that the necessary searches are performed. While the searches to be performed will vary according to the type of transaction, this chapter will explore some of the common searches that are performed in relation to corporations. Note that this is not an exhaustive discussion of all searches that may be required in any particular context. (Please refer to sources that focus on corporate transactions for this purpose.) Many of the searches that are discussed in this chapter can be performed online. Often, a law clerk may be asked to obtain these searches for the lawyer's review.

One of the first questions that Javid, Helena, Mike and Sam must ask if 1234567 Ontario Limited wants to buy the business of Entertainment Group Ltd. is a simple one – does 1234567 Ontario Limited actually exist? In Chapter 4, we discussed the concept that a corporation is a legal "person" in the law; however, even with individuals, fraud can be committed in business transactions if a person's identity is not verified. Similarly, it is critical to ensure that the corporate entity that a client is doing business with actually exists, so that there is a legal entity that is responsible for the obligations that are being negotiated in the transaction.

2. Oncorp and Cyberbahn

Online service providers such as Oncorp Direct (www.oncorp.com) and Cyberbahn & Marque D'Or (www.cybermarque.com) were introduced in Chapter 5 of this textbook. These providers have access to ONBIS (Ontario Business Information System), which is Ontario's official record of business information. They are good sources to obtain corporate search reports. Lawyers will likely use one or more of these (or other) providers for a variety of purposes – NUANS searches, incorporating online, amongst other things – so it is likely that corporate searches will be obtained from the same source that is used for other purposes.

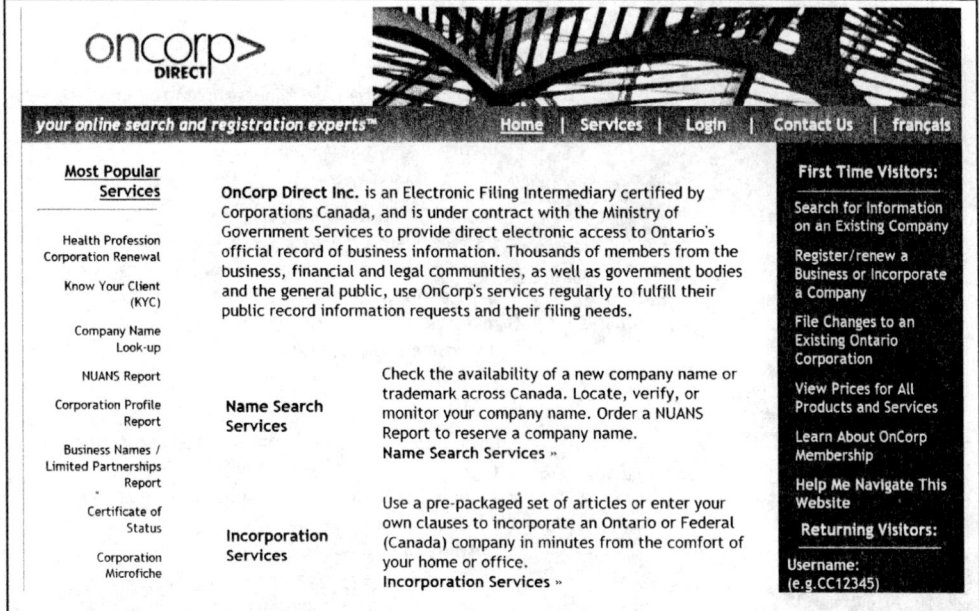

OnCorp Direct provides access to a number of popular searches on the left side of its home page. To confirm that a corporation exists, you can obtain a Certificate of Status or a NUANS Report. A Certificate of Status is a report that will indicate whether a corporation is active, dissolved or in default of government requirements. It is only available for Ontario corporations, or for extra-provincial corporations. A "clear" Certificate of Status is one that indicates that the corporation *has not been dissolved* – in other words, that it exists, according to official government records. Most corporate transactions in Ontario will require a Certificate of Status (at minimum) to confirm the existence of a corporation. (If the corporation is a federal corporation, you can refer to the Corporations Canada website, which will be discussed in part 3 of this Chapter.)

Report		
Certificate of Status	**Incorporation Services**	Use a pre-packaged set of articles or enter your own clauses to incorporate an Ontario or Federal (Canada) company in minutes from the comfort of your home or office. Incorporation Services »
Corporation Microfiche		
Initial Return / Notice of Change		
Incorporation		Search for information on an existing Ontario business name registration or register/renew your Ontario sole proprietorship / general partnership under the *Business Names Act* in minutes. Don't waste time driving to a government office and waiting in line. Small Business Name Search and Registration »
Business Name Registration / Renewal	**Small Business Name Search and Registration**	
What's New		
BizInfoTracker™ (Canada / U.S. Corporation Reports)	**Corporation Searches** ■◆■	Find matches and order reports for corporations registered in Canada or the U.S. quickly and easily with OnCorp's online corporation search services. Corporation Searches »
Electronic Due Diligence Search™		
Comprehensive Pre-Search™ (Business Name Availability)	**Corporation Filings**	Need to file a change of address or officer/director information for an Ontario incorporation? Complete an Initial Return, Notice of Change or Annual Return under the *Corporations Information Act* and update the government record for your corporation instantaneously. Corporation Filings »
About OnCorp		
	Corporate Supplies	Every corporation must maintain a minute book, and a corporate seal is required for many business transactions. OnCorp offers these and other quality products at competitive prices. Corporate Supplies »

Oncorp Direct also provides a variety of other corporation searches, for both Canadian and U.S. corporations. The BizInfoTracker is a useful tool when you are looking for information on a corporation, but its jurisdiction is unknown. It can be particularly useful for clients that engage in cross-border business (with the United States.) The following chart summarizes the corporate search reports available for Ontario corporations from Oncorp Direct. Refer to the Oncorp Direct website for pricing information.

CORPORATE SEARCH REPORT	BRIEF DESCRIPTION
Certificate of Status	Indicates whether the corporation is active, dissolved or in default; applies only to Ontario or extra-provincial corporations
Corporation Profile Report	A more thorough report summarizing the most recent information filed on or after June 27, 1992 and recorded in ONBIS; includes details such as head office address, names and addresses of active directors and officers, forms filed, and some historical information
Corporation Document List	Lists all documents filed with the Ministry of Government Services on or after June 27, 1992, including the filing date for each document
List of Current Business Names Registered by a Corporation	A list of all business names (and some related details, such as the Business Identification Number) for active and inactive business names registered or renewed by the corporation in the last five years
Business Names Report for a Trade/Style Name	A thorough report on corporation trade/style names registered on or after April 1, 1994 under the *Business Names Act*[1] (Form 2)
Corporation Point-in-Time Report	Provides the information filed by an Ontario corporation and recorded in ONBIS as of a specific date (after June 27, 1992); includes details similar to information provided in the Corporation Profile Report
Corporate Microfiche	Allows you to obtain a copy of the Articles of Incorporation for an Ontario company
Electronic Corporation Index Search	A search of all corporations registered in ONBIS, including basic information (such as corporate name and number) and some detailed information (such as previous names and links to other corporations.)
Certificate of Non-Filing	Will only be produced if no documents have been filed under the *Corporations Information Act*[2] since June 27, 1992

---

1 R.S.O. 1990, c. B.17.
2 R.S.O. 1990, c. C.39.

Statement/Certificate of No Record	Issued if there is no record of the corporation (as searched) in ONBIS[3]

Please refer to Oncorp Direct's website (www.oncorpdirect.com) for other searches that might be relevant to a client's situation, such as the Business Names/Limited Partnerships Report (which provides, amongst other things, information about the owners of a sole proprietorship or partnership.) Under the "Security Search and Registration" link, you can perform a *PPSA* search (to be discussed in part 4 of this Chapter,) as well as an Electronic Due Diligence Search (EDD). The EDD is designed to assist a legal professional in performing the searches that are required when a client is buying, investing in or financing (that is, lending money to) a business. The EDD will provide search results for searches at a number of government agencies, as well as a report of outstanding liens for a business or individual.

The Cyberbahn & Marque D'Or website – referred to generally as the Cyberbahn website at www.cybermarque.com – services different professions. Click on the Professions tab at the top of the screen and select "Legal" to view the services that are relevant to corporate law.

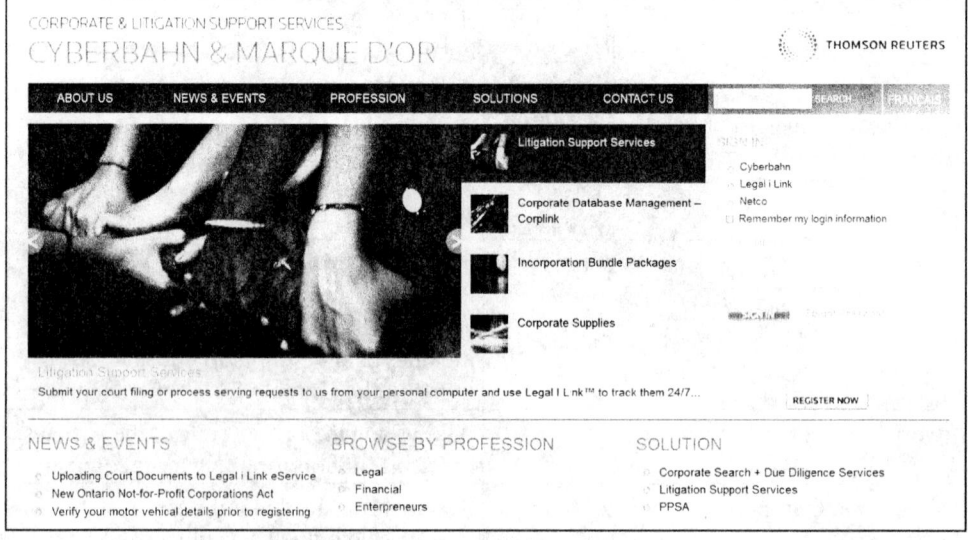

---

3 Online: Oncorp Direct <http://www.oncorpdirect.com>.

CORPORATE & LITIGATION SUPPORT SERVICES
CYBERBAHN & MARQUE D'OR

| ABOUT US | NEWS & EVENTS | PROFESSION | SOLUTIONS | CONTACT US |

Home > Profession > Legal

LEGAL

Many legal professionals have put their trust in our hands for all of their corporate and litigation needs. Conduct your corporate registrations and searches online or ask our team of clerks to do your corporate or litigation work for you. We are your go-to-provider for exceptional service in the most efficient and economical way. See our solutions for the legal industry below or contact us for information.

○ **Corporate and Business Information**
Updated information on corporations and businesses in any jurisdiction across Canada.

○ **Security Search And Diligence Information**
Updated diligence and security searches in any jurisdiction across Canada.

○ **PPSA Searches and Registrations**
Search, register, renew or amend liens in any jurisdiction across Canada and the USA.

○ **NUANS**
Verify corporate name availability prior to incorporating and obtain a mandatory NUANS® report.

○ **Articles of Incorporation**
Incorporate across Canada conveniently and efficiently.

○ **Incorporation Supplies**
Choose from a wide array of professional supplies: Minute Books, Seals, Share Certificates and more. All delivered within 24 hours of order placement.

The Cyberbahn website provides similar corporation search reports to those provided by Oncorp Direct, but also provides several security searches (which may be included in Oncorp Direct's EDD). These searches and their purpose are briefly summarized in the chart below. Note that this is not an exhaustive list; please refer to the Cyberbahn website for a full list of searches and services that may be performed. Note that a number of corporate searches are available for non-Ontario and federal corporations.

SECURITY SEARCH REPORT	BRIEF DESCRIPTION
Bank Act Search (Section 427)	Indicates whether a bank has taken security over the assets of a debtor, as provided for in section 427 of the *Bank Act*; this shows, in effect, that a bank has a preferential lien over the assets of the debtor
Superintendent of Bankruptcy/Official Receiver (National)	Shows whether proceedings have begun to declare a corporation or individual a bankrupt under the *Bankruptcy and Insolvency Act*;[4] note that, if such proceedings have begun, the debtor cannot be sued
Writs of Execution	Shows that a debtor has been successfully sued by a creditor for nonpayment of a debt
Ontario Bulk Sales Act	Required when a vendor wants to sell all, or substantially all, of its assets
Litigation Searches	Provides basic information about a court action or other legal proceeding commenced by or against a particular party
PPSA Search	Indicates whether a creditor has taken a security interest over the assets of a particular debtor

3. Corporations Canada

The Corporations Canada website (introduced in Chapter 5) allows individuals to search for a company incorporated under the *Canada Business Corporations Act*[5] and other federal legislation. (Refer to the website for a full list of legislation.) It does not include corporations created pursuant to financial legislation. Searches can be conducted by corporation number, corporation name or Business Number (BN).

---

4 R.S.C. 1985, c. B-3.
5 R.S.C. 1985, c. C-44.

4. *Personal Property Security Act*

In part 2 of this Chapter, reference was made to a *PPSA* search, which can be obtained from private online service providers like OnCorp Direct or Cyberbahn, and from the ServiceOntario website. Because *PPSA* searches are very common in business transactions, additional details about this type of search will be provided in this part of the Chapter.

A *PPSA* search is a search conducted pursuant to the *Personal Property and Security Act*[6] (known as the "*PPSA*".) The *PPSA* is designed to protect creditors – that is, individuals or businesses that lend money to others. The primary purpose of this statute is to simplify business transactions that involve security interests, and to create a system where those interests can be registered and searched. Note that the statute applies to personal property, which can include book debts, inventory, equipment, motor vehicles or other personal property. It does not apply to security taken over real property and certain other interests specified in the Act. Section 2 of the *PPSA* provides:

---

6 R.S.O. 1990, c. P.10.

Subject to subsection 4 (1), this Act applies to,

    (a) every transaction without regard to its form and without regard to the person who has title to the collateral that in substance creates a security interest including, without limiting the foregoing,

        (i) a chattel mortgage, conditional sale, equipment trust, debenture, floating charge, pledge, trust indenture or trust receipt, and

        (ii) an assignment, lease or consignment that secures payment or performance of an obligation;

    (b) a transfer of an account or chattel paper even though the transfer may not secure payment or performance of an obligation; and

    (c) a lease of goods under a lease for a term of more than one year even though the lease may not secure payment or performance of an obligation.

Assume that Entertainment Group Ltd. leases music equipment for use in Nirvana Nightclub. The term of the lease is for a period of three years. The company that owns the music equipment is called Techno Music Ltd. In return for leasing the equipment to Entertainment Group Ltd., Techno Music Ltd. will receive a certain amount of money per month; it also takes a security interest over the music equipment that is being leased, and over other assets of Entertainment Group Ltd. Why? How does this benefit Techno Music Ltd.? How does it affect Entertainment Group Ltd.?

Creditors lend money to debtors, in exchange for interest payments and eventual repayment of the capital of a loan. However, the reality is that a number of debtors will not repay some or all of the amount borrowed. To protect themselves from losing their money, creditors register a security interest[7] under the *PPSA*, which allows the creditors to seize personal property of the debtor (such as inventory, machinery, motor vehicles and other personal property) if the debtor does not repay the loan. The creditor can then sell that personal property and apply the proceeds towards repayment of the loan. The term "collateral" refers to "personal property that is subject to a security interest."[8] For example, if a creditor takes a security interest over a motor vehicle, the security interest is the right to seize the motor vehicle if the loan or other obligation is not repaid or fulfilled; collateral refers to the actual motor vehicle that can be seized by that creditor.

A critical feature of the *PPSA* is that it creates a registration system for security interests against personal property – referred to as the "Personal Property Security Registration" system ("PPSR"). Registrations under the *PPSA* and the *Repair and Storage Liens Act*[9] ("RSLA") are made in the PPSR. This is a system that creditors (or others) can search to find out if another creditor has already taken security on particular assets. Proper registration of a security interest is essential to establish the creditor's right to the

---

7 Subsection 1(1) of the *PPSA* defines "security interest" as:an interest in personal property that secures payment or performance of an obligation, and includes, whether or not the interest secures payment or performance of an obligation,(a) the interest of a transferee of an account or chattel paper, and(b) the interest of a lessor of goods under a lease for a term of more than one year; ("sûreté")

8 *Personal Property Security Act,* R.S.O. 1990, c. P.10., s. 1(1).

9 R.S.O. 1990, c. R.25.

security interest. Where there are competing claims against a debtor, the priority of claims is determined by the date and time of registration; in other words, the first person who registers a security interest over a particular asset has priority (that is, has the right to seize that asset) over the second person who registers a security interest over that asset. Similarly, people who repair or store articles and are not paid in full before giving up possession of that article, can register a claim for lien under the *RSLA*.

Assume Easy Loans Inc. lends $25,000 to Entertainment Group Ltd. to buy furniture and equipment for Nirvana Nightclub. Easy Loans Inc. takes security over the inventory and equipment of Entertainment Group Ltd. (This was negotiated by the parties in their loan agreement.) However, the manager of Easy Loans Inc. forgets to instruct its lawyer to register the security interest under the *PPSA*. Entertainment Group Ltd. realizes that it needs another $10,000 and borrows that amount from Fast Money Ltd. Fast Money Ltd. takes security over the inventory and equipment of Entertainment Group Ltd., and immediately registers its security interest under the *PPSA*. Unfortunately, after a few months, it becomes clear that Entertainment Group Ltd. cannot repay either loan. Which creditor has the right to seize Entertainment Group Ltd.'s inventory and equipment to satisfy the outstanding debt?

The Personal Property and Security Branch – which is part of the Ministry of Government Services – adminsters the *PPSA* and manages the PPSR. As of April 30, 2007, the public can access the PPSR through the "Access Now" registration and enquiry service, which is available on the ServiceOntario website. Individuals and businesses must create a Web Account to use this service. Individuals must provide a major credit card, along with credit information to a a registered Consumer Reporting Agency called Equifax Canada Inc. Businesses must apply for a Web Account by submitting two application forms to the Companies and Personal Property Security Branch; the application forms and further details are available from the ServiceOntario website.

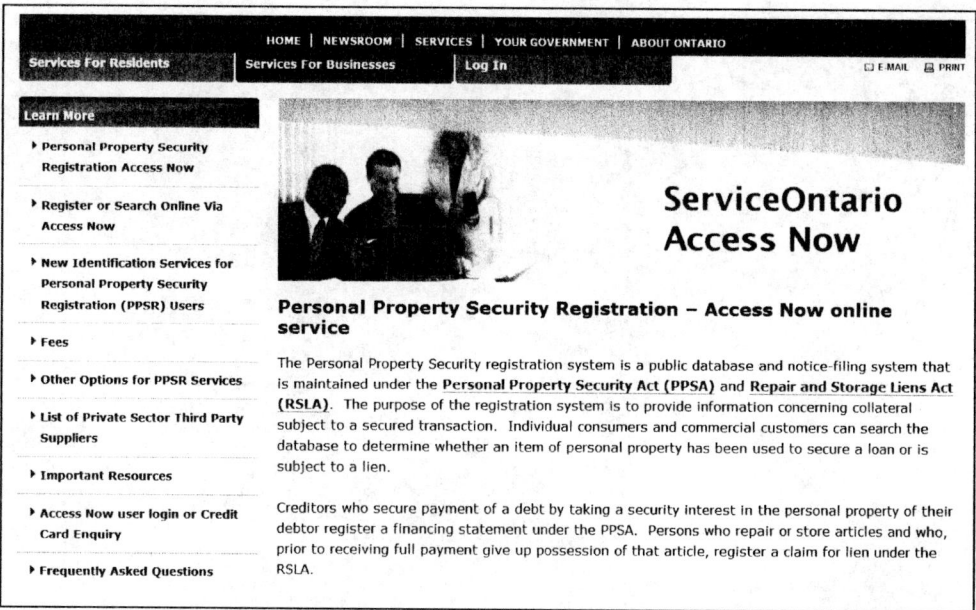

Note that a list of private sector companies that will conduct *PPSA* searches for legal professionals is also found on the ServiceOntario website. This list includes, but is certainly not limited to, OnCorp Direct and Cyberbahn.

CHAPTER 14: CORPORATE SOFTWARE – FAST COMPANY

Overview:

- Introduction
- Do Process
- Fast Company

1. Introduction

> Jonas is a general practitioner starting a new practice. He intends to provide services in a number of areas, including corporate law. He hires Antoinetta, a new graduate from the Law Clerk program at a local college, to assist him in his practice. Antoinetta took a course in corporate law during her diploma program, but she is a bit intimidated by the idea of creating minute books from scratch. Jonas, on the other hand, is concerned about running an efficient and cost effective practice, and he does not want Antoinetta to spend undue amounts of time creating minute books and other corporate documents for clients. He needs her to work independently, even though he recognizes that he must assist her and review her work. How can Jonas achieve his goal of running an efficient and cost-effective corporate law practice?

For many lawyers, an important consideration is determining what resources will assist them in running a profitable practice. Today, many of these resources relate to technology and software that is designed to assist legal practitioners. While such resources do require an investment, they can save money in the long term if there is a significant amount of work in a particular area of practice. For example, software that reduces the amount of time that a law clerk has to spend on routine matters may pay for itself in reduction of overtime pay to that law clerk. In each case, the lawyer must perform a cost-benefit analysis to determine whether such resources can be helpful. Many large law firms create internal systems that assist them in running an efficient and cost-effective practice; however, for smaller firms, software provided by external providers can achieve the same goals.

2. Do Process

While there are other competitors in the Ontario legal software market, Do Process Software LP (hereinafter referred to as "Do Process") is the dominant player. It is best known for *The Conveyancer*, a software program used for real estate transactions. Released in 1989, *The Conveyancer* is currently used in approximately 80% of the real estate transactions done in Ontario. Founded by Toronto solicitor Mitchell Brown in 1987, Do Process is now run as a limited partnership with Teranet Inc. (Teranet Inc. is the company mandated by the Province of Ontario to provide the Electronic Search and Registration system for real estate in Ontario.) The full range of products provided by Do Process includes:

- *The Conveyancer* – for real estate transactions
- *Fast Company* – for preparation of documents used in a corporate practice
- *Estate-a-Base* – for preparation of documents used in estates administration
- *WillBuilder* – for preparation of wills and powers of attorney[1]

At the beginning of 2012, the market share held by Do Process for each of these products (out of approximately 6000 law firms in Ontario) can be summarized as follows:

---

1 Greg Ham (Account Manager) *Do Process Software Background.*

- over 3600 law firms were licensed for *The Conveyancer*, and more than 80% of the real estate transactions done in Ontario are done through *The Conveyancer*

- over 1000 law firms were licensed for *Fast Company*

- over 1200 law firms were licensed for *Estate-a-Base*

- over 600 law firms were licensed for *WillBuilder*

In each area of practice, the product provided by Do Process is the most widely used by law firms in Ontario and beyond.[2]

Do Process does have competitors in the Ontario legal software market, but few have survived and none have been able to challenge the position of dominance held by Do Process. *LawyerDoneDeal* markets real estate software in both Ontario and Western Canada, and also offers a corporate program. There are also other real estate document assembly programs available in the Western provinces.[3] Given the dominance of Do Process in the legal software market, we will focus on Fast Company as a potential resource for lawyers who practice corporate law. Lawyers should, however, investigate other options that may be available to them.

3. Fast Company

Fast Company is a powerful database program which allows a lawyer, law clerk or legal secretary to manage corporate information and generate corporate documents. As clients incorporate, information about the corporation is entered into the database as a separate corporate record. There is minimal duplication of data entered – in other words, once you enter information in a corporate record (such as a director's address,) that information is automatically included in a variety of documents generated through the database. In addition, there are helpful features such as "pick lists" which give you choices to select from in relevant parts of the corporate record. For example, in the field that requests information on "type of corporation", you can click on the pick list which gives you three options: private, public and not-for profit corporation.

Once data is entered into a corporate record, a legal professional can select the documents to be generated. These documents include electronic forms (such as Articles of Incorporation) or minute book documents (such as by-laws, registers, ledgers, minutes, resolutions and share certificates.) An entire minute book can be generated through the software, as can annual minutes and other resolutions that are required from time to time. (It is important to note, however, that all documents should be reviewed and tailored as required, as each client's needs and goals must be taken into account.) Another helpful feature is the ability to generate a reporting letter, general correspondence and a Statement of Account. Finally, a link allows users to file Articles of Incorporation and Form 1 under the *Corporations Information Act*[4] (generated through Fast Company) with Oncorp Direct Inc.

In addition to generating documents required for a minute book, Fast Company allows a legal professional to manage corporate information and access:

---

2   *Ibid.*
3   *Ibid.*
4   R.S.O. 1990, c. C.39.

- specific information about a corporation
- a list of all corporate records (or a group of certain types of records)
- a list of all corporations that a particular client is now, or has ever been part of (as an incorporator, director, officer or shareholder)
- historical information, such as:
    - the effect of each successive change of directors or officers
    - a list of shareholders as of a specific date
    - transfer of shares that occurred on a specific date
    - transfer of shares involving a particular shareholder (past or present)
- a "tickler system" that notes dates related to registrations, filings, etc. which were entered into corporate records

There are essentially three steps to processing a corporate record in Fast Company:

- entering data into the corporate record
    - this can be done when the client first provides the information, and over time as additional information is acquired
- producing documents
    - Fast Company will produce electronic forms and other corporate documents (including minute book documents)
    - Articles of Incorporation and Form 1 under the *CIA* can be filed through Oncorp Direct Inc.
- using a word processor to open, edit and print the documents produced
    - documents are saved in a directory for each corporate record; these documents can then be accessed through Microsoft Word or any other word processor to edit and print the documents

The minute book documents provided in the Appendices to Chapters 9 and 10 have been generated through Fast Company. For a thorough review of the features of this software — including those that have not been summarized in this Chapter — please contact Do Process Software. Contact information can be obtained through the company's website at <http://www.doprocess.com>.[5]

---

5 Fast Company User's Guide, Version 4.01, April 2011.

Index

References given are to page numbers.